LAWS AND PROGRAMS

SMALL COPYRIGHT CLAIMS

CHALLENGES AND PROPOSALS

LAWS AND PROGRAMS

Additional books in this series can be found on Nova's website under the Series tab.

Additional E-books in this series can be found on Nova's website under the E-book tab.

LAWS AND PROGRAMS

SMALL COPYRIGHT CLAIMS

CHALLENGES AND PROPOSALS

SABRINA LOFTUS
EDITOR

nova publishers
New York

For permission to use material from this book please contact us:
Telephone 631-231-7269; Fax 631-231-8175
Web Site: http://www.novapublishers.com

Additional color graphics may be available in the e-book version of this book.

Library of Congress Cataloging-in-Publication Data

ISBN: 978-1-63117-313-4

Published by Nova Science Publishers, Inc. † New York

CONTENTS

PREFACE

This book discusses the remedies for small copyright claims provided by the Graphic Artists Guild, the Association of American Publishers, and American photographic artists.

Chapter 1 – The Constitution empowers, and the Copyright Act conveys, a system of exclusive rights for authors, for the benefit of their livelihoods, the livelihoods of other actors in the chain of commerce, and the overall public good. To protect and promote these rights, the law has always included a corresponding set of enforcement provisions allowing copyright owners to redress the unauthorized use of their works. While infringement is nothing new when it comes to the world of creative works, there is no question that it has proliferated with the ascendance of digital culture and the unprecedented desire for content. Today it is not only easy to make unauthorized copies, but to do so at virtually no cost, much to the detriment of authors and the market for their works.

As provided in the Constitution, the rights granted to authors are not merely to be articulated, but also "secur[ed]." Unfortunately, and perhaps ironically, as the rate of infringement has increased, so too have the barriers to pursuing copyright claims in the federal courts. These barriers are largely practical: federal litigation is expensive and time-consuming, and therefore out of reach for many copyright owners. The problem is especially vexing in the context of small claims, where the injury may be limited or difficult to measure. If exclusive rights are unenforceable, they are weakened as the pillars of the copyright law, and public respect for our nation's creativity is eroded in turn.

Chapter 2 – From the moment you get up in the morning, you are surrounded by graphic art. A graphic artist's job and talent is to translate society's ideas and messages from the market to you in visual form. Your sheets are designed by a textile artist, as are the fabrics you wear. The enticing labels on the food you buy at the grocery store, or the bags and containers that you get from a fast-food restaurant, are designed by graphic artists. Your morning newspaper (in print or online) or TV news program was formatted by a graphic designer or broadcast designer. The book, magazines, or newspaper you read as you commute to work are designed by graphic designers, and illustrated by artists and photographers. The logos, letterheads and brochures you see at work present visual images that enhance the written messages you receive and were also created by graphic artists. Indeed, the type fonts used in these documents were developed by graphic artists. Our society depends upon the work of graphic artists to make our products and messages interesting and attractive. Virtually all areas of commerce and communications use graphic artists.

Because graphic art is so integral to the American economy, the graphic art industry is uniquely vulnerable to copyright infringement. Protecting the creative works of graphic artists should be a vital, necessary, integral part of U.S. law. Graphic artists' livelihoods depend on their ability to claim authorship of the work they produce, and to control and set fees for use of their works in the marketplace. The ability to sell or license limited usage, or limited rights, to a creative work for a fee is not only an issue of basic fairness; it is the economic essence of copyright law that sustains the productivity of American creative professionals.

Chapter 3 – This is the Remedies for Small Copyright Claims: Additional Comments Submitted by the Association of American Publishers.

Chapter 4 – This is the Remedies for Small Copyright Claims: Response to Third Request for Comments Submitted by American Photographic Artists.

In: Small Copyright Claims: Challenges and Proposals
Editor: Sabrina Loftus
ISBN: 978-1-63117-313-4

Chapter 1

COPYRIGHT SMALL CLAIMS*

United States Copyright Office

ACKNOWLEDGMENTS

This Report reflects the efforts of a dedicated team of experts at the U.S. Copyright Office. Jacqueline C. Charlesworth, General Counsel and Associate Register, oversaw the public hearings, analysis, writing, and recommendations. She and Senior Counsel Catherine Rowland are the Report's principal authors, and I am grateful to both of them for their leadership and expertise from beginning to end. Also staffing the project were Attorney-Advisors Chris Weston and John Riley, each of whom made numerous and important contributions.

Karyn Temple Claggett, Associate Register and Director of Policy and International Affairs, reviewed the report in various iterations and offered invaluable guidance along the way. Attorney-Advisor Katie Alvarez provided timely and useful drafting assistance. The Report also benefited greatly from the research and citation skills of Counsel Kevin Amer, Attorney-Advisors Rick Marshall, Frank Muller, Steve Ruwe, Aaron Watson, and Andrea Zizzi, and Law Clerks Connie Boutsikaris, Philippa Dewey, Erica Larocque, Dawn Leung, Leo Lichtman, Jordan Reth, Michael Todd, Erik Turkman, Skyler Walker, and Susan Zucco.

I am grateful to Professors June Besek and Philippa Loengard of the Columbia School of Law for facilitating the New York City public hearings, and to Professor Doug Lichtman and Leigh Iwanaga of the UCLA School of Law for helping to arrange the hearings in Los Angeles.

Early in our process, Professor Robert Brauneis of George Washington University Law School hosted a roundtable discussion about small claims that generated a number of useful insights for both the copyright and patent systems, including in the area of constitutional law.

* This is an edited, reformatted and augmented version of the United States Copyright Office, dated September, 2013.

Finally, I would like to thank the diverse and numerous commenting parties and hearing participants, whose observations were crucial in the shaping of our recommendations.

Maria A. Pallante
Register of Copyrights and Director
U.S. Copyright Office

INTRODUCTION

The Constitution empowers, and the Copyright Act conveys, a system of exclusive rights for authors, for the benefit of their livelihoods, the livelihoods of other actors in the chain of commerce, and the overall public good.[1] To protect and promote these rights, the law has always included a corresponding set of enforcement provisions allowing copyright owners to redress the unauthorized use of their works. While infringement is nothing new when it comes to the world of creative works, there is no question that it has proliferated with the ascendance of digital culture and the unprecedented desire for content. Today it is not only easy to make unauthorized copies, but to do so at virtually no cost, much to the detriment of authors and the market for their works.

As provided in the Constitution, the rights granted to authors are not merely to be articulated, but also "secur[ed]."[2] Unfortunately, and perhaps ironically, as the rate of infringement has increased, so too have the barriers to pursuing copyright claims in the federal courts. These barriers are largely practical: federal litigation is expensive and time-consuming, and therefore out of reach for many copyright owners. The problem is especially vexing in the context of small claims, where the injury may be limited or difficult to measure. If exclusive rights are unenforceable, they are weakened as the pillars of the copyright law, and public respect for our nation's creativity is eroded in turn.[3]

The problem of modest-sized copyright claims, on the one hand, and costly enforcement, on the other, appears to be especially acute for individual creators. In comments submitted to the Copyright Office in the course of this study, the Graphic Artists Guild wrote that "[a]s a practical matter, except for large corporate copyright owners, our current copyright laws are virtually unenforceable when it comes to the infringement of visual works."[4] In a similar vein, American Photographic Artists explained that "the current system deters authors from asserting their rights, renders these cases difficult for any attorney to take on, and encourages copyright infringement by all phases of society."[5] The Alliance for Visual Artists pointed out that "[t]he traditional method of protecting copyrights ... is simply impracticable for a small business photographer with limited income."[6] Observing that "[w]e weaken markets for valuable goods at our collective peril," the Authors Guild reported that a majority of authors surveyed saw the need for a copyright small claims tribunal.[7] A representative of the Songwriters Guild of America opined that while "[s]uch small claims and random infringements may seem unimportant, ... taken in the aggregate, they have an effect on the livelihoods of individual creators akin to the infamous torture 'death by a thousand cuts.'"[8]

Creators are not alone in voicing these concerns. Citing the "hindrances that currently exist in preventing copyright owners from pursuing copyright claims of relatively small economic value," the American Bar Association's Section of Intellectual Property Law offered recommendations in support of "a much needed avenue for small copyright claims adjudication."[9] Organizations that provide *pro bono* assistance to lower-income artists, such as California Lawyers for the Arts and the New York-based Volunteer Lawyers for the Arts, emphasized what they saw as a pressing need for alternatives to federal litigation.[10]

Finally, the frustrations of those seeking to defend against claims of infringement – who themselves may be smaller actors and who also face high litigation costs – cannot be overlooked.

The Copyright Office trusts that the findings and recommendations of this Report will be helpful to Congress as it continues to explore the issue of small copyright claims.

I. EXECUTIVE SUMMARY

It appears beyond dispute that under the current federal system small copyright claimants face formidable challenges in seeking to enforce the exclusive rights to which they are entitled. The Copyright Office therefore recommends that Congress consider the creation of an alternative forum that will enable copyright owners to pursue small infringement matters and related claims arising under the Copyright Act.

In light of the state court tradition of referring to claims of modest economic value as "small claims," many have adopted that term to reference the nature of the claims that are the focus of this Report, as does the Report itself. Such claims, however, are not small to the individual creators who are deprived of income or opportunity due to the misuse of their works, and the problem of addressing lower-value infringements is not a small one for our copyright system.

But how would we structure an alternative process? Concerns of pragmatism and efficiency are core considerations, but they are not the only ones, and they must be viewed in the larger context of federal powers. Our Constitution protects both the role of the federal judiciary and the rights of those who participate in adjudicatory proceedings. These principles are enshrined in Article III and the Fifth and Seventh Amendments, and in judicial interpretations of these and other constitutional provisions. Any alternative process must fit comfortably within the constitutional parameters.

In light of the existing constitutional landscape, the challenges of the current system, and the views and insights of those who participated in this study, it appears that the most promising option to address small copyright claims would be a streamlined adjudication process in which parties would participate by consent. Perhaps not surprisingly, a number of the commenting parties viewed the Copyright Office as the logical and appropriate home for such a small claims system.

In recent years, many have emphasized the potential of voluntary solutions to certain problems of copyright enforcement.[11] In this case, a voluntary approach necessarily will fall short of a full-fledged judicial process, offering the complete panoply of copyright remedies, to which small copyright claimants could turn reliably and affordably to pursue infringers. Such a process is what our legal system would provide in an ideal world. But in the real world of constitutional and institutional limitations, a voluntary system with strong incentives for participation on both sides seems more attainable, at least in the near term. Importantly, such a voluntary approach would retain a mandatory backstop; parties who declined to consent to the alternative small claims proceeding could still be summoned to federal district court by a claimant who was able to take that path.

In brief summary, the Report makes the following recommendations:

- Congress should create a centralized tribunal within the Copyright Office, which would administer proceedings through online and teleconferencing facilities without the requirement of personal appearances. The tribunal would be staffed by three adjudicators, two of whom would have significant experience in copyright law – together having represented or presided over the interests of both owners and users of copyrighted works – with the third to have a background in alternative dispute resolution.
- The tribunal would be a voluntary alternative to federal court. Its focus would be on small infringement cases valued at no more than $30,000 in damages. Copyright owners would be required to have registered their works or filed an application before bringing an action. They would be eligible to recover either actual or statutory damages up to the $30,000 cap, but statutory damages would be limited to $15,000 per work (or $7,500 for a work not registered by the normally applicable deadline for statutory damages).
- Claimants who initiated a proceeding would provide notice of the claim to responding parties, who would need to agree to the process, either through an opt-out mechanism or by affirmative written consent. Respondents would be permitted to assert all relevant defenses, including fair use, as well as limited counterclaims arising from the infringing conduct at issue. Certain DMCA-related matters relating to takedown notices, including claims of misrepresentation, could also be considered, and parties threatened with an infringement action could seek a declaration of noninfringement.
- Parties would provide written submissions and hearings would be conducted through telecommunications facilities. Proceedings would be streamlined, with limited discovery and no formal motion practice. A responding party's agreement to cease infringing activity could be considered by the tribunal and reflected in its determination. The tribunal would retain the discretion to dismiss without prejudice any claim that it did not believe could fairly be adjudicated through the small claims process.
- Determinations of the small claims tribunal would be binding only with respect to the parties and claims at issue and would have no precedential effect. They would be subject to limited administrative review for error and could be challenged in federal district court for fraud, misconduct, or other improprieties. Final determinations could be filed in federal court, if necessary, to ensure their enforceability.

II. Study History

Congress identified the problem of small copyright claims in 2006 as an outgrowth of its consideration of orphan works.[12] As Congress considered potential solutions to the problem of orphan works, it became clear that certain claims for copyright infringement – in particular, those involving lesser amounts of damages – could not practically be pursued within the existing federal court structure. Recognizing that this concern was not limited to orphan works, in March 2006, the House of Representatives' Subcommittee on Courts, the Internet, and Intellectual Property held a separate hearing on the question of small copyright claims.[13] The hearing focused on possible alternative dispute resolution systems such as a copyright "small claims court."[14] At the hearing, witnesses, including representatives of authors, musicians, illustrators, photographers, and graphic artists, testified about the challenges of the current system and the inability to address smaller infringement matters. The Copyright Office submitted a statement to the Subcommittee in which it also observed these difficulties and suggested possible avenues to be considered.[15]

In October 2011, the House Judiciary Committee revisited the question of small copyright claims, requesting that the Copyright Office conduct a study to evaluate the issue.[16] In a letter to the Register, then-Chairman Lamar Smith asked the Office to review "the extent to which authors and other copyright owners are effectively prevented from seeking relief from infringement due to constraints in the current system."[17] Additionally, the Office was tasked to "furnish specific recommendations, as appropriate, for changes in administrative, regulatory and statutory authority that will improve the adjudication of small copyright claims and thereby enable all copyright owners to more fully realize the promise of exclusive rights enshrined in our Constitution."[18]

In response to the October 2011 request, the Office published an initial Notice of Inquiry in the Federal Register ("First Notice of Inquiry").[19] There, the Office requested public comment on how copyright owners have handled small copyright claims and the obstacles they have encountered, as well as potential alternatives to the current legal system that might better accommodate such claims. The Office received fifty-five substantive responses to its notice from a broad spectrum of interested parties, including industry associations, public interest groups, technology companies, publisher representatives, legal scholars, and individual creators.[20] Commenting parties expressed frustration with the inaccessibility of the current system, as well as concern over defendants' rights in any alternative system.

In May 2012, the Copyright Office, along with the U.S. Patent and Trademark Office ("PTO"), participated in a roundtable event sponsored by the George Washington University School of Law regarding small claims.[21] There, legal scholars and other interested parties helped to frame the issues and debated the merits of potential small claims solutions in both the copyright and patent contexts. The PTO, which is conducting its own inquiry into the area of patent small claims, has been supportive of the Copyright Office study and followed it with close interest.

The Office published a second Notice of Inquiry in August 2012 ("Second Notice of Inquiry").[22] This additional notice focused on potential alternatives to federal court litigation and identified a host of issues raised by commenting parties and the Office's own research. The Second Notice of Inquiry asked for public comment on the nature of an alternative tribunal or process, qualifications of the adjudicators, discovery parameters, available relief, treatment of frivolous claims, appeal mechanisms, and constitutional concerns, among other topics. The Office received twenty-five additional comments addressed to these issues, which provided helpful guidance as the Office continued to contemplate alternatives to federal court litigation.[23]

In November 2012, the Office held two two-day public hearings regarding the copyright small claims issue at Columbia Law School in New York City and UCLA School of Law in

Los Angeles. Each hearing was divided into seven panels addressed to the following broad topics: forum, jurisdiction, and decisionmakers; subject matter, claims, and defenses; practice and procedure; litigation alternatives; relief and appeals; constitutional issues; and moving forward (which included empirical data, funding considerations, and future assessments). At each hearing, participants representing a range of views and interests participated in lively discussions regarding potential alternative systems.[24]

Finally, the Office published a third Notice of Inquiry in February 2013 ("Third Notice of Inquiry")[25] which requested additional comments on some of the subjects raised in earlier comments and at the hearings. This Notice focused on whether an alternative system should be voluntary or mandatory, the types of copyrighted works that should be covered, the types of claims that would be appropriate, whether injunctive relief should be available, the role of attorneys, the enforceability of judgments, and other pertinent issues. The Office received twenty-seven further comments, again representing a wide variety of viewpoints, on these subjects.[26]

III. THE CURRENT SYSTEM

Copyright disputes are governed by federal law and, by statute, must be brought in federal district court.[27] United States district courts capably serve a multitude of claimants, presiding over a wide range of disputes, including highly complex litigations with significant rights and millions of dollars at stake. In many cases, federal courts offer distinct advantages over other venues. Federal judges tend to be highly skilled and are more likely to have experience in the interpretation and application of federal law, including the Copyright Act.

In recent years, the number of copyright complaints filed in the U.S. district courts has ranged from slightly above 2,000 to something over 3,000, currently representing about one out of every 100 cases initiated in the federal system.[28] But, as is discussed in more detail throughout this Report, federal court is effectively inaccessible to copyright owners seeking redress for claims of relatively low economic value, especially individual creators who are of limited resources.[29] It has been estimated that the median cost for a party to litigate a copyright infringement lawsuit with less than $1 million at stake through appeal is $350,000.[30] Such costs, of course, are not only completely disproportionate to what most individuals could invest in a lawsuit, but also to what a copyright claimant could ever hope to recover in a relatively modest infringement case.

Small copyright owners, who frequently lack experience with federal courts, often find federal litigation too difficult or expensive to pursue[31] and may be unable to navigate "the often complex procedural rules that govern federal litigation, leading to resentment and frustration."[32] Stakeholders described federal court litigation as a "very daunting task [where] it is virtually impossible to have *pro se* representation."[33] A number expressed the view that "most [infringements] will never be prosecuted because it is economically unfeasible for the creators to commence an action in federal court."[34] Moreover, because the potential for recovery of damages is limited, small claimants have less ability to retain counsel, as most attorneys are unwilling to take copyright cases that are unlikely to yield a certain level of damages.[35] Accordingly, even meritorious claims can effectively be shut out of court. For these reasons, the number of infringement actions actually filed in federal court likely significantly underrepresents the number of cases that copyright owners would choose to bring if they were able.

A. Exclusive Federal Jurisdiction

Copyright infringement claims are governed by federal law and are required to be brought in federal – not state – court.[36] In considering a case under the Copyright Act, a federal court may also exercise supplemental jurisdiction over a related state court claim,[37] such as a breach of contract action, in appropriate circumstances.[38]

In their limitation to the federal courts, copyright cases resemble patent actions, which also must be brought in federal court. But while patent cases initially are filed and heard by federal district courts, unlike copyright cases, they are appealed from the district courts to a specialized appellate court, the Court of Appeals for the Federal Circuit, which is responsible for appeals in patent cases and other specific types of matters.[39] Copyright cases, by contrast, are appealed to the courts of appeals for the circuits in which the matters are initially decided.[40]

The limitation to federal jurisdiction for copyright and patent matters differs from the treatment of trademark cases. Unlike patents and copyrights, trademarks are governed by both federal and state statutes and caselaw.[41] The federal law regarding trademarks, the Lanham Act, does not preempt all state law claims.[42] States therefore are able to provide additional protections against the misuse of unregistered marks, unfair competition, and similar wrongdoing.

Additionally, the Lanham Act allows for concurrent federal and state jurisdiction so that both federal and state courts can adjudicate federal trademark cases.[43] Conversely, federal courts often hear state law trademark claims either as a matter of supplemental jurisdiction or on diversity grounds.[44] But despite the availability of both federal and state courts to enforce trademark rights, given the option, trademark owners tend to prefer the federal system, evidently because federal judges are perceived as more knowledgeable about trademark law.[45]

B. Proceeding *Pro se* in Federal Court

Although, in theory, they can proceed *pro se*, federal court litigants typically hire attorneys to help them navigate federal procedural rules as well as the substantive law that applies in their case. When parties do proceed *pro se*, they encounter significant challenges. A recent Federal Judicial Center report on *pro se* civil litigants (the "2011 FJC Report") identified the following major issues in *pro se* cases: unnecessary or illegible submissions; problems with responses to motions; lack of knowledge about the law; failure to know when to object; and failure to understand the legal consequences of their actions or inactions.[46] Similarly, a self-help center for *pro se* litigants established by the Northern District of California notes that *pro se* litigants are less likely to succeed in federal court "because they lack the [necessary] legal knowledge, training and experience."[47] Needless to say, such fundamental limitations can have significant consequences for the outcome of an action.[48]

In light of these concerns, *pro se* litigants often receive more leeway from courts than parties represented by attorneys. For example, *pro se* pleadings generally are held to less stringent standards than those applied to attorney-drafted pleadings.[49] Courts typically review *pro se* pleadings "carefully and liberally and interpret such pleadings to raise the strongest arguments that they suggest."[50] Some districts also have local court rules designed to help *pro se* parties.[51]

The 2011 FJC Report specifically noted that effective ways to assist *pro se* litigants included the provision of "clear orders and instructions, standardized forms, prompt decisions on matters submitted to the court, and use of hearings and conferences to better understand the case and let litigants know the court has heard their case."[52] Additionally, the study identified two practices that were "especially helpful" in helping *pro se* litigants: dedicated court staff to provide specially tailored information to *pro se* litigants, including forms and instructions;[53] and *pro bono* programs, including mediation/settlement procedures and *pro se* help centers.[54]

Pro se copyright litigants occasionally find success managing the federal court system on their own.[55] Nevertheless, proceeding *pro se* in the procedurally complex federal courts can be a risky endeavor in which rights or defenses may inadvertently be waived or otherwise jeopardized due to a lack of familiarity with the court system or substantive law.

C. Federal Court Procedure

The Federal Rules of Civil Procedure ("Federal Rules") govern federal district court litigation, with the goal of "secur[ing] the just, speedy, and inexpensive determination of every action and proceeding."[56] The Federal Rules apply to a wide variety of procedural issues – from how to serve a complaint to the amount and types of permissible discovery to how to request injunctive relief. In addition to the Federal Rules, federal court litigants typically also must abide by local court rules and specific rules of the presiding judge. The Federal Rules, while helpful in laying a comprehensive logistical framework for a wide range of lawsuits, can be difficult to navigate even for experienced litigators, much less *pro se* litigants. Unlike in state court systems, there is no streamlined federal "small claims" procedure for lower-stakes disputes.

1. Initiating a Lawsuit

The Federal Rules and principles of constitutional law constrain a plaintiff's choice of forum. When initiating a lawsuit, the plaintiff must determine which court has personal jurisdiction over the parties, the proper venue for the action, and the correct method to serve notice of the lawsuit.[57] Depending upon the defendant's conduct and location, the plaintiff may not be able to hale the defendant into the preferred court. Such decisions can be complicated, especially for an inexperienced plaintiff. Additionally, service of process – to ensure that the defendant is properly notified of the action – may be costly depending on the type of service required. There are no shortcuts for copyright claimants or those with small claims – all litigants must follow the same procedures. Once a plaintiff undertakes this analysis, he or she initiates a case by filing a complaint and paying the federal court filing and administrative fees, which currently total $400.[58]

2. Discovery

After a lawsuit is initiated, parties normally engage in discovery. Under the Federal Rules, this process typically entails mandatory initial disclosures,[59] as well as depositions (including of potential experts),[60] up to twenty-five written interrogatories per party[61] (unless more are permitted by the court),[62] and potentially unlimited requests for both production of documents[63] and party admissions.[64] Document requests almost always include requests for electronically stored information, which may require extensive search and review of document files, email, and other records.

Civil litigation attorneys cite the discovery process as the primary reason for the length of federal court litigation.[65] In addition to the time it takes to respond to written discovery requests and take depositions, the parties may have discovery disputes that require motions to compel and associated hearings, adding still more time and expense to the proceeding. The discovery process provokes significant frustration due to its often substantial costs and potential for abuse by exploitative litigants.[66]

Estimates put the cost of discovery at 50% to 90% of the total cost of litigation.[67] The current state of discovery, including the forbidding cost of electronic discovery, may well persuade a party to forego bringing a lawsuit or cause a party to settle on less than ideal terms.[68] As the Supreme Court has observed, "the threat of discovery expense will push cost-conscious defendants to settle even anemic cases before reaching [even summary judgment] proceedings."[69] While sanctions for discovery abuse are available at the discretion of the court,[70] some believe that "courts have been reluctant to take a strong hand in managing the discovery process or to impose meaningful sanctions for abuses."[71]

3. Dispositive Motions and Trials

Parties may try to end a case expeditiously through a dispositive motion, such as a motion for a default judgment, a motion to dismiss,[72] a motion for judgment on the pleadings,[73] or a summary judgment motion.[74] Such motions – especially summary judgment motions – may themselves be costly and time-consuming. Apart from default motions, most dispositive motions are contested, and parties may file cross-motions that further complicate the proceedings and drive up litigation costs. While these motions can remove vexatious claims from court, at least some lawyers believe that dispositive motions – such as those for summary judgment, which are frequently denied so that the litigation continues on – are not proportionately beneficial compared to their cost.[75]

If the parties forego dispositive motions or the motions are denied, and the case is not settled, the parties proceed to trial, adding another layer of expense. Trial can be a daunting experience for lawyers, much less inexperienced litigants. Before the trial begins, parties typically must exchange exhibit and witness lists, prepare proposed exhibits, furnish evidentiary objections and replies, prepare to examine and cross-examine witnesses, prepare and object to opposing jury instructions if a jury is involved, and create demonstrative exhibits, among many other things. Trial materials and testimony generally must abide by the Federal Rules of Evidence,[76] with which litigants must be familiar in order to lodge and respond to objections during the proceedings. Litigants also must be prepared to offer procedural and substantive legal arguments in response to the plethora of issues that inevitably arise during a trial.

4. Magistrate Judges

Federal district courts rely on federal magistrate judges to ease burdens on both the district judges and the court system generally.[77] The Federal Magistrates Act[78] allows federal district courts to delegate certain pretrial matters to magistrate judges without the consent of the parties, including the ability to draft proposed findings of fact and recommendations for the resolution of nondispositive matters.[79] The magistrate judge's recommended decision stands unless a party lodges an objection within fourteen days. If there is an objection, the referring district judge will review the matter *de novo*.[80]

In addition, with the consent of the parties, magistrate judges can conduct civil trials and enter judgments in particular matters.[81] In such cases, magistrate judges, like district court judges, abide by both the Federal Rules and the Rules of Evidence.[82] Thus, while a decision may be rendered more promptly if the magistrate judge's schedule permits an earlier trial, referral to a magistrate judge may not yield any actual savings in terms of the overall complexity or cost of litigation.

5. Special Patent Procedures

Patent cases present formidable challenges for the judicial system because of the considerable resources required to construe complex patent claims and render determinations on prior art and obviousness, evaluate highly involved scientific and technological evidence, and ascertain economically appropriate damages if infringement is established. For these reasons, some federal courts have adopted specialized procedural rules to govern patent infringement cases. Courts that have taken this approach include the Southern District of New York and the Western District of Pennsylvania, both of which are also participating in a pilot program established by Congress for patent cases.[83] The modified patent rules adjust the Federal Rules to address the specific complexities of patent litigation by altering procedures for the initial scheduling conference, initial disclosures, and claim construction proceedings.[84] Another court, the Eastern District of Texas, has adopted special patent rules that are notoriously challenging but have shortened trial timelines in such a manner as to make that district a magnet for patent plaintiffs.[85] Some have expressed concern that the Eastern District of Texas's local patent rules unfairly favor plaintiffs by compressing the period in which defendants must respond even though plaintiffs may have spent significant time preparing the case before filing.[86]

D. Specific Challenges in Copyright Cases

Unlike in the patent context (at least in some jurisdictions), federal court procedural rules are not tuned to the specific needs of copyright litigants. At the same time, the Copyright Act and decisional law impose additional requirements on those seeking to pursue copyright infringement claims, which can add to the legal complexity of a case.

1. Registration Requirement

The Copyright Act states, with certain limited exceptions, that "no action for infringement of the copyright in any work shall be instituted until registration of the copyright claim has been made in accordance with this title."[87] This means that owners of United States works[88] must either register or receive a refusal of registration for the subject work prior to bringing a copyright infringement lawsuit.[89] While this requirement may impose a procedural hurdle for copyright claimants, it helps to produce a valuable public record of American creativity as well as material information to parties in litigation.[90]

The registration requirement, however, is not as straightforward as it may appear. There is a circuit court split concerning whether the copyright owner can satisfy this obligation merely by applying to register, or whether the owner instead must wait to receive the Office's registration decision before bringing suit.[91]

Regardless of whether a completed application will suffice for purposes of filing a lawsuit, a copyright plaintiff may only recover statutory damages and attorneys' fees – as opposed to actual damages and profits – if the work at issue was registered within a statutorily prescribed time frame.[92] Generally speaking, to qualify for statutory damages and attorneys' fees, the work must have been registered within three months of its publication or, if unpublished, before the act of infringement.[93] The registration requirement can be problematic for small copyright claimants, who may not be aware of the repercussions of not registering in a timely manner. Moreover, while online registration fees are relatively modest (currently $35 for a simple online application), a claimant in a hurry to go to court must pay a significantly higher fee (currently $760) to expedite the registration process.[94]

When deciding whether to register a work, individual artists and smaller entities face a difficult choice in weighing the costs of registration against the possibility of infringement and future ability to proceed in court. Individual photographers, for example, who tend to produce numerous works, may lack the administrative or financial resources to register their works within the statutory deadline.[95] Yet the inability to recover statutory damages can effectively preclude legal action against an infringer.[96]

During the course of the study, photographers and others pointed out that in some cases, actual damages for an infringement – as measured by a typical licensing fee for use a work, for example – could be several thousand dollars or less.[97] Given the costs of litigation, "[u]nless actual damages are truly substantial, the copyright holder will be without an effective remedy in federal court."[98] As one sole proprietor explained: "I had failed to register my work before the infringement occurred and was forced to decide whether to spend my hard-earned capital fighting with the infringer in court, knowing full well that my attorney's [sic] fees would not be recouped. Ultimately, after consulting with an attorney, it became clear that I simply could not afford to defend [sic] myself, even if I was on the right side of the law. The infringer got away with it and went on to win several awards with my artwork, claiming it as his own."[99]

2. Identification of Online Infringers

Before filing a federal lawsuit, a copyright owner seeking to pursue an infringement claim must first identify and locate the alleged infringer. In the internet age – where wrongdoers can act anonymously – this can be difficult. While not unique to the copyright context, the prevalence of online infringement makes this a particular concern for creators. For example, the copyright owner may want to bring a lawsuit to stop unlawful conduct on a website, but might not know who operates the website or where the operator is located.[100] Thus, the small copyright claimant might need to turn to the court for a subpoena requiring an internet service provider to identify the unknown operator.[101] Some courts, however, have been reluctant to order subpoenas to identify unknown defendants.[102] For example, while the

Digital Millennium Copyright Act ("DMCA") includes an expedited process for a copyright owner to obtain a subpoena requiring an internet service provider to identify an alleged infringer, courts have construed that provision narrowly so as to preclude issuance of a subpoena in many cases.[103]

3. Potential Bars to Recovery

Potential copyright plaintiffs also must analyze whether their infringement claims will withstand the defenses to infringement available under the Copyright Act. A primary consideration is whether the three-year statute of limitations for copyright claims has expired.[104] In cases where the infringement commenced more than three years ago, but has continued, this analysis may present challenges.[105]

In addition, a number of important limitations and exceptions to copyright protection – some of which are legally complex – may preclude a lawsuit, including: the safe harbors for qualifying online service providers available under the DMCA;[106] the applicability of a statutory license;[107] and exceptions for libraries and archives, for certain educational, religious and charitable uses, and to benefit the print disabled.[108] Additionally and apart from these exceptions, in many cases a plaintiff must assess whether the defendant may have a credible claim for fair use.[109] The fair use doctrine, embodied in section 107 of the Copyright Act, serves to protect legitimate uses of copyrighted works for purposes such as criticism, comment, teaching and research.[110]

4. Remedies

Parties may seek a variety of remedies in copyright infringement lawsuits, including monetary relief, declaratory judgments, preliminary and permanent injunctions, impoundment and destruction of infringing articles, and recovery of costs and attorneys' fees. Each of these remedies presents unique challenges for copyright litigants.

a. Damages

A plaintiff who is successful in a copyright infringement claim has the option of electing to recover either statutory damages or actual damages and profits of the defendant.[111]

Actual damages can be difficult to prove and measure in copyright cases.[112] First, information about the extent of infringement and resulting profits is unlikely to be known, or fully known, to a plaintiff and may be difficult to obtain from a defendant who did not keep records of infringing activities or is reluctant to produce them in discovery.[113] Second, it may be difficult to assess the full value of the harm caused by an infringer's unauthorized use of a work. In some cases, the use may violate not just the owner's rights but an exclusive licensing arrangement for the work, thus impacting third-party interests and the relationship between the copyright owner and licensee.[114] In other cases, a creator may not want to have the work published or used in a manner that may be harmful to the integrity of the work, an injury that is difficult to value.[115]

For these reasons, statutory damages have long played an important role in the protection of copyright interests.[116] In addition, many view statutory damages as essential to deterring infringing conduct. If all that can be recovered from an infringer at the end of a lawsuit is what the infringer would have paid for a license in the first place, exploiters of copyrighted works have little reason not to adopt a "take now, pay later" philosophy.[117]

Under the Copyright Act, standard statutory damages for copyright infringement range from $750 to $30,000 per infringed work.[118] Willful infringement can increase damages to as much as $150,000 per work, while a finding that the infringement was innocent can reduce damages to as low as $200.[119] The range of possible recovery if statutory damages are elected is therefore substantial, especially in cases involving willful infringement.

Concerning the amount of damages to be awarded, the Copyright Act mandates only that within the prescribed range, statutory damages are to be assessed "as the court considers just."[120] When a jury trial is requested, it is up to the jury to decide the amount of statutory damages.[121] Typically, in assessing statutory damages, the jury (or judge if a jury is waived) considers the range of possible damages under the law, whether the infringement was willful or innocent, and other factors such as "the nature of the infringement; the defendant's purpose and intent, the profit that the defendant reaped, if any, and/or the expense that the defendant saved; the revenue lost by the plaintiff as a result of the infringement; the value of the copyright; the duration of the infringement; the defendant's continuation of infringement after notice or knowledge of copyright claims; and the need to deter this defendant and other potential infringers."[122]

In practice, statutory damages may be more likely to be awarded to larger entities because "individual authors and small firms do not typically register their copyrights within three months of publication, ... [and thus] rarely qualify for statutory damages or attorney's fee awards."[123] Several commenters concurred with the view that the registration requirement for statutory damages places individuals and smaller entities at a disadvantage because it is difficult and burdensome for them to meet the statutory requirement for timely registration.[124]

b. Injunctive Relief

Parties may try to obtain early injunctive relief in a copyright case by filing a motion for a preliminary injunction.[125] This process requires the expense of briefing and, typically, a separate hearing. The court may issue the preliminary relief only if the moving party posts a bond or "security" in an amount large enough to cover the costs and damages of a party wrongfully restrained.[126]

Parties also may seek permanent injunctive relief following a trial on the merits. The Supreme Court's 2006 decision in *eBay Inc. v. MercExchange*,[127] though a patent infringement case, set a standard for injunctive relief that also applies in copyright actions.[128] Citing earlier copyright decisions to support its holding, the *eBay* Court rejected judicial interpretations favoring the automatic grant of an injunction upon a finding of infringement.[129] *eBay* thus held that, to secure an injunction, a plaintiff must demonstrate: (1) that it has suffered an irreparable injury; (2) that remedies available at law, such as monetary damages, are inadequate to compensate for that injury; (3) that, considering the balance of hardships between the plaintiff and defendant, a remedy in equity is warranted; and (4) that the public interest would not be disserved by a permanent injunction.[130]

c. Attorneys' Fees and Costs

The Copyright Act provides that a prevailing party in a copyright lawsuit may recover his or her costs and reasonable attorneys' fees.[131] Such fee-shifting, however, is at the discretion of a court and, if the prevailing party is a copyright owner, only if the work was registered in a timely fashion as provided in section 412.[132] One copyright law scholar has observed the importance of attorneys' fees for small claimants, stating that "[g]iven the high costs of litigation, [attorneys' fees are] crucial and indeed, for smaller litigants, may determine whether bringing an infringement action is financially viable."[133]

But an attorneys' fee award is not automatic upon a finding of infringement.[134] Rather, in considering an application for fees, courts look to a variety of factors, including "frivolousness, motivation, objective unreasonableness (both in the factual and in the legal components of the case) and the need in particular circumstances to advance considerations of compensation and deterrence."[135] Thus, a court ultimately may decline to make an award even in a case where the plaintiff has successfully pursued a legitimate claim of infringement.[136]

In weighing the possibility of litigation, a would-be copyright plaintiff also must consider that attorneys' fees are available to a "prevailing party,"[137] and that both plaintiffs and defendants in copyright suits are, under Supreme Court precedent, to be "treated alike."[138] That is, courts are to be "faithful to the purposes of the Copyright Act" and apply the relevant standard to prevailing plaintiffs and defendants "in an evenhanded manner."[139] Thus, the possibility that a defendant might collect fees if the infringement claim fails may discourage some copyright claimants from pursuing litigation.[140] And, even if the copyright owner prevails, his or her ability to recover attorneys' fees is far from assured.

5. Costs and Burden of Litigation

Copyright owners whose works are infringed often are deterred from enforcing their rights due to the burden and expense of pursuing litigation in the federal system. Especially in the case of lower-value copyright claims, the potential for monetary recovery can be quickly overcome by the costs of discovery, motion practice, and other litigation expenses. Of course the same may be true for defendants seeking to vindicate their interests in modest-sized copyright dispute.[141]

Litigation of a copyright claim in federal court requires substantial amounts of time, money, and effort. An aggrieved copyright owner must either hire a potentially costly attorney who understands federal court procedure and substantive copyright law, or attempt to enforce his or her rights *pro se*. The costs of filing, service, discovery, and transcripts can quickly compound. A court proceeding entails other costs as well, as it requires a creator plaintiff to forsake income-generating work to attend to the litigation. As one artist noted, faced with a choice between paying an attorney to pursue an infringer or continuing to focus on her work, "I am just going to work because that is the sure thing."[142]

The excessive cost of federal litigation relative to case value is an overarching issue for litigants with lower-value claims. Indeed, recent surveys confirm a widespread belief among attorneys that litigation costs are generally disproportionate to the value of "small" cases, though not necessarily disproportionate to "large" cases.[143] For example, a survey by the ABA indicated that, for attorneys representing both plaintiffs and defendants, 89% of respondents agreed that in small-value cases litigation costs were not proportional to the value of a case.[144]

If a copyright owner hires an attorney to enforce his or her copyrights, those costs can easily exceed the value of the work that is being infringed. In a 2011 email survey of 2,577 members of the American Intellectual Property Law Association ("AIPLA"), the median cost in 2010 for a party to litigate a copyright infringement lawsuit with less than $1 million at risk through to appeal was $350,000.[145] To reach even the close of discovery, the median cost was $200,000.[146] The fact that nearly two-thirds of litigation costs accrue before parties even proceed to trial demonstrates how much case preparation, discovery, and pretrial motion practice add to the total cost of a lawsuit. While the AIPLA figures do not provide a breakdown of cases in the "below $1 million" category, they attest to the high cost of enforcing copyrights, a great many of which do not begin to approach $1 million in value.

Building on the AIPLA study, the ABA IP Section attempted to determine at what perceived value a copyright attorney would agree to take a case. The section asked its members: "At what value of likely recovery (and disregarding the potential for also recovering attorneys' fees) would you consider litigation of an uncomplicated copyright claim economically justifiable ...."[147] Section members were offered a range of seven recovery amounts, from less than $10,000 at the bottom and increasing in $10,000 increments to over $60,000.[148] The results were that 32% of the respondents indicated that they would accept a case with less than $30,000 at stake, 29% of the respondents would only accept a case between $30,000 and $60,000, and 39% of respondents would only accept a case with more than $60,000 at stake.[149] The median for the responses thus indicated that an attorney would not file an uncomplicated copyright case in federal court unless the value of recovery was in the $40,000-$49,999 range.[150]

GAG also conducted a survey of its members concerning their efforts to enforce their copyrights. The survey found that 60.1% of Guild members believed that their works had been infringed.[151] Works were primarily infringed on the internet or from a printed piece[152] and in a commercial context.[153] In response to the infringement, most authors contacted the infringers themselves,[154] but most of the infringers did nothing in response.[155] Guild members offered several reasons for not hiring an attorney to pursue the infringer, including: "too much of an ordeal/I didn't want to go through with it"; "my work was not registered, and I would not recoup attorneys' fees and court costs (could not afford an attorney)"; and "the amount I would have been awarded or would ask for was less than the legal costs."[156] For those who took their cases to court, most were successful, with only 2.2% of cases lost by Guild members and 14.1% of cases dismissed or dropped.[157] From this survey, it appears that most authors in the graphic arts suffer from infringement and could be successful if they were able to bring a lawsuit, but most graphic artists do not bring cases because of the prohibitive costs and inherent difficulties of the current system. Moreover, Guild members overwhelmingly indicated that they would use an alternative system for small-value copyright infringement cases that did not require them to go to federal court or hire an attorney.[158]

6. Time to Trial

In addition to costing money, litigation of a copyright case through to resolution also takes time. From 2000 to 2012, some 39,432 copyright cases were filed in U.S. federal district courts.[159] During that period, the two districts in which most copyright cases were filed were the Central District of California, with 6,184 cases, and the Southern District of New York, with 3,588.[160] In those same years, the median time to trial in the Southern District of New York was 720 days and in the Central District of California, 589 days.[161] In districts that see the most copyright cases, it is likely to be a year and a half before the parties can get to trial.

IV. CONSTITUTIONAL ISSUES

While it is apparent that many copyright owners are effectively precluded from pursuing small claims through the existing federal court system, a workable solution will depend on constitutional considerations as much as procedural and pragmatic concerns. In contemplating potential alternatives to the current system, a number of significant constitutional issues emerge, namely: the Seventh Amendment right to a jury trial; separation of powers questions relating to the creation of non-Article III tribunals; Appointments Clause requirements; and various due process concerns, including those relating to personal jurisdiction, service of process, and the conduct of streamlined proceedings.

A. The Seventh Amendment

The Seventh Amendment provides that "[i]n Suits at common law, where the value in controversy shall exceed twenty dollars, the right of trial by jury shall be preserved ... ."[162] Until 1998, when the Supreme Court decided *Feltner v. Columbia Pictures Television, Inc.*,[163] there was no firmly established rule that a party to a copyright infringement action seeking statutory damages was entitled to a jury trial. Indeed, the language of the Copyright Act suggests otherwise, as section 504 makes no mention of a jury or jury trial but instead provides that statutory damages shall be awarded "as the court considers just."[164] Before *Feltner*, although it was understood that a party to an infringement action seeking actual damages,– a remedy at law– was entitled to a jury,[165] courts were divided on the question of whether statutory damages were equitable in nature and thus outside the purview of the Seventh Amendment.[166]

In *Feltner*, the Supreme Court laid the jury trial issue to rest. In that case, a defendant found to have infringed copyrighted television programs challenged the district court's denial of his jury trial demand and judge-determined award of statutory damages. The Supreme Court held that even though section 504 of the Copyright Act provided no right to a jury trial, the Seventh Amendment did, with respect to "all issues pertinent to an award of statutory damages," including the amount.[167]

The Court's opinion in *Feltner* is notable for its examination of the historical roots of U.S. copyright law. Although copyright law, including its rights and remedies, has long been a creature of federal statute, the Court explained that "[b]efore the adoption of the Seventh Amendment, the common law and statutes of England and this country granted copyright owners causes of action for infringement … . [C]opyright suits for monetary damages were tried in courts of law, and thus before juries."[168] Having reviewed the historical record, the Court concluded that the statutory damages provisions found in copyright laws – from Great Britain's 1710 Statute of Anne to their modern-day embodiment in title 17 – were legal, rather than equitable, in nature, as were infringement actions for damages generally.[169]

Interestingly for purposes of this report, although looking to copyright law as it stood at the time of adoption of the Seventh Amendment – which was approved by Congress in 1789 and ratified as part of the Bill of Rights in 1791[170] – the *Feltner* Court did not consider that certain cases seeking statutory damages would have been exempt from the jury trial right in that era. The first federal copyright act, enacted in 1790, provided for statutory damages of fifty cents "per sheet," far below the twenty-dollar threshold of the Seventh Amendment.[171] Thus, it would appear that the first Congress may well have been comfortable leaving certain "small" copyright claims to be decided without a jury.

While the Supreme Court's holding in *Feltner* confirms the Seventh Amendment right to a jury trial in a copyright infringement action for damages, the law is equally clear that a party can choose to waive that right. Although constitutional in stature, the right to a jury trial is considered an individual right that can be voluntarily relinquished.[172] Accordingly, while *Feltner* poses an obstacle to the creation of a mandatory forum for small copyright claims that does not include juries, it would not appear to bar a voluntary system where parties consented to proceed without a jury.[173]

B. Article III Considerations

While the Supreme Court's views concerning the right to a jury trial in a copyright damages action, and a party's ability to waive that right, seem relatively settled, its decisions concerning the constitutional parameters of non-Article III courts are less so. Although a comprehensive review of the Court's treatment of this subject is beyond the scope of this Report, a basic understanding of the jurisprudential terrain – inauspiciously referred to by one Justice as "'a darkling plain' where ignorant armies have clashed by night"[174] – is essential to any consideration of a streamlined resolution process for small copyright claims that would rely on non-Article III decisionmakers.

1. From Murray's Lessee to Northern Pipeline

Article III of the Constitution provides that "[t]he judicial Power of the United States, shall be vested in one supreme Court, and in such inferior Courts as the Congress may from time ordain and establish. The Judges, both of the supreme and inferior Courts, shall hold their Offices during good Behaviour, and shall, at stated Times, receive for their Services, a Compensation, which shall not be diminished during their Continuance in Office."[175] The Framers believed that an independent judiciary – with judges not removable at will and salaries that could not be reduced – was essential to maintain the checks and balances of their constitutional design.[176] Article III thus "serves both to protect 'the role of the independent judiciary within the constitutional scheme of tripartite government … and to safeguard litigants' 'right to have claims decided before judges who are free from potential domination by other branches of government.'"[177]

In 1855 the Supreme Court was called upon to interpret Article III in the case *Murray's Lessee v. The Hoboken Land & Improvement Co.*[178] The case concerned the constitutionality of a nonjudicial proceeding to seize property from a customs collector who owed a significant sum of money to the U.S. government. In that case, the Court recognized that not every dispute had to be decided by an Article III court, and that Congress could withhold from Article III courts certain matters "involving public rights" – such as a government action to recover public funds.[179] But at the same time the Court also observed that Congress should not be able to "withdraw from judicial cognizance" matters subject to suits at common law, in equity, or in admiralty.[180]

Over time, as the nation's governmental functions grew more complex, Congress began to create specialized tribunals with adjudicators who did not enjoy lifetime tenure or protected salaries to resolve certain types of disputes more practically or efficiently addressed outside of an Article III court. Perhaps most notable among non-Article III tribunals have been the bankruptcy courts, which perform a wide range of duties to carry out the provisions of the U.S. Bankruptcy Code. Others include the Tax Court,[181] Social Security Appeals Council,[182] Court of Appeals for Veterans Claims,[183] and Court of Federal Claims.[184] In the copyright realm, Congress has created the Copyright Royalty Board to set rates and terms and distribute royalties payable under government-established licensing schemes.[185]

The fundamental question that arises in connection with Congress' creation of such courts is whether they violate the separation of powers principle embodied in Article III. Since the time of *Murray's Lessee*, the Supreme Court has approached this issue in varying ways. As was aptly stated by Justice Rehnquist, "[t]he cases dealing with the authority of Congress to create courts other than by use of its power under Art. III do not admit of easy synthesis."[186]

In the significant 1932 case *Crowell v. Benson*, the Supreme Court considered Congress' authority to create an agency-administered process to award compensation for injuries sustained in navigable waters.[187] Departing from a strict interpretation of *Murray's Lessee*, the Court instead adopted a more flexible reading of the Constitution to uphold the congressional scheme. Even though the disputes being adjudicated involved a "private right" – that is, "the liability of one individual to another" – and thus did not fall within the narrow public rights exception articulated in *Murray's Lessee*, in light of Congress' general authority over maritime law, the Court believed that Congress could constitutionally assign the task of determining compensation awards to a specialized agency.[188]

Several decades later, in 1978, Congress enacted the Bankruptcy Reform Act, replacing the older system of bankruptcy referees with bankruptcy courts.[189] The newly formed bankruptcy courts were bestowed with expansive powers of equity, law and admiralty; they could conduct jury trials and issue any order, process, or judgment necessary to carry out the provisions of the Bankruptcy Code.[190] Because they had authority over all civil proceedings arising under title 11 and matters related to cases under title 11, they were authorized to decide claims based on state as well as federal law.[191] Their orders and judgments were reviewable by Article III courts under a clearly erroneous standard on appeal.[192]

In 1982, in the case *Northern Pipeline Construction Co. v. Marathon Pipeline Co*, the Supreme Court confronted the constitutionality of the new bankruptcy courts.[193] The specific issue in *Northern Pipeline* was whether the non-Article III bankruptcy judges could constitutionally adjudicate state law claims for breach of contract and tortious conduct asserted in the course of a bankruptcy proceeding.[194] In a plurality opinion joined by three other members of the Court, Justice Brennan took an expansive approach to the question, concluding that the courts could not adjudicate such claims and that in fact, Congress' broad grant of jurisdiction to the bankruptcy courts was unconstitutional.[195] Justice Brennan expressed the view that only three types of courts should be recognized as exempt from the constraints of Article III: territorial courts; military tribunals; and administrative tribunals falling under the public rights doctrine.[196] Drawing upon *Murray's Lessee*, Justice Brennan further suggested that the public rights doctrine should apply only to disputes between the "government and others."[197]

Justice Brennan acknowledged that "when Congress creates a statutory right … it may also provide that persons seeking to vindicate that right must do so before particularized tribunals created to perform the specialized adjudicative tasks related to that right."[198] But even if the "restructuring of debtor-creditor relations" could be considered a "public right," because many of the rights subject to adjudication by the bankruptcy courts – including the state law claims at issue in the case – were "not of Congress' creation," Justice Brennan concluded that the entire scheme was unconstitutional.[199]

Justice Brennan did not command a majority for his reading of Article III or broad invalidation of the bankruptcy courts. While two other Justices concurred in the judgment, they would have decided only the narrower question of whether the state-law based action initiated by Northern Pipeline could be adjudicated by a non-Article III court.[200] The three other Justices dissented.[201]

2. Administrative Proceedings: Thomas and Schor

Following *Northern Pipeline*, the Supreme Court continued to grapple with Article III but declined to adhere to the formalistic stance advocated by Justice Brennan, instead adopting a more pragmatic approach in subsequent cases challenging the constitutionality of non-Article III tribunals.

In the 1985 case *Thomas v. Union Carbide*, the Court was called upon to consider a mechanism adopted by Congress to resolve compensation disputes among parties who shared research data pursuant to the Federal Insecticide, Fungicide, and Rodenticide Act ("FIFRA").[202] When a party wished to rely on another party's research data to support registration of a pesticide, the relevant statutory provision required the two to negotiate and, if necessary, submit to binding arbitration to determine appropriate compensation as between them. Similar to the standard set forth in the Federal Arbitration Act,[203] the arbitrator's decision was subject to judicial review only for "fraud, misrepresentation, or other misconduct."[204]

Despite the seeming retreat by some Justices from *Crowell* in *Northern Pipeline*, all nine Justices (three in concurring opinions) agreed that the Environmental Protection Agency's arbitration scheme was compatible with Article III. Writing for the majority, Justice O'Connor expressed a considerably more flexible view of Article III than had Justice Brennan: "[T]he Court has long recognized that Congress is not barred from acting pursuant to its powers under Article I to vest decisionmaking authority in tribunals that lack the attributes of Article III courts .... Many matters that involve the application of legal standards to facts and affect private interests are routinely decided by agency action with limited or no review by Article III courts.[205]

The *Thomas* opinion was careful to limit the plurality decision in *Northern Pipeline*, explaining that the case established "only that Congress may not vest in a non-Article III court the power to adjudicate, render final judgment, and issue binding orders in a traditional contract action arising under state law, without consent of the litigants, and subject only to ordinary appellate review."[206] Moreover, the *Thomas* Court expressly rejected Justice Brennan's brightline test requiring that the federal government be a party to an action before the "public rights" exception could apply, opining instead that "practical attention to substance rather than doctrinaire reliance on formal categories should inform application of Article III."[207]

Turning to the substance of the FIFRA provision, the Court was persuaded that, in light of its relationship to the pesticide registration program, the right created by FIFRA was not purely a "private" right, but bore many characteristics of a "public" right.[208] Even though arguably akin to a state law property claim, the Court found it significant that the compensation right at issue did not in fact arise from state law.[209] The Court also pointed to Congress' desire to overcome the litigation "logjam" in the courts that was holding up the pesticide registration process, as well as the fact that the compensation decisions rendered through the agency arbitration process were subject to a limited form of Article III review.[210] Weighing all of these factors together, the Court concluded that the administrative compensation scheme at issue did not contravene Article III.[211]

In 1986, in *Commodities Futures Trading Commission v. Schor*, the Supreme Court addressed another agency-administered compensation process.[212] Under the Commodity Exchange Act ("CEA"),[213] the Commodities Futures Trading Commission ("CFTC") administered a reparations procedure through which disgruntled customers of professional commodity brokers could seek redress for brokers' violations of the CEA or of CFTC regulations. Any person so injured could apply for a reparations order from the CFTC and could enforce that order in federal district court.[214] To further the congressional goal of promoting efficient dispute resolution, the CFTC adopted a regulation that allowed it to adjudicate counterclaims "'aris[ing] out of the transaction or occurrence or series of transactions or occurrences set forth in the complaint.'"[215]

In the case, Schor had filed a complaint with the CFTC for reparations against a broker employed by ContiCommodity Services, Inc. ("Conti"). Conti asserted a state law counterclaim to recover a debit balance in Schor's account.[216] After discovery, briefing and a hearing, an administrative law judge ruled in Conti's favor on both Schor's reparations claim and Conti's counterclaim.[217] Schor appealed the ruling to the Court of Appeals for the District of Columbia Circuit, which *sua sponte* raised the question of whether the CFTC could adjudicate Conti's common law counterclaim in light of *Northern Pipeline*, ultimately concluding it could not.[218] A majority of the Supreme Court, again led by Justice O'Connor, disagreed.

Finding that the CFTC process designed by Congress was dependent upon the ability to resolve related counterclaims, the Court again took a pragmatic, rather than formalistic, approach to the Article III analysis. Observing that "Article III does not confer on litigants an absolute right to plenary consideration of every nature of claim by an Article III court," the Court explained that Article III served to protect "primarily personal, rather than structural interests," and further that, "as a personal right, Article III's guarantee of an impartial and independent federal adjudication is subject to waiver, just as are other personal constitutional rights that dictate the procedures by which civil and criminal matters must be tried."[219] Here, Schor had "indisputably" waived his right to have Conti's common law counterclaim decided by a federal district court, and "with full knowledge that the CFTC would exercise jurisdiction over that claim, chose to avail himself of the quicker and less expensive procedure Congress had provided him."[220]

While emphasizing Schor's consent to the jurisdiction of a non-Article III court as a significant factor in its analysis, the Court at the same time paid heed to the separate institutional interest served by Article III of safeguarding against encroachment upon the judicial branch. "To the extent that this structural principle is implicated in a given case, the parties cannot by consent cure the constitutional difficulty for the same reason that the parties by consent cannot confer on the federal courts subject-matter jurisdiction beyond the limitations imposed by Article III, § 2."[221] Thus, the Court proceeded to consider whether the CFTC process threatened the institutional integrity of the judicial branch, identifying several factors to be weighed: "the extent to which the 'essential attributes of judicial power' are reserved to Article III courts, and conversely, the extent to which the non-Article III forum exercised the range of jurisdiction and powers normally vested only in Article III courts, the origins and importance of the right to be adjudicated, and the concerns that drove Congress to depart from the requirements of Article III."[222]

Against this backdrop, the Court determined that the CEA's adjudication of related common law counterclaims was not fatal to the congressional scheme, as the statute left "far more of the 'essential attributes of judicial power' to Article III courts" than the portion of the Bankruptcy Act invalidated by *Northern Pipeline.*[223] Unlike the bankruptcy courts, the CFTC dealt with "one particularized area of law," its orders were enforceable only by order of the district court, and its orders were reviewable by the district court.[224] Even though Conti's counterclaim was "private" in nature, Congress had not withdrawn it from "judicial cognizance." Rather, Congress "gave the CFTC the authority to adjudicate such matters, but the decision to invoke th[e] forum [was] left entirely to the parties and the power of the federal judiciary to take jurisdiction of these matters [was] left unaffected. In such circumstances, separation of powers concerns are diminished, for it seems self-evident that just as Congress may encourage parties to settle a dispute out of court or resort to arbitration without impermissible incursions on the separation of powers, Congress may make available a quasi-judicial mechanism through which willing parties may, at their option, elect to resolve their differences."[225]

3. The Federal Magistrates Act

Another context in which the Supreme Court has considered the assignment of duties to non-Article III decisionmakers is the Federal Magistrates Act, which, as noted above, permits the assignment of certain matters by district courts to non-Article III magistrate judges.[226] The Court has upheld the ability of Article III judges to delegate responsibilities to magistrate judges under the Act on a number of occasions.[227]

In one of the Court's recent decisions considering the Act, the 2003 case *Roell v. Withrow*, a magistrate judge had presided over the trial and entered judgment in a state prisoner's section 1983 action.[228] Section 636(c)(1) of the Act provides that "[u]pon consent of the parties, a full-time United States magistrate judge … may conduct any or all proceedings in a jury or nonjury civil matter and order the entry of judgment in the case, when specially designated to exercise such jurisdiction by the district court."[229] Unlike nonconsensual referral of a pretrial matter under section 636(b) to a magistrate judge for findings and recommendations – which are reviewable *de novo* by the referring district court[230] – section 636(c)(1) gives the magistrate judge full authority over dispositive motions, conduct of the trial and the entry of final judgment, without district court review and appealable directly to a court of appeals "in the same manner as an appeal from any other judgment of a district court."[231]

The particular question before the Court in *Roell* was whether the prisoner's implied consent to trial before the magistrate judge by participating fully in the proceedings was adequate to confer "civil jurisdiction" on the magistrate judge notwithstanding a requirement in Federal Rule 73(b) that the parties' consent be in writing.[232] Drawing on earlier precedent upholding the constitutionality of the Federal Magistrates Act,[233] as well as the waiver theory articulated in *Schor,*[234] Justice Souter's practically oriented majority opinion held that the prisoner's implied consent sufficed, finding that judicial efficiency had been "served" and the Article III right "substantially honored."[235] The opinion further held that "[i]n giving magistrate judges case-dispositive civil authority, Congress hoped to relieve the district courts' 'mounting queue of civil cases' and thereby 'improve access to the courts for all groups.'"[236]

4. Bankruptcy Courts Revisited

Congress responded to the Supreme Court's invalidation of the bankruptcy courts in *Northern Pipeline* by revising the law in 1984 to provide that bankruptcy judges be appointed by the federal courts of appeals and limiting the judges' authority to enter final judgments to certain "core" bankruptcy proceedings.[237] In 1989 the Supreme Court returned to the bankruptcy arena in *Granfinanciera, S. A. v. Norberg*, which considered whether, notwithstanding Congress' designation of a fraudulent conveyance action as a "core" proceeding under the Bankruptcy Reform Act, noncreditors sued in bankruptcy court for a fraudulent conveyance were entitled to a jury trial.[238] The petitioners in *Granfinanciera*, who sought and were denied a jury trial by the bankruptcy judge, relied on the Seventh Amendment and did not invoke Article III in their constitutional challenge. In an opinion authored by Justice Brennan, however, the majority viewed the Seventh Amendment question as closely tied to the question of whether the claim could be tried in a non-Article III court: "Indeed, our decisions point to the conclusion that, if a statutory cause of action is legal in nature, the question whether the Seventh Amendment permits Congress to assign its adjudication to a tribunal that does not employ juries as fact-finders requires the same answer as the question whether Article III allows Congress to assign adjudication of that cause of action to a non-Article III tribunal."[239]

The Court then elaborated on the public rights doctrine, reaffirming its prior holding in *Thomas* that the federal government need not be a party for a case to come within that exception.[240] Rather, "[t]he crucial question, in cases not involving the Federal Government, is whether 'Congress, acting for a valid legislative purpose pursuant to its constitutional powers under Article I, [has] create[d] a seemingly 'private right' that is so closely integrated into a public regulatory scheme as to be a matter appropriate for agency resolution with limited involvement by the Article III judiciary.'"[241] In *Granfinanciera*, the Court answered this question in the negative, concluding that the bankruptcy trustee's right to recover a fraudulent conveyance was not integral to the proceedings in bankruptcy but instead "quintessentially [a] suit[] at common law."[242] The petitioners therefore were entitled to a jury trial.[243]

The Supreme Court's most recent significant opinion interpreting Article III, decided in 2011, is *Stern v. Marshall*, also emerging from the bankruptcy context.[244] In contrast to *Thomas* and *Schor*, the *Stern* opinion, authored by Chief Justice Roberts on behalf of a five-member majority, may suggest a less pragmatic inclination and at the very least, the Court's continued wariness concerning the powers granted by Congress to the bankruptcy courts.

The *Stern* case, which had already made its way to the Supreme Court once before, was part of a long-running, well-publicized dispute over the estate of J. Howard Marshall ("J. Howard"), whom Vickie Lynn Marshall (known to the public as Anna Nicole Smith) ("Vickie") had married about a year before his death.[245] Vickie, who was not included in her husband's will, had sued J. Howard's son E. Pierce Marshall ("Pierce") in Texas probate court to set aside a living trust that she claimed Pierce had fraudulently induced his father to sign.[246] After J. Howard's death, Vickie filed a petition for bankruptcy in California, and Pierce filed a complaint in the California bankruptcy proceeding contending that Vickie had defamed him by publicizing her claims of fraud, followed by a proof of claim. Vickie responded by filing a counterclaim in the bankruptcy court for tortious interference with the gift she had expected from J. Howard.[247] The bankruptcy court eventually issued a judgment in Vickie's favor, awarding her over $400 million in damages.[248]

Pierce contested the judgment, arguing that the court could not decide Vickie's counterclaim because it was not a "core" proceeding under the Bankruptcy Code. When the *Stern* case reappeared in the Supreme Court, the Court rejected the determination of the court of appeals that Vickie's counterclaim failed to qualify as a "core" proceeding, concluding that the relevant statutory provision made clear that it did.[249] But the Court further determined that Article III prohibited the bankruptcy court from entering final judgment on Vickie's counterclaim.[250]

Once again, the Court confronted the "varied formulations" of the public rights doctrine, finding that the counterclaim – a state common law claim between two private parties – did not fall within the exception. It did not "flow from a federal statutory scheme," as in *Thomas*;[251] it was not "completely dependent upon adjudication of a claim created by federal law," as in *Schor*;[252] the asserted authority to decide Vickie's claim was not limited to a "'particularized area of the law'" as in *Crowell*, *Thomas* and *Schor*;[253] and it was not "a situation in which Congress devised an 'expert and inexpensive method for dealing with a class of questions of fact which are particularly suited to examination and determination by an administrative agency specially assigned to that task.'"[254] Moreover, Pierce "did not truly consent to resolution of Vickie's claim in the bankruptcy court proceedings," because, as a creditor, he had "nowhere else to go" if he wished to recover from Vickie's estate. Thus there was no reasoning "parallel" to *Schor* to support a waiver theory.[255]

Acknowledging the elusive qualities of the public rights doctrine,[256] the Court was careful to limit its holding in *Stern* to the bankruptcy courts: "Given the extent to which this case is so markedly distinct from the agency cases discussing the public rights exception in the context of [an agency adjudicatory] regime … we do not in this opinion express any view on how the doctrine might apply in that different context."[257]

It seems, however, that in the bankruptcy context, the last chapter is always yet to be written. Another bankruptcy case raising Article III concerns, *Executive Benefits Insurance Agency v. Arkison*, is currently pending before the Supreme Court.[258] *Executive Benefits*, involving a bankruptcy court's decision in a fraudulent conveyance action, presents the question whether bankruptcy courts may exercise jurisdiction based on litigant consent, and if so, whether consent can be implied based on a litigant's conduct.[259] Of course, the Court's treatment of consent in the bankruptcy arena could have implications for other non-Article III contexts as well.

C. Relationship to a Copyright Small Claims Court

Although it is true that the Article III cases described above are not easily synthesized, some themes emerge that could be helpful in framing a small copyright claims tribunal.

1. General Observations

First, it seems that the Court has had the greatest difficulty with the broad mandate of the bankruptcy courts, including those courts' ability to decide state law claims that, even if related to a bankruptcy proceeding, are not essential to the process. The comparatively wide-ranging powers of bankruptcy courts makes them appear a lot more like federal district courts than the more limited administrative processes at issue in *Crowell*, *Thomas* or *Schor*. Indeed, Chief Justice Roberts was careful to distinguish these cases from the bankruptcy court context in his *Stern* opinion. It seems that the Court may view the bankruptcy courts as a greater potential threat to the Article III prerogative than more modest and specialized courts.

Second, the Supreme Court has moved away from the rigid interpretation of the "public rights" exception to Article III espoused by the *Northern Pipeline* plurality, which – drawing on the early case *Murray's Lessee* – posited that outside of territorial and military courts, public rights cases should be limited to those in which the government is a party. Since *Northern Pipeline*, the Court has generally embraced a more pragmatic approach to evaluating the public rights exception. The Court has acknowledged – most notably in *Thomas* and *Schor* – that even if a claim derives from or resembles a traditionally private cause of action, if the claim is closely tied to a federal statutory or regulatory scheme, it may nonetheless be amenable to determination by a non-Article III body. Notably, in *Schor*, the Court extended this principle to include a state law counterclaim where determination of the counterclaim was integral to the adjudication of the statutory entitlement. In sum, while the Court clearly remains troubled by the specter of relatively unfettered adjudication of traditional state common law causes of action by non-Article III tribunals, where Congress has articulated specific rights and remedies pursuant to a statutory scheme, the Court has been more deferential to Congress' decision to assign an adjudicatory role to a specialized agency.

Third, parties' consent to non-Article III processes, including consent as evidenced by their conduct, has played an increasingly significant role in the Court's consideration of these issues. Based upon the parties' consent, the Court has confirmed that district courts are able to delegate the conduct of entire civil trials, as well as other matters, to non-Article III magistrate judges. In the administrative context, the Court has considered parties' consent to non-Article III adjudication a critical factor favoring the constitutionality of the alternative process. While the Court in *Schor* observed that consent of a party is not itself sufficient to negate structural separation of powers concerns arising from Congress' assignment of adjudicatory functions to a non-Article III body, it also made clear that consent overcomes any personal right of the parties to have their matter heard by an Article III tribunal, and went on to uphold the alternative administrative process. A party's consent to an alternative forum thus substantially diminishes Article III concerns, especially where the Article III court remains available to that party in the first instance, and the alternative process is subject to at least limited Article III review. Even in *Stern*, where the Supreme Court determined that the bankruptcy court could not constitutionally adjudicate a state law counterclaim, the Court considered it significant that Pierce had not "truly consented" to have the claim decided by that non-Article III court.

That said, the Court's decision in *Stern* marks a departure from the more pragmatically inclined *Thomas* and *Schor*, and the Court will revisit the issue of consent in *Executive Benefits*. Depending upon the Court's analysis, the outcome of *Executive Benefits* could have an impact on Congress' approach to an alternative process for small copyright claims.

2. Copyright-Specific Considerations

As the Supreme Court has observed, "[c]opyright law is a 'creature of statute.'"[260] From the earliest days of the republic, the Court has affirmed that "[n]o one can deny that

[Congress has] the power to prescribe the conditions on which such right shall be enjoyed."[261] More recently, the Court has reiterated that the Copyright Clause "'empowers Congress to determine the intellectual property regimes that, overall, in that body's judgment, will serve the ends of the Clause.'"[262]

Congress has exercised its constitutional prerogative under the Clause since 1790, when it enacted the nation's first copyright statute.[263] For over two centuries it has defined and adjusted the rights and remedies of copyright owners under federal law, including the term of copyright, the requirements for infringement actions, and the remedies available for infringement.[264] In addition, Congress has long provided for a national system to register copyrighted works and record copyright-related transactions, to the benefit of both authors and the general public.[265]

Because the rights and remedies for copyright are fixed by Congress pursuant to an overarching statutory scheme, it would seem that under the Supreme Court's post-*Northern Pipeline* jurisprudence – most notably *Thomas* and *Schor* – at least some types of small copyright claims should be amenable to non-Article III resolution. In considering the applicability of the Seventh Amendment to statutory damages claims, *Feltner* emphasized the common law procedures for the assertion of copyright claims in the early days of the nation. But even at that time, rights and remedies of copyright owners were defined by Congress.[266]

More broadly speaking, the rights and remedies of copyright owners are statutorily created and closely tied to the national system of copyright registration and recordation. Indeed, the availability of statutory damages and attorneys' fees in cases of infringement depends upon timely registration of the work at issue,[267] and a U.S. author must have registered (or received a refusal to register from the Office) before a judicial remedy is available at all.[268] The ability and incentives to pursue infringement claims are calibrated by Congress to further the interests of the copyright system generally, and thus have a significant public dimension.

Perhaps the most fundamental question to be considered in evaluating the constitutionality of a potential small claims system is whether any such process must be based on consent, or whether it could be mandatory. Consent has been an important – and arguably determinative – factor in the Court's more recent cases addressing administrative decisionmaking. Regardless, because a process without juries would be inconsistent with *Feltner*'s holding that copyright litigants are entitled under the Seventh Amendment to a jury trial if they so choose, a mandatory approach without juries would appear to present a seemingly insuperable obstacle. For this reason, the Report need not further analyze the viability of a mandatory small claims system for purposes of Article III.

In sum, a voluntary system appears far more promising at this time. Even under a voluntary approach, however – where parties agree to waive their individual rights to an Article III forum and jury – Congress will still need to be mindful of the structural safeguards embodied in Article III and avoid undue encroachment on Article III courts. In this regard, the contrast between the bankruptcy courts' wide-ranging legal and equitable powers, and the more modest administrative schemes upheld in *Thomas* and *Schor*, is instructive. But in any event, viewing the situation in practical terms, the threat to Article III courts would appear to be substantially lessened when many of the cases that would presumably be adjudicated in an alternative system could never be practically litigated in an Article III court.

D. The Appointments Clause

Recent experience with the Copyright Royalty Board ("CRB"), an existing administrative tribunal housed within the Library of Congress whose functions are partially overseen by the Register of Copyrights, underscores the potential significance of the Constitution's Appointments Clause to the selection and supervision of those who might serve as decisionmakers in a copyright small claims system.

The Appointments Clause addresses the Framers' concerns about potential diffusion of government power by limiting Congress' authority to provide for the appointment of officers of the United States.[269] Embodied in Article II of the Constitution, it provides that "[the President] ... shall nominate, and by and with the Advice and Consent of the Senate, shall appoint ... Officers of the United States, whose Appointments are not herein otherwise provided for, and which shall be established by Law: but the Congress may by Law vest the Appointment of such inferior Officers, as they think proper, in the President alone, in the Courts of Law, or in the Heads of Departments."[270]

As defined by the Supreme Court, an "officer of the United States" – as opposed to an "employee" – is a person who "exercis[es] significant authority pursuant to the laws of the United States."[271] An inferior officer is an officer whose "work is directed and supervised at some level by others who were appointed by Presidential nomination with the advice and consent of the Senate."[272] If the officer's work is not so directed and supervised, the officer is considered a principal officer who must be appointed by the President with the advice and consent of the Senate.[273] Inferior officers may be appointed by heads of departments.[274]

The CRB, consisting of three Copyright Royalty Judges ("CRJs") appointed by the Librarian of Congress – who is in turn appointed by the President – is an administrative body that sets the rates and terms of statutory copyright licenses and distributes the royalties collected under such licenses to copyright owners.[275] In *Intercollegiate Broadcasting System v. Copyright Royalty Board*,[276] Intercollegiate, an association of noncommercial webcasters unhappy with a royalty rate determination of the CRB, challenged the constitutionality of the Board under the Appointments Clause, arguing that the CRJs constitute principal officers who can only be appointed by the President.[277]

In reviewing the responsibilities and supervision of the CRJs, the Court of Appeals for the District of Columbia Circuit concluded that, while directed in certain respects by the Librarian of Congress and Register of Copyrights, the Judges still had "vast discretion" in establishing the rates and terms for statutory licenses.[278] Moreover, they were not removable from office except for misconduct or neglect of duty.[279] Finally, the CRJs' rate determinations were not reversible or correctable by any other officer or entity within the executive branch, so their decisions – while appealable to an Article III court – were final for purposes of that branch.[280] Given the CRJs' nonremovability and the finality of their decisions, the Court of Appeals held that "the Librarian's and Register's supervision functions f[ell] short of the kind that would render the CRJs inferior officers."[281]

In light of this determination, the court declared the CRB "as currently constituted" to violate the Appointments Clause, but remedied the constitutional defect by invalidating and severing the restrictions on the Librarian's ability to remove the CRJs.[282] In the court's view, with this statutory change, the Librarian – whom the court confirmed to be a head of department – could now properly appoint the CRJs. But ensuring the Librarian's "unfettered removal power," the Librarian would be able to "direct," "'supervise'" and "exert some 'control'" over the Judges, and they would now be proper inferior officers.[283]

In establishing an alternative forum for the adjudication of small copyright claims, consideration should be given to the Appointments Clause, as well as the Court of Appeals' decision in *Intercollegiate Broadcasting*, to ensure that the decisionmakers (assuming they are not Presidential appointees) are adequately supervised and appropriately subject to removal.

E. Due Process Considerations

The Fifth and Fourteenth Amendments to the Constitution provide that "no person shall be ... deprived of life, liberty, or property, without due process of law."[284] Due process safeguards are essential to impartial adjudicative proceedings. Even in a voluntary system – where parties may choose to forego certain traditional rights – for example, by waiving objections to personal jurisdiction and formal service of process – the proceedings must be fundamentally fair both to those who bring claims and those who respond. It is therefore worthwhile to consider the basic precepts of due process as they might apply to a small copyright claims tribunal.

1. Personal Jurisdiction

It is clear that federal courts have subject matter jurisdiction over cases arising under the Copyright Act.[285] But when plaintiffs – including copyright owners alleging infringement – bring cases in federal court, they also must establish that the court has personal jurisdiction over the defendant.[286] In its simplest terms, personal jurisdiction refers to the idea that, as a matter of due process, a defendant can be sued only in a location where it is fair to require the defendant to appear in court. While it may be easy for a copyright owner to demonstrate personal jurisdiction if he or she files a lawsuit in the state or federal district where the defendant resides, it can become considerably more complicated if the plaintiff brings suit in a different jurisdiction.

Federal courts apply varying standards to determine whether a defendant is properly subject to the jurisdiction of the court, depending upon the context. As a general matter, guided by the 1945 Supreme Court decision in *International Shoe Co. v. Washington* and its progeny, courts assess whether a defendant has sufficient ties – or "minimum contacts" – with the jurisdiction to satisfy due process.[287] Under such an analysis, a court might find that it has either general or specific jurisdiction over a defendant, or both.

To establish general personal jurisdiction, a court must conclude that the defendant has had "continuous and systematic contacts" with the forum.[288] If so, the defendant is properly subject to suit. Alternatively, to find specific jurisdiction, courts typically apply a three-part test that considers whether the cause of action arose out of or resulted from the defendant's forum-related activities,[289] or the defendant purposely directed his or her activities at the forum or availed himself or herself of the privilege of conducting activities in the forum;[290] and, assuming that the answer to both of these is "yes," whether the assertion of personal jurisdiction is reasonable and does not "offend traditional notions of fair play and substantial justice."[291]

These traditional analyses of personal jurisdiction are highly fact-dependent and can become even more complicated when the case arises from online activities. If a defendant's only contact with a jurisdiction is through the internet, courts have developed additional factors to consider. In the influential case *Zippo Manufacturing Co. v. Zippo Dot Com*, the Western District of Pennsylvania announced a "sliding scale" assessment to determine when internet activity was sufficient to establish personal jurisdiction.[292] At one end of the scale are "active" websites where "the defendant clearly does business over the internet" and "enters into contracts with residents of a foreign jurisdiction that involve the knowing and repeated transmission of computer files over the internet"[293] – in which case the exercise of personal jurisdiction is proper. At the other end of the scale are "passive" websites that do "little more than make information available."[294] Such passive websites do not provide grounds for exercising personal jurisdiction. "Interactive" websites, "where a user can exchange information with the host computer," lie at the middle of the scale.[295]

Unlike a number of other federal statutes, the Copyright Act does not provide for nationwide service of process.[296] But as there appears to be interest in a centralized small claims process, perhaps administered by the Copyright Office in Washington, D.C., a question arises as to how parties from other jurisdictions might be brought before that tribunal (unless the infringing acts occurred where it was located) – including whether such a centrally located small claims facility could permit national service.

In considering where a party may be sued under a federal statutory regime that ostensibly permits nationwide service, one approach has been simply to ask whether the defendant has "minimum contacts" with the United States – rather than with a particular federal district – on the theory "that [because] the relevant sovereign is the United States, it does not offend traditional notions of fair play and substantial justice to exercise personal jurisdiction over a defendant residing within the United States."[297] This "pure minimum contacts" approach, however, has not been widely adopted. In *Republic of Panama v. BCCI Holdings*, for example, the Eleventh Circuit applied what has been called the "fairness approach."[298] Under this standard, regardless of whether the statute permits nationwide service, the court considers not only the defendant's minimum contacts with the United States, but also "balance[s] the burdens imposed on the individual defendant against the federal interest involved in the litigation."[299]

Finally, a court needs to engage in one of the above analyses only if the defendant challenges personal jurisdiction. Unlike a case in which a court lacks subject matter jurisdiction – a defect that cannot be cured by parties' consent to the forum[300] – if a nonresident defendant voluntarily submits to a court's jurisdiction, he or she waives any objection and personal jurisdiction is proper.[301]

2. Service of Process

A court's personal jurisdiction over a defendant is not complete until the defendant is properly served with process.[302] In federal court, this means that the defendant must receive notice of the lawsuit and a copy of the complaint as provided in Rule 4 of the Federal Rules. Without proper notice, the judicial proceedings are invalid as to the defendant. If service of process is defective and the defendant does not raise this defense in his answer, however, he or she is deemed to have waived the defense of insufficient service.[303]

Federal Rule 4 prescribes the requirements for the service of process on both individuals[304] and entities.[305] It includes procedures for formal service of process. As a general matter, formal service of an individual can be accomplished by delivering a copy of a summons and complaint personally to the defendant,[306] by leaving a copy of the requisite papers at the defendant's home with a resident of suitable age and discretion,[307] by delivering a copy of the papers to an agent authorized by appointment or by law to receive service of process,[308] or by following the rules for service applicable in the forum state.[309] Corporate and other entities may be served according to state rules or through an officer or authorized agent.[310] Service also may be made through an alternative process pursuant to which a defendant waives formal service by agreeing to accept notice of the action by mail or other means, in which case the defendant will benefit from additional time to respond to the complaint.[311] Rule 4 also provides for the service of foreign defendants, which is more complex and typically made pursuant to an international agreement such as the Hague Convention on the Service Abroad of Judicial and Extrajudicial Documents.[312]

3. Conduct of Proceedings

The Supreme Court has held that, at a minimum, due process consists of "notice and opportunity for a hearing appropriate to the nature of the case."[313] In the civil arena, the Court has had the opportunity to examine many elements of judicial procedure in light of due process concerns, such as assistance of counsel, provision of evidence, and availability of appellate review.

Regarding the assistance of counsel, the Court has held that a court may not arbitrarily deny a litigant the right to furnish himself or herself with counsel.[314] Additionally, the Court has ruled that the rules of evidence in effect in a given proceeding must, in order to comport with due process, provide the litigant with "a reasonable opportunity" to submit facts bearing upon his or her defense.[315]

A significant focus of inquiry has been whether due process requires appellate review of court decisions. On this question the Court has held that, provided there has been a "full and fair trial on the merits" of a case, a state is not obligated to provide for appellate review.[316] This is true in both the civil and criminal contexts.[317]

Small claims courts, by design, generally offer considerably less in the way of procedural protections than courts of plenary jurisdiction. "The rules of small claims courts emphasize conciliation and pragmatism over winning, and many rules of evidence and civil procedure have been simplified to allow maximum access to the courts by individuals unable to afford an attorney."[318] To take but one example, California small claims courts do not allow discovery or, ordinarily, the assistance of counsel.[319]

The Supreme Court has not specifically opined on what processes and opportunities must be provided by state small claims courts to comply with due process. Numerous lower federal and state courts, however, have addressed these questions, though not in any systematic way. These courts generally have held that by choosing to litigate in small claims court, plaintiffs effectively waive any due process right that may not be provided for in the abbreviated forum.[320]

Caselaw in this area analyzes questions of assistance of counsel, availability of discovery, appellate review, and the ability to cross-examine witnesses. Regarding assistance of counsel, state courts in California, Nebraska and Idaho have all found that the denial of counsel in a small claims proceeding does not violate due process where counsel is allowed if the case is tried *de novo* on review.[321] In the Virgin Islands, there is no statutory right for trial *de novo* on review, but the U.S. district court there has held that denial of counsel at the small claims level is nonetheless consistent with due process because, *inter alia*, the small claims judge has the discretion, if counsel requests, to transfer the case to a different court.[322] The overriding rule in all of these cases is that "due process requires that a party have a right to be heard through counsel at some stage."[323]

Litigants have also challenged the rule in some jurisdictions that no discovery is permitted in small claims proceedings. In Ohio, the state Court of Appeals found that such a rule does not violate due process because parties may request leave from the court to conduct interrogatories or take depositions, and because a defendant may request that the case be moved to the regular docket of the court, where discovery is permitted.[324]

Following the Supreme Court, lower federal courts and state courts are consistent in holding that appellate review of small claims verdicts is not required by due process, provided that "due process [is] accorded in the tribunal of the first instance."[325]

One due process right that some courts have held must be preserved at the small claims level is the right to cross-examine witnesses.[326] Furthermore, because one of the purposes of cross-examination is to make determinations based upon witness behavior, it has been held that testimony via telephone does not effectively preserve the right and cross-examination must be allowed to be conducted in person.[327] But notwithstanding such considerations, it is clear that the right to cross-examination, however conducted, can be waived.[328]

Alternative dispute resolution ("ADR"), specifically arbitration, is another way of settling legal conflicts through the use of abbreviated or specialized procedures. Of course, because most arbitration is conducted by private means and does not constitute "state action," it is not subject to the requirements of constitutional due process.[329] Arbitration can, however, incorporate what has been called a kind of "private due process" to protect parties against procedural unfairness.[330]

One way this is achieved is through the provisions of the Federal Arbitration Act ("FAA"), a federal statutory provision that provides for the judicial enforcement of private arbitration awards.[331] The FAA allows parties to challenge arbitral awards on a number of procedural grounds, including: where the award was due to "corruption, fraud, or undue means";[332] where there was "evident partiality";[333] where the arbitrators refused to postpone a hearing, refused to hear pertinent evidence, or were guilty of "misconduct" prejudicing the rights of the parties;[334] and where the arbitrators exceeded their powers or imperfectly exercised them so as to preclude a "mutual, final, and definite award."[335] In addition to the procedural safeguards of the FAA, courts may require arbitrators to provide a "fundamentally fair hearing," meaning "notice, opportunity to be heard and to present relevant and material evidence and argument before the decisionmakers, and that the decisionmakers are not infected with bias."[336] Courts have declined to enforce arbitral awards where an arbitral forum was not neutral,[337] one party had exclusive control over arbitrator selection,[338] the arbitration agreement was unconscionable,[339] or the arbitration rules were one-sided.[340]

V. State Courts

In addition to the federal court system described above, the United States has vibrant and essential state court systems serving each of the fifty states and the District of Columbia. There, parties litigate a huge variety of cases, from breaches of contract to divorces to serious criminal matters. As noted above, copyright cases are not currently within state court jurisdiction and thus state court judges lack expertise and experience in copyright matters. As discussed below, participants in the Copyright Office's small claims study were overwhelmingly of the view that copyright cases should continue to be the exclusive domain of federal courts or, in the case of smaller claims, perhaps some other sort of federal process. But it is nonetheless important to review the role of state courts, and state small claims procedures in particular, because they offer valuable insight into established methods to address lower-value claims in relatively streamlined fashion.

A. Courts of General Jurisdiction

The state court systems of the United States share some common characteristics. Typically, state courts have more than one level of tribunal, including trial courts and one or more appellate courts. At the trial level, states divide cases based upon monetary value and/or subject matter. Most cases are tried in state trial courts of general jurisdiction, where litigants must comply with procedural rules that can encompass significant discovery and motion practice not unlike federal court.

Many states follow a modified version of the Federal Rules,[341] which, as described above, help to structure litigation, but can also result in complex and expensive procedures, including extensive pretrial practice. As in federal courts, state court trials can be long and costly, with lay and expert witnesses, voluminous exhibits, evidentiary questions, motion practice, and juries. In fact, one survey estimated that, for some of the most common causes of action, total court costs can range from $43,000 to $122,000[342] – well above what many might consider to be the value of a small copyright claim.

Because copyright cases are reserved to the federal courts – and state court rights equivalent to federal copyright protections are preempted by the Copyright Act[343] – state courts lack expertise and experience in copyright matters. That said, state courts do sometimes address somewhat related issues involving state common law rights that have not been preempted, such as cases involving pre-1972 sound recordings (which are not subject to federal copyright protection);[344] cases involving the public performance of unfixed works (also not federally protected);[345] and certain moral rights issues, such as misattribution.[346] But, as a rule, state courts are unfamiliar with infringement and other matters that arise under the Copyright Act and lack state-developed precedents to guide them.

B. Small Claims Courts

In addition to courts of general jurisdiction, every state and the District of Columbia has a small claims process to provide better access to the legal system for citizens with low-value civil disputes.[347] Small claims systems avoid many of the technical procedural rules normally applied in state civil court proceedings, which can result in trial delays and increased costs.[348] By using simplified procedures, restricting attorney participation, and limiting the types of claims that litigants can bring, states have designed small claims systems to be accessible, low cost, and efficient.[349]

While all state small claims systems serve the same fundamental purpose, they vary in terms of structure and procedure.[350] For example, small claims may be encompassed within the civil jurisdiction of a state magistrate court or court of limited jurisdiction, as in Georgia,[351] or may be heard in a different division of the court system, such as in California or Illinois.[352] In multilevel court systems, which include New York and Massachusetts, small claims are handled within the lowest level of the civil courts, or specialized parts of those courts.[353] Although the court systems differ, one theme holds constant: separate, less formal rules of procedure govern small claims proceedings.

1. Jurisdiction

Because they employ streamlined procedural mechanisms, small claims tribunals are limited to certain types of claims. These limits turn on the monetary value or the nature of the claim asserted, or both. In some cases, states also limit the parties who may use the small claims procedure and/or attorney participation.

a. Monetary Limits

All small claims courts are limited to adjudication of claims of smaller economic value; only claims that fall under a certain dollar amount are eligible.[354] The limit varies significantly across the United States, ranging from $2,500 in Arizona and Rhode Island to $25,000 in Tennessee.[355] States sometimes also impose limits on the number of claims a single claimant may file in a given time period.[356]

States periodically evaluate whether to raise their small claims caps.[357] Supporters of higher limits principally argue that current limits are insufficient to cover basic disputes, and higher limits would help clear regular civil dockets of claims more appropriate for a small claims system.[358] Those opposed to raising limits fear that rising caps will overburden small claims systems,[359] begin to intrude on defendants' due process rights,[360] and create inequalities between one-time litigants and repeat corporate plaintiffs.[361]

b. Permissible Claims and Parties

Small claims systems adjudicate a wide variety of matters, including claims involving contracts, torts, and personal property.[362] Different states, however, have different restrictions on the claims that can be litigated in small claims court. For example, while most small claims courts hear claims arising from breach of contract, unpaid debts, and motor vehicle accidents, they do not necessarily address eviction cases, intentional torts, or defamation actions.[363] Thus, plaintiffs in different states with the same claims may have different access to their small claims courts.

Additionally, many states allow only certain types of parties to participate in small claims systems. Some states prohibit assignees, collection agencies, and/or professional lenders from bringing small claims actions.[364] These entities must instead file in the regular civil division of the applicable state court. The rationale for this prohibition is that, even without attorney representation, such repeat claimants may have an unfair advantage over a one-time defendant who is unfamiliar with court procedure.[365]

2. Attorney Representation

Most but not all states allow parties to use lawyers in small claims actions.[366] A notable exception is California, which generally prohibits attorney participation in its small claims process except when an attorney is representing himself or herself or when the suit is by or against a partnership or professional corporation of attorneys.[367] Litigants who appear *pro se*, however, may seek legal advice from attorneys to prepare their case.[368]

When attorneys are allowed to appear, small claims procedures may still limit the scope of attorney participation[369] or subject represented parties to discovery that otherwise would not be available.[370] Contrary to the usual rule requiring attorneys to represent corporations and other legal entities,[371] some states permit officers, directors, and/or employees of an entity to appear on behalf of that entity in small claims court.[372]

3. Small Claims Procedures

Small claims procedures tend to be far simpler and less formal than those applicable to ordinary civil litigation.[373] States' time-tested procedures for adjudicating lower-value claims are useful to keep in mind for a potential copyright small claims process.

a. Filing Fees

A plaintiff must pay a filing fee to initiate a claim in small claims court.[374] While such fees vary across states – for example, from $15 to $20 in New York[375] up to $150 in Massachusetts[376] – they are typically lower than those assessed by states' regular civil division counterparts, and may be graduated with respect to the amount of damages claimed.[377] In Florida, for example, a plaintiff is required to pay a fee of $50 to commence an action for damages of less than $100, but a fee of up to $380 for garnishment actions seeking more than $1000.[378]

b. Assistance to Litigants

Small claims courts typically provide information and assistance to help litigants navigate the court system and collect their judgments. Clerks may be required by statute or rule to provide materials on the small claims process to litigants.[379] Some small claims courts offer staff assistance with the preparation of initial filings. California, for example, has established special advisory services to help litigants prepare claims and defenses, while Massachusetts requires clerks to offer assistance with claims forms upon request.[380]

c. Commencement and Service of Action

In lieu of a formal pleading, a small claims plaintiff typically commences an action by filing a simple statement or using a pre-established form in which he or she provides a description of the controversy and states the amount sought in damages.[381]

Next, the claimant must serve the defendant. State small claims courts tend to have somewhat relaxed service of process rules. For example, although personal service may be used, many small claims systems allow parties to effect service by certified mail, with some courts even permitting service by regular first class mail.[382] Parties may be able to take advantage of government options such as using a sheriff, marshal, or constable to serve papers on the opposing party, or may use process servers or other disinterested adults.[383]

Once served, a defendant is expected to respond to the proceeding. Some states do not require small claims defendants to file answers, but instead only to appear at a hearing to defend against the claim.[384] Similarly, defendants do not always need to file a counterclaim, and may instead raise a counterclaim for the first time at trial.[385] In many – though not all – small claims systems, if a counterclaim exceeds the jurisdictional limit, the case will be transferred to a more general court, resulting in a more expensive and complex proceeding than may have been anticipated by the plaintiff.[386]

d. Mediation

Small claims litigants are often encouraged to mediate their claims through a court-sponsored mediation process. In some states, participation in mediation is mandatory before a trial on the merits.[387] Many states, however, merely encourage litigants to use an optional mediation procedure available at the courthouse on the day of trial.[388]

e. Pretrial Practice

The hallmark of a small claims proceeding is that traditional rules of civil procedure are significantly relaxed in order to save litigants effort and expense.[389] Modified procedures for small claims actions typically preclude or limit the use of discovery.[390] Florida's small claims court, for example, does not allow a party to make discovery requests of an unrepresented party unless the unrepresented party has himself or herself initiated discovery.[391] Other states do not permit discovery at all.[392]

Even where more traditional rules of procedure apply, they may be construed liberally by the court so litigants are not intimidated by the technicalities of formal court procedure. In most small claims settings, judges significantly control the manner in which a case proceeds, exercising considerable discretion concerning the application of procedural and evidentiary rules.[393] In some states, the judge is to decide the applicable rules and extent of discovery on an *ad hoc* basis.[394]

f. Conduct of Trial

At trial, parties will generally be asked to explain their "side" of the case, and the court may request them to provide documentary proof to support respective claims and defenses.[395] The presentation of evidence at a small claims trial, however, is generally quite curtailed in order to enable the resolution of the claim in a quick and efficient manner.[396] Judges presiding over small claims matters typically retain broad discretion to apply evidentiary rules in the interest of fairness.[397] For example, a judge may allow parties to present witness testimony telephonically[398] or may admit hearsay evidence.[399] Additionally, a judge may limit the number of witnesses or, in some states, permit an expert witness if the expert will aid the factfinder in evaluating a technical matter.[400]

g. Right to Jury

As discussed above, the Seventh Amendment of the U.S. Constitution guarantees the right to a jury trial in federal proceedings.[401] Many states, as well, have a jury trial right, and may permit litigants in a nonjury small claims proceeding to appeal to a different court for *de novo* determination of the claim before a jury.[402] Some states, including Florida,[403] Illinois,[404] and Texas,[405] allow litigants the opportunity to demand a jury in small claims court, provided they are willing to pay jury fees.[406] In other states, parties are considered to have waived their right to a jury trial by participating in the small claims forum.[407]

h. Available Relief

Full equitable relief, such as broad injunctive relief, is not widely available in state small claims systems.[408] Some states permit limited equitable relief, primarily in the form of rescission, reformation, restitution, and specific performance.[409] Equitable relief may be limited to instances where the statute giving rise to the cause of action specifically authorizes a small claims court to grant this type of relief.[410]

In many small claims courts, the prevailing party may recover reasonable costs that arise from the action, such as court fees, cost of service, and costs associated with subpoenaing a witness.[411] Consistent with the usual rule, however, attorneys' fees are typically not available unless a contractual provision authorizes such an award or a statute expressly permits it.[412]

i. Decisions and Review

In the typical small claims system, parties must appear on the day of trial, either on their own or through their attorney (if attorneys are permitted). A determination may be made at the hearing or mailed to the parties a few days to a few weeks after the case is heard.[413]

States differ in their handling of a party's failure to appear. If the plaintiff appears and the defendant does not, a default judgment may be entered for the plaintiff.[414] Before the court will issue a default judgment, however, the plaintiff may still be required to demonstrate the defendant's liability, or provide evidence to establish the accuracy of the requested damages.[415]

If the plaintiff or both parties fail to appear, the case is generally dismissed without prejudice, allowing the plaintiff to refile at a later time.[416] Default judgments generally are not appealable, but may be set aside by the court upon a showing of good cause.[417]

The Supreme Court has held that the U.S. Constitution does not require states to provide appellate review as a matter of due process.[418] States therefore may prescribe procedures for and place conditions upon the right to appeal, or decline to provide for appellate review.[419] States vary greatly as to the rules and procedures that govern small claims appeals. Some states do not permit appeals in small claims actions at all because a party is considered to have waived the appeal right by participating in the forum.[420] Other states permit aggrieved parties to appeal to a higher court.[421] Many states restrict appeals to those parties present at the small claims trial and, accordingly, in those jurisdictions, a default judgment is not appealable.[422] The states that permit appeals also differ in whether the simplified small claims procedure is carried forward to the appellate action, or if different appellate procedures apply.[423] In many states, an appeal is conducted as a trial *de novo*.[424] Alternatively, states that eschew the *de novo* approach may permit appeals on questions of law.[425]

j. Enforcement of Judgments

Once a judgment is rendered, prevailing parties generally must take additional steps to secure payment. A persistent complaint with respect to small claims courts is the difficulty in collecting on judgments.[426]

Some states now include enforcement assistance as part of their small claims programs and make a particular effort to provide information to parties about the collections process.[427] Judges may be required to explain the enforcement process and advise the prevailing party that he or she is entitled to an enforcement hearing upon request.[428] In Massachusetts, for example, courts are encouraged to hold enforcement hearings without requiring successful plaintiffs to bring a separate action to monitor whether debtors are fulfilling judgment obligations in a timely

VI. OTHER ILLUSTRATIVE MODELS AND APPROACHES

To appreciate the full range of possibilities for an alternative system to resolve small copyright claims, in addition to state judicial processes, it is instructive to highlight additional models and procedures that came to the attention of the Copyright Office during the course of its study. These systems range from federal entities such as the CRB and Trademark Trials and Appeals Board, to dispute resolution programs of nongovernment organizations, to solutions implemented in foreign jurisdictions. While disparate in their approach, each facilitates the resolution of specialized issues or smaller claims, or otherwise serves to mitigate the burdens of traditional litigation.

A. Copyright Royalty Board

The CRB comprises three full-time CRJs who are appointed by the Librarian of Congress upon consultation with the Register of Copyrights.[430] By statute, the chief CRJ is to be experienced in adjudications; a second CRJ is to have significant background in copyright law; and the third CRJ is to have significant experience in economics.[431]

Aided by two staff attorneys,[432] the CRJs are responsible for determining applicable rates and terms of various statutory licenses under the Copyright Act, including licenses for the use of musical works and sound recordings, and for the retransmission of broadcast television content by cable and satellite providers.[433] The rates and terms adopted by the CRB apply on an industry-wide basis and result in hundreds of millions of dollars in annual royalty payments.[434] Because the royalties paid under the cable and satellite licenses are collected by the Copyright Office, the CRB has the additional statutory duty to distribute those royalty pools equitably to copyright owner claimants.[435]

Because of its limited, though significant, duties to determine statutory license rates and royalty distributions, the CRB does not address the type of small copyright claims with which Congress is concerned. But its structure and responsibilities under the Copyright Act, and relationship to the Copyright Office, make it of interest for purposes of this Report.[436]

Under the Copyright Act, the CRJs are afforded independence in rendering their rate and distribution determinations,[437] but may consult with the Register of Copyrights on matters other than a question of fact,[438] and are required to consult with the Register on any novel material question of law.[439] In addition, their decisions are subject to review by the Register for legal error, and any conclusions of substantive law by the Register are binding as precedent upon the CRB in subsequent proceedings.[440]

The CRB statute and related regulations set forth detailed procedures for the conduct and determination of rate and distribution proceedings, including implementation of party settlements.[441] Proceedings may involve numerous interested parties and often take two years or longer to complete.[442]

The CRB process allows for significant discovery, including document production and depositions, though it is not as broad as discovery permitted under the Federal Rules.[443] Trials before the CRB, relatively formal in nature, typically involve multiple expert and nonexpert witnesses and voluminous economic evidence, and can last several weeks.[444] The rates and terms for statutory licenses are determined in accordance with specific statutory criteria that vary from license to license.[445]

Due to the possibility that an individual copyright owner claiming a very modest sum of royalties from a particular royalty pool can hold up the CRB's distribution of millions of dollars to others, the CRB statute includes a "small claims" process for claims of $10,000 or less, which limits the CRJs' consideration of such a claim to an abbreviated paper process.[446] Claimants who assert an inflated claim of more than $10,000 in bad faith for the purpose of avoiding the paper-based determination are to be fined "in an amount not to exceed the difference between the actual amount distributed and the amount asserted by the participant."[447]

The rate and distribution determinations of the CRB are directly appealable to the Court of Appeals for the D.C. Circuit, and are reviewable by that court to determine whether the decision was "arbitrary, capricious, an abuse of discretion, or otherwise not in accordance with law."[448]

B. Patent Courts and Procedures

1. Patent Trial and Appeal Board

With the goal of a more efficient and streamlined patent system that limits litigation costs,[449] the 2011 America Invents Act ("AIA") established the Patent Trial and Appeal Board ("PTAB") in the Patent and Trademark Office ("PTO"), replacing the Board of Patent Appeals and Interferences.[450] The PTAB, which became effective September 16, 2012, consists of the Director of the PTO, the Deputy Director, the Commissioner for Patents, the Commissioner for Trademarks, and administrative patent judges.[451] Administrative patent judges are appointed by the Secretary of Commerce in consultation with the Director of the PTO, and must have "competent legal knowledge and scientific ability."[452] The PTAB is expected to have 225 judges by the end of fiscal 2013, up from ninety-five at the beginning of 2012.[453] Each proceeding before the PTAB is heard by a panel of at least three members, as designated by the Director of the PTO.[454]

The AIA also established four new trial proceedings to take place before the PTAB: *inter partes* review; post grant review; a transitional program for covered business method patents ("TPCBM"); and derivation proceedings. An *inter partes* or post grant review involves a challenge by a third party to an issued patent, seeking to cancel that patent.[455] A TPCBM proceeding is similar to a post grant review, except a person may not file a petition for a TPCBM proceeding unless that person has been charged with infringement under the patent.[456] Lastly, a derivation proceeding determines whether an inventor named in an earlier application derived the claimed invention from an inventor named in the petitioner's application and the earlier application claiming such invention was filed without authorization.[457] In a derivation proceeding, the PTAB may correct the naming of the inventor in the patent at issue.[458]

Petitions for *inter partes* or post grant reviews must be filed with the appropriate fees and include specified information.[459] The patent owner has the right to file a preliminary response to such a petition explaining why review should not be instituted.[460] The Director of the PTO must then determine whether to institute a review based on whether the petition and response show that (in *inter partes* matters) "there is a reasonable likelihood that the petitioner would prevail with respect to at least 1 of the claims challenged in the petition"[461] or that (in post grant matters) "it is more likely than not that at least 1 of the claims challenged in the petition is unpatentable."[462]

In 2012, the PTO issued regulations governing rules of practice for the PTAB proceedings described above.[463] These rules cover filing of documents, management of the record, motion practice, testimony and production, oral argument, decision, settlement, and other matters.[464] As to representation by counsel, the regulations do not require it, but do require that if counsel is involved, the party must designate a lead and a back-up counsel.[465] The rules permit motion practice,[466] compulsion of testimony and production,[467] and depositions.[468] Oral argument may be requested by either party.[469]

A party dissatisfied with the final written decision of the PTAB following an *inter partes* or post grant review may appeal the decision only to the U.S. Court of Appeals for the Federal Circuit.[470]

Because the AIA-instituted PTAB proceedings are so new, the available statistics do not tell us much. Through July 2013 there have been 394 *inter partes* review petitions filed with the PTAB.[471] Out of these, 126 trials have been instituted, but none has proceeded to a final decision.[472] Only one post grant review petition has been filed, and that trial was terminated.[473]

2. Specialized Federal Procedures

Because patent infringement cases can be particularly formidable for courts and litigants, some federal courts have adopted special procedural rules for such actions. Courts that have taken this approach include the Southern District of New York and the Western District of Pennsylvania, both of which are participating in a pilot program established by Congress as the Patent Cases Pilot Program.[474] The modified patent rules adjust the Federal Rules to address the specific complexities of patent litigation by altering procedures for case management conferences, initial disclosures, and claim construction proceedings.[475]

Another court, the Eastern District of Texas, has adopted special patent rules that are notoriously daunting but have shortened trial timelines such that the district has become a magnet for patent plaintiffs.[476] Some have expressed concern that the Eastern District of Texas's local patent rules unfairly favor plaintiffs by compressing the time defendants have to respond, while plaintiffs may have spent significant time preparing the case before filing it in court.[477]

In addition, as noted above, patent cases are appealed from the district courts to a specialized federal tribunal, the Court of Appeals for the Federal Circuit.[478] Congress established the Federal Circuit to handle patent appeals and certain other types of appeals in part to "increase doctrinal stability in the field of patent law," which was important because the "uncertainty created by the lack of national law precedent was a significant problem, and … widespread forum-shopping [was] particularly acute."[479]

3. Small Claims Review

The PTO, in conjunction with the ABA, currently is considering whether the United States should develop a small claims process for patent disputes. In a December 2012 Federal Register notice, the PTO solicited comments on a number of issues, including whether a small claims alternative for patent enforcement is needed and what features a small patent claims process might have.[480] In addition, the PTO is reviewing a number of issues that parallel the issues considered in this Report, including "subject matter jurisdiction, venue, case management, appellate review, available remedies, and conformity with the U.S. constitutional framework (*e.g.*, Seventh Amendment)."[481] The PTO indicated that it is continuing to evaluate comments of the public and "will provide recommendations regarding the concept in due course …, in consultation with the ABA, the Federal judiciary, and other stakeholders."[482]

C. Trademark Trial and Appeal Board

PTO's Trademark Trial and Appeal Board ("TTAB") hears cases concerning the federal registration of trademarks such as *inter partes* (third party) petitions for cancellation of marks, oppositions to registration, and concurrent use and interference proceedings.[483] While the TTAB relies largely upon the Federal Rules, it is not an Article III court, and certain procedures are modified. Most notably, the TTAB offers an accelerated adjudication option that relies upon party stipulations and abbreviated procedures.[484]

The TTAB, which is staffed by a total of twenty-three administrative trademark judges,[485] the large majority of which have experience as trademark examining attorneys with the PTO,[486] has very limited jurisdiction: it only hears cases regarding whether the PTO should issue or cancel a federal trademark registration. The TTAB is not able to "determine the right to use [a trademark], nor may it decide broader questions of infringement or unfair competition."[487] Nor may it "declare any portion of … any … act of Congress … unconstitutional."[488] Matters litigated before the TTAB, however, also can be litigated in federal district court.[489]

Though the vast majority of TTAB proceedings do not address collateral issues, they sometimes touch on other subjects necessary to reach a determination related to registration. For example, the TTAB may consider whether a settlement agreement prevents a party from bringing a TTAB action.[490]

The TTAB provides only limited remedies. Essentially, in *inter partes* cases, it only may order cancellation of an existing federal trademark registration or prohibit the registration of a pending application.[491] The TTAB cannot grant any monetary relief, including costs or attorneys' fees. Additionally, it cannot grant any injunctive relief to prevent a losing trademark applicant or registrant from using the subject trademark.[492]

Each TTAB case is decided by a panel of three administrative law judges.[493] In addition to the judges, an interlocutory attorney is assigned to each case to help expedite its progress. The interlocutory attorneys handle various logistical matters and are able to decide certain non-dispositive motions, such as uncontested motions for extensions of time. They also may conduct discovery conferences.[494]

In TTAB proceedings, a party may be represented by an attorney[495] or may proceed *pro se*.[496] The TTAB will not hold any person (including attorneys) in contempt or award expenses (including attorneys' fees) to any party,[497] but other sanctions available under Rule 37(b)(2) of the Federal Rules may be ordered.[498]

To initiate a case before the TTAB, a party must file either a notice of opposition[499] or a petition to cancel,[500] serve the opposing party,[501] and pay a filing fee.[502] Pretrial practice includes potentially extensive discovery – including depositions – and motion practice similar to that in federal courts.[503]

Unlike typical federal court litigation, the TTAB does not have live trials. Instead, the parties file written trial materials, which may include deposition and other testimony, official records, and other evidence.[504] Parties may provide trial briefs and can request oral argument, which can be conducted in-person or via videoconference.[505]

Since 2008, parties have been able to submit their cases to the TTAB's Accelerated Case Resolution ("ACR") process as an alternative to a traditional TTAB hearing. ACR is designed to be a more efficient and economical form of resolution for non-complex cases and approximates a summary bench trial. Parties' agreement to use the ACR procedure allows the TTAB "to resolve issues of fact at summary judgment and to treat the parties' summary judgment motion papers and evidence as the final record and briefs on the merits of the case."[506] To facilitate the ACR process, parties may stipulate to abbreviated procedures regarding discovery, testimony, witnesses, and other matters.[507]

A party can appeal a TTAB's *inter partes* decision directly to the Court of Appeals for the Federal Circuit,[508] or to any federal district court.[509] TTAB decisions are reviewed under the deferential "substantial evidence" standard of the Administrative Procedure Act for findings of fact but *de novo* for findings of law.[510]

Notably, practitioners have voiced dissatisfaction over the length of time it takes for the TTAB to come to a final decision in an *inter partes* proceeding.[511] Statistics show that intervals between the commencement of a proceeding and final decision have increased over time.[512] Currently, TTAB scheduling orders and rules typically mean that a non-ACR case will take at least 550 days to submit for decision, assuming there are no oral arguments, motions to extend, or successful dispositive motions.[513] This would seem to be as long as or longer than some federal district court proceedings.

D. United States Tax Court

The United States Tax Court ("Tax Court") is a court formed pursuant to Article I of the Constitution and primarily is responsible for resolving taxpayer disputes concerning tax delinquency determinations of the Commissioner of Internal Revenue. Of particular note for purposes of this report is that the Tax Court has developed special rules of procedure for small tax cases.[514]

Today's Tax Court has its roots in Congress's 1925 creation of the Board of Tax Appeals[515] in response to perceived hardships for taxpayers in appealing tax assessments to federal district courts.[516] In 1969, Congress renamed this administrative body the United States Tax Court, converted it to an Article I court, and added a small case component for taxpayers with low-value disputes.[517]

The Tax Court has the power to adjudicate tax deficiency cases,[518] overpayment claims,[519] declaratory judgment actions,[520] disclosure actions,[521] and a variety of other actions. This responsibility to adjudicate tax disputes is not exclusive to the Tax Court, and is shared with the Court of Federal Claims and the several federal district courts.[522] Despite the shared jurisdiction, the Tax Court hears the vast majority of tax cases in the United States.[523] To invoke the Tax Court's small tax case procedures, the amount in dispute has to be $50,000 or less for the tax year in question and must involve income, estate, gift, or certain excise taxes.[524] The small case limit has been raised several times by Congress from the initial cap of $1,000 in 1970.[525]

Tax Court judges are appointed by the President, with the advice and consent of the Senate,[526] though they serve fifteen-year terms rather than life tenure.[527] While the Tax Court relies to some degree on the Federal Rules, its procedures are substantially different when a petitioner elects to pursue his or her case on the small case track.[528] Once a petitioner chooses the small case path, proceedings are conducted by "special trial judges" appointed by the Tax Court's Chief Judge,[529] and the standard procedural rules of the Tax Court are supplanted by the rules for small tax cases, which are designed to be as informal as possible.[530]

The principal office of the Tax Court is in the District of Columbia, but by statute the Tax Court or any of its field divisions may sit at any place within the United States.[531] Currently, there are field divisions in seventy-five different cities,[532] fifteen of which hear only small tax cases.[533]

To commence a case in the Tax Court, a party must file a petition and pay a filing fee.[534] The petitioner can request that the case be heard in Washington, D.C. or in a more convenient location.[535] If the amount in dispute is $50,000 or less, a petitioner can request to use the small tax case procedure, though a case may not be adjudicated as a small case if the decision "would provide precedent for the disposition of a substantial number of cases, or if an appellate decision is sought on a significant issue,"[536] or if it turns out the amount in dispute is above the $50,000 statutory limit.[537]

The Internal Revenue Code gives the Tax Court wide latitude over the rules of procedure and evidence and procedure to be employed in small tax cases, referred to as "S" cases.[538] The procedural rules state simply that trials are conducted as informally as possible and that "any evidence deemed by the Court to have probative value shall be admissible."[539] Small case petitions are submitted on a standardized form with checkboxes and limited areas to present narratives.[540] Neither briefs nor oral arguments are required in these cases "unless the Court otherwise directs."[541]

A petitioner in a small tax case may appear without representation or may be represented by any person – including a non-attorney – admitted to practice before the court.[542] A petitioner who prevails in a tax case in federal court, including the Tax Court, potentially can recover attorneys' fees and court costs if certain conditions are met,[543] including the exhaustion of any administrative remedies.[544] The United States, however, may not recover fees or expenses.[545]

Decisions of the Tax Court are rendered either orally from the bench or as written opinions.[546] Standard decisions can be appealed to the various U.S. courts of appeals, but small case determinations are not appealable and may not be treated as precedent in any other proceeding.[547]

E. Uniform Domain Name Dispute Resolution Policy

Several commenters suggested that the Office look to the Uniform Domain Name Dispute Resolution Policy ("UDRP") procedures governing domain name disputes as a potential model for an alternative copyright small claims process.[548] UDRP proceedings help trademark owners enforce their rights against infringing domain names in a timelier, more cost-efficient manner than they could through traditional infringement litigation.[549] The UDRP is internationally respected "as an expedient alternative to judicial opinions for resolving trademark disputes arising across multiple national jurisdictions."[550]

The UDRP was established in 1999 by the Internet Corporation for Assigned Names and Numbers ("ICANN"), the non-profit entity created for the allocation and management of the domain name system ("DNS").[551] The UDRP provides rules for handling domain name disputes, but the disputes themselves are resolved by various nongovernmental organizations ("dispute resolution providers"), including the World Intellectual Property Organization ("WIPO").[552] ICANN approves dispute resolution providers that have "demonstrated [the] ability to handle proceedings in an expedited, global, online context in an orderly and fair manner."[553] UDRP proceedings are conducted in writing and presided over remotely by one to three panelists – selected by the dispute resolution provider either alone or in conjunction with the parties[554] – who determine whether a domain name registrant has engaged in bad-faith registration of a domain name (or "cybersquatting") in violation of a third party's trademark rights.

Dispute resolution panels hear only limited types of claims that they are empowered to resolve by virtue of the contractual relationships between ICANN and the different domain name registrars (the companies that offer domain name registration services), and, by extension, those registrars' contractual relationships with individual registrants. ICANN requires that domain name registrars implement the UDRP for resolution of trademark-related disputes for generic top-level domains.[555] Registrars therefore include the UDRP in all of those domain name registration agreements, which makes submission to an administrative proceeding mandatory for disputes over registrations that are identical or confusingly similar to trademarks.[556] Thus, registrants of generic top-level domains must abide by the UDRP and are subject to UDRP proceedings.[557]

UDRP panelists to which disputes are submitted are charged only with determining whether a domain name is identical or confusingly similar to a third party's trademark, the registrant lacks rights or legitimate interests in the name, and the name was registered and is being used in bad faith.[558] UDRP panels therefore do not generally consider issues collateral to the determination of whether a registrant violated the UDRP. There are exceptions, however. A UDRP panel may need to evaluate third-party rights, usually in the context of deciding whether to cancel a registration as opposed to transferring a domain name.[559] And panels have considered the infringement of copyrighted works on a website as evidence of bad faith conduct.[560]

UDRP disputes are governed by several layers of substantive and procedural rules. First, the UDRP itself provides general requirements, including the broad standard used to determine whether a domain name was registered and used in bad faith.[561] Panels thus base their decisions on the UDRP standard and not any one country's laws.[562] All UDRP disputes also are subject to the Rules for Uniform Domain Name Dispute Resolution Policy (the "UDRP Rules"), which provide procedural rules, including specific information as to what the parties must include in their filings.[563] In addition to these requirements, each dispute resolution provider has its own procedural rules regarding logistics, including how to provide documents to the panels and word or page limits for pleadings. [564] Dispute resolution providers request that parties use an electronic submissions process, employing website forms and/or email.[565]

It is up to the complainant to propose the number of panelists that will hear a dispute but, if the complainant requests a one-member panel, the respondent can request that the matter be heard instead by a three-member panel.[566] UDRP proceedings are conducted in writing; there are no live or remotely conducted hearings other than for exceptional reasons.[567] The papers involved are the trademark owner's complaint, the domain name registrant's response, and, in some cases, a limited ability for the trademark owner to reply.[568] These pleadings contain all of the parties' factual and legal arguments, and may include extensive exhibits and, in some cases, witness declarations.[569] UDRP proceedings do not afford any opportunity for discovery.[570]

The dispute resolution provider must assemble a panel within five days of the receipt of the registrant's response,[571] and, barring exceptional circumstances, the panel must forward its written decision to the provider within fourteen days of its appointment.[572] The relief available in a UDRP proceeding is very limited. Complainants can request only that the panel cancel or transfer the relevant domain name(s); the panel cannot grant monetary relief or enjoin registrants from registering additional infringing domain names in the future.[573]

Parties to a UDRP dispute do not need to be represented by attorneys, though complainants often are.[574] UDRP fees, which ordinarily are borne by the complainant,[575] vary among the four authorized dispute resolution providers and based upon the number of panelists and the number of domain names at issue. Current fees to challenge a domain name range from about $670 (€500) to $1,500 for single-panelist consideration of a single domain name.[576] Each party bears its own attorneys' fees.[577]

The UDRP rules do not contain provisions for appeals to a dispute resolution provider or to ICANN itself, but either party can appeal a determination to a traditional government court.[578] A respondent has ten days after losing a UDRP proceeding to file a court case before the domain name is transferred or canceled by the registrar with which the name is registered during the dispute.[579] Notably, in the United States, a claimant can also bring suit before, during, or after a dispute resolution provider's UDRP decision under traditional trademark infringement theories or under the Anticybersquatting Consumer Protection Act, codified in the Lanham Act.[580]

F. Federal Court Procedures

1. The Federal Arbitration Act

The FAA[581] enacted by Congress in 1925,[582] provides a mechanism for the enforcement of private arbitration decisions through state and federal courts. The statute provides that written agreements to arbitrate are to be considered "valid, irrevocable, and enforceable, save upon such grounds as exist at law or in equity for the revocation of any contract."[583] Additionally, reflecting a broad congressional policy favoring arbitral agreements,[584] states cannot curtail the FAA's subject matter limitations or provisions limiting the revocability of arbitration agreements.[585] While parties may challenge an agreement to arbitrate under standard contract law, as reviewed above, they can only challenge an arbitration decision resulting from a valid arbitration agreement on limited procedural grounds such as fraud, evident partiality, or other misconduct.[586] Because the United States is a party to international conventions on arbitration, valid arbitration awards also are recognized in many countries throughout the world.[587]

To enforce an arbitration award under the FAA, a party may file a motion to confirm the award with the proper court, thereby reducing the award to a judgment.[588] This court can be a state court or a federal court as specified by the parties' arbitration agreement; if no court is specified, the award is enforceable by the U.S. district court for the district in which the award was made.[589] A motion to confirm an arbitration award in federal court must be accompanied by the agreement to arbitrate and any time extensions, the arbitration award and each notice, affidavit, or other paper used upon an application to confirm, modify, or correct the award,[590] as well as the applicable district court filing fee.[591] Some federal district courts require additional documentation, such as: an affidavit listing the facts underlying the arbitration award, hearing, and arbitral agreement; a proposed order; and a memorandum of law in support of the request for confirmation.[592]

A party to the arbitral proceeding has one year to apply to a court to confirm the award.[593] A party who seeks to set aside an award, however, must petition the court within three months of its issuance.[594] An award can be vacated only for the reasons specified in the FAA and parties cannot expand these statutory grounds by contract.[595]

A party seeking to overturn an arbitral award bears a "heavy burden" under the standards specified in the FAA.[596] For example, to show that an arbitrator exceeded his or her powers, "[i]t is not even enough that the [arbitration] Panel may have failed to understand or apply the law .... An arbitrator's decision must be upheld unless it is 'completely irrational,' or it constitutes a 'manifest disregard of law.'"[597] If one of the statutory exceptions does not apply, a court is obligated to confirm the award.[598] Finally, if a party refuses to abide by a valid arbitral award "in bad faith, vexatiously, or for oppressive reasons," a court may award attorneys' fees to the party attempting to enforce the valid arbitral award.[599]

2. Federal Court Alternative Dispute Resolution Processes

In recent decades, Congress has provided that various forms of ADR processes be made available to federal court litigants in order to promote innovative ways of resolving disputes, efficiently achieve settlements, and ease the backlog of federal cases.[600]

In 1988, Congress passed the Judicial Improvements and Access to Justice Act,[601] which created a pilot program allowing a limited number of federal district courts to create local procedural rules to facilitate the voluntary or mandatory referral of civil actions to non-binding arbitration.[602] The pilot program had an initial five-year term, [603] which was extended for several years[604] before the program was supplanted by The Alternative Dispute Resolution Act of 1998 ("ADRA").[605] While the ADRA expanded the reach of federal ADR – adding mediation and other potential options for litigants[606] – it eliminated mandatorily imposed arbitration, which some believed to be in tension with the Seventh Amendment.[607] Accordingly, the ADRA provides that district court rules should ensure that "(1) consent to arbitration is freely and knowingly obtained; and (2) no party or attorney is prejudiced for refusing to participate in arbitration."[608]

The ADRA instructs each U.S. district court to authorize by local rule the use of ADR in all civil actions, through processes such as early neutral evaluation, mediation, minitrial, and arbitration.[609] Local ADR rules also must require that litigants "consider" the use of ADR, and may mandate the use of mediation or early neutral evaluation in "certain cases."[610] Particular cases or categories of cases may be excluded from referral to ADR as well.[611] The ADRA provides three instances where referral to arbitration must be barred, even if the parties otherwise consent: (1) where the action concerns the violation of a constitutional right; (2) in civil rights actions pursuant to 28 U.S.C. § 1343; and (3) where $150,000 or more in money damages is sought.[612]

Every district court has implemented some form of ADR, with more than a third authorizing multiple forms of dispute resolution.[613] The most popular form of ADR is mediation, with 67% of the ninety-four district courts using it.[614] Settlement conferences are used by 38.3% of courts, and arbitration and early neutral evaluation are both employed by 24.5%.[615] District court rules vary as to how ADR referrals are handled. For example, while a judge may order mediation without the parties' consent in forty-six districts, eleven districts require consent by all parties before mediation.[616] In its 2011 review of ADR procedures the FJC garnered information on the number of ADR referrals from forty-nine district courts, and found that, for the twelve-month period ending June 30, 2011, mediation was preferred by an overwhelming amount (17,833 cases) over arbitration (2,799) and early neutral evaluation (1,320).[617]

One notable ADR program is that run by the Northern District of California, where appropriate civil cases are presumptively referred to the "ADR Multi-Option Program," under which the parties may choose among mediation, non-binding arbitration, or early neutral evaluation, with the additional options of private ADR or a settlement conference with a magistrate judge.[618] According to statistics for 2006 through 2011, mediation is consistently the most used ADR procedure in the Northern District of California, followed by settlement conferences, private ADR, and early neutral evaluation.[619] Arbitration typically represents less than 1% of referrals.[620]

3. Programs to Assist Small Copyright Litigants

Recognizing the importance and value of legal advice, some organizations provide support to unrepresented federal court litigants in the form of *pro se* education and *pro bono* representation. Examples of such organizations that assist copyright litigants that were identified in the small claims comments and hearings include California Lawyers for the Arts ("CLA") in several California locations, the Volunteer Lawyers for the Arts, Inc. ("VLA") in New York City, and the Federal Legal Assistance Self Help Center at the San Jose Courthouse ("FLASH").

CLA is an organization dedicated to serving the creative communities in San Francisco, Sacramento, and Los Angeles that offers both a lawyer referral service and ADR services to parties with copyright conflicts. CLA's lawyer referral service allows a litigant to have a thirty-minute consultation with an attorney at a nominal cost.[621] After the consultation, CLA provides a referral to a paid attorney; or if the party qualifies, CLA will identify an attorney offering *pro bono* services or an attorney participating in CLA's modest means program.[622] The modest means program connects qualifying clients with smaller or boutique firms operating on pricing tiers that are lower than those of standard copyright attorneys. Some attorneys may be willing to give "behind the scenes" advice to clients who are proceeding *pro se*.

CLA also encourages the nonjudicial resolution of disputes through mediation, conciliation, or arbitration. CLA's ADR services (Arts Arbitration and Mediation Services, or AAMS) can be made available in person or by phone, with a $25 case opening fee and further sliding-scale fees based on the income of the individual or business ranging from $25 to $1,500.[623]

VLA, based in New York City, "provides pro bono legal representation to low-income artists and nonprofit arts and cultural organizations as well as a range of other services (legal counseling, educational programs, advocacy, and ADR services) to the entire arts community, and assists in the training of lawyers."[624] From the time it was established in 1969, VLA has helped more than 265,000 low-income artists and nonprofit organizations.[625]

To access VLA's *pro bono* placement service, a client first interviews with a VLA staff attorney.[626] Over 75% of cases are resolved through advice provided at this initial meeting, and the remainder of the matters are identified in a bimonthly email list to potential volunteer attorneys at law firms or elsewhere.[627] Most cases are placed within six to twelve weeks.[628]

VLA also operates the Art Law Line, where attorneys and other volunteers take over 150 calls daily seeking legal advice.[629]

FLASH is a service of the San Jose division of the United States District Court for the Northern District of California that offers legal research and litigation guidance to qualified parties in civil cases, including copyright cases.[630] To receive assistance from FLASH, a party must be proceeding *pro se*, but the service is free for those who qualify.[631] FLASH does not represent litigants but instead "provide[s] information about legal rights and responsibilities and about the court procedures applicable to [the] civil case, limited-scope legal advice, help preparing simple pleadings, and referrals to legal, social, and government services."[632] FLASH also makes referrals to a panel consisting of experienced attorneys from large law firms who provide *pro bono* legal research and litigation guidance, but not in-court representation, to *pro se* litigants.[633]

Statistics maintained by FLASH indicate that parties referred to the *pro bono* assistance program have a success rate of 83%, as compared to the 39% rate of success for other *pro se* litigants.[634] Intellectual property claims are the third most frequent type of claim handled by FLASH's attorneys.[635]

G. International Models

A number of countries have specialized court procedures or government-sponsored ADR programs to address copyright matters. While their usefulness as models may be limited by the varying legal regimes and cultures that they serve, these international examples offer interesting points of comparison.

1. United Kingdom

In 1990, the UK established the Patents County Court ("PCC") to serve the interests of small and medium-sized enterprises by "providing an affordable forum for intellectual property litigation," including copyright, trademark, and patent cases.[636] Over time, however, it became apparent that UK intellectual property holders continued to face significant cost barriers to enforcing their rights, even in the PCC.[637]

In 2009 and 2011, successive reports by Lord Justice Rupert Jackson ("Jackson Report")[638] and Professor Ian Hargreaves ("Hargreaves Report")[639] focused attention on the problems facing UK authors, further confirming that certain intellectual property claims are not pursued in the UK due to prohibitively high litigation costs. The Jackson Report observed that because intellectual property rights played a crucial role in the UK economy, it was critical for owners of such rights to be able to "assert or defend them in the courts."[640] The Hargreaves Report found that stakeholders "identified enforcement as the most serious weakness in the UK's IP framework" [641] and noted Nokia's submission that "even a £2,000 claim for copyright infringement ... can run up costs of £20-£30k ... which dissuades people from enforcing IP at low levels."[642] The two reports agreed that small and medium enterprises lack a cost-effective legal environment for resolving intellectual property disputes,[643] and advocated for a small claims track for intellectual property disputes within the PCC.[644]

The UK government concurred with many of the studies' points regarding small intellectual property claims, with the further observation that the lack of a cost-effective environment to resolve such disputes affects parties' decisions to settle or engage in ADR.[645] New rules were thus adopted in October 2012 to create a small claims track of the PCC.

The PCC small claims track has jurisdiction over claims concerning copyright, trademark, passing off, and unregistered design rights[646] in which the value of the claim does not exceed £10,000 (or about $15,000 U.S.).[647] In addition to the jurisdictional monetary limit, the PCC does not assign cases to the small claims track if the case involves complex questions of fact, law, or evidence.[648] Within the realm of copyright cases, the UK Intellectual Property Office suggested that copyright disputes may be best suited to the small claims track when they involve instances of direct copying.[649] If a matter is factually complex, requires significant oral evidence, or the law or evidence is complicated, the case will not be allocated to the small claims track but can still be heard by the PCC.[650]

To initiate a claim in the PCC small claims track, a plaintiff may submit a complaint with a request that the case be allocated to that track.[651] The court then sends the defendant standardized forms and instructions on how to respond.[652] If a defendant objects to using the small claims track, the judge looks to the parties' submissions to determine whether the case should in fact be tried in that track regardless of the defendant's wishes.[653] If the plaintiff did not request the small claims track, but the defendant made the request, the judge also has the discretion to send it there.[654] Without a request from either party, the case is automatically assigned to a different track.[655]

Cases assigned to the PCC small claims track can proceed based on written evidence only, without any live hearings.[656] Though attorneys are permitted, the track is designed to keep costs low by allowing a party to proceed *pro se*.[657] The standard rules for discovery (or "disclosure and inspection") do not apply to the small claims track.[658] But the small claims judge has the power to issue "special directions" to parties, which may include provisions for discovery.[659] If a judge determines that a hearing is required, the hearing is conducted informally.[660] Strict rules of evidence do not apply; the court may limit cross-examination and the court need not take evidence on oath.[661] In cases where trial is not based on the written evidence alone, it will be held in the judge's chambers or sometimes in open court.[662]

In PCC small claims cases, the court can issue both monetary and final injunctive relief.[663] Preliminary injunctions, however, are not available[664] because "interim injunctions are often complex and highly contentious matters which would significantly increase costs for litigants."[665] The expectation is that the small claims track is sufficiently streamlined to alleviate the need for preliminary relief.[666]

In the UK, the usual rule is that the unsuccessful party pays the legal costs – including the attorneys' fees – of the successful party.[667] This presumption, however, is applied very restrictively in the PCC small claims context.[668] The small claims court may award the successful party limited costs, for fixed sums, in relation to issuing the claim, court fees, and the expenses related to attending the hearing.[669] Reimbursement for legal fees is limited to cases where a party is seeking an injunction or specific performance,[670] and even then may not exceed £260 (about $411 U.S.).[671]

Appeals from a PCC decision in the small claims track can be lodged only with permission from the judge who decided the case or a circuit judge sitting in the PCC.[672] When an appeal is permitted, the case proceeds first to the sitting circuit judge, then to the Court of Appeal, where it is reviewed for errors of law or construction, or on points as to the application of the law to the facts as found by the trial judge.[673]

2. Scotland

Although Scotland is part of the UK and UK substantive intellectual property law governs, Scotland represents a separate jurisdiction with its own courts, court rules, procedures, and judges. Since the same substantive laws apply, parties can choose to bring suit in England or Scotland. Scottish intellectual property cases are heard in the Outer House of the Court of Session and appealed to the Inner House of the Court of Session. The Supreme Court of the UK hears appeals from the Inner House.[674]

Scottish procedural rules governing intellectual property cases underwent a major overhaul in 2012.[675] Although the revisions did not create a small copyright claims track as in the UK PCC, significant changes were made to facilitate the resolution of smaller intellectual property claims in a more efficient fashion. These included enhanced judicial discretion to manage cases and proceed quickly to a final hearing without unnecessary preliminary procedures.[676] Judges may require disclosure of key pleadings and facts and restrict counterclaims,[677] and witness statements and evidentiary submissions may be limited to written documents.[678] In addition, an overarching provision allows the judge to make any order he or she deems fit to promote a speedy determination.[679] The 2012 revisions also permit the judge to impose procedural and monetary sanctions on disobedient parties.[680]

3. Canada

Canada's court system provides low-cost and simplified options for resolving intellectual property disputes. These include summary proceedings for copyright and moral right infringement actions.[681] The Canadian Copyright Act explicitly states that "in the case of an application, [the proceeding will] be heard and determined without delay and in a summary way."[682] This opens the door for rights holders to take advantage of Canadian court rules governing simplified proceedings with less drawn-out discovery. The main benefit of these proceedings is that evidence is filed by affidavit.[683] Affidavits are subject to cross-examination,[684] but live testimony generally is only authorized in special circumstances as determined by the court.[685]

4. Mexico

In Mexico, the National Institute for Copyrights (Instituto National del Derecho de Autor or "INDAUTOR") handles registration of copyrights and related rights in Mexico, and has the administrative authority to resolve certain violations of copyright law. For example, the agency can impose fines on violations of the moral rights of paternity and integrity, or sanction an organization purporting to be a collecting society without the proper registration.[686]

INDAUTOR engages in both conciliation[687] and arbitration proceedings. First, INDAUTOR provides conciliation procedures as an alternative to judicial actions.[688] Conciliation proceedings take place at the request of either party and are conducted by the agency's Legal Department of Consultations.[689]

To initiate the conciliation proceeding, the complainant must file a written complaint[690] that includes a brief account of the cause of action.[691] The fee for submitting a complaint is 363 Mexican pesos (about $28 U.S.). No evidence is required at this early stage, but INDAUTOR recommends that it nonetheless be included with the complaint because there is no discovery phase in the proceeding.[692] INDAUTOR notifies the adverse party in person or by certified mail of the complaint within ten days of its receipt, and the respondent has ten days to respond, including in person at a hearing. INDAUTOR also schedules a confidential hearing, which must be held within twenty days from when the complaint was filed. The hearing will be held even if the adverse party does not respond to the agency's notification.[693] If the parties do not attend the hearing, they are subject to a fine.[694]

During the hearing, INDAUTOR mediates between the parties, but cannot make any determination on the substantive issues of the case.[695] If an agreement is reached, it is considered binding and enforceable.[696] If the parties do not reach an agreement, they are encouraged to submit to arbitration proceedings.[697]

INDAUTOR receives several hundred conciliation requests a year. In 2012, 759 requests were filed. One hundred twenty-three of the proceedings filed that year reached a settlement.[698] From 2003 to 2008, the agency was successful in resolving between 25% and 41% of requests. The percentage of resolved conciliations has dropped in recent years and currently ranges from 15% to 16%.[699]

Additionally, INDAUTOR provides arbitration services when the parties have previously agreed to arbitration through a contractual provision or agree after a dispute has arisen.[700] The proceeding is overseen by a board of three arbitrators who are selected from a list published each year by INDAUTOR. The parties each pick one arbitrator from the list and the selected arbitrators then decide on a third to act as chairman.[701] The maximum arbitration proceeding runs sixty days from when the parties choose their arbitrators,[702] but the parties can choose to extend the period.[703] Evidence can be submitted and witnesses called.[704] The proceeding ends when either the board declares an award or the parties come to an agreement before the award issues.[705] The award is final, not appealable, binding, and enforceable.[706] Arbitration expenses are borne by both parties according to rates issued each year by INDAUTOR.[707]

5. Korea

Korea makes use of a governmental entity, the Korea Copyright Commission ("KCC"), to help resolve copyright disputes through conciliation, mediation, and arbitration.[708] The KCC addresses disputes arising from rights protected under Korea's Copyright Act, including disputes over moral rights,[709] economic rights,[710] neighboring rights,[711] compensation,[712] and database producers' rights.[713]

Proceedings are initiated when an individual submits an application to the KCC, at which point a conciliation division is designated and provided with the application.[714] The designated division prepares for a hearing (which must be held within three to four months) by reviewing the application and the submitted documents and contacting the parties beforehand to discuss the dispute.[715] During the hearing, the parties can make written or oral statements and submit additional evidence through witness testimony, documents, or expert opinions.[716] The proceedings are closed, and the participants' statements cannot be quoted in litigation or arbitration.[717]

The KCC conciliation proceeding is a relatively unstructured process where a neutral person facilitates communication and assists in resolving disputes, and if a settlement is reached, it is given the same weight as a court ruling.[718]

The KCC's conciliation services have become more popular over the years. The most recent conciliation statistics are from 2011, when ninety-seven applications were filed and twenty-eight cases were resolved, representing a 28.9% settlement rate. But, while applications have risen over the past few years, the actual number of conciliation-aided settlements has remained roughly the same.[719]

In addition to its conciliation service, the KCC offers free mediation services for copyright- related disputes. A single mediator is assigned after a party submits an application to the commission.[720] Proceedings may be suspended if the mediator determines that a resolution is impossible or a conciliation application is submitted for the same dispute.[721] Assuming an agreement is reached, the letter of mediation has the same effect as a civil settlement, and failure to comply must be addressed through litigation.[722]

Finally, the KCC provides arbitration services for copyright-related disputes. Disputes are resolved by a group of one to three arbitrators, one of whom must be a specialist in copyright and technology.[723] The resolution has the same legal weight as a final judgment.[724]

VII. Key Findings and Recommendations

In light of relevant constitutional and institutional considerations, the various models and approaches reviewed by the Office, and the extensive and useful comments of those who shared their views and experiences in the course of this study, the Office makes the following findings and recommendations.

A. Forum

1. Federal Courts

In theory, the existing federal court system might be able to accommodate a streamlined process for the resolution of small copyright claims. But while some commenting parties suggested modification of federal court procedures to accommodate smaller copyright claims,[725] most did not dwell on restructuring Article III courts or processes as promising alternatives. There is no precedent for either a small claims tier in the federal courts or specialized procedures for copyright claims. A revamping of the district courts to establish a small claims process for copyright cases therefore did not appear to be viewed as a particularly realistic option by most. As one commenter explained it: "There has traditionally been resistance in the federal judiciary to creating 'specialized courts.' While the copyright small claims procedure would not require a 'specialized court' within the existing federal system, it would require a specialized process. Judges and legislators might fairly question why small copyright claims should have access to such a process, while other small federal claims do not."[726]

Interestingly, Congress and the federal judiciary have, by contrast, embraced a degree of special treatment for patent cases, which are viewed as especially challenging for both courts and litigants. Although they originate in the various district courts, patent cases are appealed to a specialized court of appeals, the Federal Circuit, a court of national jurisdiction. This, of course, differs from copyright cases (and most other types of cases, for that matter), which are appealed to the court of appeals for the circuit encompassing the federal district of origin. In addition, some district courts, such as the Eastern District of Texas, the Western District of Pennsylvania, and the Southern District of New York, have adopted specialized rules of procedure for patent cases. Such processes – which can impose challenging burdens on litigants – are, however, aimed at improving courts' efficiency and speed in addressing complex, high-stakes claims, rather than at the expeditious resolution of low-value claims. Moreover, the acceleration of patent cases under such rules often comes at the price of frenetic discovery and motion practice, which can be intimidating and expensive.

To address the problem of small copyright claims through modification of federal court procedures, it would seem that at least all district courts with a meaningful number of copyright cases would have to be persuaded to adopt unprecedented, specialized rules for the streamlined handling of such claims.[727] If the treatment of patent cases is any indication, district courts would vary in their approach – some adopting local rules and many making no adjustment at all – which would result in no improvement for many litigants and possibly forum shopping by others. Perhaps most daunting would be persuading courts to adopt such rules solely for copyright cases, when such claims are but 1% of all matters before them.[728]

In a related vein, the federal judiciary might attempt to rely more heavily on referrals to magistrate judges for small claims cases.[729] But it is important to keep in mind that parties cannot be sent to trial before a magistrate judge without their consent, and magistrate judges follow the same Federal Rules as the district courts.[730] Thus, absent a more general overhaul of existing procedures, the use of magistrate judges does not in itself present an obvious solution.[731]

The creation of a general small claims tier within the Article III courts is something that Congress may wish to consider as a broader and longer term solution to the obstacles faced by small claimants seeking to vindicate their rights through the federal system. Should the federal judiciary become interested in a small claims solution for copyright (and perhaps other) cases, the Office would be pleased to provide Congress with additional suggestions in furtherance of that goal. In the meantime, the Office recommends focusing on a solution that could be more readily implemented to address the enforcement challenges faced by small copyright claimants.

2. State Courts

Another possible approach to provide small copyright claimants greater access to courts would simply be to amend federal law, which currently restricts jurisdiction in copyright cases to the federal judiciary,[732] to provide state courts with concurrent jurisdiction in copyright disputes of low economic value. The potential benefit of this approach lies in its apparent simplicity, at least in certain respects: there would be no need to draft extensive statutory or regulatory language, or to amend the Federal Rules. Moreover, as described above, state courts already have the procedural mechanisms in place to handle smaller claims with less formality.

Despite the surface appeal, however, state court systems likely are not the best option for small copyright claimants. During the Office's study, only a couple of commenting parties expressed interest in allowing state courts to hear such claims, and most of that interest was due to concern that other obstacles to alternative systems may be insurmountable.[733] By contrast, a wide range of stakeholders voiced significant opposition to state court jurisdiction, including the ABA IP Section, AIPLA, APA, Authors Guild, GAG, Getty Images, Google Inc., NPPA, PACA, SGA, NSAI and VLA.[734]

Commenter statements and the Office's own research highlight several reasons why Congress may not wish to empower state courts to hear small copyright claims. First and foremost, perhaps, is that because cases arising under title 17 are the exclusive domain of the federal courts, state courts – and state small claims courts in particular – lack experience in copyright law.[735] Federal courts have generated a wealth of copyright precedent, but it is sometimes complex and perhaps not well-suited to cursory review by a judge who is looking at issues for the first time in a state small claims court setting.[736] State court inexperience with federal copyright principles thus weighs heavily against the possibility of expanding copyright jurisdiction to state courts.[737]

Second, state small claims systems vary significantly in both the monetary limits and subject matter of the claims that they adjudicate. The range of monetary limits for claims that can be heard in state small claim systems extends from $2,500 to $25,000; thus, depending upon the size of the claim, copyright owners in some states would be denied the ability to take part in a streamlined state process while similarly situated copyrighted owners in other states would be able to move forward. As noted by one hearing participant, state small claims limits can be "very, very low" and, in fact "lower than ... most of the proposals being made [by commenters] with respect to what the [proposed alternative] copyright tribunal threshold would be."[738]

Additionally, some states restrict the types of claims that can be heard in small claims court – limiting them to such matters as breach of contract, unpaid debts, and motor vehicle accident disputes – and exclude more complicated matters. It would be up to the states to determine whether small copyright claims qualified for small claims treatment. As a result, many copyright owners who theoretically might avail themselves of a state small claims system could find themselves in the same position that they are in now because they would be forced into a more costly court of general jurisdiction.

Additionally, state small claims systems differ enormously in their procedural rules and the relief they offer. While some go so far as to exclude attorneys[739] – who might be helpful or even necessary for some copyright plaintiffs – others incorporate jury trials, either at the small claims level or on appeal.[740] Equitable relief tends to be limited but is far from uniform across small claims systems.[741] The fact that state small claims courts are inconsistent in their procedures and available relief weighs strongly against consigning them the responsibility to adjudicate substantive federal rights, which should be worthy of similar treatment no matter where they are decided.

While for these reasons state small claims systems do not appear to offer a sensible solution, a question arises as to whether those seeking to pursue such claims might benefit if they could be heard by state courts of general jurisdiction. No commenting party appeared to endorse such an approach, likely because of such courts' perceived lack of expertise with copyright matters as well as the expense of litigating in state courts of plenary jurisdiction.[742] General state court systems share many of the disadvantages of the federal court system. Litigants are required to engage in sometimes lengthy discovery, motion practice, and a full trial on the merits – the same elements that render federal court litigation long and costly. Thus, even apart from the lack of state judicial experience with federal copyright matters, merely moving small copyright claims from the federal system to state courts of general jurisdiction may not be very helpful to small claimants.

3. Administrative Tribunal

Because, at least under current conditions, there appears to be no clear path by which Congress could reliably introduce a copyright small claims process into the existing federal or state court systems, the Copyright Office proposes that Congress consider instead the creation of a specialized administrative entity for this purpose. Many of the comments and suggestions offered in the course of this small claims proceeding pointed – either implicitly or explicitly – to such an alternative process and the possibility of locating it in the Copyright Office. The Office's observations and recommendations concerning such an administrative approach are reviewed below.

B. Nature of Tribunal

1. Voluntary versus Mandatory

While commenting parties expressed strong opinions concerning the type of tribunal they would find most useful, ultimately the range of options is constrained by what is legally supportable. For the reasons set forth above, constitutional considerations suggest that an alternative system to determine small copyright claims should be voluntary, rather than mandatory, in nature. A voluntary alternative will not impinge upon the continuing availability and authority of federal district courts to decide copyright cases. And, because neither claimants nor respondents would be required to participate in the small claims process – they could still proceed in federal court if they chose – concerns about Article III would be diminished[743] and the Seventh Amendment would be honored.[744]

Of course, a voluntary system carries its own set of challenges. By what mechanism would parties consent (or decline to consent)? Would the system be able to accommodate default judgments? And perhaps most important, what incentives would there be for responding parties to participate, especially when they may believe that the odds of being pursued in district court are low?

With respect to consent, the Office believes that Congress may wish to weigh the benefits and drawbacks of both an opt-out and opt-in model of participation.[745] Under an opt-out model, a claimant would be required to serve the respondent as provided under Rule 4 of the Federal Rules – that is, in the same manner as is prescribed for federal court – unless the respondent agreed to a waiver of formal service, as is also permitted under that rule.[746] Notice provided at the time of service would advise the respondent of the nature of the action and claim and the consequences of failing to opt out of the proceeding. A properly served respondent would have sixty days to opt out of the small claims procedure by providing written notification to the small claims tribunal. If the respondent did not opt out, he or she would be considered to have consented to participate, and thus be bound by the result.

By contrast, the opt-in model would not require formal service of process but would require an affirmative written response from the respondent that the respondent agreed to participate. Only respondents who provided such notice after receiving information about the proceeding and claim against them would be considered to have consented.

The opt-out model offers the significant advantage that parties could pursue claims against uncooperative respondents. In the comments and at the hearings, copyright owners expressed considerable frustration that their cease and desist notifications to infringers often were ignored.[747] Such experiences suggest that notification of a small claims proceeding might be similarly disregarded. An opt-out system would address this concern, at least with respect to infringers who could be located and served.[748] Moreover, an opt-out system would permit aggrieved parties to seek default determinations against nonresponsive parties based upon the submission of appropriate proof of infringement and damages.[749] Because the claimant in a default case would be required to file the default determination with a district court in order to enforce it, the defaulting party would have an opportunity to set aside the default judgment before an Article III judge upon a showing of excusable neglect.

From a due process perspective, the opt-out model may be somewhat more ambitious than an opt-in model because consent would be premised not on a written agreement or affirmative conduct, but instead on the failure to respond to a properly served notice (though a respondent could subsequently demonstrate consent by participating in the proceeding). In a district court action, however, a party served in accordance with Federal Rule 4 can be held accountable and subject to a default judgment if he or she fails to respond.[750] Likewise, a party sued in state court on a claim that is also cognizable in federal court has a limited time to seek removal of the case to the federal forum; if the party fails to file for removal in a timely fashion, he or she forfeits the right to litigate in federal court.[751] Significantly, as noted, the approach proposed by the Office would provide a means to have the default determination reviewed and potentially set aside by an Article III judge, thus providing an additional safeguard for defaulting respondents.

By contrast, an opt-in model, while perhaps more appealing as a means to obtain consent, would fail to capture infringers who simply choose to ignore a claim of infringement. In some cases, this would be at the recipient's peril; a party who received notice of a proceeding and failed to respond would be taking the risk that the claimant would subsequently pursue the action in federal district court. The question is whether that risk would incentivize the named respondent to participate in thc process. While the fact that the claimant took the step of filing with the small claims tribunal would presumably demonstrate some level of commitment on the claimant's part, undoubtedly in some cases this would not be enough to trigger an opt-in. On the other hand, for more risk-averse parties who would be disinclined simply to ignore a plausible claim of infringement, resolution of the matter through a small claims process might seem considerably more attractive than the possibility of a federal court action. As discussed below, however, the relative appeal of the small claims option probably would depend largely on how the respondent viewed his or her damages exposure, and the benefits of a streamlined adjudicative process, as compared to what might be expected in federal court.

2. Decisionmakers

Throughout the Office's review, commenting parties have emphasized the importance of copyright expertise to an alternative small copyright claims system. Almost universally, commenters and hearing participants voiced a preference for a tribunal or other system administered by lawyers or judges who were knowledgeable about copyright law.[752] Copyright law is perceived by some to be "amazingly complex"[753] and "complicated"[754]; one hearing participant observed that the requirement of copyright expertise was "critical" because copyright "issues … can quickly get beyond the everyday knowledge of even the plaintiff to know what rights they may or may not have."[755] The need for knowledgeable decisionmakers presumably would be accentuated in a streamlined proceeding, which would not typically involve extensive legal research or briefing by the parties. Moreover, the participants in such a proceeding – particularly if acting *pro se* – might need guidance in focusing their claims and defenses, making the adjudicators' knowledge of applicable law that much more important.[756]

In light of this, the Office recommends that any alternative small claims system avail itself of experienced copyright lawyers. The Office proposes that it be administered by a panel of three attorneys, two of whom would be experienced in copyright infringement matters as attorneys or adjudicators. In addition, these two panel members would have between them handled matters involving both enforcement and permissible uses, and counseled clients in protecting their rights as well as in defending against allegations of copyright infringement. Such qualifications could help ensure a balanced system sensitive to both sides of infringement claims. In the Office's view, the panel also would benefit from an attorney with meaningful experience in mediation or other forms of ADR.[757] A panel that combined both copyright and ADR expertise should be able to undertake a holistic analysis of infringement claims with an eye toward the resourceful resolution of disputes.

Because the adjudicators in any such system would have significant responsibilities in administering U.S. copyright law, the Office recommends that they be appointed and supervised by a principal officer of the United States in a manner similar to the CRJs (following the changes implemented by the Court of Appeals for the D.C. Circuit in *Intercollegiate Broadcasting System* described above[758]). While the day-to-day administration of their offices would be overseen by the Register of Copyrights, for constitutional purposes, they would be appointed and removable at will, and ultimately supervised, by the Librarian of Congress.

A copyright small claims system also would benefit from the efforts of knowledgeable staff attorneys who could both assist the adjudicators and provide information to parties concerning logistical matters. Participants at the public hearings expressed support for this concept, including for purposes of identifying faulty filings.[759] For example, staff attorneys could explain tribunal requirements and rules, assist with the completion of forms, and so forth. This is not a novel idea but similar to existing models, including the FLASH program described above, which provides support to *pro se* litigants in the San Jose courthouse in the Northern District of California, and the practices of some state small claims courts, where individuals can seek help from administrative staff.[760] In addition to their public-facing duties, copyright small claims attorneys also would act as law clerks to the adjudicators by providing legal research and analysis and helping to keep cases on track.[761] As in many adjudicative systems – including the CRB – staff attorneys presumably would play a vital role in the operation of a copyright small claims system.

3. Format and Location

While a number of suggestions were raised and discussed, a large number of commenters expressed support for a centralized process relying primarily upon written submissions, without the requirement of personal appearances.[762] Under this model, proceedings would be conducted remotely via the internet, with any hearings accomplished by video or teleconference.[763] For many, the Copyright Office appeared to be the obvious home for such a process.[764]

The Office agrees that a centralized process made available by remote means probably represents the most sensible and cost-effective approach. In a non-voluntary system, a centralized system in a single location might raise concerns of personal jurisdiction. As a matter of due process, it could be problematic to subject a responding party to the mandatory jurisdiction of a faraway tribunal (though due process concerns might be substantially mitigated if all proceedings were conducted remotely). As the proposal is for a voluntary process, however, personal jurisdiction should not be an issue; parties would waive any objection to personal jurisdiction by agreeing to participate.

As in UDRP proceedings, parties' contentions and evidence would be submitted largely in written form, with suggested formats provided by the system itself. Decisions would be based primarily on documentary evidence. If necessary, the adjudicators could hold limited conferences or hearings by telephone or videoconference to address case management issues and enable the parties to elaborate on their arguments and evidence. The tribunal would be broadly accessible without elaborate procedures or the necessity of travel.

A few suggested that the CRB might be tasked with adjudicating small copyright claims in addition to its current duties.[765] While the CRB plays a vital role in the administration of various statutory copyright licenses, the Office does not believe it is well-suited to administer a small copyright claims system. The industry-wide royalty rate and distribution determinations for which it is responsible – and its necessary focus on complicated economic evidence and expert analysis – lie at the opposite end of the spectrum from small copyright claims. Moreover, at least at present, the CRB is not equipped to operate remotely, but rather requires multiple in-person appearances by parties and witnesses over the course of multiyear proceedings and typically lengthy trials. For these reasons, the Office believes that a small claims process would be largely incompatible with, and could thus detract from, the essential operations of the CRB, and that a separately constituted tribunal is advisable.

That said, the Office agrees with those who suggested that a small claims facility would be logically situated at the Copyright Office, as such an entity would fit well within the Office's overall responsibility of administering the nation's copyright system.

C. Subject Matter and Remedies

1. Eligible Claims

The written comments and public roundtables reflected a considerable amount of debate concerning the types of claims and defenses that should be encompassed by an alternative small copyright claims system. Participants espoused widely divergent views about these issues, which are at the heart of any alternative system. Although there was agreement that a primary purpose of such a small claims process obviously would be to hear smaller infringement cases, it was unclear at first blush what other claims might be considered or what defenses should be allowed.

As most copyright litigators know, copyright cases often involve multiple claims that can range from straightforward infringement claims to more complex matters intertwined with contract or trademark disputes or other issues. In federal court, these claims can be pursued in a single lawsuit, which can make litigation more efficient because all related claims between the parties are adjudicated at once. A unified proceeding makes sense in federal court, where there is extensive discovery and motion practice and the parties expend significant resources and time. The same rationale, however, may not hold true in an expedited process for small copyright claims.

In a copyright small claims system, the parties likely will not have access to extensive discovery and will instead be limited to presenting the most critical evidence. Cases will be developed using abbreviated procedures, in shorter time frames, in order to simplify and speed the process. Notably, other specialized tribunals, such as the UDRP and TTAB, typically refrain from considering issues outside of their primary purpose or jurisdiction. Even when these tribunals do review ancillary issues, such consideration is limited to that necessary to permit a judgment on the primary matter within the tribunal's jurisdiction. Similarly, to preserve the limited scope of their proceedings, the Tax Court and UK's Patents County Court exclude complex claims. The Office recommends that an alternative copyright small claims tribunal be similarly confined.

Most commenting parties generally concurred in this view. Groups as diverse as the American Photographic Artists, Association of American Publishers, Picture Archive Council of America, and the Independent Film and Television Association all agreed that tangential trademark, unfair competition, and similar claims do not belong in a small copyright claims setting.[766] At the same time, however, some observed that related contract and ownership claims should be considered when relevant to the infringement proceeding.[767] Others referenced the need for coverage for DMCA claims regarding misrepresentations in takedown notices.[768] Additionally, while not discussed at length in the comments and at the hearings, the idea of including declaratory judgment actions was positively received.[769]

The Office believes that the main focus of any small claims proceeding should be on infringement matters arising under one or more of the exclusive rights set forth in section 106 of the Copyright Act. In addition to damages determinations, a small claims system should have the ability to render declaratory judgments pertaining to either the infringement or noninfringement of a copyrighted work. In some cases, such a determination may entail consideration of contract or ownership issues, but any such consideration should be limited to that required to resolve the infringement claim at hand.

Additionally, the Office recommends that any small copyright claims system include the ability to review claims of misrepresentation in DMCA takedown notices or counter notifications under section 512(f) and that proceedings before it should qualify to prevent the reposting of removed material pursuant to section 512(g). These infringement-related matters can be quite frustrating for those involved and exceptionally uneconomical to litigate in federal court.[770] The Office therefore believes that the ability to address takedown-related disputes through a streamlined proceeding would provide significant benefits for both copyright owners and online users.

This means that the Office proposes to exclude trademark, unfair competition, and other similar claims from the purview of a small claims system, at least as an initial matter. To operate efficiently and within the scope of its expertise, the Office believes that the tribunal must focus on the copyright infringement claims – as well as defenses and related counterclaims, as discussed below – that are essential to its purpose. While limiting claims in this manner may prevent some small copyright claimants from pursuing every claim they might wish in an alternative forum, it offers the benefit of a quicker and less expensive option to address their chief concern. Such an approach is consistent with other specialized tribunals, such as state small claims systems, the TTAB, and UDRP panels, all of which seek to minimize by varying degrees the burden and costs of dispute resolution by limiting the scope of their jurisdiction.

Another issue is whether the Office should hear cases involving secondary liability under theories of contributory or vicarious infringement. Unfortunately, there is not much record evidence on this point,[771] but the Office does not see a reason for blanket exclusion of all secondary liability claims at this time. In some cases where a direct infringer is unknown or unwilling to participate in the small claims process, the claimant may be limited to proceeding against a secondary infringer who is profiting from or facilitating the infringement of the claimant's work. That said, many potential secondary liability claims involving online uses will likely be barred by one of the DMCA safe harbors set forth in section 512. To ensure against inappropriate actions, the Office therefore proposes that any claim potentially subject to a DMCA safe harbor be excluded unless it is demonstrated that a DMCA takedown notice was provided and was unsuccessful. And finally, as a more general matter, the tribunal should retain the discretion to dismiss without prejudice any secondary liability (or other) claim that cannot appropriately be adjudicated within the constraints of its streamlined process.

2. *Defenses and Counterclaims*

Although the Office is proposing a streamlined approach to small copyright claims, alleged infringers must be allowed to defend themselves vigorously. A respondent in a small claims proceeding must therefore have access to all available defenses arising under the Copyright Act or other relevant law.[772] For example, the Office recommends that alleged infringers be able to assert that they in fact are owners of or have a valid contractual right to use of a work. Such a defense, however, would only pertain to the claim of infringement before the tribunal. The construction of a licensing agreement offered as a defense to infringement, for instance, should not limit future consideration of that agreement in other contexts. Similarly, if the small claims copyright tribunal found that a respondent had rightfully purchased the copyright in a work, that finding would only lead to an order of noninfringement in that case, not a finding of ownership that the defendant could use outside of the proceedings.

This approach also would apply to the defense of fair use, typically a fact-specific defense that requires careful analysis and review. Some commenters argued that fair use is too complex to include in a small claims system.[773] Thus, some urged, a small claims system should not get involved in fair use determinations. But at the same time, participants observed that "[f]air use has to be the single biggest defense that we hear people make."[774] Because it is so frequently invoked as a defense to infringement, to eliminate it from possible consideration likely would rule out the adjudication of many meritorious claims, as many responding parties would presumably decline to proceed with a voluntary process without the ability to have it considered. As one hearing participant noted, "it is far too easy to raise a frivolous defense of fair use or even a serious defense of fair use that would automatically take these claims out."[775] Accordingly, in this participant's view, "every defense that's available in federal court, the contract defenses, fair use defenses and so on, ought to be subject to this proceeding."[776] The Office agrees and recommends that fair use be an available defense in a small claims proceeding. Apart from the logistical concern of motivating participation in a voluntary system, the Office does not see how claims of infringement can fairly be adjudicated without consideration of legitimate claims of fair use.

In this regard, the Office believes that the proposed tribunal, which would include adjudicators, with substantial experience in copyright matters, would possess the appropriate background to review fair use claims. While fair use is fact-dependent, and requires close analysis, there is a good amount of judicial precedent in this area, and most assertions of fair use should not be beyond the reach of qualified decisionmakers – especially decisionmakers whose primary job it is to evaluate claims of infringement and defenses thereto. In the unusual case where, due to the streamlined process, the tribunal could not appropriately evaluate a claim of fair use – for example, because of a lack of essential evidence – the case could be dismissed without prejudice to be litigated in federal court.

Similarly, a responding party should be able to bring certain related and necessary counterclaims in a small claims proceeding.[777] Notably, such a practice is allowed in some state small claims courts and in other specialized proceedings such as TTAB cases.[778] Specifically, respondents in copyright small claims cases should be allowed to bring counterclaims based on the same transaction or occurrence as the original claim that either arises from an exclusive right set forth in section 106 or under 512(f) of the Copyright Act, or from a related contract, such as a licensing agreement, that could affect the relief the tribunal might award the claimant. Additionally, counterclaims would have to fall within the damages limitations applicable to claimants that are discussed below. But counterclaims would not be mandatory, and would be preserved for future adjudication in a different forum if the respondent wished to pursue them elsewhere.[779]

3. Registration Requirement

Title 17 currently requires most copyright owners to register their works with (or receive a refusal from) the Copyright Office before bringing an infringement lawsuit, and works must be timely registered (generally within three months of publication) to be eligible for statutory damages.[780] In the small claims study and other contexts, many copyright owners have expressed concern over the burden of registering works as a condition to bringing a lawsuit or the ability to seek statutory damages for infringement.[781]

For example, photographers have pointed out that they create hundreds or thousands of works in short periods of time, and often lack the resources to register all of the photographs to secure the full protections of the Copyright Act.[782] These frustrations are shared by graphic artists, writers, and others, many of whom view the registration requirement as an obstacle to vindicating their rights, even apart from the significant costs of litigation once one gets to court.[783] At the same time, registration is important to our copyright system because it enhances the public record, encourages licensing opportunities, and provides baseline information for courts and others to use in assessing a copyright owners' claims.

How should the competing values be balanced in the context of a system for the resolution of lower-value copyright claims? The Office recommends that registration be required, but that the registration may be issued any time before the tribunal renders a determination. A copyright owner who had not previously registered would need only demonstrate that he or she had filed an application, deposit, and fee prior to commencing the action. This approach was suggested by several stakeholders as a potential middle ground solution,[784] and is similar to the practice already followed in some federal jurisdictions.[785] To help ensure against unwarranted claims, if a registration certificate were not issued while the small claims proceeding remained pending (that is, before a final determination), or were refused, the action would be dismissed without prejudice.

In addition, it is clear from the record in this proceeding that individual creators are discouraged from pursuing claims of infringement when they are unable to seek statutory damages. The Office suggests that, within the small claims context, a copyright owner be allowed to pursue a limited amount of statutory damages even if registration was not made within the time frame prescribed by section 412. An ability to recover limited statutory damages without extensive discovery into an infringer's activities and profits would serve a small claims system by helping to simplify and streamline the proceedings. At the same time, the system should not wholly eliminate incentives to register within the time limits of section 412. As further discussed below, under the Office's suggested approach, while late-registered works would be eligible for statutory damages (as well as actual damages up to the small claims limit), such works would be entitled to only half of the statutory damages available to timely registrants through the small claims system.

4. Remedies

a. Overall Damages Limitation

Perhaps the most obvious question to ask in connection with the possibility of creating an alternative tribunal to resolve small copyright claims is what in fact constitutes a "small" copyright claim. As might be predicted, participants in the Office's study expressed a range of opinions. Suggestions for what should be deemed "small" ranged from claims seeking damages of under $10,000[786] to those seeking a maximum of $80,000.[787] Many comments, however, suggested limits in the range of $20,000 to $30,000. For example: the ABA IP Section recommended a $25-30,000 limit; ASMP suggested $25,000; Getty Images proposed $30,000; the Kernochan Center argued for $20-30,000; GAG favored a $30,000 limit; the MPAA believed $30,000 to be reasonable; and the NPPA suggested $10-25,000.[788]

It is important to consider carefully the proper claim amount because any voluntary process must provide sufficient ability for claimants to redress typical infringements while also incentivizing respondents to participate. Indeed, as one stakeholder explained, damages are "the largest thing on the table" in considering how to persuade respondents to agree to alternative adjudication.[789] The damages ceiling also should reflect and be proportionate to the limited discovery and streamlined proceedings of a small claims process. The higher the limit, the less likely a responding party will agree to forego a federal court proceeding with the full panoply of discovery and pretrial proceedings. On the other hand, a carefully chosen lower limit should encourage voluntary participation if it meaningfully reduces exposure for damages.

Also to be considered in recommending an overall monetary cap is whether the available damages will permit small copyright claimants to retain counsel to assist them in the process. While based on a small sample size, the ABA IP Section submitted evidence that suggested most lawyers are unlikely to take copyright cases with a value of under $60,000, and only a third will take cases valued at under $30,000.[790] While these findings reflect the current reality that copyright cases must be pursued in federal court, they are nonetheless informative because they indicate a breakdown in obtaining legal representation where the need for an alternative system may be the highest – in cases valued at under $30,000.

In light of these factors, the Office suggests that, subject to future adjustment by Congress if necessary, a copyright matter be considered "small" if its overall value is no more than $30,000. Thus, parties could not pursue a case seeking more than that amount in the small claims venue. If a claimant wished to bring multiple claims in a single proceeding, the Office proposes that the $30,000 limit would apply to all claims together. As discussed below, in addition to this overall damages cap, the Office recommends further limitations with respect to the recovery of statutory damages.

A $30,000 cap for small claims proceedings corresponds to what many stakeholders proposed and also coincides with the upper limit of statutory damages available under the Copyright Act in cases of nonwillful infringement. At the same time, it is only one-fifth of the highest level of statutory damages available for willful infringement, and thus should be attractive to potential respondents.

b. Actual and Statutory Damages

Copyright law allows copyright owners to seek different types of damages: actual damages and a defendant's profits, or statutory damages within certain limits.[791] The Office recommends that there be no limit on actual damages and profits available in a small claims system other than the monetary cap applicable to the proceeding as a whole. Thus, where actual damages and profits are established for the infringement of one or more works through in a small claims proceeding, they should be recoverable up to the $30,000 limit.

Statutory damages, however, require more nuanced consideration. Under the Copyright Act, permissible statutory damages range from $750 to $30,000 for the nonwillful infringement of a work (with a reduction to as low as $200 for "innocent" infringement), and up to $150,000 in cases where the defendant's infringement is shown to have been willful.[792] Throughout the Office's study, stakeholders debated both the availability and amount of statutory damages that might be awarded by an alternative tribunal, with some taking the position that there should be none at all.[793] Indeed, in recent years, statutory damages have been the subject of more general debate in the copyright community, with potential large-scale infringers and others arguing that the possibility for high awards has a chilling effect on innovation, and copyright owners asserting that statutory damages are essential to deterring infringement.[794] In the context of small claims, some participants were concerned that statutory damages would dissuade potential defendants from agreeing to participate in a voluntary system,[795] while others emphasized the importance of statutory damages in furthering settlement discussions.[796] Others did not believe there was much difference as to whether available damages were statutory or actual so long as they fell within the applicable monetary cap.[797]

The Office suggests that a small claims system include the remedy of limited statutory damages, in addition to the ability to recover actual damages and profits. In many cases, the availability of statutory damages as an alternative to establishing actual damages and profits could serve to reduce time-consuming and potentially costly wrangling over damage-related discovery issues and calculations.[798] In this way, statutory damages would further the objectives of a small claims system.

At the same time, however, statutory damages would need to be appropriately tailored for such a system, both to reflect the lesser value of "small" claims and also to ensure that they would not deter – but rather would encourage – participation by those notified of a claim of infringement.

Accordingly, while recommending that statutory damages be available in the small claims system, the Office further suggests that the available statutory damages be only half of the $30,000 per-work maximum for nonwillful infringement applicable in federal court. Thus, for works registered within the time frame prescribed in section 412, statutory damages would be capped at $15,000 per work.[799] Applying the overall $30,000 small claims limit, a claimant could thus, for example, receive up to two $15,000 statutory damages awards or three $10,000 awards for related infringements of separate works in a single proceeding.

Additionally, in a significant departure from the rule applied in federal court, works registered after the time period provided under section 412 also would be eligible for statutory damages in a small claims proceeding. These damages, however, only would be recoverable at up to half of the amount permitted for timely registered works within the small claims system – that is, up to $7,500 per work – and with the additional caveat that no more than $15,000 in total statutory damages could be awarded for all late-registered works in any one proceeding.

Another consideration is whether the small claims court should consider willful or innocent conduct in making an award of statutory damages, as is permitted under section 504 of the Copyright Act. While there seemed to be less concern about eliminating a potential downward adjustment of awards based upon a finding of innocence,[800] some participants in the study noted that it could be difficult to establish the necessary factual predicate to support a finding of willfulness in an expedited proceeding.[801] Likewise, viewed from the opposite perspective, respondents facing a claim of wilfullness might not have a full opportunity to rebut it. Picture Archive Council of America, Inc. ("PACA") made the additional observation that the willfulness distinction could be a "distraction" in a small claims proceeding, and that willful infringers were likely to end up in federal court anyway.[802] Perhaps most significantly, with a per-work limit of $15,000 and an overall cap of $30,000, any statutory damages would be below the per-work maximum for nonwillful infringement, findings of willfulness would likely be superfluous. The Office thus concludes that while it is reasonable to consider innocence in the context of a small claim, willfulness should not be a consideration in establishing statutory damages in a small claims proceeding.

c. Injunctive and Other Equitable Relief

The Copyright Act provides for different of types of equitable relief upon a finding of infringement, including injunctions[803] and impoundment and destruction of infringing goods.[804]

For some small claimants, the primary objective of bringing an infringement action is not recovery of damages but rather to halt the unauthorized use of a copyrighted work. Unauthorized uses can dilute the value of a work, impact exclusive license relationships, or may simply be objectionable to the owner. So long as the conduct continues, the claimant continues to be harmed. As one hearing participant explained, "most of the time what artists want is … the infringement to stop or they want to get some work back that has been taken from them."[805] Another creator emphasized that injunctive relief is "vital" as "injunctions are often essential to protect the moral rights of the author" and "infringement is [frequently] continuing."[806]

Unfortunately, however, injunctive relief is not as simple as it sounds. In the wake of the Supreme Court's 2006 *eBay* decision, copyright plaintiffs must demonstrate more than the mere fact of infringement to obtain a final injunction. Rather, they must show: that they have suffered an irreparable injury; that remedies available at law are inadequate to compensate for that injury; that, considering the balance of hardships between the plaintiff and defendant, a remedy in equity is warranted; and that the public interest would not be disserved by a permanent injunction.[807] Preliminary injunctions must satisfy a similar multifactor test as well.[808] Injunctions issued at the beginning of a case involve independent briefing and, often, a separate hearing, to ensure that the injunction is justified in light of the potential harm to the copyright and considerations of due process. Some small claims hearing participants questioned the ability to establish the appropriate evidentiary basis for injunctive relief in an abbreviated small claims proceeding.[809]

A related and significant concern identified by participants in the study is the potential impact of injunctive relief in certain situations, especially those involving derivative works. If an infringer simply is reproducing a work as a whole and selling it or distributing it by itself (for example, by displaying a copyrighted image on a website or selling a product incorporating a copyrighted design), it may be fairly straightforward to require the infringer to cease infringing conduct.[810]

As discussed at the hearings, however, there are more complex situations in which the infringer has incorporated the original work into another work and the financial consequences of requiring a defendant to cease the infringing use outweigh the claimant's damages claim – and perhaps the monetary limits of the small claims forum as well.[811] For example, to halt or delay the distribution of a film incorporating another work (perhaps a screenplay or song) could cost the distributor many thousands or, in some cases, even millions of dollars in marketing expenditures and lost revenues.[812] If the author of the song demands its removal from a film, the movie studio may have to spend substantial resources to edit the movie, which may not be practicable depending on timing. In such a scenario, the songwriter might be alleging damages of several thousand dollars, but an injunction would cost the studio exponentially more money to implement.

The Office believes that compromise is necessary on this point. A voluntary system needs the participation of both parties, and alleged infringers will be less likely to consent if the consequences include potentially prohibitive injunctive relief. Moreover, in many cases, the expedited nature of the proceeding might make it difficult for the adjudicators to render the factual findings necessary to support an injunction. Even if the tribunal determined that an injunction was appropriate, the claimant could have difficulty securing compliance without the enforcement powers of a federal district court.[813] But if claimants had to apply to the district court for review and enforcement of an injunction, as some participants suggested,[814] it would probably make more sense to bring the action there in the first place.

The Office is of the view that in some cases, respondents might have reason to consent to a takedown of infringing material or cessation of infringing activity upon a finding of infringement, either at the outset or during the course of the proceeding. The system could allow adjudicators to reduce a damages award that might otherwise compensate for future use of the infringed work in exchange for a respondent's promise to cease the infringing behavior. Any such agreement could, similar to a consent judgment, be memorialized in the tribunal's final determination – which, in turn, as discussed below, could be filed with a federal court to secure enforcement. In this way, claimants would not be wholly precluded from seeking to end to infringing conduct, but the small claims tribunal would avoid the significant concerns inherent in the power to order injunctive relief.

In addition to injunctions, the Copyright Act allows for the impoundment and destruction of infringing goods. There was no groundswell of support for this option, which, even when sought, is usually seen as a secondary remedy by copyright claimants. In any event, for many of the same reasons as reviewed in connection with the availability of injunctions, the Office believes these additional equitable remedies exceed what can be expected from an administrative small claims process.

d. Attorneys' Fees and Costs

Assuming attorneys are to participate in a copyright small claims process – a matter discussed below – the question arises as to whether the system should permit recovery of attorneys' fees. The Copyright Act allows, but does not require, courts to award attorneys' fees and costs to a prevailing party.[815] In federal court, as discussed above, such fees and costs can be considerable, and can quickly overwhelm potential damages in a lower-value case.[816] The possibility of recovering (or, alternatively, having to pay) attorneys' fees may therefore be a significant factor in a plaintiff's decision whether to pursue litigation, or a defendant's evaluation of settlement options. Although the allowance for fee-shifting under the Copyright Act is generally viewed as a plaintiff-friendly rule, copyright claimants cannot be overly sanguine about recovering fees. In some cases, courts award damages to successful defendants,[817] and in many cases courts do not award fees at all.[818]

As with other issues, commenters had differing views as to whether attorneys' fees and costs should be recoverable by prevailing parties in small claims actions. In a system that allows parties to hire lawyers, there is logic to permitting recovery of attorneys' fees – not only to reimburse the winning party, but also to incentivize attorneys to take lower-value cases.[819] Such fees might be capped to reflect the smaller claims at issue and protect parties against deep-pocketed adversaries.[820] On one hand, the availability of fees might encourage attorneys to amplify what could otherwise be more expeditious proceedings.

A number of stakeholders expressed concern about the impact of attorneys' fees on parties' participation in a small claims system. Responding parties might be put off by the increased risk of a potential fee award.[821] Claimants, too, might be deterred by the prospect of having to pay fees should they lose.[822] As one copyright owner representative noted, "[w]e clearly do not want to scare off potential plaintiffs from using a system that's been developed specifically for them to be able to address small claims. But we do, of course, want to avoid harassment of defendants by what amounts to something more than frivolous and bordering on fraudulent claims. That's not fair either."[823]

A related issue is the question of what standard would apply if fee-shifting were permitted. An absolute rule awarding fees to a prevailing party could be inequitable in close cases, for example, where a responding party had a colorable but ultimately unsuccessful claim of fair use. On the other hand, a rule allowing significant discretion – as is permitted to federal judges in copyright actions under section 505 – could extend the proceeding and increase expenses by requiring independent consideration of a fee award. Moreover, as in the federal courts today, a discretionary system would offer no guarantee to a party for whom recovery of fees was critical.[824]

On the whole, while there clearly are arguments to be made on both sides, because attorneys' fees awards might upset the balance of incentives to participate in the system, and perhaps increase the length and expense of proceedings, the Office recommends against a general fee and cost-shifting provision at this time. The Office acknowledges, however, that if a small claims tribunal were to become operational, the question of fee-shifting – including how fee awards might be limited to reflect that environment – would benefit from further study.

That said, the Office does propose an exception to its general recommendation against fee-shifting in cases where it is established that a party has pursued a claim or defense in bad faith, or has summoned a respondent to the tribunal but failed to proceed with the case. In such a situation, the offending party should pay fees and costs to those adversely affected by the conduct in question. Such a rule will not only serve to compensate parties for unnecessary expense, but also help to deter the pursuit of frivolous claims. Even so, in light of the modest value of the proceedings, the Office believes that such an award should not be more than the total sum of $5,000, or for parties appearing *pro* se, consist of costs only and not exceed $2,500.

5. Eligible Works

Copyright owners with rights in all types of works may be interested in using an alternative system to seek relief. Indeed, the Office received comments from numerous creators, including photographers, graphic artists, songwriters, filmmakers, and writers, all of whom argued, sometimes passionately, for an alternative system.[825] In comments and at the public roundtables, there was near universal agreement that all types of copyrighted works should be eligible for protection through an alternative system, an approach that is endorsed by the Office. As one hearing participant explained, "anything that is eligible for copyright ought to be" eligible for a small claims system.[826]

The National Music Publishers' Association ("NMPA") and the Harry Fox Agency, Inc. ("HFA"), however, joined by ASCAP, BMI, SESAC, the Recording Industry Association of America ("RIAA"), and the American Association of Independent Music ("A2IM"), urged that music should be excluded from any small claims system, at least in the near term.[827] These organizations asserted that because music matters can be complex and involve ownership and contract disputes, and potentially frivolous claims of authorship,[828] musical works and sound recordings should not be included. NMPA and other music publisher organizations generally asserted that because they represent songwriters' interests in infringement matters, songwriters did not need access to a small claims tribunal. They also expressed concern that songwriters might invoke the small claims system to pursue breach of contract claims against their constituents.[829]

By contrast, both the Songwriters Guild of America ("SGA") and the Nashville Songwriters Association International ("NSAI") "strongly endorse the concept of establishing a forum in which individual copyright owners could pursue infringement claims that have a relatively small economic value."[830] Songwriters provided an impassioned response to the music publisher organizations seeking to exclude musical works from a potential small claims forum. As one songwriter advocate bluntly opined, the "blanket exclusion of music from the small claims process would be grossly unfair to the creators of musical works."[831] This representative pointed out that as songwriters reclaim their copyrights in musical works from music publishers under the termination provisions of the Copyright Act,[832] many more will be representing themselves and may have a need for an accessible forum in which to vindicate their rights.

Indeed, there are numerous songwriters and musicians who are self-represented and do not rely on music publishers or record labels to manage their rights.[833] In fact, VLA, which provides *pro bono* legal assistance to artists, reported that approximately 20% of the organization's clients seek music-related advice, including claims by both unrepresented songwriters and songwriters hoping to enforce their rights after a publisher has declined to take action.[834] Indeed, a music publisher representative at the Los Angeles hearing acknowledged that music publishers decline to pursue songwriter claims that are not economically practical to litigate.[835]

The Office understands that each type of work has its own world of complexities, including musical works and sound recordings. In some instances such works may benefit greatly from litigation assistance provided by music publishers, performance rights organizations, or record labels. But it is clear that this is not every case; indeed, it may well be the exception rather than the rule when it comes to smaller claims of infringement. The fact that musical works and sound recordings may be managed by intermediaries does not mean that songwriters or other musicians should be deprived on a blanket basis of the opportunity to pursue an infringement matter in an alternative small claims system if they should so choose. That said, music publisher organizations and record companies may take comfort in the small claims procedures being proposed. The system will not override private agreements, so such organizations will remain free to structure their contractual relations as they wish, which of course can address copyright enforcement responsibilities as between them and those they represent. Moreover, as explained below, the Office recommends that any small claims decisions – including with respect to ownership questions – be without preclusive effect in future proceedings. But perhaps most significantly, because the system is voluntary, music publishers and others who receive notice of a small claims action would be free to decide whether it is the appropriate forum in which to address any particular claim.

Lastly, although the Office recommends that all types of works be covered by a small copyright claims system, at least for now, it is possible that experience may show that certain types of infringement claims are too complex for a small claims system. For example, claims that involve in-depth analysis of computer software programs – should any be pursued as small claims – could require a level of technical expertise that is beyond the capacity of a small claims forum. For this reason, the Office recommends that the small claims body be allowed to dismiss *sua sponte* claims that cannot be decided due to a lack of essential witnesses, evidence, or expert analysis.

D. Practice and Procedure

1. Role of Attorneys

The question of whether attorneys should be allowed to participate in a small copyright claims system generated considerable controversy among participating parties. Notably, some state systems, including California, do not permit attorneys to appear on behalf of small claims litigants.[836] While stakeholders generally acknowledged that attorneys can be helpful to copyright litigants, some expressed concern about the imbalance that could occur if individual claimants appearing *pro se* had to face off against attorneys representing large corporate interests.[837] Others, however, pointed out that unsophisticated parties should not be deprived of the opportunity to be represented by counsel, as they are the ones who may be most in need of legal counsel.[838] Because aspects of copyright law can be complicated, many viewed the role of attorneys as potentially more important in copyright cases than in typical small claims-type disputes involving nonpayment or basic contract issues.[839]

On balance, the Office believes that, even if an alternative system is designed to enable *pro se* participation, it is preferable for parties to have access to attorneys to represent them if they wish. In the United States, there is a strong tradition – buttressed by considerations of due process – of allowing parties to be assisted by counsel if they so choose. Less sophisticated parties may need assistance in navigating copyright law and litigation procedure, and attorneys may be useful in screening out nonmeritorious claims and defenses.[840] Additionally, notwithstanding the practice in certain state small claims courts, the general default rule is that corporations and other types of business entities may only appear in court through an attorney.[841] Corporate respondents may be dissuaded from participating in an alternative system if they are deprived of representation of the attorneys who ordinarily perform this role. Finally, as a practical matter, even if attorneys were to be banned from the proceedings, it would be difficult to prevent them from preparing the written submissions that likely will be decisive in many cases.

2. Assistance to Litigants

A small claims process will be of little value if its procedures and requirements are not easily understood by the average litigant. During the small copyright claims study, participants exchanged ideas concerning how to make the system accessible to litigants, and especially to unrepresented parties. There was general consensus that any such tribunal should provide comprehensive information, in plain language, as to what is required of both claimants and respondents.[842] Such guidance might include forms with spaces to add simple narrative, document templates, and similar aids for those seeking to pursue and defend claims.[843] Good examples of such user-friendly materials include California's extensive handbook for small claims litigants[844] and WIPO's model forms setting forth basic templates for the complaint and response in UDRP proceedings.[845]

In addition, as noted above, staff attorneys could be made available to answer procedural questions and assist with the completion of forms. Outside organizations, too, such as California Lawyers for the Arts and Volunteer Lawyers for the Arts, presumably would become familiar with the process over time and might be available to help litigants either by representing them on a *pro bono* basis or offering behind-the-scenes advice.

3. Initiation of Proceeding

In any system of adjudication, due process requires that defending parties receive fair notice of the claims against them. This is no less true in a small claims setting, especially one in which the respondent must decide whether to participate. As discussed above, the Office recommends that Congress consider the relative merits of both an opt-out process and opt-in process to initiate a proceeding. An opt-out process would require more robust notice to the responding party, who would be considered subject to the proceeding unless he or she opted out. Under this approach, service of process probably should follow a procedure analogous to that prescribed by Rule 4 of the Federal Rules. Absent a defendant's waiver of formal service, this rule generally requires personal service of a defendant by a non-party over the age of eighteen by delivering a copy of notice of the action and claim to the individual personally; leaving a copy at the respondent's place of abode with a suitable resident; delivering a copy to an agent authorized to receive service; or, in the case of a corporation or other entity, serving the corporation through an officer, registered agent, or by other acceptable means.[846] The respondent would then have a period of time – for example, sixty days – in which to file an opt-out notice with the tribunal, or be bound by the result. Alternatively, under an opt-in system, the responding party could be notified less formally, but would need to submit written consent to the tribunal before he or she was considered to be participating. Many commenters suggested that claimants be required to provide *prima facie* evidence of a claim before the respondent is forced to respond to notice of a proceeding.[847] The Office generally concurs with this approach and recommends that, to commence a proceeding, the complaining party be required to set forth the nature of the claim and the material facts that support it. In addition, the claimant should certify the facts alleged. As some pointed out, a certification requirement will signal to the claimant that the claim is a serious matter and should help to deter unfounded submissions.[848] Additionally, as discussed above, the Office believes that a copyright small claims system could benefit from a process whereby staff attorneys review incoming claims to ensure that they meet certain minimum requirements – for example, that they set forth basic ownership information and the nature of the infringement alleged. Finally, the small claims tribunal should require filing fees. Although such fees will not cover the costs of the proceedings, they will offset some of these costs and serve to discourage spurious claims. As one commenter explained, "the filing fee is very important for staving off some of the meritless suits that would potentially be brought if this is a very streamlined time and cost efficient and easier process for bringing these small claims."[849]

4. Multiple Claims and Parties

A small copyright claims system should promote the efficient resolution of disputes. To this end, some stakeholders believe that a small claims system should allow multiple claims and/or parties in a single proceeding.[850] This is typical in federal court litigation, which in some circumstances requires parties to assert any related claims or join indispensable parties in one action.[851] The failure to do so can constitute a waiver of the right to litigate the foregone claim or sue the additional party.[852]

In a less formal proceeding before a voluntary tribunal, however, mandatory related claims or joinder of parties would be procedurally challenging, and in some cases, not possible. Nonetheless, in some circumstances, co-owners of an infringed work might seek to bring a claim jointly. Likewise, where multiple parties are involved in the same infringing activity or course of conduct, it could be logical to pursue them together. Finally, in a situation where the same party or parties have committed a series of related infringements, it could make sense to adjudicate the claims together. The Office sees no reason why one or more parties should not be allowed to pursue one or more claims against one or more respondents in a small claims setting, assuming all of the parties and claims are tied to the same allegedly infringing activity or a continuous course of alleged infringement.[853] In such a case, the same evidence would be at issue and the parties would be able to resolve their dispute in one proceeding. But to keep the matter small, the Office recommends that the overall monetary cap of $30,000 be maintained across all claims and parties. That is, the total damages sought by all claimants for all of the claims together should not exceed $30,000. Accordingly, if a party attempted to bring three $15,000 claims against an alleged infringer for the infringing use of three photographs on a single web page, the claims could not proceed because the aggregate amount would exceed the Office's proposed $30,000 limit.

5. Unknown Infringers

As was pointed out by participants in the small copyright claims study, in some cases – in particular, cases of online infringement – a claimant may not know the identity or location of an infringing party. Website owners can, and often do, choose to operate anonymously, and their identities may be difficult or impossible for the average citizen to ascertain. This is a vexing problem for copyright owners and others who wish to take action against online conduct. In a federal court case, upon an appropriate showing, a plaintiff may be able to obtain a subpoena against an online service provider to disclose the identity and address of a website operator.[854] As noted above, however, courts sometimes decline to order the production of such information by a third party. The Office believes that the question of whether a small claims court should provide a mechanism to permit identification of unknown online infringers is one that should await another day. While some sort of subpoena process might be beneficial, the current record does not provide much insight as to how it would be practically implemented in an administrative setting. In this regard, it is noteworthy that the statutory provisions governing the CRB provide for the issuance of subpoenas but the CRJs have never exercised this authority.[855]

Needless to say, any such procedure to determine the identity of unknown infringers would require careful analysis as to the mechanism to be employed, including the appropriate procedural safeguards to protect against unwarranted requests for disclosure. The Office therefore recommends further consideration of this issue if an alternative small claims system is adopted.

6. Discovery

Any system to adjudicate small claims must grapple with the nature and amount of discovery to be permitted. As suggested above, the broad availability of discovery and related frustration of discovery-related disputes are significant factors in the timing and expense of federal litigation. At the same time, it is difficult to resolve a dispute fairly without access to relevant information. In considering the question of whether and what discovery should be permitted in an alternative system, there is no obvious model to emulate. Discovery varies enormously across different forums – from none at all in UDRP proceedings to district court-like procedures in the TTAB. State small claims courts allow differing degrees of discovery, ranging from none to discovery in limited circumstances, usually for good cause shown.[856]

Most stakeholders offering opinions seemed to favor a middle ground with respect to discovery.[857] As one hearing participant explained, "there is definitely going to be a need for the availability of limited discovery, but … the process would benefit from having an adjudicator put limits on [it] because one of the huge obstacles and expenses in litigation is … the discovery process."[858] Discovery can be critical to actual damages claims because "overwhelmingly the evidence of actual damages and their amount will be in the possession of the defendant."[859] Many commenters, however, believed that only certain types of discovery should be allowed, proposing written discovery[860] with no depositions.[861]

The Office agrees that litigants should be able to pursue some amount of discovery in small claims actions, including production of documents, interrogatory responses, and written admissions. The Office does not believe that depositions – which are typically conducted in person, can be intimidating for litigants, and require costly transcription services – should be necessary in a small claims system. Commenting parties tended to agree that depositions would be inconsistent with the goal of achieving inexpensive and streamlined resolution of cases.[862]

The ability to learn about the other side's case may be critical to support a defense or damages claim, or help to facilitate a settlement. But any such discovery should be narrowly focused on the issues in dispute and far more modest than what is permitted under the Federal Rules (which allow for up to twenty-five interrogatories per party and unlimited requests for production of documents and admissions).[863] Nonetheless, to ensure some flexibility in the system, the tribunal should retain the authority to allow limited additional discovery if it will advance the ultimate goal of resolving a case expeditiously.

7. Motion Practice

In theory, a small claims system could provide the parties with the option to file both procedural and substantive motions, as do some of the models reviewed above. A dispositive motion, such as for summary judgment, can shorten a case if it is successful – but by the same token can extend the proceedings and waste valuable resources if it is not. Moreover, formal motion practice requires a familiarity with applicable procedural and substantive law that may be beyond the reach of most *pro se* litigants. Recognizing these concerns, some stakeholders suggested that any small claims process "strongly limit ... motion practice."[864] The Office agrees that formal motion practice would be inconsistent with the objectives of the alternative small claims system it is proposing. Any such small claims process should focus on allowing the parties to present their respective evidence and arguments in an informal yet fair manner to permit the ultimate decision on the merits. But this does not mean the parties should be altogether precluded from raising a matter that is obstructing resolution. The Office recommends that parties be allowed to make informal requests to the adjudicators during the course of the proceeding to address case management and discovery issues. In addition, should the adjudicators believe that they need more information from the parties to reach a result, they should be able request specific submissions from the parties.

8. Evidence

As in any adjudicatory system, the parties will need to submit evidence to support their positions. At the roundtables and in comments, parties suggested that any evidence should be offered in written form.[865] The Office agrees and recommends that, as a general matter, all evidence, including testimony, be submitted electronically in documentary form. Moreover, as in many small claims settings, formal rules of evidence should not apply; the adjudicators should have the discretion to consider evidentiary submissions according to their worth.

One specific point of contention during the study was whether to allow expert testimony.[866] When a court is addressing a complex topic – for example, the marketplace impact of a statutory copyright license – subject matter experts may help to identify and make sense of complicated evidence. A drawback, however, of using experts is that they are expensive and must typically be retained by both sides in a litigation to ensure that the court has a balanced view of the issue.

The Office believes that in the vast majority of cases, a copyright claim that is amenable to small claims treatment should not require the presentation of expert evidence. A default rule precluding expert witnesses is consistent with the procedures of the recently established copyright small claims court of the UK[867] At the same time, however, in the rare case where it were shown that expert evidence could be fairly introduced and would aid the tribunal in resolving a matter, the tribunal should have the discretion to consider it.

9. Frivolous Claims

Throughout the small claims study, stakeholders voiced concern about the potential filing of frivolous or harassing claims and the resulting nuisance for those required to respond. More specifically, there was a view that an alternative system would invite unfounded claims by offering cheaper and easier access than federal court. As one commenter explained, "[i]f the process for filing a complaint amounts to writing a short letter, the court will be overwhelmed with claims and many defendants will have to respond to frivolous complaints."[868] At the same time, however, it was acknowledged that not all such claims would necessarily be malicious; in some cases, a copyright owner might sincerely but mistakenly believe he or she had a legitimate claim when in fact it was barred by the statute of limitations or was based on a misunderstanding of the law.[869]

To this end, the Office proposes several strategies to guard against frivolous claims. First, as described above, the tribunal and staff attorneys should provide ample information to the public about the rules and requirements of the system. Second, a staff attorney experienced in copyright law should review incoming claims to ensure that they satisfy certain basic legal requirements. For example, a claim should identify the work at issue, the claimant's interest in the work, and the nature of the alleged infringement. If a claim failed to meet these minimal requirements, it could be returned to the claimant for amendment if possible. If the claimant were ultimately unable to provide a sufficient basis to move forward, the claim would be dismissed without prejudice. Such an approach is consistent with many stakeholder comments and presumably would screen out many unwarranted filings.

In addition, however, as discussed above, the Office suggests that, upon a proper showing, the tribunal be authorized to award aggrieved parties reasonable attorneys' fees and costs – up to a total amount of $5,000 – when a litigant has pursued a claim or defense for a harassing or improper purpose, or without a reasonable basis in fact or law.[870] A fee-shifting award could also be made in the case of a claimant who summoned a respondent to the tribunal but failed to move forward with the case. *Pro se* litigants would be eligible for such reimbursement, but for costs only of up to $2,500. Such amounts would be in addition to, and not count against, the applicable damages cap for small claims proceedings.

10. Enforcement

A small claims tribunal will not mean much if its decisions can simply be ignored. As one stakeholder put it, "[i]t would be of little use to obtain a judgment in a small copyright claim forum if there was no effective means to enforce the judgment."[871]

Because a non-Article III administrative tribunal would lack the inherent powers to enforce its determinations, claimants would need a mechanism to turn an award of relief into a court-enforceable judgment. The Office believes that the FAA provides a valuable model in this regard.[872] Under the FAA, parties who have obtained an award through private arbitration may file the award with a federal district court to have it confirmed and reduced to a judgment.[873] As discussed in more detail above, such awards are presumptively confirmed absent a showing that they were obtained by fraud or misconduct, exceed the powers of the deciding body, or fail to make a final and definite award.[874] Under the Office's proposal, relief awarded through a voluntary small copyright claims process could similarly be confirmed by a district court. A party who was having difficulty collecting damages or securing other relief awarded by the small claims tribunal would thus have the option of obtaining a federal court judgment. While it seems that many small claims respondents who agreed to participate in the process would pay up if damages were imposed, undoubtedly there would be those who would not, even if the claimant took the step of filing the determination in district court. The problem of collecting on judgments is, of course, not unique to copyright, but a perennial concern for prevailing litigants, particularly in the small claims context.[875] A successful copyright small claims litigant who had his or her judgment confirmed by a district court would, for better or worse, then need to rely on general processes for enforcement of a federal court judgment. These typically would include filing the judgment with a federal or state court in the respondent's jurisdiction and possibly seeking garnishment or similar court-sanctioned relief.[876]

11. Review

While presumably the outcome of a small claims proceeding should be subject to some form of review, the benefits of a streamlined system would quickly evaporate if decisions could be extensively reconsidered, especially by an Article III court. Losing parties with substantial resources could essentially seek to relitigate the matter in federal court. Taking the examples of the bankruptcy courts and CRB, such Article III review could be either *de novo* at the district court level or by direct appeal to a federal court of appeals. Like district court litigation, federal appellate review can be procedurally complex, time-consuming and costly.[877] In either case, a litigant who could not afford the burden or expense of federal court and was forced to litigate an appeal would be back at square one. As one hearing participant predicted, "[i]f [the award] is appealable afterwards, [a] large corporation is going to take it. And if they don't like the ruling, they are going to appeal it …."[878] Another commenting party observed that if appeals were not sufficiently limited, the small claims process could become "an exercise in futility for indigent plaintiffs or small plaintiffs who prevail and then are subjected to an appellate process."[879]

At the same time, as a matter of basic fairness, a litigant before a small claims tribunal should have some ability to challenge and correct a faulty determination. As a middle ground, the Office therefore proposes that the system provide for review of decisions in a limited manner that will not defeat the purpose of the small claims system. First, as is common in many adjudicatory settings, parties should be able to seek reconsideration by the decisionmakers based on a material error or technical mistake.[880] If reconsideration is denied, upon payment of an additional fee, a party should be permitted to appeal the denial to the Register of Copyrights, who would be empowered to remand the case for further proceedings if she believed the denial of reconsideration was erroneous.[881] Finally, regardless of whether an aggrieved party exercised his or her right to appeal to the Register, the party could challenge the enforceability of the decision in a manner analogous to that permitted under the FAA – that is, the party could seek to have the decision set aside for fraud, misconduct, or on similar grounds.[882] Parties subject to a default judgment or subject to a fee award could also seek review by the district court to have the award set aside upon a showing of excusable neglect.

12. Effect of Decisions

A critical question with respect to any alternative adjudication process is what effect its decisions should have. Commenting parties were near universal in their opinion that decisions of an alternative small claims tribunal should not be preclusive, or serve as precedent, in future proceedings.[883] As one stakeholder explained it: "The goals of a small claims court ...

should not include influencing the direction of copyright law: decisions of the court will often be made quickly, based on a superficial record, without the benefit of briefing by counsel."[884] Another noted that "the decisions should not have any precedential effect beyond the immediate dispute which should lessen any impact on what decisional law the tribunal should follow."[885]

The Office strongly concurs. Because the small claims tribunal would rely on abbreviated procedures, including limited discovery and argument, it would be inappropriate for its decisions to be binding beyond the particular parties and disputes it adjudicates. Any specific factual or legal issue addressed in a determination – for example, a question of copyright ownership or fair use – should be of no future effect. Similarly, the determinations of a streamlined small claims tribunal should not carry precedential weight, either in federal court or in future matters before it. Notably, this approach is similar to that in UDRP proceedings, which do not accord previous panel decisions any persuasive weight.

Although nonbinding and nonprecedential in effect, however, in the interest of the transparency and maintenance of a public record, the Office believes that the decisions of any alternative small claims process should be publicly available, consistent with the general rules applicable to government proceedings.[886]

13. Settlement and Alternative Dispute Resolution

Most stakeholders emphasized the need for a system that could render binding decisions and were not enthusiastic about mediation or other forms of ADR as a viable solution to the problem of small claims. To quote one participant on this subject: "I think the reality is no one takes you seriously until you file .... Every defendant I know in my own copyright cases are [sic] like 'Whatever.'"[887] Asked about the possibility of requiring parties to submit to a mediation process before seeking an adjudicative decision, some expressed concern that it would simply increase the time and expense necessary to resolve a claim.[888] In addition to the difficulties of reaching a resolution through mediation, parties also noted the considerable costs of traditional arbitration, where parties are typically required to pay the arbitrators' fees.[889] In light of these reactions, it appears that, at least at this time, stakeholders are most interested in an adjudicative process that results in binding decisions rather than one that relies on ADR.

But the Office does not believe that the possibility of mediation or other ADR procedures should be abandoned completely. Mediation can be effective when all parties are committed to resolving a dispute.[890] At the very least, any small claims process should encourage settlement when possible. For example, participants should have the ability to request a supervised settlement conference if they believe it would be helpful. For these reasons, as discussed above, the Office believes that an alternative small claims process could benefit substantially from a decisionmaker who has meaningful background and experience in ADR. If a small claims process is adopted, further consideration should be given to the question of whether it should also offer mediation or similar services in addition to performing its adjudicative functions.

And finally, to alleviate some of the burdens on federal district courts, the Office suggests that any small claims tribunal be expressly designated as a qualified ADR process under the ADRA so that eligible cases can be referred to the tribunal for streamlined resolution upon parties' consent.[891]

E. Implementation and Additional Study

In their written comments and at the hearings, stakeholders expressed the view that any small claims process would need to be evaluated and potentially adjusted after it had been in effect for a period of time. As with any unprecedented program, it is difficult to predict all of the contingencies that might arise once it becomes operational. Commentators noted in different ways that "a pilot program is probably a good idea."[892]

For these reasons, the Office believes that much of the fine-tuning of any such system should be accomplished through regulation, rather than attempted by legislation. While the forum, subject matter, jurisdiction, available remedies, and other fundamental features of the process should be prescribed by statute, the details should be left to the rulemaking capabilities of the Copyright Office. To this end, Congress should ensure that the Office has the regulatory authority to implement the small claims system within the statutory parameters. In addition, after three years of operation, the Office should report to Congress on the efficacy of the system, including in relation to eligible works and claims, damages limitations, fee-shifting authority, identification of unknown infringers, and possible inclusion of mediation or similar ADR services.

VIII. LEGISLATIVE PROPOSAL

Based on the above findings and recommendations, the Copyright Office has prepared a draft of proposed legislation to implement a small claims system, as well as a section-by-section analysis of the proposal, both of which are set forth below. The draft legislation includes alternative provisions to implement the system on either an opt-out or opt-in basis.

A. Discussion Draft

§ 1401 – Copyright Claims Board and Staff

a) Copyright Claims Board. – There shall be established within the U.S. Copyright Office a Copyright Claims Board, which shall serve as an alternative forum in which parties may voluntarily seek to resolve certain copyright claims, as further provided in this chapter.

b) Officers and Staff. –

   1) Copyright Claims Officers. – Upon consultation with the Register of Copyrights, who shall recommend qualified candidates, the Librarian of Congress shall appoint 3 full-time Copyright Claims Officers to serve on the Copyright Claims Board.

   2) Copyright Claims Attorneys. – The Register of Copyrights shall appoint no fewer than 2 full-time Copyright Claims Attorneys to assist in the administration of the Copyright Claims Board.

   3) Qualifications. –

      A) Copyright Claims Officers. – Each Copyright Claims Officer shall be an attorney with no less than 7 years of legal experience. Two of the Copyright

Claims Officers shall have substantial experience in the evaluation, litigation or adjudication of copyright infringement claims and, between them, shall have represented or presided over a diversity of copyright interests, including those of both owners and users of copyrighted works. The third Copyright Claims Officer shall have substantial experience in the field of alternative dispute resolution, including the resolution of litigation matters through such means.

B) Copyright Claims Attorneys. – Each Copyright Claims Attorney shall be an attorney with no less than 3 years of substantial experience in the field of copyright law.

4) Compensation. – Each Copyright Claims Officer shall be compensated at not less than the basic minimum and not more than the basic maximum rate of pay for SL employees (or the equivalent) of the federal government. Each Copyright Claims Attorney shall be compensated at not more than the basic rate of pay for level 10 of GS-15 of the General Schedule (or the equivalent).

5) Term. – Copyright Claims Officers shall serve for 6-year terms that are automatically renewable by the Librarian of Congress upon consultation with the Register of Copyrights; provided, however, that the terms for the initial Copyright Claims Officers appointed hereunder shall be as follows: one Copyright Claims Officer shall be appointed for 4 years; the second shall be appointed for 5 years; and the third shall be appointed for 6 years.

6) Vacancies and Incapacity. –

A) Vacancy. – If a vacancy shall occur in the position of Copyright Claims Officer, the Librarian of Congress shall, upon consultation with the Register of Copyrights who shall recommend qualified candidates, act expeditiously to appoint a Copyright Claims Officer for that position. An individual appointed to fill a vacancy occurring before the expiration of the term for which his or her predecessor was appointed shall be appointed to serve for a 6-year term.

B) Incapacity. – If a Copyright Claims Officer is temporarily unable to perform his or her duties, the Librarian of Congress shall, upon consultation with the Register of Copyrights who shall recommend qualified candidates, act expeditiously to appoint an interim Copyright Claims Officer to perform such duties during the period of such incapacity.

7) Supervision and Removal. – Subject to section 1402(b), the Copyright Claims Officers and Copyright Claims Attorneys shall be supervised and removable by the Librarian of Congress.

8) Administrative Support. – The Register of Copyrights shall provide the Copyright Claims Officers and Copyright Claims Attorneys with necessary administrative support, including technological facilities, to carry out their duties under this chapter.

9) Location in Copyright Office. – The offices of the Copyright Claims Officers and Copyright Claims Attorneys shall be located at the Copyright Office.

§ 1402 – Authority and Responsibilities of the Copyright Claims Board

a) Functions. –

1) Copyright Claims Officers. – Subject to the provisions of this chapter and applicable regulations, the functions of the Copyright Claims Officers shall be as follows:
   A) To render determinations on such civil copyright claims, counterclaims and defenses as are permitted to be brought before them under this chapter, and to certify such determinations for confirmation by the United States District Court for the District of Columbia;
   B) To ensure that claims and counterclaims are properly filed and otherwise appropriate for resolution by the Copyright Claims Board;
   C) To manage the proceedings before them and render rulings pertaining to the consideration of claims, including scheduling, discovery, evidentiary, and other matters;
   D) To request the production of information and documents relevant to the resolution of a claim, defense, or counterclaim from participants in a proceeding and from nonparticipants;
   E) To conduct hearings and conferences;
   F) To facilitate parties' settlement of claims and counterclaims;
   G) To include in its determinations a requirement of cessation or mitigation of infringing activity, including takedown or destruction of infringing materials, where the party to undertake such measures has so agreed;
   H) To provide information to the public concerning the procedures and requirements of the Copyright Claims Board;
   I) To maintain records of the proceedings before them and make public the determinations in individual proceedings;
   J) To carry out such other duties as are prescribed in this chapter; and
   K) When not engaged in performing their duties as prescribed in this chapter, to perform such other duties as may be assigned by the Register of Copyrights.
2) Copyright Claims Attorneys. – Subject to the provisions of this chapter and applicable regulations, the functions of the Copyright Claims Attorneys shall be as follows:
   A) To provide assistance to the Copyright Claims Officers in the administration of their duties under this chapter;
   B) To provide assistance to members of the public with respect to the procedures and requirements of the Copyright Claims Board; and
   C) When not engaged in performing their duties as prescribed in this chapter, to perform such other duties as may be assigned by the Register of Copyrights.

b) Independence in Determinations. – The Copyright Claims Officers shall render their determinations in individual proceedings independently on the basis of the records in the proceedings before them and in accordance with the provisions of this title, judicial precedent and applicable regulations of the Register of Copyrights. The Copyright Claims Officers and Copyright Claims Attorneys may consult with the Register of Copyrights on general issues of law, but, subject to section 1405(w), not with respect to the facts of any particular matter pending before them or the application of law thereto. Notwithstanding any other provision of law or any regulation or policy of the Library of Congress or Register of Copyrights, no performance appraisal of a Copyright Claims Officer or Copyright Claims Attorney shall consider the substantive result of any individual determination reached by the Copyright Claims Board as a basis for appraisal except insofar as it may relate to an actual or alleged violation of an ethical standard of conduct.

c) Direction by Register. – Subject to subsection (b), the Copyright Claims Officers and Copyright Claims Attorneys shall be generally directed in the administration of their duties by the Register of Copyrights.
d) Inconsistent Duties Barred. – No Copyright Claims Officer or Copyright Claims Attorney may undertake duties that conflict with his or her duties or responsibilities in connection with the Copyright Claims Board.
e) Recusal. – A Copyright Claims Officer shall recuse himself or herself from participation in any proceeding with respect to which the Copyright Claims Officer has reason to believe that he or she has a conflict of interest.
f) Ex Parte Communications. – Except as may otherwise be permitted by applicable law, any party to a proceeding before the Copyright Claims Board shall refrain from ex parte communications with the Copyright Claims Officers concerning the substance of any proceeding before the Copyright Claims Board; provided, however, that Copyright Claims Attorneys may provide information and assistance to parties concerning the procedures and requirements of the Copyright Claims Board.
g) Judicial Review. – Actions of the Copyright Claims Officers and Register of Copyrights under this chapter in connection with the rendering of individual determinations are subject to judicial review as provided under section 1407(c) and not under chapter 7 of title 5.

§ 1403 – Nature of Proceedings

a) Voluntary Participation. – Participation in a Copyright Claims Board proceeding shall be on a voluntary basis in accordance with this chapter, and the right of any party to instead pursue a claim, counterclaim or defense in a United States district court or any other court, and to seek a jury trial, shall be preserved.
b) Statute of Limitations. –
    1) In General. – No proceeding shall be maintained before the Copyright Claims Board unless it is commenced before the Copyright Claims Board within three years after the claim that is the basis for the proceeding accrued.
    2) Tolling. – Subject to section 1406(a), a proceeding commenced before the Copyright Claims Board shall toll the time permitted under section 507(b) of this title for commencement of an action on the same claim in a federal district court during the time it remains pending.
c) Permissible Claims, Counterclaims and Defenses. – The Copyright Claims Officers may render determinations with respect to the following claims, counterclaims and defenses, subject to such further limitations and requirements, including with respect to particular classes of works, as may be set forth in regulations adopted by the Register of Copyrights:
    1) A claim for infringement or a declaration of infringement of an exclusive right of copyright provided under section 106 of this title asserted by the legal or beneficial owner of such exclusive right at the time of infringement pursuant to which the claimant seeks damages, if any, within the limitations set forth in subsection (d)(1).

2) A claim for a declaration of noninfringement of an exclusive right of copyright provided under section 106 of this title pursuant to which the claimant seeks damages, if any, within the limitations set forth in subsection (d)(1), where an actual controversy exists as evidenced by a documented threat of legal action against the claimant.
3) Notwithstanding any other provision of law, a claim pursuant to 512(f) for misrepresentation in connection with a notification of claimed infringement or a counter notification seeking to replace removed or disabled material; provided, however, that any remedies in such a proceeding before the Copyright Claims Board shall be limited to those available under this chapter.

Note: A conforming amendment to section 512(f) may be advisable.

4) A counterclaim asserted solely against the claimant or claimants in a proceeding pursuant to which the counterclaimant or counterclaimants seek damages, if any, within the limitations set forth in subsection (d)(1), and that –
   A) Arises under section 106 or section 512(f) of this title and out of the same transaction or occurrence that is the subject of a claim of infringement brought under paragraph (1) or a claim of misrepresentation under paragraph (3); or
   B) Arises under an agreement pertaining to the same transaction or occurrence that is the subject of a claim of infringement brought under paragraph (1) and could affect the relief awarded to the claimant.
5) A legal or equitable defense, pursuant to this title or otherwise available under law, in response to a claim or counterclaim asserted under this subsection.
6) A single claim or multiple claims permitted under paragraphs (1), (2) or (3) by one or more claimants against one or more respondents; provided, however, that all claims asserted in any one proceeding arise out of the same allegedly infringing activity or a continuous course of alleged infringement and do not in the aggregate result in a claim for damages in excess of the limitation provided in subsection (d)(1)(D).
7) Excluded Claims. – The following claims and counterclaims are not subject to determination by the Copyright Claims Board:
   A) A claim or counterclaim that is not a permissible claim or counterclaim under subsection (c);
   B) A claim or counterclaim already pending before, or finally adjudicated by, a court of competent jurisdiction;
   C) A claim or counterclaim by or against a federal or state government entity;
   D) A claim or counterclaim asserted against a person or entity residing outside of the United States; and
   E) A claim or counterclaim dismissed by the Copyright Claims Board pursuant to section 1405(f)(3).

d) Permissible Remedies.
   1) Damages for Infringement. –
      A) Actual and Limited Statutory Damages. – Subject to the limitation on total damages set forth in subparagraph (D), with respect to a claim or

counterclaim for infringement of copyright, the Copyright Claims Board may award –

(i) Actual damages and profits of the infringing party determined in accordance with section 504(b) of this title, which determination shall include in appropriate cases consideration of whether the infringing party has agreed to cease or mitigate the infringing activity as provided in subsection (d)(2); or

(ii) Limited statutory damages, which shall be determined in accordance with section 504(c) of this title, subject to the following conditions:

(I) With respect to works timely registered under section 412 of this title such that they are eligible for an award of statutory damages under that section, such limited statutory damages shall not exceed $15,000 per work infringed;

(II) With respect to works not timely registered under section 412 of this title but eligible for an award of statutory damages under section 1404(b), limited statutory damages shall not exceed $7,500 per work infringed, or a total of $15,000 in any one proceeding;

(III) The Copyright Claims Board shall not make any finding or consider whether the infringement was committed willfully in making an award of limited statutory damages; and

(IV) The Copyright Claims Board may consider as an additional factor in awarding limited statutory damages whether the infringer has agreed to cease or mitigate the infringing activity as provided in subsection (d)(2).

B) Election of Damages. – With respect to a claim or counterclaim of infringement, the claimant or counterclaimant shall after the close of discovery and in accordance with the schedule adopted by the Copyright Claims Board pursuant to section 1405(j) elect to pursue either actual damages and profits or limited statutory damages as provided in subparagraph (A).

C) Other Damages. – Damages for claims and counterclaims other than infringement claims shall be awarded in accordance with applicable law and shall be subject to the limitation set forth in subparagraph (D).

D) Limitation on Total Damages. – Notwithstanding any other provision of law, a party who pursues any one or more claims or counterclaims in any single proceeding before the Copyright Claims Board may not seek or recover in such proceeding total damages of whatever type that exceed the sum of $30,000, exclusive of any attorneys' fees and costs that may be awarded under section 1405(x)(2).

2) Requirement to Cease Infringing Activity. – In any proceeding where a party agrees to cease activity that is found to be infringing, including by removal or disabling of access to, or destruction of, infringing materials, and such agreement is reflected in the record, the Copyright Claims Board shall include in its determination a requirement that such party, if found to have infringed, cease his or her infringing conduct to the extent agreed.

3) Costs and Attorneys' Fees. – Notwithstanding any other provision of law, except in the case of bad faith conduct as provided in section 1405(x)(2), the parties to proceedings before the Copyright Claims Board shall bear their own costs and attorneys' fees.

§ 1404 – Registration Requirement

a) No claim or counterclaim alleging infringement of an exclusive right of copyright may be asserted before the Copyright Claims Board unless the owner of the copyright has first delivered a completed application, deposit and the required fee for registration to the Copyright Office and either a registration certificate has been issued or has not been refused.

b) Notwithstanding any other provision of law, a claimant or counterclaimant in a proceeding before the Copyright Claims Board shall be eligible to recover actual damages and profits or limited statutory damages for infringement of a copyrighted work under this chapter if the requirements of subsection (a) have been met; provided, however, that –

1) The Copyright Claims Board shall not render a determination in the proceeding until a registration certificate has been issued by the Copyright Office, submitted to the Copyright Claims Board and made available to the other parties to the proceeding, and the other parties have been provided an opportunity to address it;

2) If a proceeding cannot proceed further due to an outstanding registration certificate, it shall be held in abeyance pending submission of the certificate to the Copyright Claims Board; but if held in abeyance for more than 6 months, the Copyright Claims Board may, upon providing written notice to the parties' and 30 days to respond, dismiss the proceeding without prejudice; and

3) If the Copyright Claims Board receives notice that registration has been refused by the Copyright Office, the proceeding shall be dismissed without prejudice.

c) Where a certificate shows that registration of a work was made before or within five years of its first publication, the presumption set forth in section 410(c) of this title shall apply in a proceeding before the Copyright Claims Board.

§ 1405 – Conduct of Proceedings

a) In General. – Proceedings of the Copyright Claims Board shall be conducted in accordance with this chapter and regulations as implemented by the Register of Copyrights.

b) Record. – The Copyright Claims Board shall maintain records documenting the proceedings before it.

c) Centralized Process. – Proceedings before the Copyright Claims Board shall be conducted without the requirement of personal appearances by parties or others at the offices of the Copyright Claims Board, and shall take place by means of written submissions and through hearings and conferences accomplished via internet-based applications and other telecommunications facilities; provided, however, that in cases where physical or other nontestimonial evidence material to a proceeding cannot be furnished to the Copyright Claims Board through available telecommunications facilities, the Copyright Claims Board shall have the discretion to make alternative arrangements for the submission of such evidence that do not prejudice another party to the proceeding.

d) Representation. – A party to a proceeding before the Copyright Claims Board may but is not required to be represented by an attorney.

e) Commencement of Proceeding. – To commence a proceeding, a claimant shall, subject to such additional requirements as may be prescribed in regulations adopted by the Register of Copyrights, file a claim with the Copyright Claims Board, that –
   1) Includes a statement of material facts in support of the claim;
   2) Is certified in accordance with section 1405(x)(1);
   3) Is accompanied by a filing fee in such amount as may be prescribed in regulations adopted by the Register of Copyrights, which amount shall be at least $100, shall not exceed the cost of filing an action in federal district court, and shall be established to further the goals of the Copyright Claims Board.

Note: A conforming amendment to section 708 may be advisable.

f) Review of Claims and Counterclaims. –
   1) Claims. – Upon filing, a claim shall be reviewed by a Copyright Claims Attorney to ensure that it complies with the provisions of this chapter and applicable regulations. If the claim –
      A) Is found to comply, the claimant shall be so notified and instructed to proceed with service of the claim as provided in subsection (g).
      B) Is found not to comply, the claimant shall be notified that the claim is deficient and permitted to file an amended claim within 30 days of the date of such notice without the requirement of an additional filing fee. If the claimant files a compliant claim within that period, he or she shall be so notified and instructed to proceed with service of the claim. If the claim is refiled within the 30-day period but still fails to comply, the claimant will again be notified that the claim is deficient and provided a second opportunity to amend it within 30 days without the requirement of an additional filing fee. If the claim is refiled again within the second 30-day period and is compliant, the claimant shall be so notified and instructed to proceed with service, but if the claim still fails to comply, upon confirmation of its noncompliance by a Copyright Claims Officer, the proceeding shall be dismissed without prejudice. The Copyright Claims Board shall also dismiss without prejudice any proceeding in which a compliant claim is not filed within the applicable 30-day time period.
      C) For purposes of this paragraph, a claim against an online service provider for infringement by reason of the storage at the direction of a user of material residing on a system or network controlled or operated by the service provider that may be subject to the provisions of 512(c) of this title, or by reason of the service provider referring or linking users to an online location containing infringing material that may be subject to the provisions of section 512(d) of this title, shall be considered noncompliant unless the claimant affirms in the statement required under subsection (e)(1) that he or she has previously notified the service provider of the claimed infringement

in accordance with section 512(c)(3) of this title and the service provider failed to remove or disable access to the material within 5 business days of the date of provision of such notice; provided, however, that if a claim is found to be noncompliant under this subparagraph, the Copyright Claims Board shall provide the claimant with information concerning the service of a notice pursuant to section 512(c)(3) of this title.

2) Counterclaims. – Upon filing and service of a counterclaim, the counterclaim shall be reviewed by a Copyright Claims Attorney to ensure that it complies with the provisions of this chapter and applicable regulations. If the counterclaim is found not to comply, the counterclaimant and other parties shall be notified that it is deficient and the counterclaimant permitted to file and serve an amended counterclaim within 30 days of the date of such notice. If the counterclaimant files and serves a compliant counterclaim within that period, the counterclaimant and other parties shall be so notified. If the counterclaim is refiled and served within the 30-day period but still fails to comply, the counterclaimant and other parties will again be notified that it is deficient and the counterclaimant provided a second opportunity to amend it within 30 days. If the counterclaim is refiled and served again within the second 30-day period and is compliant, the counterclaimant and parties shall be so notified, but if the counterclaim still fails to comply, upon confirmation of its noncompliance by a Copyright Claims Officer, the counterclaim, but not the proceeding, shall be dismissed without prejudice.

3) Dismissal for Good Cause. – If upon reviewing a claim or counterclaim in a particular proceeding the Copyright Claims Board concludes that it is unsuitable for determination by the Copyright Claims Board due to the failure to join a necessary party, the lack of an essential witness, evidence or expert testimony, or for other good cause, the Copyright Claims Board shall dismiss the proceeding without prejudice.

Opt-Out Alternative

g) Service of Notice and Claims. – To proceed with a claim against a respondent, a claimant must within 90 days of receiving notification to proceed with service file proof of service on the respondent with the Copyright Claims Board. To effectuate service on a respondent, the claimant must cause notice of the proceeding and a copy of the claim to be served on the respondent, either by personal service or pursuant to a waiver of personal service, as prescribed in regulations adopted by the Register of Copyrights. Such regulations shall include the following requirements and conditions:

1) The notice of the proceeding shall adhere to a prescribed form and shall set forth the nature of the Copyright Claims Board and proceeding, the respondent's right to opt out, and the consequences of opting out and not opting out.
2) The copy of the claim served on the respondent shall be as it was filed with the Copyright Claims Board.
3) Personal service of a notice and claim may be effected by an individual who is not a party to the proceeding and is over the age of 18.
4) An individual, other than a minor or incompetent individual, may be served by:

A) Following state law for serving a summons in an action brought in courts of general jurisdiction in the state where service is made; or

B) Doing any of the following:

(i) Delivering a copy of the notice and claim to the individual personally;

(ii) Leaving a copy of each at the individual's dwelling or usual place of abode with someone of suitable age and discretion who resides there; or

(iii) Delivering a copy of each to an agent authorized by appointment or by law to receive service of process.

5) A corporation, partnership or unincorporated association that is subject to suit in courts of general jurisdiction under a common name may be served by:

A) Following state law for serving a summons in an action brought in courts of general jurisdiction in the state where service is made; or

B) Delivering a copy of the notice and claim to an officer, a managing or general agent or any other agency authorized by appointment or by law to receive service of process in an action brought in courts of general jurisdiction and, if the agent is one authorized by statute and the statute so requires, by also mailing a copy of each to the respondent.

6) To request a waiver of personal service, the claimant may notify a respondent by first-class mail or other reliable means that a proceeding has been commenced, as follows:

A) Any such request shall be in writing and addressed to the individual respondent, and be accompanied by the prescribed notice and as-filed copy of the claim, as well as by two copies of a prescribed form for waiver of personal service, and a prepaid or costless means of returning the form; and

B) The request shall state the date it was sent and provide the respondent 30 days to return one copy of the signed waiver form, which signed waiver shall constitute proof of service for purposes of filing under this subsection.

7) A respondent's waiver of personal service shall not constitute a waiver of the respondent's right to opt out of the proceeding; provided, however, that a respondent who waives personal service and does not opt out shall be allowed an additional 30 days beyond the amount of time normally permitted under the applicable procedures of the Copyright Claims Board to submit a substantive response to the claim, including any defenses and counterclaims.

8) A minor or an incompetent individual may only be served by following state law for serving a summons or like process on such an individual in an action brought in the courts of general jurisdiction of the state where service is made; and

9) Service of a claim and waiver of personal service may only be effected within the United States.

h) Opt-Out Procedure. – Upon receipt of a properly served notice and claim the respondent shall have 60 days from the date of service in which to provide written notice to the Copyright Claims Board, in accordance with regulations adopted by the Register of Copyrights, of his or her desire to opt out of the Copyright Claims Board proceeding. If proof of service has been filed by the claimant and the respondent does not submit an opt-out notice to the Copyright Claims Board within 60 days of service, the proceeding shall be deemed an active proceeding and the respondent shall be bound by the result to the extent provided under section 1406(a). If the respondent opts out during that period, the proceeding shall be dismissed without prejudice.

Opt-In Alternative

g) Service of Notice and Claims. – To proceed with a claim against a respondent, a claimant must within 60 days of receiving notification to proceed with service file proof of service on the respondent with the Copyright Claims Board. To effectuate service on a respondent, the claimant must provide notice of the proceeding and a copy of the claim to the respondent in a manner prescribed in regulations adopted by the Register of Copyrights. The notice of the proceeding shall adhere to a prescribed form and shall set forth the nature of the Copyright Claims Board and proceeding, the respondent's right to choose not to opt in and the consequences of opting in and not opting in.

h) Opt-In Procedure. – Upon receipt of a notice and claim the respondent shall have 60 days from the date of service in which to provide written notice to the Copyright Claims Board, as prescribed in regulations adopted by the Register of Copyrights, that he or she chooses to opt in to and participate in the proceeding. If proof of service has been filed by the claimant and the respondent submits an opt-in notice to the Copyright Claims Board during the 60-day period, the proceeding shall be deemed an active proceeding and the respondent shall be bound by the result to the extent provided in section 1406(a). If the respondent fails to provide a written opt-in notice during that period, the proceeding shall be dismissed without prejudice.

i) Service of Other Documents. – Other documents submitted or relied upon in the proceeding shall be served as provided in regulations adopted by the Register of Copyrights.

j) Scheduling. – Upon confirmation that a proceeding has become an active proceeding, the Copyright Claims Board shall issue a schedule for future conduct of the proceeding. A schedule issued by the Copyright Claims Board may be amended by the Copyright Claims Board for good cause.

k) Conferences. – One or more Copyright Claims Officers may hold a conference to address case management or discovery issues in a proceeding; provided, however, that such conference shall not be addressed to ultimate issues of fact or law. Any such conference shall be noted upon the record of the proceeding and may be recorded or transcribed.

  l) Party Submissions. – There shall be no formal motion practice in a Copyright Claims Board proceeding; provided, however, that, subject to applicable regulations and the procedures of the Copyright Claims Board –

    1) The parties to a proceeding shall be permitted to make requests to the Copyright Claims Board to address case management and discovery matters, and responses thereto; and

    2) The Copyright Claims Board may request or permit parties to make submissions addressing relevant questions of fact or law, or other matters, and offer responses thereto.

m) Discovery. – Discovery shall be limited to the production of relevant information and documents, written interrogatories, and written requests for admission, as further provided in regulations adopted by the Register of Copyrights; provided, however –

1) That upon request of a party, and for good cause shown, the Copyright Claims Board shall have the discretion to approve additional limited discovery in particular matters, and may request specific information and documents from participants and nonparticipants in the proceeding; and
2) After providing notice and an opportunity to respond, and upon good cause shown, the Copyright Claims Board may apply an adverse inference with respect to disputed facts against a party who has failed timely to provide discovery materials in response to a proper request for materials that could be relevant to such facts.

n) Evidence. – The Copyright Claims Board may consider the following types of evidence, which may be admitted without application of formal rules of evidence:
1) Documentary and other nontestimonial evidence that is relevant to the claims, counterlaims or defenses in a proceeding; and
2) Testimonial evidence, submitted under penalty of perjury and in accordance with subsection (o), limited to written statements of the parties and nonexpert witnesses, that is relevant to the claims, counterclaims and defenses in a proceeding; provided, however, that in exceptional cases expert witness testimony or other forms of testimony may be permitted by the Copyright Claims Board for good cause shown.

o) Hearings. – The Copyright Claims Board may conduct a hearing to receive oral presentations on issues of fact or law from parties and witnesses to a proceeding, provided that –
1) Any such hearing shall be attended by at least two of the Copyright Claims Officers;
2) The hearing shall be noted upon the record of the proceeding and may be recorded or transcribed; and
3) A recording or transcript of the hearing shall be made available to a Copyright Claims Officer who is not in attendance.

p) Voluntary Dismissal. –
1) By Claimant. – Upon written request of a claimant received prior to a respondent's filing of a response to a claim, the Copyright Board shall dismiss the proceeding, or a claim or respondent, as requested, such dismissal to be without prejudice.
2) By Counterclaimant. – Upon written request of a counterclaimant received prior to a claimant's filing of a response to a counterclaim, the Copyright Board shall dismiss the counterclaim, such dismissal to be without prejudice.

q) Settlement. – At any time in an active proceeding some or all of the parties may –
1) Jointly request a conference with a Copyright Claims Officer for the purpose of facilitating settlement discussions; or
2) Submit to the Copyright Claims Board an agreement providing for settlement and dismissal of some or all of the claims and counterclaims in the proceeding, which submission may also include a request that the Copyright Claims Board adopt some or all of the terms of the parties' settlement in a final determination.

r) Factual Findings. – Subject to subsection (m)(2), the Copyright Claims Board shall make factual findings based upon a preponderance of the evidence.

s) Determinations. –

1) Nature and contents. – A determination rendered by the Copyright Claims Board in a proceeding shall –
   A) Be reached by a majority of the Copyright Claims Board;
   B) Be in writing, and include an explanation of the factual and legal basis of the decision therein;
   C) Pursuant to section 1403(d)(2), set forth any terms of by which a respondent or counterclaim respondent has agreed to cease infringing activity;
   D) Pursuant to subsection (q)(2) and to the extent agreed by the parties, set forth the terms of any settlement to the extent requested by the parties; and
   E) Include a clear statement of all damages and other relief awarded, including pursuant to paragraphs C and D.
2) Dissent. – A Copyright Claims Officer who dissents from a decision contained in a determination may append a statement setting forth the grounds for his or her dissent.
3) Publication. – Final determinations of the Copyright Claims Board shall be made available on a website maintained by the Copyright Claims Board that is publicly accessible.

Opt-Out Alternative

t) Respondent's Default. – Where a proceeding has been deemed an active proceeding but the respondent has failed to appear or has ceased participating in the proceeding, as demonstrated by his or her failing to meet one or more deadlines or requirements set forth in the schedule adopted by the Copyright Claims Board pursuant to subsection (j) without justifiable cause, the Copyright Claims Board may enter a default determination, as follows and in accordance with such other requirements as the Register of Copyrights may prescribe by regulation:
   1) The Copyright Claims Board shall require the claimant to submit relevant evidence and other information in support of his or her claim and any asserted damages and, upon review of such evidence and any other requested submissions from the claimant, shall determine whether the materials so submitted are sufficient to support a finding in favor of the claimant under applicable law and, if so, the appropriate relief and damages, if any, to be awarded;
   2) If the claimant has met his or her burden under paragraph (1), the Copyright Claims Board shall prepare a proposed default determination and provide written notice to the respondent at all addresses, including email addresses, reflected in the records of the Copyright Claims Board, concerning the pendency of a default determination by the Copyright Claims Board and the legal significance of such determination. Such notice shall be accompanied by the proposed default determination and provide that the respondent has 30 days from the date of the notice to submit any evidence and other information in opposition to the proposed default determination;
   3) If the respondent responds to the notice provided under paragraph (2) within the 30-day period, the Copyright Claims Board shall consider respondent's submissions and, after allowing the other parties to address such submissions, maintain or amend its determination as appropriate, and the resulting determination shall not be a default determination; and

4) If the respondent fails to respond to the notice provided under paragraph (2), the Copyright Claims Board shall proceed to issue the default determination as a final determination. Thereafter, a respondent may only challenge such determination to the extent permitted under section 1407(c).

u) Claimant's Failure to Proceed. –

1) Failure to Complete Service. – If a claimant fails to complete service on a respondent within the 90-day period as prescribed in subsection (g), that respondent shall be dismissed from the proceeding without prejudice; and if a claimant fails to complete service on all respondents within the 90-day period, the proceeding shall be dismissed by the Copyright Claims Board without prejudice.

2) Failure to Prosecute. – If a claimant fails to proceed in an active proceeding, as demonstrated by his or her failing to meet one or more deadlines or requirements set forth in the schedule adopted by the Copyright Claims Board pursuant to subsection (j) without justifiable cause, the Copyright Claims Board may, upon providing written notice to the claimant and 30 days to respond, issue a determination dismissing the claimants' claims, which shall include an award of attorneys' fees and costs if appropriate under subsection 1405(x)(2).

Opt-In Alternative

t) Respondent's Default. – Where the proceeding has been deemed an active proceeding but the respondent has ceased participating in the proceeding, as demonstrated by his or her failing to meet one or more deadlines or requirements set forth in the schedule adopted by the Copyright Claims Board pursuant to section 1405(j) without justifiable cause, the Copyright Claims Board may enter a default determination, as follows and in accordance with such other requirements as the Register of Copyrights may prescribe by regulation:

1) The Copyright Claims Board shall require the claimant to submit relevant evidence and other information in support of his or her claim and any asserted damages and, upon review of such evidence and any other requested submissions from the claimant, shall determine whether the materials so submitted are sufficient to support a finding in favor of claimant under applicable law and, if so, the appropriate relief and damages, if any, to be awarded;

2) If the claimant has met his or her burden under paragraph (1), the Copyright Claims Board shall prepare a proposed default determination and provide written notice to the respondent at all addresses, including email addresses, reflected in the records of the Copyright Claims Board, concerning the pendency of a default determination by the Copyright Claims Board and the legal significance of such determination. Such notice shall be accompanied by the proposed default determination and provide that the respondent has 30 days from the date of the notice to submit any evidence and other information in opposition to the proposed default determination;

3) If the respondent responds to the notice provided under paragraph (2) within the 30-day period, the Copyright Claims Board shall consider respondent's submissions and, after allowing the other parties to address such submissions,

maintain or amend its determination as appropriate, and the resulting determination shall not be a default determination; and

4) If the respondent fails to respond to the notice provided under paragraph (2), the Copyright Claims Board shall proceed to issue the default determination as a final determination. Thereafter, a respondent may only challenge such determination to the extent permitted under section 1407(c).

u) Claimant's Failure to Proceed. –

1) Failure to Complete Service. – If a claimant fails to complete service on a respondent within the 60-day period as prescribed in subsection (g), that respondent shall be dismissed from the proceeding without prejudice; and if a claimant fails to complete service on all respondents within the 60-day period, the proceeding shall be dismissed by the Copyright Claims Board without prejudice.

2) Failure to Prosecute. – If a claimant fails to proceed in an active proceeding, as demonstrated by his or her failing to meet one or more deadlines or requirements set forth in the schedule adopted by the Copyright Claims Board pursuant to subsection (j) without justifiable cause, the Copyright Claims Board may, upon providing written notice to the claimant and 30 days to respond, issue a determination dismissing the claimants' claims, which shall include an award of attorneys' fees and costs if appropriate under subsection (x)(2). Thereafter, the claimant may only challenge such determination to the extent permitted under section 1407(c).

v) Reconsideration. – A party may, within 14 days of the date of issuance of a final determination by the Copyright Claims Board, submit a written request for reconsideration of, or an amendment to, such determination if the party identifies a clear error of law or fact material to the outcome, or a technical mistake. After providing the other parties an opportunity to address such request, the Copyright Claims Board shall respond by denying the request or issuing an amended final determination.

w) Review by Register. – A party who has been denied reconsideration by the Copyright Claims Board may, within 14 days of the date of such denial, request review by the Register of Copyrights in accordance with regulations adopted by the Register of Copyrights, which regulations shall provide for a reasonable filing fee. The Register's review shall be limited to consideration of whether the Copyright Claims Board abused its discretion in denying reconsideration. After providing the other parties an opportunity to address the request, the Register shall respond by denying the request or remanding the proceeding to the Copyright Claims Board for reconsideration of identified issues and issuance of an amended final determination, which amended final determination shall not be subject to further consideration or review other than pursuant to section 1407(c).

Note: A conforming amendment to section 708 may be advisable.

x) Conduct of Parties and Attorneys. –

1) Certification. – The Register of Copyrights shall adopt regulations concerning certification of the accuracy and truthfulness of statements made by participants in proceedings before the Copyright Claims Board.
2) Bad Faith Conduct. – Notwithstanding any other provision of law, in any proceeding in which a determination is rendered and –
   A) It is established that a party pursued a claim, counterclaim or defense for a harassing or other improper purpose, or without reasonable basis in law or fact; or
   B) The claimant's claim is dismissed for failure to prosecute pursuant to subsection (u)(2), unless inconsistent with the interests of justice, the Copyright Claim Board shall in such determination award reasonable attorneys' fees and costs to any adversely affected party or parties in a total amount not to exceed $5,000; provided, however, that if an adversely affected party appeared *pro se* in the proceeding, the award to that party shall be of costs only and no more than $2,500.

§ 1406 – Effect of Proceeding

a) Determination. – Subject to the reconsideration and review processes afforded by section 1405(v) and (w) and section 1407(c), the rendering of a final determination by the Copyright Claims Board in a proceeding, including a default determination or determination based on failure to prosecute, shall, solely with respect to the parties to such determination, preclude relitigation before any court or tribunal, or before the Copyright Claims Board, of the claims and counterclaims asserted and finally determined by such determination, and may be cited or relied upon in a future action or proceeding for such purpose; provided, however, that –
   1) A determination of the Copyright Claims Board shall not preclude litigation or relitigation as between the same or different parties before any court or tribunal, or the Copyright Claims Board, of the same or similar issues of fact or law in connection with different claims or counterclaims not asserted and finally determined by the determination of the Copyright Claims Board;
   2) A determination of ownership of a copyrighted work for purposes of resolving a matter before the Copyright Claims Board shall not be relied upon, and shall have no preclusive effect, in any other action or proceeding before any other court or tribunal, including the Copyright Claims Board; and
   3) Except to the extent permitted in this subsection and section 1407, no determination of the Copyright Claims Board shall be cited or relied upon as legal precedent in any other action or proceeding before any court or tribunal, including the Copyright Claims Board.
b) Other Materials in Proceeding. – Except as permitted under this section and section 1407, a submission or statement of a party or witness made in connection with a proceeding before the Copyright Claims Board, including a proceeding that is dismissed, shall not be cited or relied upon in, or serve as the basis of, any action or proceeding before any court or tribunal, including the Copyright Claims Board.
c) With Respect to Section 512(g) of Title 17. – Notwithstanding any other provision of law, the commencement of a proceeding by a claimant before the Copyright Claims Board against a subscriber of a service provider that seeks a declaration of

infringement concerning material that has been removed or to which access has been disabled by the service provider in response to a notification of claimed infringement by the claimant pursuant to section 512(c)(1)(C) of this title shall be a basis to preclude the replacement of such material by the service provider pursuant to section 512(g) of this title if notice of the commencement of the Copyright Claims Board proceeding is provided by the claimant to the service provider's designated agent not less than 10 nor more than 14 business days following receipt of a counter notification by the service provider pursuant that subsection.

Note: A conforming amendment to section 512(g)(2)(C) may be advisable.

d) Stay of District Court Proceedings. – A federal district court shall order a stay of proceedings or such other relief as it deems appropriate with respect to any claim brought before it that is already the subject of a pending active proceeding before the Copyright Claims Board.
e) Failure to Assert Counterclaim. – The failure or inability to assert a counterclaim in a proceeding before the Copyright Claims Board shall not preclude its assertion in a subsequent court action or proceeding before the Copyright Claims Board.

Opt-Out Alternative

f) Opt-Out or Dismissal of Party. – If a party has timely opted out of a proceeding under section 1405(h) or is dismissed from a proceeding prior to the issuance of a final determination by the Copyright Claims Board, the determination shall not be binding upon and shall have no preclusive effect with respect to that party.

Opt-In Alternative

f) Failure to Opt In or Dismissal of Party. – If a party declines to opt in or is dismissed from a proceeding prior to the issuance of a final determination by the Copyright Claims Board, the determination shall not be binding upon and shall have no preclusive effect with respect to that party.

§ 1407 – Review and Confirmation by District Court

a) In General. – In any proceeding in which a party has failed to pay damages or otherwise comply with the relief awarded in a final determination of the Copyright Claims Board, including a default determination or a determination based on failure to prosecute, the aggrieved party may, within one year of the issuance of such final determination or resolution of any reconsideration by the Copyright Claims Board or review by the Register of Copyrights, apply to the United States District Court for the District of Columbia for an order confirming the relief awarded and reducing such relief to judgment. The court shall grant such order and direct entry of judgment unless the determination is vacated, modified or corrected as permitted under subsection (c). Such judgment shall be docketed as if it were rendered in an action in the United States District Court for the District of Columbia, and shall be subject to all the provisions of law relating to, and of the same force and effect as if it had been rendered in, an action in the United States District Court for the District of Columbia.
b) Filing Procedures. –

1) Notice of the application for confirmation of a determination of the Copyright Claims Board and entry of judgment shall be provided to all parties to the proceeding before the Copyright Claims Board, in accordance with the procedures applicable to service of a motion in United States District Court for the District of Columbia. If a party to be served is a nonresident, then notice of the application shall be served by the marshal of any district within which such party may be found in the same manner as other process of the court.
2) The application shall include a certified copy of the final determination of the Copyright Claims Board that is to be confirmed and rendered to judgment as reflected in the records of the Copyright Claims Board following any process of reconsideration or review by the Register of Copyrights, as well as a declaration by the applicant under penalty of perjury that it is a true and correct copy of such determination and the date it was issued.

c) Challenges to the Determination. –
   1) Bases for Challenge. – Upon application of a party to the Copyright Claims Board proceeding within 90 days of the issuance of a final determination by the Copyright Claims Board, the United States Court for the District of Columbia may issue an order vacating, modifying or correcting a determination of the Copyright Claims Board in the following cases:
      A) Where the determination was issued or as a result of fraud, corruption, or undue means, or as a result of misconduct;
      B) Where the Copyright Claims Board exceeded its authority or so imperfectly executed its duties that a final and definite determination concerning the subject matter at issue was not made; or
      C) In the case of a default determination or determination based on failure to prosecute, where it is established that the default or failure was due to excusable neglect.
   2) Procedure to Challenge. –
      A) Notice of the application to challenge a determination of the Copyright Claims Board shall be provided to all parties to the proceeding before the Copyright Claims Board, in accordance with the procedures applicable to service of a motion in United States District Court for the District of Columbia. If a party to be served is a nonresident, then notice of the application shall be served by the marshal of any district within which such party may be found in the same manner as other process of the court.
      B) The application shall include a certified copy of the final determination of the Copyright Claims Board that is the subject of the application as reflected in the records of the Copyright Claims Board following any process of reconsideration or review by the Register of Copyrights, as well as a declaration by the applicant under penalty of perjury that it is a true and correct copy of such determination, the date it was issued, and the basis for challenge under subsection (c)(1). For the purposes of the application any judge who might make an order to stay the proceedings in an action brought in the same court may make an order, to be served with the notice of application, staying proceedings to enforce the award.

§ 1408 – Referral of Cases by District Courts

The Copyright Claims Board shall qualify as an alternative dispute resolution process under section 651 of title 28 for purposes of referral of eligible cases upon consent of the parties by United States district courts.

§ 1409 – Implementation by Copyright Office

a) Regulations. – The Register of Copyrights shall adopt regulations to implement the Copyright Claims Board as contemplated by this chapter.
b) Necessary Facilities. – Subject to applicable law, the Register of Copyrights may retain outside vendors to establish internet-based, teleconferencing and other facilities required to operate the Copyright Claims Board.
c) Study. – Not later than 3 years after the issuance of the first determination by the Copyright Claims Board, the Register of Copyrights shall deliver a study to Congress that addresses –
    1) The use and efficacy of the Copyright Claims Board in resolving copyright claims;
    2) Whether adjustments to the authority of the Copyright Claims Board, including eligible claims and works and applicable damages limitations, are necessary or advisable;
    3) Whether greater allowance should be made to permit awards of attorneys' fees and costs to prevailing parties, including potential limitations on such awards;
    4) Potential mechanisms to assist copyright owners with small claims in ascertaining the identity and location of unknown online infringers;
    5) Whether the Copyright Claims Board should be expanded to offer mediation or other nonbinding alternative dispute resolution services to interested parties; and
    6) Such other matters as the Register of Copyrights believes may be pertinent concerning the Copyright Claims Board.

§ 1410 – Funding

There are authorized to be appropriated such sums as may be necessary to pay the costs incurred under this chapter not covered by the filing fees collected under this chapter, including the costs of establishing the Copyright Claims Board and its facilities.

§ 1411 – Technical amendments

[Conforming amendments as noted above and otherwise identified]

§ 1412 – Definitions

a) As used in this chapter, "party" refers to both a party and the party's attorney, as applicable.
b) As used in this chapter, "person" (including "his" and "her") refers to both an individual and an entity that is amenable to legal process under applicable law.
c) "United States" has the meaning given in section 101 of this title.

B. Section-by-Section Summary

§ 1401 – Copyright Claims Board and Staff

This section establishes the Copyright Claims Board ("Board") as an optional alternative forum within the U.S. Copyright Office to resolve certain copyright claims and sets forth the qualifications, compensation, and term of the Board and staff. The Board consists of three experienced attorneys called Claims Officers. The Librarian of Congress, after consulting with the Register of Copyrights, appoints the Claims Officers and Claims Attorneys. The Claims Officers must have at least seven years of legal experience, with two Claims Officers having copyright litigation or adjudication experience and the third having alternative dispute resolution experience. The Claims Officers are paid at the level of compensation for SL government employees. They have six-year terms, but their initial terms are staggered at four, five, and six years. The Claims Officers are assisted by two or more Claims Attorneys appointed by the Register of Copyrights. The Claims Attorneys are paid at up to grade 15 of the General Schedule for government employees. This section also provides for supervision and removal of the Claims Officers and filling of vacancies on the Board.

§ 1402 – Authority and Responsibilities of the Copyright Claims Board

This section sets forth the duties and powers of the Claims Officers and Claims Attorneys. The Claims Officers' primary duty is to make determinations on eligible copyright claims. The Claims Officers are also to review cases to make sure they are properly before the Board, manage the proceedings and render rulings on matters relating to the consideration of claims, request the production of information necessary to the resolution of claims, conduct hearings and conferences, facilitate parties' settlements, provide information to the public, and maintain records of their proceedings. They may also be assigned other duties by the Register of Copyrights. Claims Attorneys assist the Claims Officers in performing their duties, provide assistance to members of the public concerning the procedures and requirements of the Board, and engage in any other duties assigned by the Register of Copyrights. Although subject to general direction by the Register of Copyrights, the Board is to be independent in making its determinations in proceedings and the Claims Officers and Claims Attorneys cannot engage in conduct that would be inconsistent with their duties. Claims Officers and Claims Attorneys must recuse themselves from any proceedings in cases where they perceive a conflict of interest. Parties are not permitted to have *ex parte* communications with a Claims Officer, but Claims Attorneys may communicate with parties to provide assistance with Board procedures and requirements.

§ 1403 – Nature of Proceedings

This section establishes that proceedings before the Board are voluntary, provides for a three-year statute of limitations with a tolling provision, and sets forth the permissible claims, counterclaims, defenses and remedies available to parties coming before the Board. It confirms that parties retain the right to proceed in federal court instead of before the Board if they choose. Subject to applicable monetary limits, parties may bring the following types of claims to the Board: a claim for infringement, or a declaration of noninfringement, of one of the exclusive rights under section 106 of the Copyright Act; a claim of misrepresentation under section 512(f) of the Digital Millennium Copyright Act ("DMCA"); and certain limited counterclaims arising under sections 106 and 512(f) of the Copyright Act or an agreement concerning the same transaction or occurrence. In addition, parties can assert any legal or equitable defenses to any such claims or counterclaims. Claims can be brought by one or more claimants against one or more respondents if all of the claims arise out of the same activity or a continuous course of conduct and the total damages do not exceed the applicable monetary limit for a Board proceeding. Some claims and counterclaims are specifically excluded from Board determination, including claims that are already pending before or adjudicated by a court, claims against a federal or state government entity, claims against a person or entity residing outside of the United States, and claims dismissed by the Board for good cause. The Board can award a number of limited remedies. The Board can award monetary damages, including actual damages and profits, or limited statutory damages where infringement is shown. Limited statutory damages are capped at $15,000 per work for works timely registered pursuant to section 412 of the Copyright Act (generally speaking, within three months of publication), and $7,500 per work for works that are later registered in accordance with section 1404 (but not more than a total of $15,000 for all such works). After the close of discovery, the party seeking damages is to elect to pursue either actual damages and profits or limited statutory damages. The Board will not consider whether the infringement was willful in assessing limited statutory damages, but it can take into account an infringer's willingness to cease or mitigate infringing activities. The Board cannot make a total monetary award in a single proceeding of more than $30,000, exclusive of any attorneys' fees and costs awarded for bad faith conduct under section 1405 (which are capped at $5,000). In addition to monetary awards, the Board can include in its determination a requirement for an infringer to cease or mitigate infringing conduct if the infringer has agreed to do so (which agreements can be the basis for an adjustment of damages).

Costs and attorneys' fees are not available except in cases where it is established that a party has proceeded (or failed to proceed) in bad faith.

§ 1404 – Registration Requirement

Parties need not have a finalized registration from the Copyright Office for the work at issue before bringing a claim before the Board (though the timing of registration affects the range of available statutory damages). A party must apply for a registration of the work with the Copyright Office, however, before bringing the claim. The Board will not render a determination until a registration certificate is issued by the Copyright Office. The Board will delay rendering a determination for a period of time if the registration has not yet issued, but will dismiss the case if it does not issue or is refused within a certain period. Finally, if a copyright was registered before or within five years of publication, the Board will apply the presumptions of section 410 of the Copyright Act that the registration is valid and the information in the registration is accurate.

§ 1405 – Conduct of Proceedings

Generally, proceedings are conducted by the Board from the Copyright Office based on written submissions, with no requirement of personal appearances, and hearings conducted by internet and other telecommunications facilities. Parties do not need to be represented by an attorney, but attorney representation is permitted. The Board will maintain records documenting its proceedings.

Proceedings are initiated by submitting a statement of facts in support of the claim, certified by the claimant, and a filing fee established by the Register (which can be no less than $100). When a claim or counterclaim is initiated, it is reviewed by a Claims Attorney to make sure that it complies with Board requirements and can be served on the respondent. Parties who submit noncompliant claims and counterclaims are provided limited opportunities to correct errors and submit amended filings. When a claim is asserted against an online service provider for activity that may be covered by the section 512(c) or 512(d) safe harbors, before the Board will allow the claim to proceed, the claimant must certify that he or she served a DMCA takedown notice and the service provider failed to remove or disable access to the infringing material within five business days. If this is not the case, the Board will provide the claimant with information as to how to serve a DMCA notice.

Opt-Out Alternative

Within 90 days of receiving the Board's direction to proceed with service, the claimant must serve formal notice of the proceeding and claim on the respondent in accordance with rules modeled on Rule 4 of the Federal Rules of Civil Procedure. As under Rule 4, the respondent may waive formal service and agree to accept informal service (for example, by mail), but such waiver of formal service does not constitute a waiver of the respondent's right to opt out of the proceeding. The content of the notice served on the opposing party will explain the nature of the Board and proceeding, the respondent's right to opt out, and the consequences of opting out and not opting out. The respondent has 60 days to file an opt-out notice with the Board. If the respondent does not opt out within 60 days of service, the proceeding is deemed an active proceeding and the respondent will be bound by the result. Otherwise, the proceeding will be dismissed without prejudice.

Opt-In Alternative

Within 60 days of receiving the Board's direction to proceed with service, the claimant must provide notice of the proceeding and claim to the respondent, but formal service is not required. The content of the notice served on the opposing party will explain the nature of the Board and proceeding, the respondent's right to opt in, and the consequences of opting in and not opting in. The respondent has 60 days to file an opt-in notice with the Board. If the respondent opts in within 60 days of service, the proceeding is deemed an active proceeding and the respondent will be bound by the result. Otherwise, the proceeding will be dismissed without prejudice.

Once a proceeding is active, the Board will issue a scheduling order to govern the proceedings. The Board may hold conferences as well as hearings to receive oral presentations on issues of fact or law. There is no formal motion practice in a Board proceeding, but the parties can request that the Board address case management and discovery issues and the Board can ask the parties to make submissions addressing relevant questions of fact or law, or other matters. Discovery is allowed but ordinarily limited to the production of relevant information and documents, written interrogatories, and written requests for admission, with more particular limitations to be imposed by regulation. The Board can approve additional discovery and request specific information from parties and nonparties if good cause is shown. If a party does not provide discovery documents in a timely manner, the Board can draw appropriate inferences against that party. The Board will accept both documentary and testimonial evidence without application of formal rules of evidence.

Testimonial evidence is normally limited to written statements of the parties and nonexpert witnesses, but in exceptional cases expert evidence may be accepted. The Board renders factual findings based on a preponderance of evidence standard.

Final determinations will be issued in writing by a majority of the Board, will explain the factual and legal reasoning for the decision, and will include a clear statement of all relief awarded, including any agreement to cease infringing activity or settlement terms. A dissenting Claims Officer may issue a dissenting opinion. Determinations will be made available to the public on the Board's website. A party can request that the Board reconsider and amend a determination if the party identifies a clear error of law or fact that is material to the outcome, or a technical mistake. Additionally, a party who has been denied reconsideration may, for an additional fee, seek review of the denial by the Register of Copyrights under an abuse of discretion standard. If the Register finds that reconsideration should have been granted, she will remand the matter to the Board for its further review of specific concerns and issuance of an amended determination. Parties can agree to settle claims and counterclaims, and claims and counterclaims can be voluntarily dismissed before a response is filed. The Board may dismiss claims and counterclaims for good cause, including for failure to join a necessary party, or the lack of an essential witness, evidence or expert testimony. The Board may issue default determinations as well as determinations based upon failure to prosecute.

Opt-Out Alternative

If a respondent has been properly served and not opted out and the proceeding is active, but the respondent fails to appear or ceases participation in the proceeding, then the Board may issue a default determination in favor of the claimant provided that the claimant can establish his or her claim and provide evidence to support a damage award. Before the Board can enter a default, it must attempt to notify the respondent and provide an opportunity to respond.

The Board may also issue a determination in cases where a claimant fails to prosecute by ceasing participation in a proceeding, which may also provide for attorneys' fees and costs to responding parties.

Opt-In Alternative

Following the same procedures as above, a default determination can be entered against a respondent who has opted in but has ceased participation in the proceeding, and a determination can be entered against a claimant who fails to prosecute a proceeding.

Unless it does not serve the interests of justice, the Board must award attorneys' fees and costs against a party who is shown to have acted in bad faith (for a harassing or improper purpose or without reasonable basis in law or fact), or a claimant who fails to prosecute a proceeding. The Board may not award more than a total of $5,000 to all adversely affected parties (and no more than $2,500 for costs only to a party acting *pro se*).

§ 1406 – Effect of Proceeding

As between the parties to a final determination, the determination precludes relitigation of the claims and counterclaims asserted and determined by the Board before any court, tribunal or the Board. But it does not preclude litigation as between the same or different parties of the same or similar issues of fact or law in connection with claims or counterclaims not determined by the Board, and it has no later preclusive effect as to copyright ownership issues. Decisions of the Board may not be cited or relied upon as legal precedent, except to the extent the proceeding is reviewed by a district court in accordance with section 1407.

If a party brings a Board proceeding against the subscriber of an online service provider within the applicable time frame seeking a declaration of infringement concerning material subject to a DMCA takedown notice and timely notifies the service provider of the proceeding, then the proceeding will satisfy section 512(g) of the DMCA and preclude the service provider from replacing the material that was subject to the takedown notice.

A federal court is to stay proceedings or order other appropriate relief when a party files a claim that is already the subject of an active proceeding before the Board. There are no compulsory counterclaims before the Board, and failure to plead a counterclaim has no preclusive effect.

Opt-Out Alternative

If a party timely opts out or is dismissed from a proceeding before the issuance of a final determination, the determination shall not be binding upon the party.

Opt-In Alternative

If a party declines to opt in or is dismissed from a proceeding before the issuance of a final determination, the determination shall not be binding upon the party.

§ 1407 – Review and Confirmation by District Court

Parties who obtain a Board determination can file the determination within one year of its issuance for confirmation by the United States District Court for the District of Columbia in a manner similar to filing an arbitration award under the Federal Arbitration Act. Such confirmation renders the determination an enforceable judgment. Within 90 days of the issuance of a determination by the Board, an aggrieved party can seek to challenge the determination on the ground that it was issued or resulted from fraud, corruption, or undue means, or as a result of misconduct; or where the Board exceeded its authority or so imperfectly executed its duties that no final or definite determination was made; or, in the case of a default determination or determination based on failure to prosecute, that the default or failure was due to excusable neglect.

§ 1408 – Referral of Cases by District Courts

The Board qualifies as an alternative dispute resolution process under 28 U.S.C. § 651 for purposes of referring cases from the federal courts.

§ 1409 – Implementation by Copyright Office

The Copyright Office has authority to adopt regulations to implement the Board and may retain outside vendors to establish the necessary facilities. Once the Board has been in operation for three years, the Copyright Office is to issue a study regarding the use and efficacy of the Board and whether any adjustments are needed.

§ 1410 – Funding

This section authorizes appropriations to fund the Board.

§ 1411 – Technical amendments

This section allows for conforming amendments to existing statutory provisions.

§ 1412 – Definitions

This section contains definitions for certain key terms.

APPENDIX A. U.S. COPYRIGHT OFFICE STATEMENT ON SMALL COPYRIGHT CLAIMS (2006)

MATERIAL SUBMITTED FOR THE HEARING RECORD

PREPARED STATEMENT OF THE HONORABLE HOWARD L. BERMAN, A REPRESENTATIVE IN CONGRESS FROM THE STATE OF CALIFORNIA, AND RANKING MEMBER, SUBCOMMITTEE ON COURTS, THE INTERNET, AND INTELLECTUAL PROPERTY

Mr. Chairman,

It is especially good timing to have this hearing on alternative dispute resolution mechanisms immediately after the orphan works hearing. ADR was raised by some in the orphan works context as a way to begin addressing some of the inequities that could result from a statutory change. However, there are multiple instances in the copyright context as well in which parties could benefit from forums other than federal court to resolve copyright infringement claims. Today will provide an opportunity to discuss the advantages of offering alternative methods of resolving small copyright claims even outside the scope of the orphan works provision.

As the cost of litigation rises, oftentimes a copyright owner has to make a calculation that is entirely independent from whether the owner will prevail on the merits of the case. The owner must ask: Is it worth it to pursue full scale litigation when the damages or remedies wouldn't even cover the cost of the proceeding, much less provide any relief from infringing conduct?

A number proposals for resolving this dilemma have been suggested, ranging from the establishment of a small claims court to expanding the jurisdiction of Copyright Royalty Judges to determine copyright claims in an administrative dispute resolution proceeding. I would caution that the goal here should not be to create an opportunity for forum-shopping as a result of substance, but merely a to create more simplified procedures that will resolve disputes at a lower cost. I look forward to hearing the witnesses describe circumstances in which they may forgo a remedy because of the cost of bringing suit, and whether they have any suggestions for reform. I doubt this is the last we will hear on this issue.

I also would like to work with the Chairman in pursuing a Copyright Office study on this issue. It is encouraging that in its written testimony, the Office offers to study both 1) how and to what extent copyright owners are hindered from seeking relief due to the cost of litigation, and 2) what changes in the law might be advisable to remedy the problem.

PREPARED STATEMENT OF THE UNITED STATES COPYRIGHT OFFICE

The Copyright Office is pleased to present the Subcommittee with its observations on the issue of remedies for small copyright claims.

In preparing the Report on Orphan Works which the Office released two months ago, the Office was told by a representative of photographers that a new mechanism is needed to adjudicate small copyright infringement claims because the cost of litigating in federal courts is prohibitively expensive in many cases.[1] While the Office did not believe that this issue relates directly to the problem of orphan works or to the Office's proposed solution to that problem, the Office observed in its Report on Orphan Works that:

> We are sympathetic to the concerns of individual authors about the high cost of litigation and how, in many cases, the individual creator may have little practical recourse in obtaining relief through the court system, particularly against

[1] See Comment of Professional Photographers of America, March 25, 2005, pp. 11–13, submitted in Copyright Office Study on Orphan Works [available on the Copyright Office website at *http://www.copyright.gov/orphan/comments/OW0642-PPA.pdf*] [hereinafter "PPA Comment"].

> infringements involving small amounts of actual damages. This problem, however, has existed for some time and goes beyond the orphan works situation, extending to all types of infringement of the works of individual authors. While there are some mechanisms in place to help address the problem, such as enforcement by collective organizations or timely registration to secure the availability of statutory damages and attorneys fees, we believe that consideration of new procedures, such as establishment of a "small claims" or other inexpensive dispute resolution procedure, would be an important issue for further study by Congress. It is not, however, within the province of this study on orphan works.[2]

In subsequent discussions over proposed legislation to address the orphan works problem, photographers have repeated their assertion that a new procedure and forum for adjudicating small copyright claims is necessary. While the Office does not believe that it is necessary or even advisable to address this issue in the context of orphan works legislation, the Office continues to believe that the issue deserves the attention of Congress. If the Subcommittee believes it would be helpful, the Office would be pleased to study the issue in a way similar to the way in which the Office studied the orphan works problem itself, and to report to Congress its findings as to (1) whether, how, and to what extent authors and copyright owners are hindered or even prevented from seeking relief for infringements of their copyrights due to the cost of litigation under the current system, and (2) if the current system does not provide adequate procedures and remedies for the adjudication of small copyright claims, what changes in the law would be advisable to ensure that authors and copyright owners are able, as a practical matter, to seek remedies for infringements of their works.

Anyone who has litigated a case—whether as a party or as counsel—in the federal courts knows that the costs of litigation are beyond the means of many Americans. Attorneys typically charge hundreds of dollars per hour for their services, and it is our understanding that contingency fee arrangements in copyright cases are relatively rare. In a typical civil case, after pleadings, discovery, motion practice and trial (as well as possible appeals), attorney's fees can run to tens of thousands of dollars or more, and other costs can run to thousands of dollars or more.[3] If, as the Professional Photographers of America have told us, photographers generally earn about $30,000 a year,[4] then assertions that they are unable to take advantage of the remedies offered by the federal courts may well be credible.[5] It is legitimate to ask whether the federal courts are hospitable to most small claims.

Of course, there are provisions built into the copyright law that are designed in part to provide even the copyright owner of modest means with a reasonable prospect of recovering not only compensation for infringement but also the expenses of litigation in a successful infringement suit. Unlike most areas of the law, copyright law permits a court to award a reasonable attorney's fee to a successful plaintiff (or defendant).[6] Moreover, a copyright owner may elect to receive an award of statutory damages of up to $30,000 per infringed work—and up to $150,000 per work in cases of willful infringement—in lieu of actual damages and profits.[7]

It is reasonable to ask whether these provisions offer sufficient incentive and sufficient assurance that the copyright owner will be able to afford the cost of litigation. In the past couple of weeks we have asked representatives of authors and "small" copyright owners about their experience in litigating infringement claims. We have heard assertions that in many cases it simply is not worthwhile to bear the expense of federal litigation no matter how meritorious the claim may be. We are not in a position at this time to evaluate the accuracy of those assertions, but it is not difficult to imagine that in many cases an author or copyright owner engaging in a rational analysis of the costs and benefits of litigation will conclude that in light of the modest value of his or her infringement claim and the relatively high cost of litigation, it makes no sense to pursue that claim.

Although the copyright law offers the advantages described above to copyright owners who pursue claims of infringement, another provision of the law arguably

---

[2] United States Copyright Office, *Report on Orphan Works* 114 (Jan. 2006)

[3] If expert witnesses are used, as is not uncommon in copyright cases, additional thousands of dollars or more in expenses can be incurred.

[4] PPA Comment 10.

[5] It may be worth noting that in diversity actions, the minimum amount in controversy required to invoke the jurisdiction of the federal courts is $75,000. 28 U.S.C. § 1332(a).

[6] 17 U.S.C. § 505.

[7] 17 U.S.C. § 504(c). Attorney's fees and statutory damages are available to plaintiffs only in cases where the copyright in the work was registered prior to the commencement of the infringement or within three months after first publication of the work. 17 U.S.C. § 412.

Web site exactly as they are received, along with names and organizations. If electronic submission of comments is not feasible, please contact the Office at 202–707–8380 for special instructions.

For Further Information Contact: Catherine Rowland, Counsel, Office of Policy and International Affairs, by telephone at 202–707–8350 or by electronic mail at *crowland@loc.gov.*

Supplementary Information:

I. Background

The Copyright Act (the ''Act''), 17 U.S.C. 101 *et seq.,* protects a wide variety of works of authorship, ranging from individual articles or photographs that may not have a high commercial value to motion pictures worth hundreds of millions of dollars in the marketplace. Copyright owners of all of these works may seek remedies under the federal Copyright Act in the event of infringement. Not all of these copyright owners, however, have the same resources to bring a federal lawsuit, which can require substantial time, money, and effort. To the extent an infringement results in a relatively small amount of economic damage, the copyright owner may be dissuaded from filing a lawsuit because the potential award may not justify the expense of litigation. Even where statutory damages and attorney fees are possible, they are not available until the conclusion of the litigation. Moreover, awards of statutory damages may be as low as $750 (or, in cases of innocent infringement, $200), and may not always make the copyright owner whole.

In light of these challenges, the House of Representatives' Subcommittee on Courts, the Internet, and Intellectual Property held a hearing in March 2006 to learn more about the problems faced by small copyright claimants (the ''Small Claims Hearing'').[893] The hearing focused on possible alternative dispute resolution systems such as a copyright ''small claims court'' or other mechanism. The testimony also addressed some of the problems that small copyright claim owners have with the current system, as well as concerns about defendants' rights in an alternative system. The Copyright Office submitted a statement to the Subcommittee regarding the small copyright claims issue, noting these difficulties, proposing to review potential alternatives, and welcoming the possibility of further study.[894] The Copyright Office also identified some of these ''small claims'' challenges in its 2006 Report on Orphan Works,[895] and proposed legislation in 2006 and 2008 addressing orphan works included provisions that specifically directed the Copyright Office to conduct a study addressing remedies for small claims, but the legislation ultimately did not become law.[896]

The Chairman of the House Judiciary Committee has recently asked the U.S. Copyright Office to study the obstacles facing small copyright claims disputes, as well as possible alternatives. In a letter dated October 11, 2011, Chairman Lamar Smith requested that the Office ''undertake a study to assess: (1) The extent to which authors and other copyright owners are effectively prevented from seeking relief from infringements due to constraints in the current system; and (2) furnish specific recommendations, as appropriate, for changes in administrative, regulatory and statutory authority that will improve the adjudication of small copyright claims and thereby enable all copyright owners to more fully realize the promise of exclusive rights enshrined in our Constitution.''

The Office therefore seeks comments on how parties—both copyright owners and those alleged to have infringed— view the current system, what their experiences with the current system have been, and what types of alternatives would be helpful and viable.

A. Challenges of the Current Legal System

Currently, copyright owners interested in bringing a lawsuit to enforce their copyrights must do so in federal district courts, which have exclusive jurisdiction over copyright claims. 28 U.S.C. 1338. This is true regardless of the monetary value of the copyright claim. Vesting exclusive jurisdiction in federal courts is generally beneficial because copyright law is federal law, and federal courts have become familiar with copyright analysis and thus should bring a level of consistency to copyright cases. Additionally, the Act aids some copyright claimants by permitting awards of reasonable attorney's fees and statutory damages to the prevailing party, but a plaintiff may recover statutory damages and attorney's fees only if the work was timely registered. 17 U.S.C. 412, 504, 505.

Despite the benefits of the current system, there are some drawbacks to requiring copyright owners and defendants to engage in potentially extensive federal litigation for all copyright disputes. One of the major impediments to federal lawsuits is the cost of litigation. Although copyright owners could proceed *pro se* in federal court, they often need the assistance of a lawyer to understand and handle federal procedures and substantive law. This is especially true because, unlike in the state court system, there is no streamlined ''small claims'' process for claims with a lower monetary value. If a copyright owner hires a lawyer, the expenses can add up quickly. Contingency fee arrangements are relatively rare in copyright lawsuits; thus most copyright owners will have to pay an hourly fee for representation. Lawyers charge hundreds of dollars per hour, which could reach a total of tens or hundreds of thousands of dollars when a case does not immediately settle and instead requires discovery, motion practice, and trial. In fact, one recent survey found that, as of 2011, the median cost for litigating a copyright infringement lawsuit with less than $1 million at risk was $350,000. Am. Intellectual Prop. Law Ass'n ("AIPLA"), Report of the Economic Survey 2011 35 (2011). Even if a copyright owner proceeds *pro se,* litigation itself includes court costs and fees, which can add up to a not insignificant sum. Many individual copyright owners simply do not have the resources to fund expensive litigation. Moreover, even though the Act allows some awards of attorney's fees, other costs, and statutory damages, these awards are not guaranteed—and may not be available at all depending on the timeliness of copyright registration—and are only awarded at the end of litigation, likely after a copyright owner has made significant out of pocket payment to cover legal fees and court costs. Additionally, an award of attorney's fees—assuming that it is collectible— will not necessarily reimburse the copyright owner for all fees expended in prosecuting a claim.

In federal litigation, the period of time between the filing of a case and the final determination can be lengthy. The Federal Rules of Civil Procedure allow parties to engage in extensive discovery and motion practice, which often take far more than a year to complete. In fact, the median time for all cases that went to trial—not just copyright suits—was twenty-three months in 2009–2010.[897] This lengthy time frame requires litigants to expend energy and effort throughout a relatively long period of time. This investment of time, not to mention the associated expenses, may not be feasible for individual authors, who may not be able to dedicate sufficient time to handle all of the litigation burdens.

B. Potential Alternatives for Small Copyright Claims

The Office is interested in learning about alternatives to the current legal system that might help alleviate some of the burdens associated with pursuing small copyright claims. Some alternatives were identified at the Small Claims Hearing, including: (1) Using the current Copyright Royalty Board (a panel of administrative law judges established under Chapter 8 of Title 17 that sets rates and terms for statutory licenses and decides how to distribute certain statutory license royalties); (2) creating a federal "small claims court" or otherwise streamlining federal procedures; (3) developing a staff of dedicated administrative law judges to specialize in small copyright claims; (4) amending the Act to allow state courts (including small claims courts) to hear small copyright claims; and (5) allowing trade associations or other group representatives to bring a single, large filing on behalf of a sizeable group of small copyright owners. While these alternatives deserve balanced discussion, there may be other potentially suitable options that were not discussed at the Small Claims Hearing.

There are, of course, a variety of issues that require further consideration. These include:

Degree of Difficulty Litigating Small Copyright Claims in the Current System: Before analyzing various alternatives to the current system, it is important to further explore the obstacles that the district court process presents in small copyright claim cases. This would help focus future analysis and any potential alternative legal processes.

State Court Involvement: State courts do not have expertise in copyright jurisprudence. As noted above, Section 1338 of Title 28 of the U.S. Code vests federal courts with exclusive jurisdiction over copyright claims. Moreover, Section 301 of the Act explicitly preempts state claims "that are equivalent to any of the exclusive rights within the general scope of copyright as specified by section 106 in works of authorship that are fixed in a tangible medium of expression and come within the subject matter of copyright as specified by sections 102 and 103." Thus, state courts are not experienced in the nuances of copyright law and may not have sufficient resources to devote to a claim's intricacies, especially when limited in a small claims court context. Nevertheless, state courts commonly handle small disputes, and thus they likely have the structure to handle the logistics of such claims. State court involvement, however, is only one possible avenue to explore and there are also several federal options that should be considered in the discussion.

Location of Federal Court/Tribunal: Creating a federal "small claims court" or administrative judge panel would create logistical rather than jurisdictional challenges, including where the court(s) and panel(s) would be located. If there are several courts or panels located throughout the country, it may provide more convenience to the parties, but it may also reduce consistency and add to administrative costs. Alternatively, if there is only one court or panel, the guiding rules could allow for liberal use of telephone conferences and videoconferences, and the procedures could focus more on a paper practice with fewer (if any) hearings. The court or tribunal could also limit the types and amount of discovery in the interest of expediency.

Affiliation with the Copyright Office or Copyright Royalty Board: The Copyright Office administers the Copyright Act, is a substantive expert on provisions of copyright law, and has statutory responsibilities in both litigation and administrative law. It may thus be appropriate for the Office to be associated with a new process. Similarly, the Copyright Royalty Board is already proficient in handling administrative procedures under the Act, and it may have the capability of expanding its scope to handle additional claims.

Determination of ''Small'' Copyright Claims: Although many copyright owners are concerned about the cost of litigating ''small'' copyright claims in federal court, the definition of ''small'' is unclear. Any changes in legal process must take a balanced approach to determine which claims are deemed ''small'' enough to fit into the new system.

Voluntary or Mandatory: A major question is whether a new small copyright claim process would be voluntary or mandatory. Copyright owners may want the option of choosing which type of court hears a claim, and defendants might similarly wish to remove a claim filed in a new court or panel to federal district court. Additionally, the question arises about how to appeal an adverse decision—and to what court or other body.

Fair Use: The affirmative defense of fair use defense is extremely fact-specific and typically requires courts to examine decades of judicial precedent. The ability to present and have heard a fair use defense is therefore a concern.

Defendants' Appearance: It has been suggested that defendants should not be required to appear at a small copyright claim proceeding until the copyright owner provides a *prima facie* case of infringement. This ostensibly would prevent a copyright owner from dragging a defendant into a legal proceeding without cause. It is unclear whether this would be necessary, or whether an alternative small copyright claims proceeding might instead rely upon a rule akin to Federal Rule of Civil Procedure 11, which requires plaintiffs to certify the veracity of the claim.

Available Remedies: Because a small copyright claim process likely would be limited to reduce costs and time, it is unclear what types of remedies should be offered. The Act itself offers a number of infringement remedies, including injunctions, monetary relief (including statutory damages), impounding of infringing copies and of the articles by means of which infringing copies may be reproduced, costs and attorney's fees. Consideration should be given to whether an alternative small claims process could or should provide this whole panoply of remedies, and whether the new system would also allow preliminary relief to prevent impending or continuing infringement, similar to a temporary restraining order or preliminary injunction under Federal Rule of Civil Procedure 65.

These are but a few of the factors to analyze before deciding whether to move forward with a new small copyright claim system, and, if so, what that new process might be.

II. Subjects of Inquiry

The Office seeks comment on how copyright small owners and defendants use the current legal system for small copyright claims, including information on the obstacles and benefits of using federal district courts. Additionally, the Office requests comment on potential alternatives for handling copyright claims that have a relatively small economic value. The Office is interested in comment on the logistics of potential alternatives, as well as the benefits and risks presented by different types of processes.

III. Conclusion

The Office hereby seeks comment from the public on factual and policy matters related to the treatment of small copyright claims. If there are any additional pertinent issues not discussed above, the Office encourages interested parties to raise those matters in their comments. In addition, the Office is considering having one or more roundtables or formal hearings on the matters raised above in the coming months. It is also likely that, following receipt of the comments in response to this Notice, the Office will publish a further Notice of Inquiry posing specific questions and possibly exploring additional alternatives.

Dated: October 24, 2011.

Maria A. Pallante,
Register of Copyrights.

LIBRARY OF CONGRESS
Copyright Office
[Docket No. 2011–10]
Remedies for Small Copyright Claims:
Additional Comments

Agency: Copyright Office, Library of Congress.

Action: Notice of inquiry.

Summary: This is the second request for public comment pertaining to a study undertaken by the U.S. Copyright Office at the request of Congress on the topic of adjudicating small copyright claims. The study will assess whether and, if so, how the current legal system hinders or prevents copyright owners from pursuing claims that have a relatively small economic value and will discuss, with appropriate recommendations, potential changes in administrative, regulatory, and statutory authority. At this time, the Office seeks additional comments on some of the possible alternatives. The Copyright Office also announces two public meetings following the comment period, to be held during November 2012 in New York and Los Angeles, respectively.

Dates: Comments are due September 26, 2012.

Addresses: All comments and reply comments shall be submitted electronically. A comment page containing a comment form is posted on the Office Web site at *http://www.copyright.gov/docs/small claims*. The Web site interface requires commenting parties to complete a form specifying name and organization, as applicable, and to upload comments as an attachment via a browser button. To meet accessibility standards, commenting parties must upload comments in a single file not to exceed six megabytes (MB) in one of the following formats: the Adobe Portable Document File (PDF) format that contains searchable, accessible text (not an image); Microsoft Word; WordPerfect; Rich Text Format (RTF); or ASCII text file format (not a scanned document). The form and face of the comments must include both the name of the submitter and organization. The Office will post the comments publicly on the Office's Web site exactly as they are received, along with names and organizations. If electronic submission of comments is not feasible, please contact the Office at 202–707–8350 for special instructions.

Public Meetings: The public meeting in New York will be held in the Jerome Greene Annex of Columbia Law School, 410 West 117th Street, New York, New York 10027, on November 15, 2012 from 9:30 a.m. to 5:30 p.m. and on November 16, 2012 from 9:30 a.m. to 3:30 p.m. The public meeting in Los Angeles will be held in Room 1314 of the UCLA School of Law, 405 Hilgard Avenue, Los Angeles, California 90095, on November 26, 2012 from 9:30 a.m. to 5:30 p.m. and on November 27, 2012 from 9:30 a.m. to 3:30 p.m. The agendas and the process for submitting requests to participate in or observe one of these meetings will be published on the Copyright Office Web site no later than October 15, 2012.

For Further Information Contact: Jacqueline Charlesworth, Senior Counsel, Office of the Register, by email at *jcharlesworth@loc.gov* or by telephone at 202–707–8350; or Catherine Rowland, Counsel, Office of Policy and International Affairs, by email at *crowland@loc.gov* or by telephone at 202–707–8350.

Supplementary Information:

I. Background

At the request of Congress, the Copyright Office is conducting a study to assess whether and, if so, how the current legal system hinders or prevents copyright owners from pursuing copyright infringement claims that have a relatively small economic value (''small copyright claims'' or ''small claims''), and to recommend potential changes in administrative, regulatory, and statutory authority to improve the adjudication of such claims. The Office published a general Notice of Inquiry in the fall of 2011 and received numerous comments regarding the current environment in which small copyright claims are (or are not) pursued and possible alternatives to address concerns about the current system. See the original Notice of Inquiry, 76 FR 66758 (Oct. 27, 2011), and comments received in response thereto, which are posted on the Copyright Office Web site, at http://www.copyright.gov/docs/smallclaims/comments/. The Copyright Office also notes the roundtable discussion on small claims sponsored by George Washington University Law School (''GW'') on May 10, 2012. The GW discussion covered topics ranging from constitutional considerations to the definition of a ''small claim'' to potential features of a streamlined adjudicatory process, and included the participation of both the Copyright Office and the Patent and Trademark Office. *See* http://www.uspto.gov/blog/ director/entry/ uspto_co_sponsors_ip_small.

At this time, the Copyright Office seeks further input concerning how a copyright small claims system might be structured and function. Accordingly, the Office seeks responses on the specific subjects below (some of which were identified by the Office in its earlier Notice), including from parties who did not previously address those subjects, or those who wish to amplify or clarify their earlier comments or respond to the comments of others. (The Office has studied and will take into consideration the comments already received, so there is no need to restate previously submitted material.) A party choosing to respond to this Notice of

Inquiry need not address every subject below, but the Office requests that responding parties clearly identify and separately address each subject for which a response is submitted.

Subjects of Inquiry

Assuming a system for small copyright claims is created:

1. *Nature of tribunal/process.* Provide a general description of the small claims system you believe would work best. Should it be a streamlined process within the existing Article III court structure, or an alternative process administered by the Copyright Office, the Copyright Royalty Judges, and/or some other type of tribunal? If an alternative process, should it include a right of review by an Article III court? Should the process be adjudicatory in nature, or instead consist of, or include, arbitration or mediation, or be some combination of these? (See below for more specific questions on review/ appeals and the potential role of arbitration and/or mediation.)
2. *Voluntary versus mandatory participation.* Explain whether the small claims process would best be structured as a voluntary or mandatory system. Should a prospective plaintiff with a claim that meets the small claims criteria retain the option of choosing the existing federal district court process instead? Should a defendant be permitted to opt out of the small claims forum in favor of federal district court? If one or both parties' participation in the small claims process is voluntary, what incentives—such as damages limitations, attorneys' fees awards, or other features—might be instituted to encourage voluntary participation by plaintiffs and/or defendants?
3. *Arbitration.* Explain what role, if any, arbitration might play in the small claims process. Should matters be decided through some sort of specialized arbitration? Would such arbitration be binding? If so, how would the arbitrator's award be enforced and under what circumstances, if any, could it be set aside (and how might the Federal Arbitration Act, 9 U.S.C. 1 *et seq.,* apply)? How would arbitrators be trained and selected? Are there any existing arbitration models that might be especially useful as a model for arbitrating small copyright claims?
4. *Mediation.* Explain what role, if any, mediation might play in the small claims system. Should parties be required to participate in mediation before proceeding with a more formal process? Would it be useful to offer a copyright-focused voluntary mediation service? How would mediators be trained and selected?
5. *Settlement.* Please comment on how the small claims process might be structured to encourage voluntary settlements in lieu of litigated proceedings. Should a plaintiff be required to make a settlement offer to a prospective defendant before proceeding with a claim? Should the defendant be required to respond?
6. *Location of tribunal(s).* Could the small claims tribunal be centrally located, or should there be regional venues? If centrally located, where should it be? If in multiple locations, what should those be?
7. *Qualifications and selection of adjudicators.* Who should the adjudicators be? If the small claims system is a streamlined process within the Article III court structure, is there a role for magistrate judges or staff attorneys? If it is an alternative process, what qualifications should the adjudicators have, and how should they be selected?

8. *Eligible works.* Are some types of copyrighted works more amenable to, or in need of, a small claims system than others? Should the small claims process be limited to certain classes of works, for example, photographs and illustrations, or should it be available for all types of copyrighted works?
9. *Permissible claims.* Discuss the types of claims that could or should be eligible for the small claims process. For example, should the process be limited solely to claims of infringement, or should it be possible to bring a related claim arising out of the same dispute, such as a Lanham Act claim? What about an infringement claim that is tied to a contractual issue, as in the case where the defendant is alleged to have infringed by exceeding the terms of a license? Should issues of copyright ownership be amenable to decision through the small claims process? What about a user's claim that a takedown notice contained a material misrepresentation in violation of the Digital Millennium Copyright Act (''DMCA''), 17 U.S.C. 512(f)?
10. *Permissible claim amount.* Assuming there would be a cap on the amount of damages that could be sought by a plaintiff or counterclaimant in the small claims process, what should that amount be? What is the rationale for the cap proposed? Should there be any independent analysis of the damages claim by the tribunal? Should it be permissible for a copyright owner to pursue multiple claims in the same proceeding provided that, either individually or, alternatively, in the aggregate, they do not exceed the cap? What if, during the course of the proceeding, additional infringements are discovered such that the plaintiff's potential damages exceed the cap? What if a defendant asserts a counterclaim that exceeds the cap?
11. *Permissible defenses and counterclaims.* Discuss what limitations, if any, there should be on the types of defenses and counterclaims that could be decided through the small claims process. For example, could a defense of fair use or independent creation be adjudicated through the process? What about defenses or counterclaims arising under the DMCA, such as an assertion that the plaintiff's claim is subject to one of the safe harbor provisions of 17 U.S.C. 512(a) through (d), or that a takedown notice violated 17 U.S.C. 512(f)? To the extent such defenses or counterclaims were not subject to adjudication through the small claims process and would require removal of the action to federal district court, would this provide defendants with a means to ''opt out'' of the small claims system in a substantial number of cases?
12. *Registration.* Should registration of the allegedly infringed work be required in order to initiate a claim through the small claims process or, alternatively, should proof of filing of an application for registration suffice? Should the process permit claims to be brought for unregistered works? Should the registration status of a work affect the availability of statutory damages or recovery of attorneys' fees, assuming such remedies are available through the small claims process?
13. *Filing fee.* Discuss the merits of requiring a filing fee to pursue a claim through the small claims process and the amount, if any, that would be appropriate. Should the filing fee vary with the size of the claim? Are there existing standards that might be informative?
14. *Initiation of proceeding.* Explain what would be required to initiate a proceeding. Should some sort of attestation and/or a *prima facie* showing of infringement be required of a copyright owner with the initial filing? Should a copyright owner need

to establish a *prima facie* case of infringement before the defendant is required to appear and, if so, how would it be determined that this requirement had been met? By what means would the defendant be served or otherwise notified of the action? Should a defendant that is sued in federal district court for copyright infringement be permitted to transfer the matter to the small claims tribunal if the plaintiff's alleged damages are within the small claims damages cap? Should a party who has been put on notice of an alleged infringement be able to initiate an action by seeking a declaratory judgment of no infringement?

15. *Representation.* Describe the role of attorneys or other representatives, if any, in a small claims copyright system. Should individual copyright owners be permitted to be represented by an attorney and/or a non-attorney advocate, in addition to appearing *pro se*? Should corporations and other business entities be permitted to appear through employees instead of attorneys?
16. *Conduct of proceedings.* Describe how the small claims proceeding would work. Could the process be conducted by paper submission, without the requirement of personal appearances? Should the tribunal have the option to hold teleconferences or videoconferences in lieu of personal appearances? Should non-party witnesses be permitted to participate and, if so, by what means? Should expert witnesses be permitted? Should the tribunal have any sort of subpoena power? Should there be an established time frame for adjudication of the matter?
17. *Discovery, motion practice and evidence.* Explain what types of discovery, if any, should be permitted in the small claims system. For example, should depositions (either oral or by written question), requests for production of documents, interrogatories and/or requests for admission be permitted and, if so, to what extent? Should motion practice be allowed and, if so, to what extent? What types of testimony and/or evidence should be accepted (e.g., written, oral, documentary, etc.), and what standards of admissibility, if any, should apply?
18. *Damages.* Describe the damages that would be available through the small claims system. Should damages be limited to actual damages, or could statutory damages also be awarded? If statutory damages were available, should they adhere to the existing statutory damages framework of 17 U.S.C. 504(c) (subject to any cap applicable in the small claims system), or could an alternative approach be adopted, such as a fixed amount to be awarded in the case of a finding of infringement?
19. *Equitable relief.* Describe the equitable relief, if any, that should be available through the small claims system. Should the small claims tribunal be able to grant declaratory relief, issue an injunction to halt the infringing use of a work, impose license terms (such as for the continued distribution of a derivative work) and/ or award other forms of equitable relief?
20. *Attorneys' fees and costs.* Explain how attorneys' fees and costs might be handled within the small claims system. Should a prevailing plaintiff and/or defendant be entitled to recover its attorneys' fees and costs? If so, should such fees and costs be awarded according to the standards that have evolved under 17 U.S.C. 505, should they be awarded as a matter of course, or should other criteria apply? Should there be a limit on the amount of attorneys' fees that could be sought and/ or awarded in the small claims system?

21. *Record of proceedings.* Describe the record of proceedings that should be kept by the tribunal. Should decisions of the tribunal be rendered in writing? Should they include factual findings, legal explanation and/or other analysis? Should the records be publicly available?
22. *Effect of adjudication.* Explain the nature and effect of a small claims adjudication. Should a decision of the small claims tribunal constitute a final and enforceable judgment (subject to any further review or appeal)? Should it be published and/or carry any precedential weight? Should it have any *res judicata* or collateral estoppel effect, or should it be limited to the specific activities at issue and parties in question?
23. *Enforceability of judgment.* With respect to monetary judgments and any equitable or other relief awarded by the small claims tribunal, through what means would such remedies be enforceable? Should there be any special procedures for enforcement? Are there existing judicial or nonjudicial resources that might be useful in this regard?
24. *Review/appeals.* Should there be a right of review or appeal and, if so, under what circumstances, and by or to what body or court? What would be the appropriate standard of review (e.g., *de novo,* clearly erroneous, abuse of discretion, etc.)? Aside from any applicable filing fee, should there be any conditions for seeking review (such as posting of a bond)? Should a prevailing party in a review or appeal process be entitled to recover its attorneys' fees or costs?
25. *Group claims.* Should multiple copyright owners or a trade association or other entity acting on behalf of copyright owners be permitted to pursue multiple infringement claims against a single defendant, or multiple defendants, in a single proceeding? Should there be specialized rules of standing or procedures to permit this within the small claims system?
26. *Frivolous claims.* How might the small claims system deter frivolous and unwarranted filings? What measures— such as the awarding of attorneys' fees or other financial sanctions, or the barring of copyright owners that have repeatedly pursued frivolous claims from further use of the small claims process—might be taken to discourage the assertion of bad faith or harassing infringement claims, defenses and counterclaims?
27. *Constitutional issues.* Comment on whether a small claims system might implicate any one or more of the following constitutional concerns—or any other constitutional issue—and, if so, how the particular concern might be addressed:
    a. Separation of powers questions arising from the creation of specialized tribunals outside of the Article III framework, including how a right of review by an Article III court might impact the analysis;
    b. The Seventh Amendment right to have a copyright infringement case tried to a jury, as confirmed in *Feltner* v. *Columbia Pictures Television, Inc.,* 523 U.S. 340 (1998);
    c. Constitutional requirements for a court's assertion of personal jurisdiction, in particular when adjudicating claims of a defendant located in another state; and/or
    d. Due process considerations arising from abbreviated procedures that impose limitations on briefing, discovery, testimony, evidence, appellate review, etc.

28. *State court alternative.* As an alternative to creating a small claims system at a federal level, should the statutory mandate of exclusive federal jurisdiction for copyright claims be altered to allow small copyright claims to be pursued through existing state court systems, including traditional state small claims courts? What benefits or problems might flow from such a change?
29. *Empirical data.* Commenting parties are invited to cite and submit further empirical data (in addition to the anecdotal and survey information already cited or submitted to the Copyright Office in connection with this proceeding) bearing upon:
    a. Whether copyright owners are or are not pursuing small infringement claims through the existing federal court process, and the factors that influence copyright owners' decisions in that regard, including the value of claims pursued or forgone;
    b. The overall cost to a plaintiff and/ or a defendant to litigate a copyright infringement action to conclusion in federal court, including costs and attorneys' fees, discovery expenditures, expert witness fees and other expenses (with reference to the stage of proceedings at which the matter was concluded);
    c. The frequency with which courts award costs and/or attorneys' fees to prevailing parties pursuant to 17 U.S.C. 505, and the amount of such awards in relation to the underlying claim or recovery; and/or
    d. The frequency with which litigants decline to accept an outcome in state small claims court and seek *de novo* review (with or without a jury trial) or file an appeal in a different court.
30. *Funding considerations.* Aside from filing fees, by what means might a small claims system be partially or wholly self-supporting? Should winning and/or losing parties be required to defray the administrative costs of the tribunal's consideration of their matter, in all or in part? If so, by what means? If the system consists of or includes arbitration or mediation, should parties bear the cost of these alternatives?
31. *Evaluation of small claims system.* Should the small claims system be evaluated for efficacy and, if so, how? Should it be subject to periodic review or adjustment? Should it be launched initially as a pilot program or on a limited basis?
32. *Other issues.* Are there any additional pertinent issues identified above that the Copyright Office should consider in conducting its study?

Dated: August 20, 2012.
Maria A. Pallante,
Register of Copyrights.

LIBRARY OF CONGRESS
United States Copyright Office
[Docket No. 2011–10]
Remedies for Small Copyright Claims: Third Request for Comments

Agency: U.S. Copyright Office, Library of Congress.

Action: Notice of inquiry.

Summary: The United States Copyright Office is requesting public comment for the third time on the topic of adjudicating small copyright claims. The Office is studying whether and, if so, how the current legal system hinders or prevents copyright owners from pursuing copyright claims that have a relatively small economic value and will discuss, with appropriate recommendations, potential changes in administrative, regulatory, and statutory authority. At this time, the Office seeks additional comments on possible alternatives to the current system to improve the adjudication of such claims.

Dates: Comments are due April 12, 2013.

Addresses: All comments are to be submitted electronically. A comment page containing a comment form is posted on the Office Web site at http://www.copyright.gov/docs/smallclaims. The Web site interface requires commenting parties to complete a form specifying name and organization, as applicable, and to upload comments as an attachment via a browser button. To meet accessibility standards, commenting parties must upload comments in a single file not to exceed six megabytes (MB) in one of the following formats: The Adobe Portable Document File (PDF) format that contains searchable, accessible text (not an image); Microsoft Word; WordPerfect; Rich Text Format (RTF); or ASCII text file format (not a scanned document). The form and face of the comments must include both the name of the submitter and organization. The Office will post the comments publicly on the Office's Web site exactly as they are received, along with names and organizations. If electronic submission of comments is not feasible, please contact the Office at 202–707–8350 for special instructions.

For Further Information Contact: Jacqueline Charlesworth, Senior Counsel, Office of the Register, by email at jcharlesworth@loc.gov or by telephone at 202–707–8350; or Catherine Rowland, Senior Counsel, Office of Policy and International Affairs, by email at crowland@loc.gov or by telephone at 202–707–8350.

Supplementary Information:

I. Background

At the request of Congress, the Copyright Office is conducting a study to assess whether and, if so, how the current legal system hinders or prevents copyright owners from pursuing copyright infringement claims that have a relatively small economic value (''small copyright claims'' or ''small claims''), and to recommend potential changes in administrative, regulatory, and statutory authority to improve the adjudication of such claims. To aid with this study, the Office has published two prior Notices of Inquiry seeking public comment, and the Office also has held public hearings on small copyright claims issues. The Office's first general Notice of Inquiry, published in the fall of 2011, generated numerous comments regarding the current environment in which small copyright claims are (or are not) pursued, and possible alternatives to address concerns about the current system. *See* the original Notice of Inquiry, 76 FR 66758 (Oct. 27, 2011), and comments received in response thereto, which are posted on the Copyright Office Web site, at http:// www.copyright.gov/docs/smallclaims/ comments/. The Copyright Office published a second Notice of Inquiry in the summer of 2012 that announced public hearings and set forth a list of specific topics relating to the small copyright claims process, which resulted in additional public comments. *See* the second Notice of Inquiry, 77 FR 51068 (Aug. 23, 2012), and comments received in response thereto, posted on the Copyright Office Web site, at http://www.copyright.gov/docs/smallclaims/ comments/noi_10112012/ index.html. Finally, in November 2012, the Office held two two-day public hearings on small copyright claims in New York City and Los Angeles, during which participants provided their views on the adjudication of small copyright claims.

At this time, the Copyright Office seeks additional comments regarding how a small copyright claims system might be structured and function, including from parties who have not previously addressed these issues, or those who wish to amplify or clarify their earlier comments, or respond to the comments of others. The Office is interested in additional comments about the potential benefits and risks of creating a new procedure for adjudicating small copyright claims, as well as how such a system might be implemented—for example, as a new adjudicative body, as part of the existing federal court system, by extending the jurisdiction of state courts, or as some form of arbitration or mediation system. Based on its review of previously submitted comments and statements at the public hearings, the Office in particular seeks further commentary on the specific subjects set forth below, as the Office believes they warrant further analysis.

While commenting parties may address any matter pertinent to the adjudication of small copyright claims, they should be aware that the Office has studied and will take into consideration the comments already received, so there is no need to restate previously submitted material. A party choosing to respond to this Notice of Inquiry need not address every topic below, but the Office requests that responding parties clearly identify and separately address those subjects for which a response is submitted.

II. Subjects of Inquiry

1. *Voluntary versus mandatory participation.* Stakeholders voiced opinions in their comments and at the Office's two public hearings regarding the benefits and risks of voluntary versus mandatory small copyright claim resolution systems. Specifically, members of the public expressed conflicting views concerning the efficacy of incentives for participation in a voluntary system and the constitutional implications of a mandatory system. The Office is interested in learning more about the feasibility and constraints of voluntary and mandatory systems, and how these alternatives might be implemented. Among other questions, the Office is interested in whether a voluntary system could be implemented on an ''opt out'' basis—that is, whether a properly served defendant might be deemed to consent to participate in the voluntary process unless he or she affirmatively opts out within a certain time frame. Some stakeholders suggested that such a framework might be helpful to address the

problem of alleged infringers who fail to respond to notices of infringement and thus might also be unlikely to respond to notice of a lawsuit.

2. *Eligible works.* The previous round of comments and public hearings explored the issue of what types of works should be covered by a small copyright claims process; that is, whether the procedure should cover only certain types of copyrighted works, such as photographs, illustrations, and textual works, or should cover all types of works. For example, certain music organizations proposed that musical works and sound recordings be excluded from the process (at least for the time being) as, in their view, music publishers, performing rights societies, and record companies already adequately address small copyright claims on behalf of the songwriters and recording artists they represent. At the same time, others pointed out that some songwriters and recording artists—for example, those who are self- represented—may not have access to such resources and, even if they are represented through a larger organization, may not be successful in convincing that organization to take legal action. The Office invites further comment on whether musical works, sound recordings, or any other type of copyrighted work should be excluded from the small claims process and, if so, how it might impact individual and small copyright owners of that type of work.
3. *Permissible claims.* Some of the comments and public hearing participants analyzed what types of claims should be eligible for the small copyright claims process. These comments and discussions raised questions regarding how to define what claims might or might not be amenable to the small copyright claims procedure. While it seems clear that a copyright small claims tribunal would address infringement matters, some infringement claims are intertwined with other issues, such as contractual or ownership disputes, thus suggesting a need for any such tribunal to address these additional types of claims and defenses as well. Some commenters indicated that plaintiffs should be limited to asserting infringement claims, with contractual or ownership issues to be adjudicated only when raised as defenses. Others suggested that certain types of issues, such as ownership disputes, should be excluded from the small claims process altogether. The Office is interested in further thoughts on the types of claims that should be included in a small copyright claims process and how the system might address situations where an allegedly infringing act implicates an additional cause of action or defense, such as breach of contract, an ownership issue, a trademark violation, or some other claim.
4. *Injunctive relief.* In the comments and during the public hearings, some stakeholders argued strongly that any small claims system should include the possibility of injunctive relief to end infringing behavior, including in situations where the infringing conduct exploits the work in a manner that the copyright owner would not license, or violates an exclusive arrangement between the copyright owner and a third party. However, others noted that injunctive relief could be a complicated undertaking in a small claims context, partly if the unauthorized use is but one part of a larger work such as a film, book, or sound recording. It was suggested that in such a case, a plaintiff's monetary damages might be small but the economic consequences of an injunction may be considerably larger, perhaps exceeding in value any damages cap adopted for the small claims process. Stakeholders expressed

differing views as to whether injunctive relief should be available through a small claims system and, if so, how the nature or scope of such relief might be tailored to the small claims context. Particular concerns raised in the comments and at the hearings included: whether preliminary injunctive relief is compatible with a small claims process; the procedural safeguards that would adequately protect parties against whom injunctive relief was sought; whether injunctive relief awarded through the small claims process should be reviewable by an Article III court; and whether Article III review would be a practical alternative for parties of limited means. A related consideration is how the question of injunctive relief might be affected by whether the small claims process is voluntary or mandatory. The Office welcomes additional thoughts on these issues.

5. *Secondary liability.* Although much of the public commentary and discussion of small copyright claims has focused on direct infringement, it has also touched upon issues of secondary liability, including the relationship of a small claims procedure to the notice and takedown requirements of Section 512 of the Copyright Act, 17 U.S.C. 512. The Office is interested in further views concerning the intersection of a small claims process with Section 512 and, more generally, any recommended approaches to claims of contributory and vicarious infringement within the small claims context.
6. *Role of attorneys.* Written comments and discussion at the two hearings revealed a range of opinions as to the role of attorneys in a small copyright claims system. Some believe attorneys should be excluded from the proceedings as the ability to retain counsel would tend to favor defendants with greater resources over small copyright owner plaintiffs who are compelled to proceed *pro se*. Other commenters believe that access to legal representation would be important to both sides—especially in cases with a degree of legal complexity—and the system should be designed to encourage attorneys to take lower-value cases by offering fee awards. It was further suggested that such fee awards might be capped to reflect the streamlined procedures and lower recoveries of a small claims process. The Office welcomes further consideration of these issues.
7. *Guiding law.* If the small claims tribunal was to be centrally located (or even if it were in multiple locations), what decisional law should it follow? In addition to the United States Supreme Court, should it look primarily to copyright decisions of any particular circuit—for example, based upon its location, the location of the infringing conduct, or the location of the parties? Should its own decisions have any precedential effect, at least with respect to future decisions of the small claims tribunal? In this regard, some expressed the concern that if small claims decisions had effect beyond the immediate dispute, defendants might be inclined to opt out of a voluntary system. The Office invites further thoughts on the decisional law that should guide the small claims tribunal.
8. *Willful and innocent infringement.* At the hearings, it was suggested by some that a small claims process should not include a potential finding of willfulness, in part because it could be more difficult to establish the appropriate evidentiary record to support such a finding under a streamlined procedure. In addition, a damages cap for small copyright claims appreciably below the existing $150,000 maximum in

statutory damages for willful infringement—for example, a ceiling of $30,000, as has been suggested by some—would limit the economic significance of a willfulness finding. *See* 17 U.S.C. 504(c)(2). If the willfulness element were to be eliminated in the small claims context, a question also arises as to whether the ''innocent infringer'' distinction—which permits a court to reduce statutory damages to as low as $200 for a defendant who was not aware and had no reason to believe his or her actions were infringing— should remain. *See id.* Should the small claims procedure eliminate distinctions as to the nature of the infringement, along with their potential impact on damages awards?

9. *Service of process.* At the hearings, participants shared views on how potential small claims defendants might be notified of the action. A particular concern is that copyright owners of limited means may have difficulty effectuating traditional service on distant or elusive defendants. It was suggested that Federal Rule of Civil Procedure 4, including the provision that permits a defendant to be notified of an action by mail or other means via a waiver of formal service of process, could be appropriate for the small claims system. *See* Fed. R. Civ. P. 4. It was also suggested that a Web site might properly be served by sending electronic notice to an agent designated to receive notifications of infringement pursuant to Section 512 of the Copyright Act. *See* 17 U.S.C. 512(c)(2). In addition, it was observed that the small claims tribunal might handle service of defendants, as is sometimes the case in other contexts (including in some state courts). The Office seeks further comments on potential procedures to notify defendants that an action has been filed.
10. *Offers of judgment.* Some commenters have suggested that a process such as that contemplated by Federal Rule of Civil Procedure 68— which allows a defendant to make an offer of judgment and recover certain costs if the plaintiff rejects the offer and fails to obtain a more favorable outcome—could play a useful role in the small claims setting. *See* Fed. R. Civ. P. 68. Others feel that once a plaintiff has filed an action, pretrial settlement procedures would merely delay the process in most cases. The Office is interested in additional comments as to whether and how a mechanism akin to Rule 68 might be useful in the small claims context.
11. *Default judgments.* Current federal district court procedures allow a plaintiff to seek default judgments if a lawfully served defendant fails to appear. The Office is interested in whether such a procedure should be available in a small copyright claim proceeding. If plaintiffs are able to seek default judgments, what are the procedural safeguards that should apply, what type of remedies should be available, and what type of showing should be required to justify relief?
12. *Enforceability of judgments.* A primary concern of commenters and participants at the small claims hearings is that a small claims judgment—in particular one rendered through a voluntary system—should be enforceable. In addition to monetary damages, such a judgment might include some form of injunctive relief. Participants offered a range of suggestions on the matter of enforcement. Some indicated that the Federal Arbitration Act, 9 U.S.C. 1 *et seq.*, might to some degree serve as a model for obtaining an enforceable federal court judgment following adjudication by the small claims tribunal. Participants also commented on the practical aspects of collecting on judgments. Noting that the challenges of enforcing a judgment, once

obtained, are not unique to the copyright context, some suggested that successful small claims plaintiffs could avail themselves of existing federal and state court procedures. The Office welcomes further discussion of existing or potential mechanisms that successful plaintiffs might employ to enforce small claims judgments without incurring prohibitive costs.

13. *Unknown defendants.* Some hearing participants observed that in many instances—especially in the case of internet-based infringement—the infringer's identity may not be known and/or the infringer may be difficult to locate. Web sites may lack usable contact data and/or may be registered anonymously. Should the small claims procedure permit parties to pursue claims against ''John Doe'' defendants, including, when appropriate, the means to subpoena an internet service provider to learn the identity and location of such a defendant? The Office invites comments on how such a process might work, with reference to existing practices in other courts as appropriate.
14. *Multiple tracks or proceedings.* During the hearings, some participants discussed the possibility of having more than one type of small copyright claims proceeding—a highly simplified process for straightforward claims with perhaps only a few hundred or few thousand dollars at stake, and a more robust process for matters of greater complexity or economic consequence that are still too small to be practically pursued in federal district court. Stakeholders considered whether, even within the small claims context, there should be a greater amount of discovery and procedure in certain types of cases, for example, when an injunction is sought. The Office seeks further comment on whether a tiered system would be desirable, or whether a single, unified approach to small claims is the better alternative, perhaps with the possibility of developing additional ''tracks'' over time if warranted.
15. *Constitutional issues.* The Office continues to be interested in learning more about the constitutional impact of any small copyright claims procedure. Thus, the Office requests additional comments on whether a small copyright claims system might implicate any one or more of the following constitutional concerns—or any other constitutional issue—and, if so, how the particular concern might be addressed:
    a. Separation of powers questions arising from the creation of specialized tribunals outside of the Article III framework, including how a right of review by an Article III court might impact the analysis;
    b. The Seventh Amendment right to have a copyright infringement case tried by a jury, as confirmed in *Feltner* v. *Columbia Pictures Television, Inc.,* 523 U.S. 340 (1998);
    c. Constitutional requirements for a court's assertion of personal jurisdiction, in particular when adjudicating claims of a defendant located in another state; and/or
    d. Due process considerations arising from abbreviated procedures that impose limitations on briefing, discovery, testimony, evidence, appellate review, etc.
16. *International issues.* At the public hearings, some participants sought to ensure that the small claims procedure would be available to foreign plaintiffs seeking redress for infringing activity in the United States, as well as to U.S. plaintiffs seeking to take action against foreign defendants, as is permitted under the existing federal

system. The operation of a small copyright claims system could have implications for the United States' rights and responsibilities under the Berne Convention, the Agreement on Trade-Related Aspects of Intellectual Property Rights (TRIPS), and other instruments. The Office welcomes additional comments on the international implications of a small claims system, including how the voluntary or mandatory nature of such a system might affect the analysis.

17. *Empirical data.* Previous comments provided helpful empirical data relevant to the adjudication of small copyright claims, including surveys by the American Bar Association Section on Intellectual Property Law and the Graphic Artists Guild. The Office welcomes additional surveys and empirical studies bearing upon:
    a. Whether copyright owners are or are not pursuing small infringement claims through the existing federal court process, and the factors that influence copyright owners' decisions in that regard, including the value of claims pursued or forgone;
    b. The overall cost to a plaintiff and/ or a defendant to litigate a copyright infringement action to conclusion in federal court, including costs and attorneys' fees, discovery expenditures, expert witness fees and other expenses (with reference to the stage of proceedings at which the matter was concluded);
    c. The frequency with which courts award costs and/or attorneys' fees to prevailing parties pursuant to 17 U.S.C. 505, and the amount of such awards in relation to the underlying claim or recovery; and/or
    d. The frequency with which litigants decline to accept an outcome in state small copyright claims court and seek *de novo* review (with or without a jury trial) or file an appeal in a different court. Parties considering the submission of additional survey or empirical data may wish to review the studies mentioned above, which are available at http:// www.copyright.gov/docs/smallclaims/.
18. *Other issues.* Please comment on any other issues the Copyright Office should consider in conducting its small copyright claims study.

Dated: February 20, 2013.

Maria A. Pallante,
Register of Copyrights.

APPENDIX C. COMMENTING PARTIES AND ROUNDTABLE PARTICIPANTS

Parties Who Responded to First Notice of Inquiry

1. American Intellectual Property Law Association (AIPLA)
2. Alliance of Visual Artists (AVA) (on behalf of Evidence Photographers International Council (EPIC), Professional Photographers of America (PPA), and Student Photographic Society (SPS))

3. American Society of Composers, Authors and Publishers (ASCAP) and SESAC, Inc. (SESAC)
4. American Society Of Media Photographers (ASMP)
5. American Photographic Artists (APA)
6. Association of American Publishers (AAP)
7. Atkinson, Dale
8. Authors Guild
9. Beasley, Joe
10. Broadcast Music, Inc. (BMI)
11. Broeder, Kay
12. Byron, Robert
13. California Lawyers for the Arts (CLA)
14. Cannings, James (on behalf of himself and Our Own Performing Society, Inc.)
15. Chu, Lynn
16. Copyright Alliance
17. Craig, M. Tom
18. D'Angelo, Steven
19. Damstra, Emily S.
20. Donald A. Gardner Architects, Inc.
21. Gilmartin, Robert E.
22. Google Inc.
23. Graphic Artists Guild (GAG)
24. Gray Matters
25. Hoch, Judy
26. Illustrators' Partnership of America (IPA)
27. Independent Film & Television Alliance (IFTA)
28. Keck, Cheryl
29. Kernochan Center for Law, Media and the Arts
30. Koenig III, C. Frederick
31. McDermott Medical Illustration
32. McGowan, Michael
33. Michelsen, SJ
34. Microsoft Corporation
35. National Music Publishers' Association (NMPA), American Society of Composers, Authors and Publishers (ASCAP), and SESAC, Inc. (SESAC)
36. National Press Photographers Association (NPPA)
37. National Writers Union (UAW Local 1981, AFL-CIO) (NWU)
38. New Media Rights
39. OnLock Digital Authentication
40. Pepi, Eugene
41. Perry4Law
42. Picture Archive Council Of America, Inc. (PACA)
43. Planetemeraldjungle LLC
44. Public Knowledge (PK), Electronic Frontier Foundation (EFF), and Future of Music Coalition (FMC)

45. R. Kunstadt, P.C. (on behalf of Robert Kunstadt and Fritjof Haft)
46. Recording Industry Association of America (RIAA) and American Association of Independent Music (A2IM)
47. Rosen, Barry
48. Rosenthal, Morris
49. Schnackel, Cindy
50. Sherwin, Brian
51. The Songwriters Guild of America (SGA) and The Nashville Songwriters Association International (NSAI)
52. Traynor, Michael, Spelman, Katherine C., and Cohen, Sophie
53. Westwood, William B.
54. Williamson, Miryam Ehrlich
55. ZipCourt, Inc.

Parties Who Responded to Second Notice of Inquiry

1. Alliance of Visual Artists (AVA) (on behalf of Professional Photographers of America (PPA) and Student Photographic Society (SPS))
2. American Bar Association's Section of Intellectual Property Law (ABA IP Section)
3. American Photographic Artists (APA)
4. American Society of Composers, Authors & Publishers (ASCAP), American Association of Independent Music (A2IM), Broadcast Music, Inc. (BMI), National Music Publishers Association (NMPA), Recording Industry Association of America (RIAA), and SESAC, Inc. (SESAC)
5. American Society of Media Photographers (ASMP)
6. Association of American Publishers (AAP)
7. Blitch, Michael
8. Cannings, James (on behalf of himself and Our Own Performing Society, Inc.)
9. Dreyfus, Rochelle C. (Pauline Newman Professor of Law and Co-Director, Engelberg Center on Innovation Law & Policy)
10. Gear Publishing Company
11. Getty Images
12. Graphics Artists Guild (GAG)
13. Gunewardene, R
14. Hegazy, Eman
15. Independent Book Publishers Association (IBPA)
16. Independent Film & Television Alliance (IFTA)
17. Kernochan Center for Law, Media and the Arts
18. Kirk, Thaddeus S.
19. National Press Photographers Association (NPPA)
20. New Media Rights
21. Picture Archive Council of America, Inc. (PACA)
22. The Songwriters Guild of America (SGA)
23. Soulen, Julie Magers

24. Southworth, William
25. Starstone Media

Parties Who Responded to Third Notice of Inquiry

1. American Photographic Artists (APA)
2. American Society Of Media Photographers (ASMP)
3. Association of American Publishers (AAP)
4. Blum, Richard
5. Cifrino, Christopher
6. Devorah, Carrie
7. Federal Legal Assistance Self Help Center (FLASH)
8. Firth, Sheana
9. Hibberd, Rick
10. Hollaar, Dr. Lee A. (Professor in the School of Computing at the University of Utah in Salt Lake City, representing himself)
11. Getty Images
12. Graphic Artists Guild (GAG)
13. Motion Picture Association of America, Inc. (MPAA)
14. National Music Publishers' Association, Inc. (NMPA), The Harry Fox Agency, Inc. (HFA), American Society of Composers, Authors and Publishers (ASCAP), Broadcast Music, Inc. (BMI), SESAC, Inc. (SESAC), and the Church Music Publishers Association (CMPA)
15. National Press Photographers Association (NPPA)
16. National Writers Union (UAW Local 1981, AFL-CIO) (NWU)
17. Nelson and McCulloch LLP
18. Odyssey Entertainment, Inc.
19. Peterson, Elsa
20. Picture Archive Council of America, Inc. (PACA)
21. Sisk, Lorene Leftwich
22. The Songwriters Guild of America (SGA)
23. Studio 1, Inc.
24. Sun-Glo Records, Inc. and Upward Bound Music Company, Inc.
25. VIPO Inc.
26. Volunteer Lawyers for the Arts, Inc. (VLA)
27. Umans, Rudy

Participants in New York Hearings

1. Badavas, Christos (The Harry Fox Agency, Inc.)
2. Cannings, James (Our Own Performance Society, Inc.)
3. Chaitovitz, Ann (U.S. Patent & Trademark Office)
4. Davis, Susan (National Writers Union)

5. DiMona, Joseph (Broadcast Music, Inc.)
6. Fertig, Rachel (Association of American Publishers)
7. Holland, Brad (Illustrators' Partnership of America)
8. Lehman, Bruce (Former Assistant Secretary of Commerce and Commissioner of Patents and Trademarks 1993-1999)
9. Leichtman, David (Volunteer Lawyers for the Arts, Inc.)
10. Loftus, Mary Fran (We Research Pictures, LLC)
11. Mopsik, Eugene (American Society of Media Photographers)
12. Osterreicher, Mickey (National Press Photographers Association)
13. Perlman, Victor (American Society of Media Photographers)
14. Rosenthal, Jay (National Music Publishers Association)
15. Sanders, Charles (The Songwriters Guild of America)
16. Shaftel, Lisa (Graphic Artists Guild)
17. Taylor, Randy (Copyright Defense League, LLC)
18. Willmer, Lisa (Getty Images)
19. Wolff, Nancy (Picture Archive Council of America, Inc.)

Participants in Los Angeles Hearings

1. Brennan, Lorin (Linde Law Firm)
2. Bristol, Erica (Mediator)
3. Calzada, Alicia (National Press Photographers Association)
4. Chaitovitz, Ann (U.S. Patent & Trademark Office)
5. Cleary, Susan (Independent Film & Television Alliance)
6. Clinton, George (Musician)
7. Cohan, Timothy A. (Peermusic)
8. Field, Corey (Ballard Spahr, LLP)
9. Grecco, Michael (American Photographic Artists)
10. Hasbrouck, Edward (National Writers Union)
11. Knappen, Molly (Designer and Developer)
12. Kunze, Erin (California Lawyers for the Arts)
13. Neil, Art (New Media Rights)
14. Reed, Kendall (Mediator, Arbitrator, Attorney)
15. Robinson, Alma (California Lawyers for the Arts)
16. Tommaselli, Kim (Independent Film & Television Alliance)
17. Traynor, Michael (Cobalt, LLP)
18. Wright, Carolyn (Law Offices of Carolyn E. Wright, LLC)

Appendix D. Summary of State Small Claims Procedures

State[1]	Courts	Monetary Limit ($000s)	Equitable Relief	Attorney Representation for Individuals	Simplified Pleadings	Answer Required	Counterclaims Must Be Filed In Advance of Hearing	Filing Fees ($)	Costs Recoverable	Specialized Procedure	Discovery	Evidentiary Rules	Jury Trials	Appeals
Cal.[2]	Small Claims Court (Division of Superior Court)	10	Limited	Not permitted	Yes	No	Required	30-100	Yes	Yes	Not Permitted	Relaxed	Not allowed	By Defendants
Fla.[3]	County Courts	5	Not Available	Permitted	Yes	No	Required	50-295	Yes	Yes	Limited	Relaxed	Available	By Either Party
Ga.[4]	Magistrate Courts	15	Not Available	Permitted	Yes	Yes	Permitted	< 22	Yes	Yes	By Leave of Court	Traditional w/ liberal construction	Not allowed	By Either Party
Ill.[5]	County Circuit Courts	10	Available	Permitted	Yes	No	Permitted	10-150	Yes	Yes	By Leave of Court	Relaxed	Available	By Either Party
Mass.[6]	District Court Department and Boston Municipal Court Department	7	Available	Permitted	Yes	No	Permitted	20-140	Yes	Yes	Not Permitted unless good cause shown	Relaxed	Not allowed	By Defendants
Mich.[7]	District Court	5	Limited	Not permitted	Yes	No	Permitted	25-65	Yes	Yes	Not Permitted	Relaxed	Not allowed	None, unless appealing from a magistrate
N.Y.[8]	New York City Civil Courts, City Courts outside New York City, District Courts, and Justice Courts (Small Claims Parts)	3 or 5	Not Available	Permitted	Yes	No	Required	10-20	Yes	Yes	Not Permitted Without a Court Order	Relaxed	Defendant may request	None, unless no substantial justice.
Pa.[9]	Magisterial District Judges	12	Not Available	Permitted	Yes	No	Required	30-75	Yes	Yes	Depositions & Interrogatories Not Permitted	Traditional	Not allowed	Either Party
Tenn.[10]	Court of General Sessions	25	Limited	Permitted	Yes	No	Required	42	Yes	Yes	Available	Traditional	Not allowed	Either Party
Tex.[11]	Justice Courts	10	Limited	Permitted	Yes	Yes	Required	25	Yes	Yes	Limited	Relaxed	Available	Either Party

[1] The ten states represented in this chart contain the ten district courts in which the most copyright-related cases were filed from 2000-2012. *Copyright Cases Filed by Year*, LEX MACHINA, https://winslow.lexmachina.com/court/tableTop (last visited Jul. 16, 2013).

[2] CAL. CIV. PROC. CODE § 116.210 (2013) (courts); *id.* § 116.221 (monetary limit) (for natural persons in most situations); *id.* §§ 116.220(a)(5), 116.220(b) (equitable relief); *id.* § 116.530 (attorney representation); *id.* §§ 116.310(a), 116.320(b) (simplified pleadings); *id.* § 116.330 (answer required); *id.* § 116.360 (2013) (advanced counterclaim); *id.* § 116.230(b)-(c) (filing fees); *id.* § 116.610(g)(1) (costs recoverable); *id.* § 116.110-.950 (specialized procedure); *id.* § 116.310(b) (discovery); *id.* § 116.520 (evidentiary rules); *Crouchman v. Superior Court*, 755 P.2d 1075, 1077 (Cal. 1988) (jury trials); CAL. CIV. PROC. CODE § 116.710 (2013) (appeals).

[3] FLA. SM. CL. R. 7.010(a) (courts); *id.* R. 7.010(b) (monetary relief); *id.* (equitable relief); *id.* R. 7.020(b) (attorney representation); *id.* R. 7.050(a)(1) and R. 7.300 (simplified pleadings); *id.* R. 7.090(c) (answer required); *id.* R. 7.100 (advanced counterclaim); FLA. STAT. § 34.041(1)(a) (2013) (filing fees); FLA. SM. CL. R. 7.175 (costs recoverable); *id.* R 7.010 – 7.350 (specialized procedure); *id.* R. 7.020(b) (discovery); *id.* R. 7.140(f) (evidentiary rules); *id.* R. 7.150 (jury trials); *id.* R. 7.230 (appeals).

[4] GA. CODE ANN. § 15-10-2(5) (2013) (courts); *id.* (monetary limit); GA. CONST. art. VI, § IV (equitable relief); GA. UNIF.MAGISTRATE CT. R. 7.1 (attorney representation); GA. CODE ANN. §§ 15-10-43(a),10-48 (2013) (simplified pleadings); *id.* § 15-10-43(c) (answer required); *id.* § 15-10-45(a)-(b) (advanced counterclaim); *id.* § 15-10-80(a) (filing fees); *id.* § 15-10-80(d) (costs recoverable); *id.* § 15-10-42 (specialized procedure); GA. UNIF.MAGISTRATE CT. R. 40 (discovery); GA. CODE ANN. § 15-10-44(b) (2013) (evidentiary rules); *id.* § 15-10-41 (jury trials); *id.* § 15-10-41(b)(1) (appeals).

[5] ILL. SUP. CT. R. 282 (courts); *id.* at § 281 (monetary limit); ILL. CONST. art. VI, § 9 (2013), *see also Wicks v. Bank of Belleville*, 371 N.E.2d 1007 (Ill. App. 1977) (noting that small claims court procedures govern but, where silent, general procedural rules govern), *see also Iowa-Illinois Gas & Electric Co. v. Fisher*, 114 N.E.2d 581, 584 (Ill. App. 1953) (finding that Illinois circuit courts derive original jurisdiction in all equity cases from section 12 of article 6 of the constitution, and that the legislature cannot validly limit those powers) (equitable relief); ILL. SUP. CT. R. 282, Illinois Attorney General, Small Claims Court, *Things You Should Know About*, http://illinoisattorneygeneral.gov/consumers/smlclaims.html (attorney representation); ILL. SUP. CT. R. 282(a) (simplified pleadings); *id.* R. 286(a) (answer required); *see id.* (advanced counterclaim); 705 ILL. COMP. STAT. 105/27.1a - 105/27.2a (2013) (filing fees); ILL. SUP. CT. R. 281, 19TH JUDICIAL CIR. CT. R. 7.07 (costs recoverable); *id.* R. 281 – 89 (specialized procedure); *id.* R. 287(a) (discovery); *id.* R. 286(b) (evidentiary rules); *id.* R. 285 (jury trials); *id.* R. 301 (appeals).

[6] MASS. GEN. LAWS ch. 218, § 21 (2013) (courts); *id.* (monetary limit); Mass. Unif. Small Cl. Standards § 702 (equitable relief); MASS. UNIF. SM. CL. R. 7(g) (attorney representation); MASS. GEN. LAWS ch. 218, § 22 (2013) (simplified pleadings); MASS. UNIF. SM. CL. R. 3(b) (answer required); *id.* R. 3(c) (advanced counterclaim); MASS. GEN. LAWS ch. 218, § 22 (2013) (filing fees); Mass. Unif. Small Cl. Standards § 7:05 (costs recoverable); MASS. GEN. LAWS ch. 218, § 21 (2013) (specialized procedure); MASS. UNIF. SM. CL. R. 5 (discovery); Mass. Unif. Sm. Cl. Standards § 6:10 (evidentiary rules); MASS. GEN. LAWS ch. 218, § 23 (2013) (jury trials); *id.* (appeals).

[7] MICH. COMP. LAWS § 600.8401 (2012) (courts); *id.* (monetary limit); *id.* § 600.8302(1) (equitable relief); *id.* § 600.8408(1) (attorney representation); MICH. CT. R. 4.302 (simplified pleadings); MICH. COMP. LAWS §§ 600.8404 (2013) (answer required); *id.* § 600.8422 (advanced counterclaim); *id.*§ 600.8420(1) (filing fees); *id.* § 600.8421 (costs recoverable); *id.* §§ 600.8401-.8427 (specialized procedure); MICH. CT. R. 2.302(A)(3) (discovery); MICH. R. EVID. 1101(b)(5) (evidentiary rules); MICH. COMP. LAWS § 600.8411(2) (2013) (jury trials); *id.* §§ 600.8412, 600.8427 (appeals).

[8] N.Y. UNIFORM DIST. CT. ACT § 1802 (Consol. 2013), N.Y. UNIFORM JUST. CT. ACT § 1802 (Consol. 2013), N.Y. UNIFORM CITY CT. ACT § 1802 (Consol. 2013), N.Y. CITY CIV. CT. ACT § 1802 (Consol. 2013) (courts); N.Y. CITY CIV. CT. ACT § 1801 (Consol. 2013), N.Y. UNIFORM CITY CT. ACT § 1801 (Consol. 2013), N.Y. UNIFORM DIST. CT. ACT § 1801 (Consol. 2013), N.Y. UNIFORM JUST. CT. ACT § 1801 (Consol. 2013) (monetary limit); *Cucinotta v. Hanulak*, 647 N.Y.S.2d 625, 626 (N.Y. App. Div. 1996) (equitable relief); N.Y. CITY CIV. CT. R. § 208.41(f), N.Y UNIFORM CITY CT. R. § 210.41(f)(1), N.Y. UNIFORM DIST. CT. R. § 212.41(f)(1), N.Y. UNIFORM JUST. CT. R. §214.10(h), (j) (attorney representation); N.Y. UNIFORM DIST. CT. ACT § 1803 (Consol. 2013), N.Y. UNIFORM JUST. CT. ACT § 1803 (Consol. 2013), N.Y. UNIFORM CITY CT. ACT § 1803 (Consol. 2013), N.Y. CITY CIV. CT. ACT § 1803 (Consol. 2013) (simplified pleadings); N.Y. UNIFORM DIST. CT. ACT § 1803 (Consol. 2013), N.Y. UNIFORM JUST. CT. ACT § 1803 (Consol. 2013), N.Y. UNIFORM CITY CT. ACT § 1803 (Consol. 2013), N.Y. CITY CIV. CT. ACT § 1803 (Consol. 2013) (answer required); N.Y. UNIFORM DIST. CT. ACT § 1803(c) (Consol. 2013), N.Y. UNIFORM JUST. CT. ACT § 1803(c) (Consol. 2013), N.Y. UNIFORM CITY CT. ACT § 1803(c) (Consol. 2013), N.Y. CITY CIV. CT. ACT § 1803(c) (Consol. 2013) (advanced counterclaim); N.Y. UNIFORM DIST. CT. ACT § 1803(a) (Consol. 2013), N.Y. UNIFORM JUST. CT. ACT § 1803(a) (Consol. 2013), N.Y. UNIFORM CITY CT. ACT § 1803(a) (Consol. 2013), N.Y. CITY CIV. CT. ACT § 1803(a) (Consol. 2013) (filing fees); N.Y. UNIFORM DIST. CT. ACT § 1901(c) (Consol. 2013), N.Y. UNIFORM CITY CT. ACT § 1901(c) (Consol. 2013), N.Y. CITY CIV. CT. ACT § 1901(c) (Consol. 2013) (costs recoverable); N.Y. UNIFORM DIST. CT. ACT § 1801-15 (Consol. 2013), N.Y. UNIFORM JUST. CT. ACT § 1801-15 (Consol. 2013), N.Y. UNIFORM CITY CT. ACT § 1801-15 (Consol. 2013), N.Y. CITY CIV. CT. ACT § 1801-15 (Consol. 2013) (specialized procedure); N.Y. UNIFORM DIST. CT. ACT § 1804 (Consol. 2013), N.Y. UNIFORM JUST. CT. ACT § 1804 (Consol. 2013), N.Y. UNIFORM CITY CT. ACT § 1804 (Consol. 2013), N.Y. CITY CIV. CT. ACT § 1804 (Consol. 2013) (discovery); N.Y. UNIFORM DIST. CT. ACT § 1804 (Consol. 2013), N.Y. UNIFORM JUST. CT. ACT § 1804 (Consol. 2013), N.Y. UNIFORM CITY CT. ACT § 1804 (Consol. 2013), N.Y. CITY CIV. CT. ACT § 1804 (Consol. 2013) (evidentiary rules); N.Y. UNIFORM DIST. CT. ACT § 1806 (Consol. 2013), N.Y. UNIFORM JUST. CT. ACT § 1806 (Consol. 2013), N.Y. UNIFORM CITY CT. ACT § 1806 (Consol. 2013), N.Y. CITY CIV. CT. ACT § 1806 (Consol. 2013) (jury trials); N.Y. UNIFORM DIST. CT. ACT § 1807 (Consol. 2013), N.Y. UNIFORM JUST. CT. ACT § 1807 (Consol. 2013), N.Y. UNIFORM CITY CT. ACT § 1807 (Consol. 2013), N.Y. CITY CIV. CT. ACT § 1807 (Consol. 2013) (appeals).

[9] 42 PA. CONS. STAT. §§ 1123(a)(4), 1515(a)(3) (2013) (courts); *id.* § 1515(a)(3) (monetary limit); *id.* (equitable relief); PA. R.C.P.D.J. NO. 207(A)(1) - (2) (attorney representation); *id.* No. 304 (simplified pleadings); *id.* No. 305 (answer required); *id.* No. 315 (advanced counterclaim); 42 PA. CONS. STAT. § 1725.1 (a) (2013) (filing fees); PA.R.C.P.D.J. No. 206(B) (costs recoverable); *id.* No. 201 – 324 (specialized procedure); *id.* No. 210 (discovery); *id.* No. 321 (evidentiary rules); 42 PA. CONS. STAT. § 1123(a)(4) (2013) (defendant has no right to jury trial in municipal court but has to right jury trial on appeal) (jury trials); PA.R.C.P.D.J. No. 1002 (appeals).

[10] TENN. CODE ANN. § 16-15-501(d)(1) (2013) (courts); *id.* (monetary limit); *id.* (equitable relief); *see, e.g.,* TENN. SHELBY CNTY, GEN. SESS. CT. R. 7 (attorney representation); TENN. CODE ANN. § 16-15-710 (2013) (simplified pleadings); *see id.* § 16-15-714 and SE. TENN. LEGAL SERVS. 3, *General Sessions Court: Advice for Persons Who Want to Represent Themselves*, *available at* http://www.selegal.org/Self-Help/Booklets/GENERAL%20SESSIONS%20COURT%20BOOKLET.pdf (answer required); TENN. CODE ANN. § 16-15-724 (2013) (advanced counterclaim); *id.* § 8-21-401(f)(1) (filing fees); *id.* § 20-12-101 (costs recoverable); *id.* §§ 16-15-501 to -15-502, 16-15-710 to -15-735, 16-15-901 to -15-905, TENN. R. CIV. P. 1 (specialized procedure); TENN. CODE ANN. § 24-9-102(a) (discovery); *id.* § 16-15-721 (evidentiary rules); TENN. R. CIV. P. 38.03 (jury trials available only if case is removed by appeal or otherwise from the Court of General Sessions) (jury trials); TENN. CODE ANN. § 27-5-108 (2013) (appeals).

[11] TEX. GOV'T CODE ANN. § 27.060(a) (West 2013) (courts); TEX. R. CIV. P. 500.3(a) (monetary limit); SMU LAW LIBRARY, SMALL CLAIMS COURT – TEXAS, http://library.law.smu.edu/Research-Tools/Research-Guides/Texas-Law-%28300%29/307-Small-Claims-Court---Texas (equitable relief); TEX. R. CIV. P. 500.4(a)(3), (b)(3) (attorney representation); *id.* 502.2(a) (simplified pleadings); *id.* 502.5(a) (answer required); *id.* 502.6(a) (requiring that counterclaims be served in accordance with TEX. R. CIV. P. 501.4 (requiring that any counterclaim be filed three days prior to any hearing)) (advanced counterclaim); TEX. GOV'T CODE ANN. § 101.151 (a)(1)(B) (West 2013) (filing fees); TEX. R. CIV. P. 505.1(d) (costs recoverable); *id.* 500 – 507 (specialized procedure); *id.* 500.9(a) (discovery); *id.* 500.3(e) (evidentiary rules); *id.* 504.1(a) (jury trials); *id.* 506.1 (appeals).

End Notes

[1] *See* U.S. CONST. art. I, § 8, cl. 8 (Congress empowered "[t]o promote the Progress of Science ... by securing for limited Times to Authors ... the exclusive Right to their respective Writings…."); 17 U.S.C. §§ 101 *et seq.*

[2] U.S. CONST. art. I, § 8, cl. 8.

[3] *See* Letter from Hon. Lamar Smith, Chairman of the U.S. House of Representatives Judiciary Committee, to Hon. Maria A. Pallante, Register of Copyrights and Director, U.S. Copyright Office (Oct. 11, 2011) ("Smith Letter").

[4] Graphic Artists Guild ("GAG"), Comments Submitted in Response to U.S. Copyright Office's Oct. 27, 2011 Notice of Inquiry at 3 (Jan. 16, 2012) ("GAG First Notice Comments").

[5] American Photographic Artists ("APA"), Comments Submitted in Response to U.S. Copyright Office's Oct. 27, 2011 Notice of Inquiry at 3 (Jan. 17, 2012) ("APA First Notice Comments").

[6] Alliance of Visual Artists ("AVA"), Comments Submitted in Response to U.S. Copyright Office's Aug. 23, 2012 Notice of Inquiry at 2 (Oct. 19, 2012) ("AVA Second Notice Comments").

[7] Authors Guild, Comments Submitted in Response to U.S. Copyright Office's Oct. 27, 2011 Notice of Inquiry at 2-3 (undated) ("Authors Guild First Notice Comments") (citing survey showing 55% of authors favor small claims court).

[8] Songwriters Guild of America ("SGA") & Nashville Songwriters Association International ("NSAI"), Comments Submitted in Response to U.S. Copyright Office's Oct. 27, 2011 Notice of Inquiry at 1 (undated) ("SGA & NSAI First Notice Comments").

[9] *See* American Bar Association ("ABA") Section of Intellectual Property Law ("ABA IP Section"), Comments Submitted in Response to U.S. Copyright Office's Aug. 23, 2012 Notice of Inquiry at 1, 10 (Oct. 19, 2012) ("ABA IP Section Second Notice Comments").

[10] *See* California Lawyers for the Arts ("CLA"), Comments Submitted in Response to U.S. Copyright Office's Oct. 27, 2011 Notice of Inquiry (undated) ("CLA First Notice Comments"); Volunteer Lawyers for the Arts, Inc. ("VLA"), Comments Submitted in Response to U.S. Copyright Office's Feb. 26, 2013 Notice of Inquiry (Apr. 12, 2013) ("VLA Third Notice Comments").

[11] *See The Role of Voluntary Agreements in the U.S. Intellectual Property System Before the Subcomm. on Courts, Intellectual Property, and the Internet of the H. Comm. on the Judiciary*, 113th Cong. (2013) (discussing various voluntary initiatives to combat copyright infringement); Center for Copyright Information, *The Copyright Alert System*, http://www.copyrightinformation.org/the-copyright-alert-system/ (click on embedded video) (explaining recently implemented U.S. Copyright Alert System, a voluntary system established by content owners and internet service providers ("ISPs") by which consumers are warned against infringing conduct through participating ISPs); *see also* THE DEPARTMENT OF COMMERCE INTERNET POLICY TASK FORCE, COPYRIGHT POLICY, CREATIVITY, AND INNOVATION IN THE DIGITAL ECONOMY App. A at 102-03 (July 2013) (noting Task Force's desire to support development of voluntary enforcement initiatives).

[12] "Orphan works" is a term used to describe the situation where the owner of a copyrighted work cannot be identified or located by someone who wishes to make use of the work in a manner that requires permission of the copyright owner. U.S. COPYRIGHT OFFICE, REPORT ON ORPHAN WORKS (2006), *available at* http://www.copyright.gov/orphan/orphan-report-full.pdf ("Orphan Works Report").

[13] *See Remedies for Small Copyright Claims, Before the Subcomm. on Courts, the Internet, and Intellectual Property of the H. Comm. on the Judiciary*, 109th Cong. (2006), *available at* http://www.gpo.gov/fdsys/pkg/CHRG-109hhrg26767/pdf/CHRG-109hhrg26767.pdf ("2006 Hearing"). The statement submitted by Register of Copyrights Marybeth Peters on behalf of the Copyright Office is attached as Appendix A.

[14] 2006 Hearing at 2.

[15] *Id.* at 45 (statement of the United States Copyright Office). The Office also identified "small claims" challenges in its Orphan Works Report, and proposed orphan works legislation in 2006 and 2008 included provisions that specifically directed the Copyright Office to conduct a study addressing remedies for small claims. *See* Orphan Works Report at 114; Shawn Bentley Orphan Works Act of 2008, S. 2913, § 5, 110th Cong. (2008); Orphan Works Act of 2008, H.R. 5889, § 6, 110th Cong. (2008); Orphan Works Act of 2006, H.R. 5439, § 4, 109th Cong. (2006).

[16] *See* Smith Letter.

[17] *Id.*

[18] *Id.*

[19] Remedies for Small Copyright Claims, 76 Fed. Reg. 66,758 (Oct. 27, 2011). This Notice of Inquiry is attached, along with the Office's two additional Federal Register notices, as Appendix B.

[20] These comments are posted on the Office's website at http://www.copyright.gov/docs/smallclaims/comments/. Additionally, lists of the parties who responded to each of the Office's Notices of Inquiry, as well as the participants in the Office's public hearings, can be found in Appendix C.

[21] *See* The George Washington University Law School, *Event Videos*, http://www.law.gwu.edu/Academics/FocusAreas/IP/Pages/Videos.aspx (hyperlinks for videos of the proceedings are under the heading "The IP Small Claims Roundtable, May 20, 2012").

[22] Remedies for Small Copyright Claims: Additional Comments, 77 Fed. Reg. 51,068 (Aug. 23, 2012) (included in Appendix B).

[23] These comments are posted on the Office's website at http://www.copyright.gov/docs/smallclaims/comments/noi_10112012/index html. A list of parties who responded to the Second Notice of Inquiry is included in Appendix C.

[24] Transcripts of the hearings are available on the Office's website at http://www.copyright.gov/docs/smallclaims/transcripts/. A list of participants in the public hearings is included in Appendix C.

[25] Remedies for Small Copyright Claims: Third Request for Comments, 78 Fed. Reg. 13,094 (Feb. 26, 2013) (included in Appendix B).

[26] These comments are posted on the Office's website at http://www.copyright.gov/docs/smallclaims/comments/noi_02263013/. A list of parties who responded to the Third Notice of Inquiry is included in Appendix C.

[27] *See* 17 U.S.C. § 301; 28 U.S.C. § 1338.

[28] *See* ADMINISTRATIVE OFFICE OF THE UNITED STATES COURTS, STATISTICAL TABLES FOR THE FEDERAL JUDICIARY, TABLE C-2: U.S. DISTRICT COURTS-CIVIL CASES COMMENCED, BY BASIS OF JURISDICTION AND NATURE OF SUIT, DURING THE 12-MONTH PERIODS ENDING DECEMBER 31, 2011 AND 2012, *available at* http://www.uscourts.gov/uscourts/Statistics/StatisticalTablesForTheFederalJudiciary/2012/december/C02Dec12.pdf. The 3,266 copyright claims filed in federal district courts in 2012 – a number which appears to be on the rise – comprised approximately 1.2% of the 267,990 civil cases filed overall. *Id.* In 2011, the number of federal district court copyright filings was 2,375. *Id.* In 2010, there were 2,033 copyright cases, and in 2009, the number was 2,018. *See* ADMINISTRATIVE OFFICE OF THE UNITED STATES COURTS, STATISTICAL TABLES FOR THE FEDERAL JUDICIARY, TABLE C-2: U.S. DISTRICT COURTS-CIVIL CASES COMMENCED, BY BASIS OF JURISDICTION AND NATURE OF SUIT, DURING THE 12-MONTH PERIODS ENDING DECEMBER 31, 2009 AND 2010, *available at* http://www.uscourts.gov/uscourts/Statistics/StatisticalTablesForTheFederalJudiciary/2010/dec10/C02Dec10.pdf.

[29] For example, on average, most individual professional photographers earn $50,000 or less per year. *See* APA First Notice Comments at 3. Similarly, the median pay for writers and authors in 2010 was $55,420 annually. *See* BUREAU OF LABOR STATISTICS, OCCUPATIONAL OUTLOOK HANDBOOK: WRITERS AND AUTHORS (2012), *available at* http://www.bls.gov/ooh/media-and-communication/writers-and-authors htm.

[30] *See* AMERICAN INTELLECTUAL PROPERTY LAW ASSOCIATION ("AIPLA"), REPORT OF THE ECONOMIC SURVEY 2011, at 35 (2011) ("AIPLA Report").

[31] *See* GAG, Comments Submitted in Response to Third Notice of Inquiry at 2 (Apr. 10, 2013) ("GAG Third Notice Comments") ("[The] existing court system is unaffordable and impractical for most occurrences of typical infringement. The result is a significant and seriously detrimental loss of income to American visual creators …."); VLA Third Notice Comments at 3 ("The cost, time and resources that need to be devoted to federal court litigation often exceed the amount in controversy in a small copyright matter, which discourages authors and artists from bringing such claims.").

[32] PUBLIC COUNSEL, THE PUBLIC COUNSEL FEDERAL PRO SE CLINIC ANNUAL REPORT FEBRUARY 2009-FEBRUARY 2010, at 1, *available at* http://www.publiccounsel.org/tools/publications/files/Public-Counsel-Federal-Pro-Se-Clinic-Annual-Report-2009-2010.pdf.

[33] Tr. at 26:08-11 (Nov. 15, 2012) (Bruce Lehman, Former Asst. Sec'y of Commerce and Comm'r of Patents & Trademarks). Throughout theis Report, transcripts of the Office's public hearings are cited with the abbreviation "Tr." along with the page and line numbers, and date, of the cited material. These citations also include the name of the speaker and organization (if any) with which the speaker is affiliated.

[34] National Press Photographers Association ("NPPA"), Comments Submitted in Response to First Notice of Inquiry at 7 (Jan. 16, 2012) ("NPPA First Notice Comments").

[35] *See* ABA IP Section Second Notice Comments at 7 (survey results indicating that less than one-third of surveyed copyright attorneys would accept an uncomplicated copyright infringement case with under $30,000 at stake).

[36] 28 U.S.C. § 1338(a). Additionally, the Copyright Act preempts all state law claims that "are equivalent to any of the exclusive rights within the general scope of copyright as specified by section 106 in works of authorship that are fixed in a tangible medium of expression and come within the subject matter of copyright as specified by sections 102 and 103 …." 17 U.S.C. § 301(a). Nevertheless, states can provide for claims that protect rights that fall *outside* of the Copyright Act, including some claims that are somewhat similar to copyright matters. For example, some states protect unfixed works, moral rights (beyond the limited rights set forth in 17 U.S.C. § 106A), and pre-1972 sound recordings.

[37] 28 U.S.C. § 1367.

[38] *See* 3 MELVILLE B. NIMMER & DAVID NIMMER, NIMMER ON COPYRIGHT § 12.01[B][2] (rev. ed., 2013) ("NIMMER") ("When federal jurisdiction exists over at least one count of a complaint, the district court may entertain other pendent counts (as to which federal jurisdiction would be lacking were they brought independently) involving the same parties and arising 'from the same nucleus of operative facts.' For example,

supplemental jurisdiction will lie as to a contract action for breach of a publishing agreement where the facts of such breach also give rise to a claim for copyright infringement.").

[39] 28 U.S.C. § 1295. In addition to patent appeals, the Federal Circuit hears appeals from various other tribunals, including certain matters from the Trademark Trial and Appeal Board and the Patent Trial and Appeal Board.

[40] 28 U.S.C. § 1291. But note that "[o]ccasionally, the Federal Circuit will hear copyright infringement claims brought as part of patent appeals." WILLIAM F. PATRY, 3 PATRY ON COPYRIGHT § 9:278 (2013) ("PATRY").

[41] While the Constitution specifically provides that Congress can enact laws regarding patents and copyrights in Article I, Section 8, Clause 8, federal trademark law is grounded in Congress' more general authority under the Commerce Clause. U.S. CONST. art.1, § 8, cl. 3; 1-1 ANNE GILSON LALONDE, GILSON ON TRADEMARKS § 1.04[2][b] (3d ed. 2013) ("GILSON").

[42] 2-7 GILSON § 7.04 (noting that Lanham Act does not occupy the field of trademark infringement entirely, as states may themselves regulate trademark activity "in the absence of a clear conflict with the Act or the attributes of federal trademark registration.").

[43] 6 J. THOMAS MCCARTHY, MCCARTHY ON TRADEMARKS AND UNFAIR COMPETITION § 32:1 (4th ed. 2013) ("MCCARTHY") ("[A] plaintiff wishing to file suit for violation of a provision of the Lanham Act has a choice to sue on the claim in either federal or state court").

[44] *Id.* §§ 32:20, 32:33.

[45] *Id.* § 32:1 ("As a matter of litigation strategy, however, most plaintiffs appear to bring such cases in the federal courts, perhaps on the assumption that federal judges are more likely to be familiar with problems of trademark infringement under a federal statute."); *see also* Aurelio Lopez-Tarruella Martinez & Fabrizio Miazzetto, *The Community Trade Mark and Design Court of Alicante and Forum Shopping Regarding European Community Intellectual Property Rights Litigation*, 95 TRADEMARK REP. 1308, 1316 n.21 (2005) ("Taking the example of the United States: it is reported that the great majority of litigants prefer to file trade mark cases in the federal courts instead of state courts because the former 'have far more experience in adjudicating trademark cases than do the state courts.'") (citation omitted).

[46] DONNA STIENSTRA, JARED BATAILLON & JASON A. CANTONE, FED. JUDICIAL CTR., ASSISTANCE TO PRO SE LITIGANTS IN U.S. DISTRICT COURTS: A REPORT ON SURVEYS OF CLERKS OF COURT AND CHIEF JUDGES vii (2011), *available at* www fjc.gov/public/pdf.nsf/lookup/proseusdc.pdf/$file/proseusdc.pdf ("STIENSTRA ET AL.").

[47] Federal Legal Assistance Self Help Center ("FLASH"), Comments Submitted in Response to Third Notice of Inquiry at 1-2 (Apr. 1, 2013) ("FLASH Third Notice Comments").

[48] For example, despite noting that "the right to a jury trial is constitutionally protected and casual waivers are not to be presumed," a court held that a *pro se* defendant had waived his right to a jury trial when he participated in a bench trial without objection. *CoxCom, Inc. v. Chaffee*, 536 F.3d 101, 110-11 (1st Cir. 2008); *see also* Tr. at 75:12-20 (Nov. 15, 2012) (Jay Rosenthal, National Music Publishers' Association ("NMPA")) ("[W]e were very concerned about the idea that a plaintiff in *pro se* represent themselves [in a music-related matter], as well as a defendant going *pro se*, not really understanding the complexities of the compulsory license or the complexities of the consent decree with BMI or ASCAP or authorship claims against each other, fair use, first use, rights of termination, on and on and on.").

[49] *See Haines v. Kerner*, 404 U.S. 519, 520 (1972) (per curiam).

[50] *Bauer v. Yellen*, 548 F. Supp. 2d 88, 92 (S.D.N.Y. 2008).

[51] For example, the Southern and Eastern Districts of New York require opposing counsel to provide *pro se* parties with unreported cases cited in submissions to the court as well as special notices in connection with motions to dismiss or for summary judgment. *See* S.D.N.Y. & E.D.N.Y L.R. 7.2, 12.1, 56.2.

[52] STIENSTRA ET AL., at 34.

[53] *Id.* at vi.

[54] *Id.* at 17.

[55] *See, e.g.*, *Macklin v. Mueck*, 373 F. Supp. 2d 1334 (S.D. Fla. 2005) (awarding *pro se* plaintiff a $300,000 default judgment that represented the maximum statutory damages for infringement of his poetry).

[56] FED. R. CIV. P. 1.

[57] Personal jurisdiction and service of process are discussed further in Part IV.E, *infra*.

[58] *See* 28 U.S.C. § 1914 (providing for $350 filing fee); ADMINISTRATIVE OFFICE OF THE U.S. COURT MISCELLANEOUS FEE SCHEDULE (May 1, 2013) (additional $50 administrative fee to be charged by district court for filing of civil action), *available at* http://www http://www.uscourts.gov/FormsAndFees/ Fees/DistrictCourt MiscellaneousFeeSchedule.aspx.

[59] FED. R. CIV. P. 26(a).

[60] *Id.* 27.

[61] *Id.* 33.

[62] *Id.* 26(b)(2).

[63] *Id.* 34.

[64] *Id.* 36.

[65] *See* ABA SECTION OF LITIGATION, MEMBER SURVEY ON CIVIL PRACTICE: FULL REPORT 12 (2009) ("ABA 2009 SURVEY"), *available at* http://www.americanbar.org/content/dam/aba/migrated/litigation/survey/docs/ report_ aba_re port.authcheckdam.pdf ("Discovery is the reason most often picked by respondents as the primary cause of delay. 48% picked that reason, while the next most popular reason (delayed rulings on motions) garnered only 25%.").

[66] *See* Hon. Frank H. Easterbrook, *Discovery as Abuse*, 69 B.U. L. REV. 635, 637 (1989) (outlining both the frustration parties have over discovery and the perspective that some litigators value discovery "not by its contribution to an anticipated judgment but by its contribution to an anticipated settlement").

[67] Administrative Office of the U.S. Courts, *Judicial Conference Adopts Rules Changes -Confronts Projected Budget Shortfalls* (Sept. 15, 1999), *available at* http://www.uscourts.gov/News/NewsView/99-09-15/Judicial_Conference_Adopts_Rules_Changes_-_Confronts_Projected_Budget_Shortfalls.aspx; *see also* T. WILLGING ET. AL., FED. JUDICIAL CTR. DISCOVERY AND DISCLOSURE PRACTICE, PROBLEMS AND PROPOSALS FOR CHANGE: A CASE-BASED NATIONAL SURVEY OF COUNSEL IN CLOSED FEDERAL CIVIL CASES, 15 (Table 4) (1997) (even before the rise of electronic discovery, the median percentage of clients' total litigation expenses accounted for by discovery was 50%), *available at* http://www.fjc.gov/public/pdf nsf/lookup/discovry.pdf/$file/discovry.pdf.

[68] *See* JOHN H. BEISNER, U.S. CHAMBER INSTITUTE FOR LEGAL REFORM, THE CENTRE CANNOT HOLD: THE NEED FOR EFFECTIVE REFORM OF THE U.S. CIVIL DISCOVERY PROCESS 2 (2010) ("BEISNER") ("[T]he effort and expense associated with electronic discovery are so excessive that settlement is often the most fiscally prudent course – regardless of the merits of the case."), *available at* http://www.uscourts.gov/uscourts/RulesAnd Policies/ rules/Duke %20Materials/Library/John%20Beisner,%20The%20Centre%20Cannot%20Hold.pdf.

[69] *Bell Atlantic Corp. v. Twombly*, 550 U.S. 544, 559 (2007).

[70] *See* FED. R. CIV. P. 16(f), 37(b)(2).

[71] BEISNER, at 3. This sentiment appears to be echoed by practitioners. *See* ABA 2009 SURVEY, at 67 ("86.5% of all lawyers agree ... that sanctions allowed by the discovery rules are seldom imposed."), *available at* http://www.americanbar.org/content/dam/aba/migrated/litigation/survey/docs/report_aba_report.authcheckdam .pdf.

[72] FED. R. CIV. P. 12(b).

[73] *Id.* 12(c).

[74] *Id.* 56.

[75] *See* ABA 2009 SURVEY, at 114 ("62.2% of plaintiffs' lawyers believe that summary judgment increases costs and delays without proportionate benefit, while defense lawyers agree only 10.9% of the time"); Tr. at 158:20-159:05 (Nov. 26, 2012) (Lorin Brennan, Linde Law Firm) ("There's always a motion for summary judgment that says, 'My gosh. The plaintiff made a tiny error in the registration certificate. This is fraud on the Copyright Office. Bands must play. Dirges must sound. The solar system must stop. And the plaintiff must be kicked out' for what turns out to be essentially trivial claims.").

[76] FED. R. EVID. 101, 1101.

[77] In addition to magistrate judges, courts sometimes also appoint special masters to assist the court in exceptional situations. FED. R. CIV. P. 53(a). A special master can hold trial proceedings in a nonjury matter or handle complex findings of fact or difficult damages computations. *Id.* 53(a)(1)(B).

[78] Pub. L. No. 90-578, 82 Stat. 1113 (1968) (codified as amended at 28 U.S.C. §§ 631-39). For further discussion of the role of federal magistrates, *see* Part III.C.4, *infra*.

[79] 28 U.S.C. § 636(b)(1)(B).

[80] *Id.* § 636(b)(1)(C).

[81] 28 U.S.C. § 636(c)(1).

[82] *See, e.g.*, FED. R. CIV. P. 72 (Magistrate judges: pretrial order); i*d.* 73 (Magistrate judges: trial by consent; appeal); FED. R. EVID. 1101(a) ("These rules apply to proceedings before ... magistrate judges").

[83] *See* Pub. L. No. 111-349, 124 Stat. 3674 (2011).

[84] *See, e.g.*, S.D.N.Y. PATENT L.R. 2 (initial scheduling conference), 6-8 & 10-12 (initial disclosures), 12 (claim construction hearing).

[85] *See generally* E.D. TEX. P.R. (local rules for patent cases in the Eastern District of Texas); *see also* Michael C. Smith, *Feature: Rocket Docket: Marshall Court Leads Nation in Hearing Patent Cases*, 69 TEX. B.J. 1045, 1046 (2006).

[86] *See* Yan Leychkis, *Of Fire Ants and Claim Construction: An Empirical Study of the Meteoric Rise of the Eastern District of Texas as a Preeminent Forum for Patent Litigation*, 9 YALE J.L. & TECH. 193, 219 (2007).

[87] 17 U.S.C. § 411(a). Although the registration requirement is not jurisdictional, it is a precondition to a suit. *See Reed Elsevier, Inc. v. Muchnick*, 559 U.S. 154, 163-66 (2010).

[88] Non-U.S. works need not be registered prior to bringing a lawsuit, but they must be timely registered if the copyright owner wishes to seek statutory damages, attorneys' fees, and/or costs. *See, e.g.*, *Football Ass'n Premier League Ltd. v. YouTube, Inc.*, 633 F. Supp. 2d 159, 162 (S.D.N.Y. 2009) ("[Section 411(a)] allows suits to be brought upon foreign works without registration of them; but it does not impair the operation of

Section 412, which forbids the recovery of statutory damages in *any* infringement action (except, among others, those under Section 411(c) concerning live broadcasts) unless the work has been registered.").

[89] *See* 17 U.S.C. § 411(a).

[90] *See* AVA Second Notice Comments at 4 ("As means of preserving the mission of the Copyright Office and Library Congress, access to this alternative body, like the federal courts, should be contingent upon registration of the infringed photograph(s)."); *see also* Motion Picture Association of America, Inc. ("MPAA"), Comments Submitted in Response to Third Notice of Inquiry at 5 (Apr. 12, 2013) ("MPPA Third Notice Comments") ("Generally speaking, a fully-populated registration system aids in searches by potential users of others' copyrighted works. A small claims system should not be designed in such a way as to lessen the incentive to register, which would lead to various negative outcomes, including an increase in the volume of potential orphan works. Moreover, in the litigation context, it is vitally important for a defendant to know exactly what it is he is accused of infringing."). Because the registration process requires that claimants deposit copies of the works for which registration is sought, the registration requirement also contributes substantially to the unequaled collection of the U.S. Library of Congress. U.S. COPYRIGHT OFFICE, ANNUAL REPORT OF THE REGISTER OF COPYRIGHTS: FISCAL YEAR ENDING SEPT. 30, 2011 29-30 (2011) (showing that the average annual value of materials transferred from the Copyright Office to the Library of Congress from 2007 through 2011 was $33 million).

[91] *Compare La Resolana Architects, PA v. Clay Realtors Angel Fire*, 416 F.3d 1195, 1205 (10th Cir. 2005), *abrogated on other grounds by Reed Elsevier, Inc.,* 559 U.S. 154 ("[W]e reject the proposition that § 411 confers federal court jurisdiction for an infringement action upon mere submission of a copyright application to the Copyright Office. In our view, the statute requires more: actual registration by the Register of Copyrights. Until that happens, an infringement action will not lie in the federal courts.") *with Apple Barrel Prods., Inc. v. R.D. Beard*, 730 F.2d 384, 386-87 (5th Cir.1984) (allowing suit to proceed upon Copyright Office's receipt of application, payment of required fee, and deposit of work in question).

[92] *See* 17 U.S.C. § 412.

[93] *See id.*

[94] *See* 37 C.F.R. § 201.3.

[95] *See* AVA, Comments Submitted in Response to First Notice of Inquiry at Attachment A (Jan. 17, 2012) ("AVA First Notice Comments") (noting that in a survey of photographers, 84% never register their works and of those who do not register, 25% said they never heard about it, 24% said it was too time consuming, and 13% said it was too expensive); Kernochan Center for Law, Media and the Arts ("Kernochan Center"), Comments Submitted in Response to Second Notice of Inquiry at 3 (Oct. 19, 2012) ("Kernochan Second Notice Comments") ("Requiring that a plaintiff wait for a registration certificate to be issued or denied before bringing an action ... would seem to run counter to the goals of a small claims proceeding. Many potential plaintiffs would have to choose between a significant delay or a significant payment (for faster processing of its application) before commencing an action."); Tr. at 40:22-41:04 (Nov. 15, 2012) (Nancy Wolff, PACA) (noting that photographers have difficulty registering because they produce photographs in large numbers).

[96] American Society of Media Photographers ("ASMP"), Comments Submitted in Response to First Notice of Inquiry at 5 (Jan. 16, 2012) ("ASMP First Notice Comments") ("[O]ne of the impediments to professional photographers' access to the current copyright enforcement system is the requirement of copyright registration before litigation can be instituted (and earlier, for eligibility for an award of attorney fees and/or statutory damages)."); Tr. at 141:07-09 (Nov. 15, 2012) (Randy Taylor, Copyright Defense League, LLC ("CDL")) ("[S]tatutory damages are an essential and major element in getting the other side to actually talk to you."); Tr. at 272:10-17 (Nov. 16, 2012) (Lisa Wilmer, Getty Images) (noting that untimely registration eliminates the option of statutory damages and leaves the challenging option of seeking only actual damages, which are not a deterrent to defendants).

[97] Tr. at 255:24-256:06 (Nov. 16, 2012) (Nancy Wolff, PACA) (noting that even though an exclusive license may only cost a few thousand dollars, widely distributing that image online is an infringement can affect the market for that image and should be subject to some sort of damages multiplier); Tr. at 261:02-07 (Nov. 16, 2012) (Bruce Lehman, Former Asst. Sec'y of Commerce and Comm'r of Patents & Trademarks) ("I think if the damages are $300, if an illustrator, photographer licenses a work for some kind of a use for $300 or $500, which wouldn't be totally uncommon for particularly a secondary use, you know, that's hardly worth their time.").

[98] Alma Robinson, *Small Copyright Claimants Need Access to Justice*, CALIFORNIA ARTS BLOG (Feb. 20, 2013), http://www.calawyersforthearts.org/california_arts_blog?mode=PostView&bmi=1213811.

[99] Sheana Firth, Comments Submitted in Response to Third Notice of Inquiry at 1. Another commenter noted that "[i]n many instances, works created by individuals or other small copyright owners will not have been registered until the infringement is found, eliminating any statutory damages or attorney's fees." Copyright Alliance, Comments Submitted in Response to First Notice of Inquiry at 2 (Jan. 17, 2012) ("Copyright Alliance First Notice Comments").

[100] *See* Getty Images, Comments Submitted in Response to Third Notice of Inquiry at 2 (Apr. 12, 2012) ("Getty Images Third Notice Comments") ("We frequently encounter infringement of images on websites where the

infringer's identity is unknown, often because the domain name has been registered through a proxy and there is no valid contact information."); National Writers Union ("NWU"), Comments Submitted in Response to First Notice of Inquiry at 11 (Jan. 16, 2012) ("NWU First Notice Comments") ("[I]nfringers...may be located in cyberspace rather than at any readily identifiable geographic location"); Tr. at 54:10-18 (Nov. 15, 2012) (Christos Badavas, Harry Fox Agency, Inc. ("HFA")) (noting that even when a plaintiff finds an infringing company, sometimes that plaintiff still cannot identify any owners of that company); Tr. at 143:20-24 (Nov 15, 2012) (Randy Taylor, CDL) (estimating that 15% of unauthorized users on the internet are using private online systems and are "going out of their way to make it very difficult to find who the infringer actually is"); Tr. at 204:18-205:07 (Nov. 26, 2012) (Carolyn Wright, Law Offices of Carolyn E. Wright, LLC) (noting that infringers on the internet are hard to find).

[101] FED. R. CIV. P. 45 (subpoenas generally); 17 U.S.C. § 512(h) (specific provision relating to online service providers).

[102] *See Art of Living Found. v. Does 1-10*, No. 10-CV-05022-LHK, 2011 WL 5444622, at *8-10 (N.D. Cal. Nov. 9, 2011) (granting motion to quash a subpoena to protect defendant's right to "anonymous speech"); *LaFace Records, LLC v. Does 1-38*, No. 5:07-CV-298-BR, 2008 WL 544992, at *3 (E.D.N.C. Feb. 27, 2008) (quashing all but one of thirty-eight subpoenas to identify unknown defendants allegedly using a peer-to-peer network); *Millenium TGA Inc. v. Does 1-800*, No. 10-C-5603, 2011 WL 10468128, at *2 (N.D. Ill. Mar. 31, 2011) (severing 800 defendants as being improperly joined, then granting single remaining defendant's motion to quash subpoena due to lack of personal jurisdiction). *But see Maverick Entm't Grp., Inc. v. Does 1-2,115*, 810 F.Supp.2d 1, 7-9 (D.D.C. 2011) (denying fifty-two motions to quash subpoenas issued to ISPs for the purpose of identifying defendants accused of infringing plaintiff's copyrighted works).

[103] *See* 17 U.S.C. § 512(h); *Recording Indus. Ass'n of Am. v. Verizon Internet Servs.*, 351 F.3d 1229, 1233 (D.C. Cir. 2003) (finding that "a subpoena may be issued only to an ISP engaged in storing on its servers material that is infringing or the subject of infringing activity," and not to an ISP that is a mere conduit for infringing material); *Recording Indus. Ass'n of Am. v. Charter Commc'ns, Inc.*, 393 F.3d 771, 777 (8th Cir. 2005) (adopting reasoning of *Verizon* court).

[104] 17 U.S.C. § 507.

[105] *Compare Taylor v. Meirick*, 712 F.2d 1112, 1118 (7th Cir. 1983) (allowing a copyright infringement suit arising from acts outside the statute of limitations to proceed because the infringing activities continued) *with Roley v. New World Pictures*, 19 F.3d 479, 481 (9th Cir. 1994) (affirming the district court's summary judgment order and rejecting the theory that a continuing wrong tolls the statute of limitations).

[106] *See* 17 U.S.C. § 512.

[107] *See, e.g., id.* §§ 114, 115, 118.

[108] *See id.* §§ 108, 110, 121.

[109] *See* 17 U.S.C. § 107; Tr. at 171:07-08 (Nov. 15, 2012) (Randy Taylor, CDL) ("The [defendant's] initial response [to a claim of copyright infringement] ... always includes fair use.").

[110] Section 107 provides that the fair use of a copyrighted work

> for purposes such as criticism, comment, news reporting, teaching ..., scholarship, or research, is not an infringement of copyright. In determining whether the use made of a work in any particular case is a fair use the factors to be considered shall include –
>
> (1) the purpose and character of the use, including whether such use is of a commercial nature or is for nonprofit educational purposes;
>
> (2)the nature of the copyrighted work;
>
> (3)the amount and substantiality of the portion used in relation to the copyrighted work as a whole;
>
> (4)and the effect of the use upon the potential market for or value of the copyrighted work.
>
> .... 17 U.S.C. § 107.

[111] *Id.* § 504.

[112] *See Sony BMG Music Entm't v. Tenenbaum*, No. 07-11446, 2012 WL 3639053, at *4 (D. Mass. 2012) ("Congress gave a Copyright Act plaintiff the right to elect statutory in lieu of actual damages, in part because it recognized that actual damages are extremely difficult to measure and prove in a copyright case.") (citations omitted); Tr. at 37:11-12 (Nov. 15, 2012) (Charles Sanders, SGA) ("[P]roving actual damages is really, really expensive.").

[113] *See, e.g.*, 2 PAUL GOLDSTEIN, GOLDSTEIN ON COPYRIGHT §14.0 at 14:1 (3d ed. 2006 Supp.) (Copyright Act "anticipates that copyright owners will sometimes encounter difficulty in establishing actual damages and profits, and so entitles the copyright owner to elect statutory damages instead"); 6 PATRY § 22:153 (2013) (statutory damages were adopted "to give the owner of a copyright some recompense for injury done him, in a case where the rules of law render difficult or impossible proof of damages or discovery of profits.") (citing *Douglas v. Cunningham* 294 U.S. 207, 209 (1935)).

[114] Tr. at 121:19-22 (Nov. 15, 2012) (Lisa Shaftel, GAG).

[115] *See* Tr. at 46:06-19 (Nov. 27, 2012) (Alicia Calzada, NPPA) ("For artists who produce work, the ability to control their work is not just about money. It is about how their work is used. ... [T]he ability to control your work is just as important as money for some situations.").

[116] Great Britain's first copyright act, the 1710 Statute of Anne, provided for statutory damages of "'one Penny for every Sheet which shall be found in [the infringer's] custody.'" *Feltner v. Columbia Pictures Television, Inc.*, 523 U.S. 340, 349 (1998) (quoting 8 Anne ch. 19 (1710)). The amount and availability of statutory damages are topics of longstanding debate among copyright stakeholders. *See, e.g.*, THE DEPARTMENT OF COMMERCE INTERNET POLICY TASK FORCE, COPYRIGHT POLICY, CREATIVITY, AND INNOVATION IN THE DIGITAL ECONOMY App. A at 102 (July 2013) (Task Force will seek to conduct dialogue regarding application of statutory damages in certain contexts).

[117] *See* Tr. at 263:2-6 (Nov. 16, 2012) (Charles Sanders, SGA) (asking whether adopting a "reasonable compensation" damages regime would "set up a situation where you have to catch me if you can? My liability is what I would have paid . . . had I actually licensed, but otherwise I am not going to pay until you ask?").

[118] 17 U.S.C. § 504(c)(1).

[119] *Id.* § 504(c)(2).

[120] *Id.* § 504(c)(1).

[121] *Feltner*, 523 U.S. at 342.

[122] *Sony BMG Music Entm't v. Tenenbaum*, 660 F.3d 487, 503-04 (1st Cir. 2011).

[123] Pamela Samuelson & Tara Wheatland, *Statutory Damages in Copyright Law: A Remedy in Need of Reform*, 51 WM. & MARY L. REV. 439, 454 (2009).

[124] NWU, Comments Submitted in Response to Third Notice of Inquiry at 3 (Apr. 12, 2013) ("NWU Third Notice Comments") ("The lack of any means of effective redress for copyright infringement genuinely accessible and affordable to most individual writers makes the investment of time and money in the attempt to satisfy copyright registration formalities an economically unjustifiable investment of writers' time and money, and a diversion from revenue-generating creative work."); Tr. at 41:17-20 (Nov. 15, 2012) (Nancy Wolff, PACA) ("[O]ften the reason that an individual creator cannot afford to go to federal court is because they can't afford to register all their work[s] as they create them.").

[125] FED. R. CIV. P. 65. They may also seek a temporary restraining order. *Id.*

[126] *Id.* 65(c).

[127] *eBay Inc. v. MercExchange, L.L.C.*, 547 U.S. 388 (2006).

[128] Courts have adapted and applied the *eBay* test to the preliminary injunction context as well. *See, e.g.*, *Flava Works, Inc. v. Gunter*, 689 F.3d 754, 755 (7th Cir. 2012) (though *eBay* "was a case about patents rather than copyrights and about permanent rather than preliminary injunctions, we are persuaded ... that *eBay* governs a motion for a preliminary injunction in a copyright case, as well"); *Salinger v. Colting*, 607 F.3d 68, 77 (2d Cir. 2010) ("We hold today that *eBay* applies with equal force (a) to preliminary injunctions (b) that are issued for alleged copyright infringement.").

[129] *eBay*, 547 U.S. at 392-93 (noting that "this Court has consistently rejected invitations to replace traditional equitable considerations with a rule that an injunction automatically follows a determination that a copyright has been infringed.") (citations omitted).

[130] *Id.* at 391.

[131] 17 U.S.C. § 505 ("In any civil action under this title, the court in its discretion may allow the recovery of full costs ... the court may also award a reasonable attorney's fee to the prevailing party as part of the costs.").

[132] *Id.* § 412 (registration generally must be made within three months of publication or, for unpublished works, before the commencement of infringement).

[133] Jane Ginsburg, *The U.S. Experience With Mandatory Copyright Formalities: A Love/Hate Relationship*, 33 COLUM. J.L. & ARTS 311, 339 (2010). Similarly, as one court explained, "[a]n award of attorney's fees helps to ensure that all litigants have equal access to the courts to vindicate their statutory rights. It also prevents copyright infringements from going unchallenged where the commercial value of the infringed work is small and there is no economic incentive to challenge an infringement through expensive litigation." *Quinto v. Legal Times of Wash., Inc.*, 511 F. Supp. 579, 581 (D.D.C. 1981).

[134] *See* 5 NIMMER § 14.10[D] ("The most difficult question presented in connection with attorney's fees is when a court should exercise its discretion to make such an award. In the words of one appellate decision, '[a]lthough attorney's fees are awarded in the trial court's discretion, they are the rule rather than the exception and should be awarded routinely.' Nevertheless, in view of the Supreme Court's later rejection of categorical rules in favor of the trial court's discretion, that statement should no longer be taken as prescriptive. Even where the prevailing party has in fact incurred no attorney's fees at all, as where he represents himself *pro se*, an award of reasonable attorney's fees may be justified (although some decisions tacitly assume the contrary).").

[135] *Fogerty v. Fantasy, Inc.*, 510 U.S. 517, 535 n.19 (1994) (internal quotation omitted).

[136] *See* 5 NIMMER § 14.10[D]; *see also, Nat'l Football League v. Primetime 24 Joint Venture*, 131 F. Supp. 2d 458, 485 (S.D.N.Y. 2001) (declining to award a plaintiff attorneys' fees due to the novelty and complexity of the issue, the lack of bad faith on the part of defendant, and the adequacy of the statutory damages already awarded to plaintiff); *LZT/Filliung P'ship, LLP v. Cody/Braun & Assocs., Inc.*, 117 F. Supp. 2d 745, 753 (N.D. Ill. 2000) (reasoning that plaintiff should not be awarded attorneys' fees because defendant's counterclaim was not frivolous and "was motivated by sound litigation strategy," even though it was not ultimately successful); *Alexander v. Chesapeake, Potomac, and Tidewater Books, Inc.*, 60 F. Supp. 2d 544,

551 (E.D. Va. 1999) (noting that attorneys' fees should not be awarded to plaintiff because there was no evidence of willful infringement, defendant's arguments were objectively reasonable, the facts did "not call for deterrence of future frivolous claims or infringing conduct").

[137] *Compare* 17 U.S.C. § 505 ("the court in its discretion may allow the recovery of full costs … the court may also award a reasonable attorney's fee to the prevailing party as part of the costs.") *with* 35 U.S.C. § 285 (for patent cases, "The court in exceptional cases may award reasonable attorney fees to the prevailing party."), *and* 15 U.S.C. § 1117(a) (for trademark cases, "The court in exceptional cases may award reasonable attorney [sic] fees to the prevailing party.").

[138] *Fogerty*, 510 U.S. at 534.

[139] *Id.* at 535 n.19 (internal quotation omitted). *But see* New Media Rights, Comments Submitted in Response to Second Notice of Inquiry (Oct. 19, 2012) ("New Media Rights Second Notice Comments") at 2-3 ("Despite the *Fogerty* decision, there has not been a fundamental alteration in the application of § 505. Prevailing plaintiffs are routinely able to access attorney's fees simply by having registered the copyright according to the statute, whereas a prevailing defendant often must show that a plaintiff's claims or conduct during the litigation are frivolous or brought in bad faith in order to earn attorney's fees. Although *Fogerty* has made it somewhat easier for prevailing defendants to win fee awards, defendants are not on equal footing under § 505 as currently interpreted.").

[140] *See, e.g.*, Tr. at 284:25-289:19 (Nov. 16, 2012) (David Leichtman, VLA).

[141] New Media Rights, Comments in Response to First Notice of Inquiry at 18 (undated) ("New Media Rights First Notice Comments") at 2 (noting that small-scale defendants can be "intimidated by the threat of federal litigation.").

[142] Tr. at 112:16-19 (Nov. 26, 2012) (Molly Knappen, designer and developer); *see also* Tr. at 92:25-93:10 (Nov. 15, 2012) (Joseph DiMona, Broadcast Music, Inc. ("BMI")) ("I suspect that even if there were a small claims court, a modestly cheaper way to do it, that songwriters would not have the wherewithal and really wouldn't want to have to spend their time bringing 10,000 small claims proceedings, even if they were cheap. That's not what songwriters want to do. They want to create, perform, and that's why they have turned to publishers, and in some cases record labels and PROs to manage the business side."); *see also Quinto*, 511 F. Supp. at 581 ("[A] pro se litigant must forego other activities in order to prepare and pursue his case.").

[143] EMERY G. LEE III & THOMAS E. WILLGING, FED. JUDICIAL CTR., ATTORNEY SATISFACTION WITH THE FEDERAL RULES OF CIVIL PROCEDURE: REPORT TO THE JUDICIAL CONFERENCE ADVISORY COMMITTEE ON CIVIL RULES, 10 (Mar. 1, 2010) (surveying members of the American College of Trial Lawyers, the ABA Section of Litigation, and the National Employment Lawyers Association), *available at* SSRN: http://ssrn.com/abstract=1606885 or http://dx.doi.org/10.2139/ssrn.1606885. The survey did not define "large" versus "small" matters.

[144] ABA 2009 SURVEY, at 153.

[145] AIPLA Report, at 35 (2011).

[146] *Id.* App. I-163.

[147] ABA IP Section Second Notice Comments at 7.

[148] *Id.*

[149] *Id.* at 6-7 (noting limited sample pool of thirty-one members who responded to the survey).

[150] *Id.* at 7.

[151] GAG, Comments Submitted in Response to Second Notice of Inquiry App. at 7 (Oct. 18, 2012) ("GAG Second Notice Comments").

[152] *Id.* App. at 8 (70.7% and 49.4% respectively; responses were not mutually exclusive).

[153] *Id.* App. at 9 (64.3%).

[154] *Id.* App. at 10 (68.3%).

[155] *Id.* App. at 11 (51.7%).

[156] *Id.* App. at 13.

[157] *Id.* App. at 12 (21.7% of claims were won by Guild members and collected on, 14.1% of claims were won but the infringer did not pay, and 50% of claims were settled out of court).

[158] *Id.* App. at 14 (80.3% would use such a system, 1.3% would not, 18.5% responded "maybe").

[159] LEX MACHINA, https://lexmachina.com/ (last visited May 30, 2013).

[160] *Id.*

[161] *Id.*

[162] U.S. CONST. amend. VII.

[163] 523 U.S. 340 (1998).

[164] 17 U.S.C. § 504(c).

[165] *Video Views, Inc. v. Studio 21, Ltd.*, 925 F.2d 1010, 1014 (7th Cir.1991) ("There is little question that the right to a jury trial exists in a copyright infringement action when the copyright owner endeavors to prove and recover its actual damages ….") (citation omitted), *overruled on other grounds by Fogerty v. Fantasy, Inc.*, 510 U.S. 517 (1994).

[166] *Compare Cass County Music Co. v. C.H.L.R., Inc.*, 88 F.3d 635, 642 (8th Cir. 1996) (holding that "[s]tatutory damages ... are unquestionably money damages and ... the assessment of money damages by a jury is a fundamental component of common-law trial by jury") *and Gnossos Music v. Mitken, Inc*., 653 F.2d 117, 119-20 (4th Cir.1981) (parties were due a jury trial as copyright infringement was similar to a claim of tortious interference with property and statutory damages analogous to civil actions for debt) *with Video Views, Inc.*, 925 F.2d at 1014 ("It is ... clear that it is for the district court and not for a jury to determine the appropriate award of statutory damages."), *Twentieth Century Music Corp. v. Frith*, 645 F.2d 6, 7 (5th Cir. 1981) (per curiam) (after plaintiffs requested minimum statutory damages, court determined that "[t]he whole case before the Court was equitable in nature as to which the appellant had no constitutional or statutory right to a jury trial") *and Sid & Marty Krofft Television Prods., Inc. v. McDonald's Corp.*, 562 F.2d 1157, 1178 (9th Cir. 1977) (finding that an award of statutory damages is within the sole discretion of the court).

[167] *Feltner*, 523 U.S. at 355.

[168] *Id.* at 348-49.

[169] *Id.* at 350-53. The Statute of Anne provided for damages of one penny for every "Sheet" in the infringer's custody, half of which were to be paid to the Crown, and half to the copyright owner. *Id.* at 349 (citing 8 Anne ch. 19 (1710)).

[170] *See* U.S. NATIONAL ARCHIVES & RECORDS ADMINISTRATION, A MORE PERFECT UNION: THE CREATION OF THE U.S. CONSTITUTION (2013), http://www.archives.gov/exhibits/charters/constitution_history html.

[171] Half of the statutory damages were payable to the copyright owner, and half to the United States. Act of May 31, 1790, ch. 15, §§ 2, 6, 1 Stat. 124, 125; *see also Feltner*, 523 U.S. at 351. With the passage of the 1831 Copyright Act, Congress increased statutory damages to one dollar per sheet. Act of Feb. 3, 1831, ch. 16, § 7, 4 Stat. 436, 438; *see also Feltner*, 523 U.S. at 352 (citing mid-nineteenth century cases with jury-awarded damages ranging from $200 to over $2,000).

[172] *Commodity Futures Trading Comm'n v. Schor*, 478 U.S. 833, 848-49 (1986) (explaining that personal constitutional rights can be waived, including the right of trial by jury in civil cases); *Seaboard Lumber Co. v. U.S.*, 903 F.2d 1560, 1563 (Fed. Cir. 1990) ("The Supreme Court has long recognized that a private litigant may waive its right to a jury and to an Article III court in civil cases."); *Civil v. Waterman S.S. Corp*., 217 F.2d 94, 97 (2d Cir. 1954) ("[T]he right of jury trial is personal to the litigant, who may waive it by his action or nonaction.") (citations omitted).

[173] Kernochan Center, Comments Submitted in Response to First Notice of Inquiry at 5 (Jan. 17, 2012) ("Kernochan First Notice Comments") ("One way of preserving jury trial rights is to have the small claims system be completely voluntary.").

[174] *Northern Pipeline Constr. Co. v. Marathon Pipeline Co.*, 458 U.S. 50, 91 (1982) (Rehnquist, J., concurring).

[175] U.S. CONST. art. III, § 1.

[176] *See Stern v. Marshall*, 131 S. Ct. 2594, 2608-09 (2011); *Northern Pipeline Constr. Co.*, 458 U.S. at 57-60.

[177] *Schor*, 478 U.S. at 848 (quoting *Thomas v. Union Carbide Agric. Prods. Co.*, 473 U.S. 568, 583 (1985), and *United States v. Will*, 449 U.S. 200, 218 (1980)).

[178] 59 U.S. (18 How.) 272.

[179] *Id.* at 284.

[180] *Id.*

[181] *See* 26 U.S.C. § 7441.

[182] *See* 42 U.S.C. § 405.

[183] *See* 38 U.S.C. §§ 7251-52.

[184] *See* 28 U.S.C. § 171.

[185] *See* 17 U.S.C. § 801 *et seq.* The Copyright Royalty Board, established in 2004, was preceded by the Copyright Arbitration Royalty Panels, in effect from 1993 to 2004, and the Copyright Royalty Tribunal, in effect from 1976 to 1993. *See* Copyright Royalty and Distribution Act of 2004, Pub. L. No. 108-419; Copyright Royalty Tribunal Reform Act of 1993, Pub. L. No. 103-198, 107 Stat. 2304; 118 Stat. 2341; H.R. REP. No. 94-1733, at 60 (1976).

[186] *Northern Pipeline*, 458 U.S. at 91 (Rehnquist, J., concurring).

[187] 285 U.S. 22, 49-54 (1932).

[188] *Id.* at 51-53.

[189] *Northern Pipeline*, 458 U.S. at 52-53.

[190] *Id.* at 55.

[191] *Id.* at 54.

[192] *Id.* at 55 & n.5.

[193] *Id.* 50.

[194] *Id.* at 56-57.

[195] *Id.* at 87.

[196] *Id.* at 63-70.

[197] *Id.* at 69 (quoting *Ex parte Bakelite Corp.*, 279 U.S. 438, 451 (1929)).

[198] *Id.* at 83.

[199] *Id.* at 71, 84.
[200] 458 U.S. at 91-92 (Rehnquist, J., concurring).
[201] In his dissent, Chief Justice Burger observed that the Court's holding should be understood not as a declaration that the bankruptcy courts were inherently unconstitutional, but rather as a more limited determination that "a 'traditional' state common-law action, not made subject to a federal rule of decision, and related only peripherally to an adjudication of bankruptcy under federal law, must, absent the consent of the litigants, be heard by an 'Art. III court' if it is to be heard by any court or agency of the United States." *Id.* at 92 (Burger, C.J., dissenting).
[202] 473 U.S. 568.
[203] *See* 9 U.S.C. § 10(a) (arbitral awards may be vacated for corruption, fraud, undue means, evident partiality, misconduct, or exceeding the powers delegated to the arbitrators).
[204] *Thomas*, 473 U.S. 568 (quoting FIFRA, § 3(c)(1)(D)(ii)).
[205] *Id.* at 583.
[206] *Id.* at 584.
[207] *Id.* at 585-87.
[208] *Id.* at 589.
[209] *Id.* at 584-85.
[210] *Id.* at 573, 590, 592-93.
[211] *Id.* at 589, 594.
[212] 478 U.S. at 833.
[213] 7 U.S.C. § 1 *et seq.*
[214] *Schor*, 478 U.S. at 836.
[215] *Id.* at 837 (quoting 17 C.F.R. § 12.23(b)(2) (1983)).
[216] *Schor v. Commodity Futures Trading Comm'n*, 740 F.2d 1262, 1265 (1984).
[217] *Schor*, 478 U.S. at 838.
[218] *Id.* at 838-39.
[219] *Id.* at 848-49.
[220] *Id.* at 849-50. Schor had unsuccessfully sought to stay or dismiss Conti's separately pending action in federal district court in favor of the administrative proceeding. The action was subsequently dismissed by Conti. *Id.* at 837-38.
[221] *Id.* at 850-51.
[222] *Id.* at 851.
[223] *Id.* at 852.
[224] *Id.* at 853.
[225] *Id.* at 854-55.
[226] The current version of the Federal Magistrates Act is codified at 28 U.S.C. §§ 631-39.
[227] *See, e.g., Roell v. Withrow*, 538 U.S. 580 (2003) (holding that a magistrate judge can preside over civil trial where parties have given implied consent); *Peretz v. United States,* 501 U.S. 923 (1991) (litigant can waive the right to have a court conduct *voir dire* and instead consent to a magistrate judge-directed jury selection); *United States v. Raddatz*, 447 U.S. 667 (1980) (delegation of certain fact-finding and recommendation functions to a magistrate judge does not violate article III so long as the ultimate decision is made by the district court); *see also* Magistrate Judges Division of the Administrative Office of the United States Courts, *A Constitutional Analysis of Magistrate Judge Authority*, 150 F.R.D. 247 (1993) (reviewing cases).
[228] 538 U.S. at 580.
[229] 28 U.S.C. § 636(c)(1).
[230] *Id.* § 636(b).
[231] *Id.* § 636(c)(1).
[232] *Roell*, 538 U.S. at 586-87; FED. R. CIV. P. 73(b).
[233] *Roell*, 538 U.S. at 590-91 (citing *Raddatz*, 447 U.S. at 676 n.3, a case in which the Court upheld the ability of a magistrate judge to preside over a suppression hearing against an Article III challenge, for the proposition that the Court should "eschew" an interpretation of the Federal Magistrates Act that would "'frustrate the plain objective of Congress to alleviate the increasing congestion of litigation in the district courts.'") (citation omitted).
[234] *Id.* at 590 (citing *Schor* for the proposition that a litigant can waive his right to an Article III court by seeking relief in an alternative forum).
[235] *Id.*
[236] *Id.* at 588 (citing S. REP. NO. 96-74, at 4 (1979)).
[237] *Stern*, 131 S. Ct. 2594 at 2610.
[238] 492 U.S. 33 (1989).
[239] *Id.* at 53.
[240] *Id.* at 54.
[241] *Id.* at 54 (quoting *Thomas*, 473 U.S. at 593-94).

[242] *Id.* at 56, 60.

[243] In so concluding, the Court distinguished the bankruptcy context from the CFTC proceeding in *Schor*, where the investor could have elected to pursue his claim in an Article III forum instead. Thus there could be no "parallel" concept of waiver to apply in *Granfinanciera*. *Id.* at 59 n.14.

[244] 131 S. Ct. 2594.

[245] *Id.* at 2600.

[246] *Id.* at 2601.

[247] *Id.*

[248] *Id.*

[249] *Id.* at 2604-05. The Court additionally found that even though the statute provided that personal injury torts should be tried by a district court rather than the bankruptcy court, Pierce's assertion that the bankruptcy court lacked the authority to enter final judgment on his defamation claim was defeated by the fact that he had consented to the bankruptcy forum. *Id.* at 2606-08.

[250] *Id.* at 2608.

[251] *Id.* at 2614.

[252] *Id.*

[253] *Id.* at 2615.

[254] *Id.*

[255] *Id.* at 2614 (citing *Thomas*, 473 U.S. at 584-85, and *Schor*, 478 U.S. at 833, 855-56).

[256] *Id.* at 2615.

[257] *Id.*

[258] 702 F.3d 553 (9th Cir. 2012), *cert. granted*, No. 12-1200, 133 S.Ct. 2880 (June 4, 2013).

[259] SCOTUSBlog, *Executive Benefits Ins. Agency v. Arkison*, http://www.scotusblog.com/case-files/cases/executive-benefits-insurance-agency-v-arkison/. The Ninth Circuit held that the implied consent of the insurance agency, which had failed to object to the bankruptcy forum, was a sufficient basis for the bankruptcy court's exercise of jurisdiction in the fraudulent conveyance action. 702 F.3d at 567-70.

[260] *Stewart v. Abend*, 495 U.S. 207, 251 (1990); *see also Authors Guild, Inc. v. Hathitrust*, 902 F. Supp. 2d 445, 451 (S.D.N.Y. 2012) (same, citing *Stewart*).

[261] *Wheaton v. Peters*, 33 U.S. (8 Pet.) 591, 663-64 (1834). In *Wheaton*, the Court rejected a common law of copyright applicable to published works because Congress had created protections for such works under the Copyright Act. *Id.* at 661-62 ("Congress, then, by this act, instead of sanctioning an existing right, as contended for, created it. This seems to be the clear import of the law, connected with the circumstances under which it was enacted.").

[262] *Golan v. Holder*, 132 S. Ct. 873, 876 (2012) (quoting *Eldred v. Ashcroft*, 537 U.S. 186, 222 (2003)).

[263] Act of May 31, 1790, ch. 15, 1 Stat. 124.

[264] *See* Act of May 31, 1790, ch. 15, 1 Stat. 124; Act of Feb. 3, 1831, ch. 16, 4 Stat. 436; Act to Amend and Consolidate the Acts Representing Copyright of 1909, Pub. L. No. 60-349, 35 Stat. 1075; Copyright Act of 1976, Pub. L. No. 94-553, 90 Stat. 251; Berne Convention Implementation Act of 1988, Pub. L. No. 100-568, 102 (Stat. 2853, 2860; Digital Millennium Copyright Act of 1998, Pub. L. No. 105-304, 112 Stat. 2860, 2887; Digital Theft Deterrence and Copyright Damages Improvement Act of 1999, Pub. L. No. 106-160, 113 Stat. 1774; *see also Golan*, 132 S. Ct. 873 (affirming Congress's authority to extend copyright protection to certain foreign works that had entered the public domain in the U.S.); *Eldred*, 537 U.S. 186 (affirming Congress's authority to lengthen the term of copyright for existing works).

[265] *See* 17 U.S.C. §§ 205, 408; COPYRIGHT OFFICE, CIRCULAR 1A, UNITED STATES COPYRIGHT OFFICE A BRIEF INTRODUCTION & HISTORY, *available at* http://www.copyright.gov/circs/circ1a.html.

[266] *Granfinanciera* suggested in dicta that the question of whether the Seventh Amendment attaches to a claim – as *Feltner* held it did with respect to copyright damages actions – is tied to whether Congress may properly assign the claim to a non-Article III tribunal. 492 U.S. at 51-52. The *Granfinanciera* Court also observed a distinction between statutorily defined "public rights" that can be determined outside of Article III courts and "quintessential" state common law causes of action. *Id.* at 56. A claim of copyright infringement arises under federal statutory law; indeed, equivalent state law claims are expressly preempted by the Copyright Act. *See* 17 U.S.C. § 301. Thus, it is unclear exactly how the reasoning of *Granfinanciera* would apply in the copyright context. Also noteworthy is the fact that the *Granfinanciera* Court did not have occasion to consider the role of consent in its analysis – another important element in Article III jurisprudence – as the complaining party did not agree to the forum in that case. *See supra* note 243.

[267] 17 U.S.C. § 412.

[268] *Id.* § 411 (also allowing copyright owners to bring cases based on preregistration).

[269] *Freytag v. Comm. of Internal Revenue*, 501 U.S. 868, 883-84 (1991).

[270] U.S. Const., art. II, § 2, cl. 2.

[271] *Buckley v. Valeo*, 424 U.S. 1, 125-26 (1976).

[272] *Intercollegiate Broad. Sys., Inc. v. Copyright Royalty Bd.*, 684 F.3d 1332, 1338 (D.C. Cir. 2012) (quoting *Edmond v. United States*, 520 U.S. 651, 663 (1997)).

[273] *Id.* at 1340.
[274] *Free Enter. Fund v. Public Co. Accounting Oversight Bd.*, 130 S. Ct. 3138, 3151-53 (2010).
[275] *See* 17 U.S.C. § 801 *et seq.*
[276] *Intercollegiate Broad. Sys., Inc.*, 684 F.3d 1332.
[277] *Id.* at 1336.
[278] *Id.* at 1338-39. *Cf. Freytag*, 501 U.S. at 881-82 (special trial judges of U.S. Tax Court were inferior offices who exercised "significant discretion" in light of their ability to take testimony, conduct trials, rule on the admissibility of evidence, and enforce discovery orders).
[279] *Intercollegiate Broad. Sys., Inc.*, 684 F.3d at 1339-40.
[280] *Id.* at 1340.
[281] *Id.* at 1339.
[282] *Id.* at 1340-42.
[283] *Id.* at 1341-41 (quoting *Edmond*, 520 U.S. at 662-64).
[284] U.S. CONST. amend. V & XIV.
[285] *See* 28 U.S.C. § 1338.
[286] Only federal – and not state – courts have subject matter jurisdiction over statutory copyright infringement suits. *See id.* While subject matter jurisdiction concerns the court's authority over the subject of the suit, personal jurisdiction addresses the court's authority over the parties.
[287] *See International Shoe v. Washington*, 326 U.S. 310, 317 (1945); *see also, World-Wide Volkswagen Corp. v. Woodson*, 444 U.S. 286, 291 (1980).
[288] *International Shoe*, 326 U.S. at 316.
[289] This factor is derived from *Burger King Corp. v. Rudzewicz*, 471 U.S. 462 (1985).
[290] This factor is derived from *World-Wide Volkswagen Corp.*, 444 U.S. 286.
[291] *International Shoe,* 326 U.S. at 316. Examples of federal courts employing this three-part test include *O'Connor v. Sandy Lane Hotel*, 496 F.3d 312, 317 (3d Cir. 2007); *Panavision Int'l, L.P. v. Toeppen*, 141 F.3d 1316 (9th Cir. 1998); *Dudnikov v. Chalk & Vermillion Fine Arts, Inc.*, 514 F.3d 1063, 1071 (10th Cir. 2008). *But see Oldfield v. Pueblo De Bahia Lora, S.A.*, 558 F.3d 1210, 1221 n.28 (11th Cir. 2009) (applying a different three-factor test for intentional torts where personal jurisdiction is appropriate if the defendant "(1) committed an intentional tort (2) that was directly aimed at the forum, (3) causing an injury within the forum that the defendant should have reasonably anticipated."); *Burlington Indus., Inc. v. Maples Indus., Inc.*, 97 F.3d 1100, 1102 (8th Cir. 1996) (applying the following five-factor test: "(1) the nature and quality of contacts with the forum state; (2) the quantity of such contacts; (3) the relation of the cause of action to the contacts; (4) the interest of the forum state in providing a forum for its residents; and (5) convenience of the parties").
[292] *Zippo Mfg. Co. v. Zippo Dot Com*, 952 F. Supp. 1119, 1124 (W.D. Pa. 1997).
[293] *Id.*
[294] *Id.*
[295] *Id.* Other courts have found that while the internet may inject some novel factual elements into the personal jurisdiction question, there is no need to abandon the traditional "minimum contacts" personal jurisdiction factors derived from *International Shoe*. For example, the Seventh Circuit has explicitly rejected the *Zippo* approach, reasoning that "[u]sing a separate test for internet-based contacts would be inappropriate" when traditional personal jurisdiction analysis "remains up to this more modern task." *uBID, Inc. v. GoDaddy Group*, 623 F.3d 421, 431 n.3 (7th Cir. 2010).
[296] *Compare* 28 U.S.C. § 1338 (granting district courts original jurisdiction over civil copyright actions, but not mentioning national service of process) *with* 15 U.S.C. § 78aa (authorizing national service of process for violations of the Securities Exchange Act), 29 U.S.C. § 1132(e)(2) (authorizing national service of process for violations of the Employee Retirement Income Security Act) *and* 18 U.S.C. § 1965(a) (authorizing national service of process for violations of the Racketeer Influenced and Corrupt Organizations Act).
[297] *Busch v. Buchman, Buchman & O'Brien*, 11 F.3d 1255, 1258 (5th Cir. 1994) (holding that Texas district court had jurisdiction over New York law firm that allegedly violated the Securities Exchange Act of 1934 because the firm wrote a tax opinion that was included in a nationwide promotional mailing).
[298] 119 F.3d 935 (11th Cir. 1997); *see also* 4 CHARLES A. WRIGHT & ARTHUR R. MILLER, FED. PRAC. & PROC. § 1068.1 (3d ed. 2013) ("WRIGHT & MILLER").
[299] *BCCI Holdings*, 119 F.3d at 946.
[300] *See, e.g., United States v. Cotton*, 535 U.S. 625, 630 (2002) ("This ... concept of subject-matter jurisdiction, because it involves a court's power to hear a case, can never be forfeited or waived.").
[301] *See* FED. R. CIV. P. 12(b)(2) (defense of lack of personal jurisdiction) and 12(h)(1) (waiver of defenses).
[302] 4 WRIGHT & MILLER § 1063.
[303] *See* FED. R. CIV. P. 12(b)(4) (defense of insufficient process); FED. R. CIV. P. 12(h)(1) (waiver of defenses); *see also Farm Credit Bank of Baltimore v. Ferrera-Goitia*, 316 F.3d 62, 68 (failure to raise deficiencies with summons in district court bars defense on appeal).
[304] FED. R. CIV. P. 4(e) & (f).
[305] *Id.* 4(h) & (i).

[306] *Id.* 4(e)(2)(A).
[307] *Id.* 4(e)(2)(B).
[308] *Id.* 4(e)(2)(C).
[309] *Id.* 4(e)(1).
[310] *Id.* 4(h).
[311] *Id.* 4(d); *id.*12(a)(1)(A).
[312] *See* FED. R. CIV. P. 4(f)(1).
[313] *Mullane v. Cent. Hanover Bank & Trust Co.*, 339 U.S. 306, 313 (1950).
[314] *Powell v. Alabama*, 287 U.S. 45, 69 (1932) ("If in any case, civil or criminal, a state or federal court were arbitrarily to refuse to hear a party by counsel, employed by and appearing for him, it reasonably may not be doubted that such a refusal would be a denial of a hearing, and, therefore, of due process in the constitutional sense."). It also has held that, in some situations – particularly those where a defendant's liberty interest is at stake – the court must appoint counsel for an indigent litigant. *Lassiter v. Dept. of Social Services*, 452 US 18, 25 (1981).
[315] *Bailey v. Alabama*, 219 U.S. 219, 239 (1911).
[316] *M.L.B. v. S.L.J.*, 519 U.S. 102, 114 (1996) (citing *Lindsey v. Normet*, 405 U.S. 56, 77 (1972)).
[317] *See, e.g.*, *Griffin v. Illinois*, 351 U.S. 12, 18 (1956) (holding, in criminal context, that states are not constitutionally compelled to provide for appellate review).
[318] Bruce Zucker & Monica Herr, *The People's Court Examined: A Legal and Empirical Analysis of the Small Claims Court System*, 37 U.S.F. L. REV. 315, 317-18 (Winter 2003) (quoting Marc Anthony Douthit, *Humbling Experiences: Trials of Small Claims*, 27 LITIG. 27 (2000)).
[319] *Id.* at 347; *see also* Summary of State Small Claims Procedures, attached as Appendix D, at col. Attorney Representation.
[320] *See Fox v. Cal. Franchise Tax Board*, 443 Fed. Appx. 354, 361 (10th Cir. 2011) (choosing to be heard in a small claims forum that does not provide for appeal by plaintiff did not deprive plaintiff of his right to notice and opportunity to be heard, because he chose that forum); *Keeffe v. Tax Appeals Tribunal*, 627 N.Y.S.2d 851, 853 (1995) ("By voluntarily entering into an agreement for the resolution of a dispute in a manner which dispenses with certain constitutional rights, a party can be deemed to have waived due process requirements.").
[321] *Prudential Ins. Co. v. Small Claims Court*, 76 Cal. App. 2d 379, 382 (1946); *Simon v. Lieberman*, 193 Neb. 321, 324 (1975); *Foster v. Walus*, 81 Idaho 452, 459 (1959).
[322] *Carr v. Pena*, 432 F. Supp. 828, 833 (D.V.I. 1977).
[323] *Id.*
[324] *Powell v. Killian*, No. 01AP-85, 2001 Ohio App. LEXIS 4154, at *6 (Ohio Ct. App. Sept. 18, 2001).
[325] *Keeffe*, 627 N.Y.S.2d 851; *see also Blair v. Supreme Ct. of Wyo.*, 671 F.2d 389, 391 (11th Cir. 1982).
[326] *Graves v. Am. Express*, 669 N.Y.S.2d 463 (1997) ("Although the procedures in Small Claims Court are relaxed, the rules of substantive law must be followed and a person's constitutional right to due process of law includes the basic right to cross-examine witnesses.").
[327] *Hughes v. Elliott*, 768 N.Y.S.2d 74 (2003).
[328] *See, e.g.*, *Lonzollo v. Weinberger*, 534 F.2d 712, 714 (7th Cir. 1976) (noting that waiver of right to cross-examine must be "clearly expressed or strongly implied from the circumstances").
[329] *See, e.g.*, Peter B. Rutledge, *Whither Arbitration?*, 6 GEO. J.L. & PUB. POL'Y 549, 563 (2008); Paul R. Verkuil, *Privatizing Due Process*, 57 ADMIN. L. REV. 963, 964 (2005).
[330] Verkuil, at 983.
[331] 9 U.S.C. § 1 *et seq.*
[332] 9 U.S.C. § 10(a)(1).
[333] *Id.* § 10(a)(2).
[334] *Id.* § 10(a)(3).
[335] *Id.* § 10(a)(4).
[336] *Bowles Fin. Grp., Inc. v. Stifel, Nicolaus & Co., Inc.*, 22 F.3d 1010, 1013 (10th Cir. 1994); *see also* Jill I. Gross, *AT&T Mobility and the Future of Small Claims Arbitration*, 42 SW. L. REV. 47, 68-69 (2012).
[337] *Walker v. Ryan's Family Steak Houses, Inc.*, 400 F.3d 370, 385-86 (6th Cir. 2005).
[338] *McMullen v. Meijer, Inc.*, 355 F.3d 485, 494 (6th Cir. 2004).
[339] *Murray v. United Food and Commercial Workers Int'l Union*, 289 F.3d 297, 303-305 (4th Cir. 2002).
[340] *Hooters of Am., Inc. v. Phillips*, 173 F.3d 933, 938 (4th Cir. 1999).
[341] *See* John B. Oakley & Arthur F. Coon, *The Federal Rules in State Courts: A Survey of State Court Systems of Civil Procedure*, 61 WASH. L. REV. 1367, 1425 (1984) (noting 23 jurisdictions that use near replicas of the Federal Rules, 4 jurisdictions that use rules substantially the same as the Federal Rules, and several other jurisdictions that have differing degrees of variance with the Federal Rules (such as the pleading standard), but still retain many aspects of the Federal Rules). *But see* Roger Michael Michalski, *Tremors of Things To Come: The Great Split Between Federal and State Pleading Standards*, 120 YALE L.J. ONLINE 109, 114 (2010) (noting recent trend of states creating rules of procedure that diverge from Federal Rules).

[342] *See* Paula Hannafor-Agor & Nicole L. Waters, *Estimating the Cost of Civil Litigation*, National Center for State Courts, Court Statistics Project, (2013), *available at* http://www.courtstatistics.org/~/media/Microsites/Files/CSP/DATA%20PDF/CSPH_online2.ashx. This monetary range is indicative of the six causes of action that "comprise nearly 60 percent of non-domestic relations civil cases filed in state courts." Although the data thus does not represent an average of *all* civil litigation costs, it confirms that the costs of most state court civil cases can be very high.

[343] 17 U.S.C. § 301 (As of January 1, 1978, "all legal or equitable rights that are equivalent to any of the exclusive rights within the general scope of copyright as specified by section 106 ... are governed exclusively by [the Copyright Act]. Thereafter, no person is entitled to any such right or equivalent right in any such work under the common law or statutes of any State.").

[344] *Id.* § 301(c) ("With respect to sound recordings fixed before February 15, 1972, any rights or remedies under the common law or statutes of any State shall not be annulled or limited by this title until February 15, 2067."); *see also* U.S. COPYRIGHT OFFICE, REPORT ON FEDERAL COPYRIGHT PROTECTION FOR PRE-1972 SOUND RECORDINGS (2011), *available at* http://www.copyright.gov/docs/sound/pre-72-report.pdf.

[345] 17 U.S.C. § 301(b)(1) (state law with respect to works of authorship not fixed in any tangible medium of expression not preempted).

[346] *See* H.R. REP. NO. 101-514, at 21 (1990) ("[federal] law will not preempt a cause of action for a misattribution of a reproduction of a work of visual art").

[347] *See* JOHN C. RUHNKA, STEVEN WELLER & JOHN A. MARTIN, SMALL CLAIMS COURTS: A NATIONAL EXAMINATION 2 (1978); Arthur Best et al., *Peace, Wealth, Happiness, and Small Claim Courts: A Case Study*, 21 FORDHAM URB. L.J. 343, 343-44 (1994); Bruce Zucker & Monica Herr, *The People's Court Examined: A Legal and Empirical Analysis of the Small Claims System*, 37 U.S.F. L. REV. 315, 317 (2003).

[348] *See* RUHNKA ET AL., at 1.

[349] *See id.* at 2-3 (discussing goals of small claims process in terms of accessibility, speed, low cost, simplicity, self-representation, fairness, and effectiveness); Josephine Y. King, *Small Claims Practice in the United States*, 52 ST. JOHN'S L. REV. 42, 43 (1977) (explaining that small claims reformers sought to avoid expense and delay caused by complex procedures while permitting self-representation); Zucker & Herr, at 317 ("Although the financial claims limits, methods of procedure, and overall structure vary from state to state, the concept is essentially the same: relatively minor disputes involving dollar amounts that are insufficient to warrant processing the case through normal court procedure justify expedited and simplistic handling.").

[350] *See* Zucker & Herr, at 317 (2003). For purposes of this Report, the Office focused primarily on small claims systems in ten different states: California, Florida, Georgia, Illinois, Massachusetts, Michigan, New York, Pennsylvania, Tennessee, and Texas. These states were selected by consulting the Lex Machina online database (https://lexmachina.com) to determine the states containing the federal districts that have heard the most copyright disputes during the past twelve years.

[351] *See* THOMAS E. MARTIN, JR., CIVIL PRACTICE IN MAGISTERIAL DISTRICT COURTS 4 (2012); WAYNE M. PURDOM, GEORGIA MAGISTRATE COURT HANDBOOK § 1-1 (4th ed. 2002).

[352] *See* Paula Hannafor-Agor & Nicole L. Waters, *Estimating the Cost of Civil Litigation*, National Center for State Courts, Court Statistics Project, (2013), *available at* http://www.courtstatistics.org/~/media/Microsites/Files/CSP/DATA%20PDF/CSPH_online2.ashx.

[353] *See* Appendix D (summarizing state small claims practices).

[354] *See id.* (summarizing monetary limits).

[355] ARIZ. REV. STAT. ANN. § 22-503(A) (2013); R.I. GEN. LAWS § 10-16-1 (2012); TENN. CODE ANN. § 16-15-501(d)(1) (2013); *see also* Appendix D (summarizing monetary limits).

[356] *See, e.g.*, CAL. CIV. PROC. CODE § 116.231(a) (2013) (limiting number of claims over $2,500 a party may file within a calendar year); MICH. COMP. LAWS § 600.8407(2) (2012) (limiting the number of claims a party may file in one week).

[357] *See, e.g.*, FLA. S. COMM. ON THE JUDICIARY, REVIEW OF THE SMALL CLAIMS PROCESS IN FLORIDA, S. REP. NO. 2009-121, Interim Rep., at 6-7 (2008), *available at* http://archive.flsenate.gov/data/Publications/2009/Senate/reports/ interim_reports/pdf/2009-121ju.pdf; N.Y. LOCAL COURTS ADVISORY COMM., REPORT OF THE ADVISORY COMMITTEE ON LOCAL COURTS, at 28 (2003), *available at* http://www.nycourts.gov/ip/judiciaryslegislative/LocalC ourts_03.pdf.

[358] *See, e.g.*, MICH. S. JUDICIARY COMM., SMALL CLAIMS COURT JURISDICTION BILL ANALYSIS, 2011-2012 Leg. Sess., at 2 (2011) ("MICH. ANALYSIS"), *available at* http://www.legislature.mi.gov/documents/2011-2012/billanalysis/senate/pdf/2011-SFA-0269-A.pdf.

[359] *See, e.g.*, FLA. S. COMM. ON THE JUDICIARY, REVIEW OF THE SMALL CLAIMS PROCESS IN FLORIDA, S. REP. NO. 2009-121, Interim Rep., at 7 (2008), *available at* http://archive.flsenate.gov/data/Publications/2009/Senate/reports/in terim_reports/pdf/2009-121ju.pdf (in five years following Florida's increase from $2,500 to $5,000, small claims caseload increased 89.5 percent).

[360] *See, e.g.*, CAL. S. JUDICIARY COMM., S.B. 221 ANALYSIS, 2005-2006 Reg. Sess., at 7-8 (2005), *available at* http://www.leginfo.ca.gov/pub/11-12/bill/sen/sb_0201-0250/sb_221_cfa_20110620_105740_asm_comm.html.

[361] *See, e.g.*, MICH. ANALYSIS, at 3.

[362] *See, e.g.*, FLA. SM. CL. R 7.010(b) (permitting "all actions at law of a civil nature"); GA. CODE. ANN. § 15-10-2(5) (2013) (permitting "[t]he trial of civil claims ... in which exclusive jurisdiction is not vested in the superior court"); N.Y. CITY CIV. CT. ACT § 1801 (Consol. 2013) (allowing "any cause of action for money only not in excess of $5,000").

[363] *See, e.g.*, MICH. COMP. LAWS § 600.8424 (2012) (actions of fraud and actions of libel, slander, assault, battery, or other intentional torts may not be brought in the small claims division).

[364] *See* RALPH WARNER, EVERYBODY'S GUIDE TO SMALL CLAIMS COURT 138, 281 (13th ed. 2010) ("WARNER"); *see also, e.g.* CAL. CIV. PROC. CODE § 116.420(a) (2013); MICH. COMP. LAWS § 600.8407 (1) & (3) (2012); N.Y. UNIFORM DIST. CT. ACT § 1809 (Consol. 2013); N.Y. UNIFORM JUST. CT. ACT § 1809 (Consol. 2013); N.Y. UNIFORM CITY CT. ACT § 1809 (Consol. 2013); N.Y. CITY CIV. CT. ACT § 1809 (Consol. 2013).

[365] *See* MICH. ANALYSIS, at 2-3.

[366] *See* WARNER, at 138; *see also* Appendix D (summarizing several states' treatment of attorney representation).

[367] CAL. CIV. PROC. CODE § 116.530(b) (2013).

[368] *See, e.g.*, *id.* § 116.530(c) (allowing attorneys to provide advice before or after commencement of an action, to testify to facts, or to appear in order to enforce a judgment or on appeal); WARNER, at 138 (noting that most courts allow attorney participation in a small claims proceeding, but even those courts that do not permit in-court attorney representation allow parties to consult an attorney outside of court).

[369] *See, e.g.*, MASS. UNIF. SM. CL. R. 7(g) (limiting attorney participation "in a manner consistent with the simple and informal adjudication of the controversy").

[370] *See, e.g.*, FLA. SM. CL. R. 7.020(b) (subjecting represented parties to discovery pursuant to the Florida Rules of Civil Procedure, while unrepresented parties are not subject to discovery unless they seek discovery).

[371] This rule dates back to the common law. *See Strong Delivery Ministry Ass'n v. Bd. of Appeals,* 543 F.2d 32, 33 (7th Cir. 1976) (recognizing that "[a]t common law '... a plea by a corporation aggregate, which is incapable of a personal appearance, must purport to be by attorney.'") (quoting 1 CHITTY ON PLEADING 550 (12th Am.ed.1855)).

[372] *See, e.g.*, TEX. R. CIV. P. 500.4(b) (setting forth possible representatives for corporations in court actions); PA.R.C.P.D.J. NO. 207(A)(2)-(3) (same).

[373] *See Rosenberg v. Superior Court*, 79 Cal. Rptr. 2d 365, 368 (Cal. Ct. App. 1998) (explaining state's intent to formulate a small claims procedure that would remove the expense and delay associated with ordinary methods of litigation, which "[grew] out of the demand for more simple, less expensive, and more speedy decisions of cases involving small amounts") (quoting *Leuschen v. Small Claims Court*, 191 Cal. 133, 138 (1923)).

[374] *See* WARNER, at 168; *see also* Appendix D (summarizing filing fees).

[375] N.Y. UNIFORM DIST. CT. ACT § 1809 (Consol. 2013); N.Y. UNIFORM JUST. CT. ACT § 1809 (Consol. 2013); N.Y. UNIFORM CITY CT. ACT § 1809 (Consol. 2013); N.Y. CITY CIV. CT. ACT § 1809 (Consol. 2013) (filing fees based on amount of claim).

[376] MASS. GEN. LAWS ch. 218, § 22 (2013) (graduating fees based on the amount of the claim).

[377] *See* Appendix D (summarizing filing fees).

[378] FLA. STAT. § 34.041 (2013) (graduating filing fees based on the amount of claim, with additional $85 fee for garnishment, attachment, replevin, and distress proceedings).

[379] *See, e.g.*, CAL. CIV. PROC. CODE § 116.930 (2013); GA. UNIF. MAGISTRATE CT. R. 17; N.Y. UNIFORM DIST. CT. ACT § 1803(b) (Consol. 2013); N.Y. UNIFORM JUST. CT. ACT § 1803(b) (Consol. 2013); N.Y. UNIFORM CITY CT. ACT § 1803(b) (Consol. 2013); N.Y. CITY CIV. CT. ACT § 1803(b) (Consol. 2013).

[380] *See* CAL. CIV. PROC. CODE §§ 116.260, 116.940(b)(1) (2013) statutorily established small claims advisory service helps prepare claims and defenses); MASS. UNIF. SM. CL. R. 2(a) (directing court clerk to assist small claims plaintiff in completing court's claim form, if requested); *see also* FLA. SM. CL. R. 7.050(c) (directing clerk to assist parties in preparing statement of claim and other papers upon request).

[381] *See* Appendix D (summarizing various simplified pleadings).

[382] *See* WARNER, at 180-85.

[383] *See id.* at 180.

[384] *See* Appendix D (summarizing answer requirements).

[385] *See id.*

[386] *See* RUHNKA ET AL., at 119 (except for two courts examined in a two-year study, all courts required the case to be transferred when the counterclaim exceeded the jurisdictional limit; in the other two jurisdictions, counterclaims in excess of the limit remained in small claims court).

[387] *See* Heather Scheiwe Kulp, *Increasing Referrals to Small Claims Mediation Programs: Models To Improve Access To Justice*, 14 CARDOZO J. CONFLICT RESOL. 361 (2013).

[388] *See id.* at 375-80 (sampling court annexed mediation for litigants in small claims systems); *see, e.g.*, FLA. S. COMM. ON THE JUDICIARY, REVIEW OF THE SMALL CLAIMS PROCESS IN FLORIDA, S. REP. NO. 2009-121, Interim Rep., at 7 (2011), *available at* http://archive flsenate.gov/data/Publications/2009/Senate/reports/ interim_reports/pdf/ 2009-121ju.pdf (some judges may highly encourage or require pretrial mediation).

[389] *See, e.g.*, MASS. GEN. LAWS ch. 218, § 22 (2013) (both parties must consent to mediation); *see also* Appendix D (summarizing various specialized procedures).

[390] *See* Appendix D (summarizing discovery practices).

[391] FLA. SM. CL. R. 7.020(b).

[392] *See, e.g.*, CAL. CIV. PROC. CODE § 116.310(b) ("The pretrial discovery procedures described in Section 2019.010 are not permitted in small claims actions."); N.Y. CITY CIV. CT. ACT § 1804 (Consol. 2013) (noting that "[d]isclosure shall be unavailable in small claims procedure except upon order of the court on showing of proper circumstances").

[393] *See, e.g.*, MASS. UNIF. SM. CL. R. 7(f); TEX. R. CIV. P. 500.3(e).

[394] *See* Appendix D (summarizing discovery practices).

[395] *See* WARNER, at 244.

[396] *See Sanderson v. Niemann*, 110 P.2d 1025, 1030 (Cal. 1941); *see also* Appendix D (summarizing evidentiary rules); Zucker & Herr, at 317.

[397] *See, e.g.*, MASS. UNIF. SM. CL. R. 6.10 ("The court should not require strict adherence to the rules of evidence in small claims trials."); TEX. R. CIV. P. 500.3(e) ("The other Rules of Civil Procedure and the Rules of Evidence do not apply except: (1) when the judge hearing the case determines that a particular rule must be followed to ensure that the proceedings are fair to all parties; or (2) when otherwise specifically provided by law or these rules.").

[398] *See, e.g.*, CAL. CIV. PROC. CODE § 116.520(a) (2013); FLA. SM. CL. R. 7.140(f); TEX. R. CIV. P. 502.4(d)(1)(C).

[399] *See, e.g.*, *Houghtaling v. Superior Court*, 21 Cal. Rptr. 2d 855, 856 (Cal. App. 4th Dist. 1993); MASS. UNIF. SM. CL. STANDARDS § 6:10.

[400] *See, e.g.*, FLA. STAT. ANN. § 90.702 (2013); TEX. R. CIV. P. 503.4(a)(4).

[401] 7 AM. JUR. 2D *Jury* § 5 (2013); *see supra* Part IV.A.

[402] *See* Nancy M. King, Annotation, *Small Claims: Jury Trial Rights in, and on Appeal From, Small Claims Court Proceeding*, 70 A.L.R.4th 1119, § 5 (2008); *see also* GA. CODE. ANN. § 15-10-41(b)(1) (2013); MASS. GEN. LAWS ch. 218, § 23 (2013) (providing defendants right to appeal to a jury); 42 PA. CONS. STAT. § 1123(4) (2013).

[403] FLA. SM. CL. R. 7.150.

[404] ILL. SUP. CT. R. 285.

[405] TEX. R. CIV. P. 504.1(a).

[406] *See* Appendix D (summarizing the availability of jury trials); *see also* Ill. Sup. Ct. R. 285; MASS. GEN. LAWS ch. 218, § 23 (2013); N.Y. CITY CIV. CT. ACT § 1806 (Consol. 2013); TEX. R. CIV. P. 504.1(b).

[407] *See* Nancy M. King, Annotation, *Small Claims: Jury Trial Rights in, and on Appeal From, Small Claims Court Proceeding*, 70 A.L.R.4th 1119, § 3(b) (2008).

[408] *See* Appendix D (summarizing availability of equitable relief).

[409] *See* WARNER, at 83-85.

[410] *See, e.g.*, CAL. CIV. PROC. CODE § 116.220(a)(5) (2013) (small claims court has jurisdiction "[f]or an injunction or other equitable relief only when a statute expressly authorizes a small claims court to award that relief").

[411] *See* Appendix D (summarizing recoverable costs); WARNER, at 251-52.

[412] *See, e.g.*, MASS. UNIF. SM. CL. STANDARDS § 7:05 cmt; TEX. CIV. PRAC. & REM. CODE § 38.001 (2013).

[413] *See* WARNER, at 360 ("[D]espite the fact that an occasional person may be upset, some judges are willing to announce and explain their decisions in court, on the theory that both parties are entitled to know why a particular decision was reached.").

[414] *See id.* at 238.

[415] *See, e.g.*, CAL. CIV. PROC. CODE § 116.520(b) (2013) (requiring plaintiff to present evidence to prove the claim); GA. CODE. ANN. § 15-10-43(e)(1) (2013) (requiring plaintiff to prove unliquidated damages); TEX. R. CIV. P. 503.1(a)(2), 503.6(c) (requiring plaintiff to provide damages evidence; if plaintiff cannot prove damages, judge must render judgment for the defendant when defendant fails to file and answer).

[416] *See* WARNER, at 242; *see, e.g.*, FLA. SM. CL. R. 7.160(b) (within judges' discretion to keep open or dismiss for want of prosecution); GA. CODE. ANN. § 15-10-43(e)(3) (2013) (dismissing with or without prejudice is discretionary).

[417] *See* WARNER, at 240; *see, e.g.*, GA. CODE. ANN. § 15-10-41(b)(2) (2013).

[418] *Nat'l Union of M. C. & S. v. Arnold*, 348 U.S. 37, 43 (1954) (while statutory right of review "is important and must be exercised without discrimination, such a review is not a requirement of due process") (citations omitted).

[419] *See Lott v. Pittman*, 243 U.S. 588, 591 (1917) (noting that the right to an appeal in a criminal case is "not essential to due process" and observing that "[i]t was, therefore, competent for the State to prescribe the procedure and conditions [to rehear the case]"); *McKane v. Durston*, 153 U.S. 684, 688 (1894) (noting, in a criminal case, that "the right of appeals may be accorded by the State ... upon such terms as in its wisdom may be deemed proper.").

[420] *See* Appendix D (summarizing appeals).

[421] *See id.* (summarizing appeals).

[422] *See* WARNER, at 368; *see, e.g.*, CAL. CIV. PROC. CODE § 116.710(d) (2013); GA. CODE. ANN. § 15-10-41(b)(2) (2013).

[423] *Compare, e.g.*, CAL. CIV. PROC. CODE § 116.770 (2013) (small claims appeals conducted informally) *with* FLA. SM. CL. R. 7.230 (appeals governed by Florida Rules of Appellate Procedure).

[424] *See, e.g.*, CAL. CIV. PROC. CODE § 116.770 (2013); GA. CODE. ANN. § 15-10-41(b)(1) (2013); MICH. COMP. LAWS § 600.8427 (2012); Pa. R.C.P.D.J. No. 1007 (A); TEX. R. CIV. P. 506.3.

[425] *See* WARNER, at 369-70.

[426] *See* FLA. S. COMM. ON THE JUDICIARY, REVIEW OF THE SMALL CLAIMS PROCESS IN FLORIDA, S. REP. NO. 2009-121, Interim Rep., at 10-11 (2011), *available at* http://archive.flsenate.gov/data/Publications/2009/Senate/reports/int erim_reports/pdf/2009-121ju.pdf.

[427] *See, e.g.*, N.Y. UNIFORM DIST. CT. ACT § 1812(b) (Consol. 2013) ("[T]he judgment creditor shall be entitled to commence an action against said judgment debtor for treble the amount of such unsatisfied judgment, together with reasonable counsel fees, and the costs and disbursements of such action."); MASS. UNIFORM SMALL CLAIMS RULE 9 (2013) ("[T]he court should take an active role in the enforcement of judgments.").

[428] FLA. S. COMM. ON THE JUDICIARY, REVIEW OF THE SMALL CLAIMS PROCESS IN FLORIDA, S. REP. NO. 2009-121, Interim Rep., at 10-11 (2011), *available at* http://archive.flsenate.gov/data/Publications/2009/Senate/reports/int erim_reports/pdf/2009-121ju.pdf. ("Judges also aid in judgment collection by attempting to curb the expectations of pro se litigants who believe that they will automatically receive payment once the court enters the judgment order. Upon entry of a judgment, judges may also explain that the plaintiff may be entitled to a hearing in aid of execution of the judgment.").

[429] MASS. UNIF. SM. CL. STANDARDS § 9:00-:02, *available at* http://www mass.gov/courts/admin/legal/smclstandards2002.pdf.

[430] 17 U.S.C. § 801.

[431] *Id.* § 802(a)(1).

[432] *See id.* § 802 (b) & (e)(2). Three full-time staff members support the Copyright Royalty Judges in performing their functions. Although not mandated by the statute, in practice the first two staff members have been attorneys, and the third provides administrative support.

[433] *Id.* § 801; *see also* U.S. Copyright Royalty Board, *Copyright Royalty Judges* (Mar. 8, 2008), http://www.loc.gov/crb/background/.

[434] *See* U.S. Copyright Office, Licensing Division, Financial Statement (Nov. 2012), http://www.copyright.gov/licensing/FIN-11-2012.pdf (showing distributions for cable, satellite, jukebox, and digital audio recording technology royalties); *see also SoundExchange, Inc. v. Librarian of Cong.*, 571 F.3d 1220, 1226 (D.C. Cir. 2009) (Kavanaugh, J., concurring) ("[B]illions of dollars and the fates of entire industries can ride on the Copyright Royalty Board's decisions.").

[435] 17 U.S.C. §§ 801(b)(3), 803(d)(2)(C).

[436] As noted above, the appointment process for the CRJs recently was found to be unconstitutional under the Appointments Clause – but was also cured – in a recent opinion of the D.C. Circuit Court of Appeals. *See supra* Part IV.D.

[437] 17 U.S.C. § 802(f)(1)(A)(i).

[438] *Id.*

[439] *Id.* § 802(f)(1)(B).

[440] *Id.* § 802(f)(1)(D).

[441] *See id.* §§ 801-05 & 37 C.F.R. §§ 350-54.

[442] *See* Determination of Rates and Terms for Preexisting Subscription and Satellite Digital Audio Radio Services, 76 Fed. Reg. 591 (Dec. 22, 2010) (announcing commencement of proceedings in Docket No. 2011–1 CRB PSS/Satellite II); Determination of Rates and Terms for Preexisting Subscription Services and Satellite Digital Audio Radio Services, 78 Fed. Reg. 23,054 (Apr. 17, 2013) (to be codified at 37 C.F.R. pt. 382) ("2013 Determination") (completing entry of Final Rule over two years after commencement of proceedings were announced in Docket No. 2011–1 CRB PSS/Satellite II); *see also* Distribution of the 2004 and 2005 Cable Royalty Funds, 73 Fed. Reg. 40,623 (July 15, 2008) (announcing commencement of Phase I proceedings in Docket No. 2007–3 CRB CD 2004–2005 to distribute cable royalty funds); Distribution of the 2004 and 2005 Cable Royalty Funds, 75 Fed. Reg. 57,063 (Sept. 15, 2010) (distributing Phase I of 2004 and 2005 cable royalty funds in Docket No. 2007–3 CRB CD 2004–2005 over two years later).

[443] *Compare* 37 C.F.R. § 351.5(b)(1) ("A participant in a royalty rate proceeding may request of an opposing participant nonprivileged documents that are directly related to the written direct statement or written rebuttal statement of that participant."), *and* 37 C.F.R. 351.6 ("In a distribution proceedings… parties may request of an opposing party nonprivileged underlying documents related to the written exhibits and testimony."), *with* FED. R. CIV. P. 26(b)(1) ("Unless otherwise limited by court order, the scope of discovery is as follows: Parties may obtain discovery regarding any nonprivileged matter that is relevant to any party's claim or defense….").

[444] *See, e.g.*, 2013 Determination at 23,054 ("In all, the Judges heard evidence and oral argument for a period of 19 days. The parties presented 32 fact and expert witnesses.").

[445] *See* 17 U.S.C. § 801(b)(1).
[446] *Id.* § 803(b)(4)(A).
[447] *Id.* § 803(b)(4)(B).
[448] 5 U.S.C. § 706(2); *see also* 17 U.S.C. § 803(d)(3) ("Jurisdiction of court. – Section 706 of title 5 shall apply with respect to review by the court of appeals under this subsection."); *Intercollegiate Broad. Sys. v. Copyright Royalty Bd.*, 684 F.3d 1332, 1336 (D.C. Cir. 2012) (determining that challenges for lack of compliance with a statutory provision are "evaluated under the familiar APA arbitrary and capricious standard").
[449] Rules of Practice for Trials Before the Patent Trial and Appeal Board and Judicial Review of Patent Trial and Appeal Board Decisions, Final Rule, 77 Fed. Reg. 48,612 (Aug. 14, 2012) ("PTAB Final Rule").
[450] America Invents Act of 2011, § 7, Pub. L. No. 112-29, 125 Stat. 284 ("AIA").
[451] 35 U.S.C. § 6(a).
[452] *Id.*
[453] Gene Quinn, *AIPLA 2012 Annual Meeting Begins*, IPWATCHDOG (Oct. 25, 2012), http://www.ipwatchdog.com/2012/10/25/aipla-2012-annual-meeting-begins/id=29280/.
[454] 35 U.S.C. § 6(c).
[455] *Id.* §§ 311-319 (*inter partes* review); *id.* §§ 321-329 (post grant review).
[456] AIA, § 18(a)(1)(B).
[457] 35 U.S.C. § 135(a).
[458] *Id.* § 135(b).
[459] *Id.* § 312 (*inter partes* review); *id.* § 322 (post grant review). The fee for filing an *inter partes* review petition challenging up to twenty claims is $27,200, and the fee for the same number of challenged claims in a post grant review petition is $35,800. 37 C.F.R. § 42.15.
[460] 35 U.S.C. § 313 (*inter partes* review); 35 U.S.C. § 323 (post grant review).
[461] *Id.* § 314(a).
[462] *Id.* § 324(a). A petition for post grant review may also be authorized on a showing that the petition "raises a novel or unsettled legal question that is important to other patents or patent applications." *Id.* § 324(b).
[463] PTAB Final Rule.
[464] 37 C.F.R. Part 42.
[465] *Id.* at § 42.10.
[466] *Id.* at §§ 42.20-42.25.
[467] *Id.* at § 42.52. Note that the Federal Rules of Evidence generally apply. *Id.* at C.F.R. § 42.62.
[468] *Id.* at. § 42.53.
[469] *Id.* at § 42.70.
[470] 35 U.S.C. § 141(c).
[471] U.S. Patent and Trademark Office, AIA Proceeding Statistics, http://www.uspto.gov/ip/boards/bpai/stats/aia_trial_proceedings.pdf.
[472] *Id.*
[473] *Id.*
[474] Pub. L. No. 111-349, 124 Stat. 3674 (2011); ADMINISTRATIVE OFFICE OF THE UNITED STATES COURTS, DISTRICT COURTS SELECTED FOR PATENT PILOT PROGRAM (Jun. 7, 2011) http://www.uscourts.gov/news/newsview/11-06-07/District_Courts_Selected_for_Patent_Pilot_Program.aspx (selected districts included the Eastern District of New York, Southern District of New York, Western District of Pennsylvania, District of New Jersey, District of Maryland, Northern District of Illinois, Southern District of Florida, District of Nevada, Eastern District of Texas, Northern District of Texas, Western District of Tennessee, Central District of California, Northern District of California, and Southern District of California).
[475] *See, e.g.*, U.S. DIST. CT. FOR THE E. DIST. OF TEX. LOCAL CIV. RULES, APP. M; E.D. TEX. P.R. 1-1 through 4-6; S&E D.N.Y PATENT L.R. 2, 6-8,10-12; W.D. Pa. LPR 2.1, 2.3, 4.1-4.5.
[476] *See, e.g.*, E.D. TEX. P.R. 3-1 (ten days for service); P.R. 4-2 (twenty days for claim term exchange); Michael C. Smith, Feature, *Rocket Docket: Marshall Court Leads Nation in Hearing Patent Cases*, 69 TEX. B.J. 1045, 1046 (2006).
[477] *See* Yan Leychkis, *Of Fire Ants and Claim Construction: An Empirical Study of the Meteoric Rise of the Eastern District of* Texas *as a Preeminent Forum for Patent Litigation*, 9 YALE J.L. & TECH. 193, 219 (2007).
[478] 28 U.S.C. § 1295.
[479] S. REP. NO. 275 at 5, 97th Cong., 1st Sess. 1981, 1982 U.S.C.C.A.N. 11.
[480] Request for Comments on a Patent Small Claims Proceeding in the United States, 77 Fed. Reg. 74,830 (Dec. 18, 2012). Comments were due April 30, 2013. Extension of Comment Period for Request for Comments on a Patent Small Claims Proceeding in the United States, 78 Fed. Reg. 14,515, 14,516 (Mar. 6, 2013). Twenty-two comments were received. *Office of Policy and External Affairs – Patents,* U.S. PATENT & TRADEMARK OFFICE, http://www.uspto.gov/ip/global/patents/index.jsp#heading-1.
[481] Request for Comments on a Patent Small Claims Proceeding in the United States, 77 Fed. Reg. 74,830, 74,830 (Dec. 18, 2012).

[482] U.S. Intellectual Property Enforcement Coordinator, *2013 Joint Strategic Plan on Intellectual Property Enforcement* 25 (Jun. 2013), *available at* http://www.whitehouse.gov/sites/default/files/omb/IPEC/2013-us-ipec-joint-strategic-plan.pdf.

[483] The TTAB also hears *ex parte* cases concerning trademark examining attorneys' rejections of applications for the federal registration of marks. This report focuses on the TTAB's treatment of *inter partes* cases, which involve a two-party dispute regarding a trademark application or registration, because they are most similar to traditional copyright infringement lawsuits.

[484] U.S. Pat. & Trademark Office, U.S. Dep't of Commerce, *Trademark Trial & Appeal Board Manual of Procedure*, § 528.05(a)(2) (3d ed. Rev. 1, June 2012) ("TBMP").

[485] The applicable statute does not provide for a set number of judges. *See* 15 U.S.C. § 1067(b) ("The Trademark Trial and Appeal Board shall include … administrative trademark judges who are appointed by the Secretary of Commerce, in consultation with the Director."). As of 2012, there were twenty-three appointed judges. *See* John L. Welch, The TTABlog: Keeping Tabs on the TTAB, "Updated Roster of TTAB Administrative Trademark Judges" (Oct. 30, 2012), http://thettablog.blogspot.com/2012/10/updated-roster-of-ttab-administrative.html ("Welch").

[486] Of the administrative judges assigned to the TTAB as of 2012, eighteen (78%) were formerly trademark examining attorneys, fourteen (61%) were TTAB interlocutory attorneys, and fourteen (61%) had experience in private practice. Of the three TTAB judges who had no prior experience as an examining or interlocutory attorney, one was formerly an arbitrator and judge pro tem and the other two were in private practice. *See* Welch.

[487] TBMP § 102.01.

[488] *Id.*

[489] 15 U.S.C. § 1119 ("In any action involving a registered mark the court may determine the right to registration, order the cancelation of registrations, in whole or in part, restore canceled registrations, and otherwise rectify the register with respect to the registrations of any party to the action.").

[490] *See Selva & Sons, Inc. v. Nina Footwear, Inc.*, 705 F.2d 1316, 1324 (Fed. Cir. 1983) ("[A]lthough other courts would be the proper tribunals in which to litigate a cause of action for enforcement or breach of the contract here involved, that is not sufficient reason for the board to decline to consider the agreement, its construction, or its validity if necessary to decide the issues properly before it in this cancellation proceeding, including the issue of estoppel.").

[491] 15 U.S.C. § 1119.

[492] *See General Mills Inc. v. Fage Dairy Processing Indus. SA*, 100 U.S.P.Q.2d 1584, 1591 (TTAB 2011) (finding that the Board does not have the power to grant injunctive relief).

[493] *See* 37 C.F.R. §§ 2.129(a) & 2.142(e)(1).

[494] *Id.* at. § 2.120(a)(2).

[495] *Id.* at § 2.11.

[496] *Id.* at § 11.14 (e).

[497] *Id.* at § 2.127(f).

[498] *Id.* at § 2.120(g)(1).

[499] *Id.* at. § 2.101.

[500] *Id.* at § 2.111.

[501] *Id.* at § 2.119(b) & (d) (setting forth appropriate service methods that include some options similar to the Federal Rules, but with additional methods such as serving via overnight courier).

[502] *Id.* at § 2.6(a) (16-18) (filing fee per petition to cancel or oppose, per class, is $300.00 and $100 for an *ex parte* appeal).

[503] *Id.* at §§ 2.120 (discovery), 2.127 (motions).

[504] *Id.* at §§ 2.122 (matters in evidence), 2.123 (trial testimony in *inter partes* cases).

[505] *Id.* at §§ 2.128 (briefs at final hearing), 2.129 (oral argument); TBMP, § 802.03 ("Oral hearings are almost exclusively held at the offices of the Board. However, parties may request attendance at the hearings remotely via video conference. A video conference will be conducted in the same manner as if conducted entirely in the hearing room.").

[506] TBMP, § 528.05(a)(2).

[507] *Id.* at § 528.05(a)(2).

[508] 37 C.F.R. § 2.145.

[509] 15 § U.S.C. 1071(b)(1).

[510] 5 U.S.C. § 706; *Glendale Int'l. Corp. v. USPTO*, 374 F. Supp. 2d 479, 485 (E.D. Va. 2005) ("[D]ecisions of the TTAB are reviewed de novo with respect to conclusions of law and for 'substantial evidence' with respect to findings of fact."); TBMP, § 906.01.

[511] James R. Robinson & Kathleen E. McCarthy, *An Introduction to the New Trademark Trial and Appeal Board Rules*, 97 TRADEMARK REP. 1380, 1381 (2007).

[512] A 2004 review of TTAB cases found that the median time between the start of an opposition or cancellation proceeding until a final decision of the TTAB was approximately 38.4 months. John M. Murphy, *Playing the*

Numbers: *A Quantitative Look at Section 2(d) Cases Before the Trademark Trial and Appeal Board*, 94 TRADEMARK REP. 800, 801 (2004). Delay in the TTAB has not significantly improved since 2004 as the median total pendency for all trial cases before the TTAB in 2010, 2011, and 2012 were 46.8, 49.1, and 46.8 months respectively. U.S. PAT. & TRADEMARK OFFICE, TTAB NEW FILINGS AND PERFORMANCE MEASURES (FISCAL YEAR 2013), http://www.uspto.gov/trademarks/process/appeal/TTAB_New_Filings_and_Performance_Measures.jsp (last visited Jul. 3, 2013, data on years prior to 2012 have since been removed from this page).

[513] Robinson & McCarthy, at 1389.

[514] *See* 26 U.S.C. §§ 7436(c), 7463 (small tax cases are cases before the Tax Court that involve a specialized set of adjudicatory procedures which are only available for petitioners who have both certain kinds of tax disputes and also involve claims of less than $50,000 at stake); T.C.R. PRAC. & P. 170-74.

[515] *See* Revenue Act of 1924, Pub. L. No. 68-176, 43 Stat. 253 (1924).

[516] S. REP. NO. 68-398 at 8-9 (1924).

[517] The Tax Reform Act of 1969, Pub. L. No. 91-172, 83 Stat. 487 (1969).

[518] 26 U.S.C. §§ 6212-14.

[519] *Id.* at § 6512(b).

[520] *Id.* at §§ 7476 (retirement plans), 7477 (certain gifts), 7478 (certain governmental obligations), 7479 (installment payments), & 7428 (status and classification of certain organizations).

[521] *Id.* at § 6110.

[522] 28 U.S.C. §§ 1330-1369 (jurisdiction of federal district courts, generally); 26 U.S.C. § 7402 (jurisdiction of district courts specifically in tax cases, which is broader than the Tax Court); 28 U.S.C. §§ 1491-1509 (jurisdiction of United States Court of Federal Claims, generally).

[523] Theodore Tannenwald, Jr., *The Tax Litigation Process: Where It Is and Where It Is Going*, 44 REC. ASS'N B. CITY OF N.Y. 825, 827 (1989) (by 1989, the Tax Court heard 95% of tax cases).

[524] 26 U.S.C § 7463(a).

[525] The Tax Reform Act of 1969, Pub. L. No. 91-172, § 957(a), 83 Stat. 487, 733 (1969) (law became effective Dec. 30, 1970).

[526] 26 U.S.C. § 7443(a)-(b) (the Tax Court is comprised of nineteen judges).

[527] *Id.* at § 7443(e).

[528] The small tax case procedure is optional. T.C.R. PRAC. & P. 171(a) ("A petitioner who wishes to have the proceedings in the case conducted as a small tax case may so request at the time the petition is filed.").

[529] 26 U.S.C. § 7443A. Appointment of these special trial judges faced a constitutional challenge in the context of a non-small claims proceeding, but was found to not be a violation of the Appointments Clause of the Constitution. *Freytag v. Comm. of Internal Revenue*, 501 U.S. 868, 892 (1991). Further discussion of the Appointments Clause is found in section IV. D. at 42.

[530] T.C.R. PRAC. & P. 174(b).

[531] 26 U.S.C. § 7445.

[532] T.C.R. PRAC. & P. FORM 5.

[533] *Id.*

[534] *Id.* App. II. The fee, currently $60, can be waived in small tax cases if the petitioner is unable to pay. *Id.* 173(a)(2).

[535] *Id.* Form 5.

[536] 26 U.S.C § 7463; T.C.R. PRAC. & P. 171.

[537] 26 U.S.C § 7463(d).

[538] *Id.* at § 7463(a) ("proceedings shall be conducted in accordance with such rules of evidence, practice, and procedure as the Tax Court may prescribe").

[539] T.C.R. PRAC. & P. Form 174(b).

[540] *Id.* 173(a) and Form 2 (Petition (Simplified Form)).

[541] *Id.* 174(c).

[542] *Id.* 24(a)(4-5) (the general rule for appearance and representation before the Tax Court allows non-attorneys to practice, including law students who provide assistance with cases, and incorporates Rule 200, which allows for non-attorneys to practice); *id.* 172 ("A petitioner in a small tax case may appear without representation or may be represented by any person admitted to practice before the Court. As to representation, see Rule 24."); *id.* 200(b) (allowing for non-attorneys to practice if that person passes an examination performed by the Tax Court.).

[543] 26 U.S.C. § 7430.

[544] *Id.* § 7430(b)(1).

[545] *See id.* § 7430(b)(2).

[546] *Id.* § 7459(b); T.C.R. PRAC. & P. 152 (allowing for non-precedential, oral findings of fact except in actions for declaratory judgment or for disclosure).

[547] 26 U.S.C. § 7463(b) ("A decision entered in any case in which the proceedings are conducted under this section shall not be reviewed in any other court and shall not be treated as a precedent for any other case.").

[548] ABA IP Section Second Notice Comments at 3; Copyright Alliance First Notice Comments at 5; Microsoft Corp., Comments Submitted in Response to First Notice of Inquiry at 4 (Jan. 17, 2012) ("Microsoft First Notice Comments"); Michael Traynor *et al.*, Comments Submitted in Response to First Notice of Inquiry at 7 (Jan. 13, 2012) ("Traynor *et al.* First Notice Comments"); PACA, Comments Submitted to Second Notice of Inquiry at 7 (Oct. 18, 2012) ("PACA Second Notice Comments").

[549] Prior to implementation of the UDRP procedures, the Internet Corporation for Assigned Names and Numbers, World Intellectual Property Institute, and the Department of Commerce all recognized that "[e]xisting mechanisms for resolving conflicts between trademark owners and domain name holders are often viewed as expensive, cumbersome, and ineffective." World Intellectual Property Organization, *The Management of Internet Names and Addresses: Intellectual Property Issues, Final Report of the WIPO Internet Domain Name Process*, ¶ 131 (Apr. 30, 1999), http://www.wipo.int/export/sites/www/amc/en/docs/report-final1.pdf.

[550] Internet Corporation for Assigned Names and Numbers, *Final GNSO Issue Report on the Current State of the Uniform Dispute Resolution Policy*, 12 (Oct. 3, 2011), http://gnso.icann.org/issues/udrp/udrp-final-issue-report-03oct11-en.pdf.

[551] When drafting the UDRP, ICANN relied heavily on a report by the World Intellectual Property Organization report *The Management of Internet Names and Addresses: Intellectual Property Issues, Final Report of the WIPO Internet Domain Name Process*, 131 (Apr. 30, 1999), http://www.wipo.int/export/sites/www/amc/en/docs/report-final1.pdf.

[552] ICANN, *List of Approved Dispute Resolution Service Providers*, http://www.icann.org/en/help/dndr/udrp/providers (dispute resolution providers include: the Asian Domain Name Dispute Resolution Centre, Czech Arbitration Court Arbitration Center for Internet Disputes, National Arbitration Forum ("NAF"), WIPO, and starting on January 1st, 2014, the Arab Center for Domain Name Dispute Resolution).

[553] ICANN, *Information Concerning Approval Process for Dispute-Resolution Service Providers*, http://www.icann.org/en/help/dndr/udrp/provider-approval-process.

[554] If the parties have a single-member panel, the dispute resolution provider chooses the panelist. If there is a three-member panel, each party proposes a list of potential panelists, with the dispute resolution provider selecting one panelist from each of the complainant's and respondent's lists and picking the third panelist separately. ICANN, *Rules for Uniform Domain Name Dispute Resolution Policy* § 6 (Oct. 30, 2009), http://www.icann.org/en/help/dndr/ udrp/rules ("UDRP Rules").

[555] ICANN, *Registrar Accreditation Agreement*, 3.8 (May 21, 2009), http://www.icann.org/en/resources/registrars/raa/ra-agreement-21may09-en.htm#3.

[556] ICANN, Uniform Domain-Name Dispute-Resolution Policy, § 4 (Aug. 26, 1999), http://www.icann.org/en/help/dndr/udrp/policy. While these proceedings are mandatory for registrants, a registrant also can invoke the jurisdiction of a court to decide a domain name dispute. UDRP § 4(k) ("The mandatory administrative proceeding requirements set forth in Paragraph 4 shall not prevent either you or the complainant from submitting the dispute to a court of competent jurisdiction for independent resolution before such mandatory administrative proceeding is commenced or after such proceeding is concluded."); If the registrant invokes the jurisdiction of a court before or during a UDRP proceeding, the UDRP tribunal has "discretion to decide whether to suspend or terminate the administrative proceeding, or to proceed to a decision." UDRP Rules § 18(a).

[557] ICANN, *Domain Name Dispute Resolution Policies*, http://www.icann.org/en/help/dndr (this includes all the domain names that end in .aero, .asia, .biz, .cat, .com, .coop, .info, .jobs, .mobi, .museum, name, net, .org, .pro, .tel and .travel).

[558] UDRP § 4(a).

[559] An example of this occurred when a UDRP panel refused to transfer a domain name containing both the trademark of the claimant and its nonparty competitor because transferring the domain name to the claimant might violate the nonparty competitor's rights. *See Lilly ICOS LLC v. Tudor Burden, Burden Mktg.*, Case No. D2004-0794 (WIPO Dec. 20, 2004) (the domain name at issue was cialis-viagra.info and Pfizer Inc. owns the trademark to Viagra, but was not a party to the proceedings).

[560] *See, e.g, Wintershall Holding GMBH v. Tracey Morgan*, Case No. D2011-1456 (WIPO Oct. 20, 2011) (while the panel noted that "assessing copyright infringement is beyond the scope of the Policy," citing prior decisions that found copyright infringement to be evidence of bad faith, the panel still found that using the disputed domain name to place an infringing copy of the advertising content found on the complainant's website was evidence of bad faith).

[561] UDRP § 4(a).

[562] *See, e.g., Anomaly Action Sports S.R.L. Con Sigla AAS S.r.l. v. Kruse*, Case No. D2013-0276 at ¶ 6.22 (WIPO March 15, 2013) ("[T]his Panel is of the opinion that the importation into the Policy of local law doctrines based upon the location of the parties is both unwarranted and misconceived."); M. Scott Donahey, 1 INTERNET L. & PRACTICE § 16:6 (2013) ("While panelists' approaches to choice of law are not consistent, the general practice is, where both parties are from the same country, to apply the law of that country. Where parties are from different countries, panelists tend to rely entirely on the UDRP and the Uniform Rules and do not apply any national law.").

[563] UDRP §§ 3-5 ("complaints" and "responses").

[564] WIPO, *World Intellectual Property Organization Supplemental Rules for Uniform Domain Name Dispute Resolution*, § 11 (Dec. 14, 2009), http://www.wipo.int/amc/en/domains/supplemental/eudrp/ (5,000 word limit); Arbitration Center for Internet Disputes; *CAC's UDRP Supplemental Rules of the Czech Arbitration Court*, § 13, https://udrp.adr.eu/arbitration_platform/udrp_supplemental_rules.php (5,000 word limit); The Asian Domain Name Dispute Resolution Centre, *Supplemental Rules to the Internet Corporation for Assigned Names and Numbers (ICANN) Uniform Domain Name Dispute Resolution Policy and the Rules for the Domain Name Dispute Resolution Policy*, art. 13.1 (Jul. 26, 2012), https://www.adndrc.org/doc/Supplemental_Rules_26-07-2012_en.pdf (3,000 word limit); National Arbitration Forum, *The National Arbitration Forum's Supplemental Rules to ICANN's Uniform Domain Name Dispute Resolution Policy*, §§ 4(a), 5(a) (Mar. 1, 2010), http://domains.adrforum.com/users/icann/res ources/UDRP%20Supplemental%20Rules%20eff%20March%201%202010.pdf (fifteen page limit).

[565] *See, e.g.*, WIPO, *Online Complaint Filing Form Complaints under the Uniform Domain Name Dispute Resolution Policy (UDRP)*, www.wipo.int/amc/en/domains/filing/udrp/eudrpcomplaint.jsp; National Arbitration Forum, *Online Filing for Uniform Domain Dispute Resolution Policy (UDRP) Cases*, https://secure.arb-forum.com/ddfiling/default.aspx?Ruleset=UDRP.

[566] UDRP Rules §§ 3(b)(iv), 5(b)(iv)-(v), 6.

[567] UDRP Rules § 13; *Mary's Futons, Inc. v. Texas Int'l Prop. Assocs.*, Claim Number FA0706001012059 (National Arbitration Forum) (Aug. 13, 2007) ("In the thousands of cases which have now been determined by both WIPO and NAF, there has been no occasion on which an in-person hearing has been ordered.").

[568] Typically most providers do not allow submission of additional documents. However, the National Arbitration Forum allows for one additional written statement to be submitted within five days of a Response if it does not amend the Complaint or Response. *See The National Arbitration Forum's Supplemental Rules to ICANN's Uniform Domain Name Dispute Resolution Policy,* § 7 (Mar. 1, 2010), http://domains.adrforum.com/users/icann/resources/UDRP%20Supplemental%20Rules%20eff%20March%201%202010.pdf. While submission of additional documents is uncommon, dispute resolution providers may allow a trademark owner an additional submission in the case of new evidence.

[569] UDRP Rules §§ 3(b), 5(b).

[570] Kristan B. Burch, *Domain Name Disputes: Why Are So Many Disputes Resolved Administratively?*, 59 FED. LAWYER 20, 22 (2012) ("The parties in a UDRP proceeding cannot participate in discovery").

[571] UDRP Rules § 6.

[572] *Id.* § 15(b).

[573] *Id.* § 4(i) ("The remedies available to a complainant pursuant to any proceeding before an Administrative Panel shall be limited to requiring the cancellation of your domain name or the transfer of your domain name registration to the complainant.").

[574] WIPO, *Guide to the Uniform Domain Name Dispute Resolution Policy (UDRP)*, http://www.wipo.int/amc/en/do mains/guide/#b6 ("While the assistance of a lawyer may be helpful, there is no requirement that the Complaint be prepared or submitted by a lawyer.").

[575] UDRP § 4(g). A respondent may, however, share the costs of the proceeding if the respondent participates in the adjudicatory process and opts to have three panelists where the complainant has requested one.

[576] *See* WIPO, *Schedule of Fees under the UDRP* (Dec. 1, 2002), http://www.wipo.int/amc/en/domains/fees/index.ht ml. ($1,500 for single-panelist review of up to five domain names); National Arbitration Forum, *The National Arbitration Forum's Supplemental Rules to ICANN's Uniform Domain Name Dispute Resolution Policy*, § 17 (Mar. 1, 2010), http://domains.adrforum.com/users/icann/resources/UDRP%20Supplemental%20Rules%20eff%20March %201%202010.pdf ($1,300 for single-panelist review of up to two domain names); Arbitration Center for Internet Disputes, *Fees of the Czech Arbitration Court (CAC),* https://udrp.adr.eu/arbitration_platform/fees.php (€500 for single-panelist review of up to five domain names); Asian Domain Name Dispute Resolution Centre, *Supplemental Rules to the Internet Corporation for Assigned Names and Numbers (ICANN) Uniform Domain Name Dispute Resolution Policy and the Rules for the Domain Name Dispute Resolution Policy*, art. 15 (Jul. 26, 2012), https://ww w.adndrc.org/doc/Supplemental_Rules_26-07-2012_en.pdf ($1,300 for single-panelist review of up to two domain names).

[577] *See* UDRP § 4(i).

[578] *Id.* § 4(k). The UDRP procedural rules, to which complainants agree by virtue of bringing a complaint and registrants agree pursuant to the registration agreement with the registrar, mandate that the complainant "will submit, with respect to any challenges to a decision in the administrative proceeding canceling or transferring the domain name, to the jurisdiction of the courts in at least one specified Mutual Jurisdiction." *Id.* § 3(xiii). A "Mutual Jurisdiction" is "a court jurisdiction at the location of either (a) the principal office of the Registrar… or (b) the domain-name holder's address as shown for the registration of the domain name in Registrar's WhoIs database at the time the complaint is submitted to the Provider." UDRP § 1. A "WhoIs" database reflects the registration information of the domain name registrant and typically is publicly available on the registrar's website as well as on other websites.

[579] UDRP § 4(k).

[580] *See* 15 U.S.C. § 1125(d)(1) (cause of action for trademark owners seeking transfer of the domain name against the alleged cybersquatter); *id.* § 1125(d)(2) (cause of action for trademark owners against the domain name *in rem* when the domain name owner cannot be located); 15 U.S.C. § 1114(2)(D)(v) (creating a civil cause of action for domain name owners seeking to restore rights to a domain name when the domain name has been suspended, disabled, or transferred under a policy prohibiting the registration of a domain name that is identical to, confusingly similar to, or dilutive of another's mark (for example, the UDRP)).

[581] 9 U.S.C. §§ 1-16.

[582] The modern FAA derived from the United States Arbitration Act, which was in effect from 1925 until it was replaced by the current FAA in 1947. Act of Feb. 12, 1925, ch. 213, §§ 1-15, 43 Stat. 883-86 (repealed by FAA, 9 U.S.C. §§ 1-16 (1947)).

[583] 9 U.S.C. § 2.

[584] *See Southland Co. v. Keating*, 465 U.S. 1, 11 (1984) (noting "broad principle of enforceability" under FAA).

[585] *See Moses H. Cone Mem'l Hosp. v. Mercury Const. Corp.*, 460 U.S. 1, 24 (1983).

[586] 9 U.S.C. § 10.

[587] Inter-American Convention on International Commercial Arbitration, Jan. 30, 1975, S. TREATY DOC. No. 97-12 (1981); Convention on the Recognition and Enforcement of Foreign Arbitral Awards, art. I(3), June 10, 1958, 21 U.S.T. 2517; 9 U.S.C. § 304.

[588] 9 U.S.C. § 9.

[589] *Id.* All fifty states and the District of Columbia have provisions for the enforcement of arbitral awards. *See* Susan Weins & Roger Haydock, *Confirming Arbitration Awards: Taking the Mystery Out of a Summary Proceeding*, 33 WM. MITCHELL L. REV. 1293, 1294 n.5 (2007) (listing all state arbitration laws).

[590] 9 U.S.C. § 13.

[591] This fee varies in federal district court. *Compare* United States District Court Eastern District of Pennsylvania, *District Court Miscellaneous Fee Schedule*, http://www.paed.uscourts.gov/documents/fees/dcfees.pdf (the Eastern District of Pennsylvania categorizes the confirmation of arbitration awards as miscellaneous actions and charges a fee of $46), *with* United States District Court Southern District of New York, *District Court Fee Schedule and Related Information*, http://www.nysd.uscourts.gov/fees (Southern District of New York requires parties to pay the full fee for a new civil action of $400 in order to confirm an arbitration award).

[592] *See* Weins & Haydock, at 1305.

[593] 9 U.S.C. § 9.

[594] *Id.* § 12.

[595] *Hall Street Assocs., L.L.C. v. Mattel, Inc.*, 552 U.S. 576, 584 (2008).

[596] *Oxford Health Plans LLC v. Sutter*, 133 S. Ct. 2064, 2068 (2013) (referring to the "exceeded their powers" standard specifically, but also noting generally that "[u]nder the FAA, courts may vacate an arbitrator's decision 'only in very unusual circumstances.'") (citation omitted).

[597] *French v. Merrill Lynch, Pierce, Fenner & Smith, Inc.*, 784 F.2d 902, 906 (9th Cir.1986) (citations omitted).

[598] *See Hall Street Assocs.*, 552 U.S. at 587 ("There is nothing malleable about 'must grant,' which unequivocally tells courts to grant confirmation in all cases, except when one of the 'prescribed' exceptions applies."); *see also Dean Witter Reynolds, Inc. v. Byrd*, 470 U.S. 213, 218 (1985) ("By its terms, the Act leaves no place for the exercise of discretion by a district court, but instead mandates that district courts *shall* direct the parties to proceed to arbitration on issues as to which an arbitration agreement has been signed.").

[599] *Int'l Union of Petrol. & Indus. Workers v. W. Indus. Maint., Inc.*, 707 F.2d 425, 428 (9th Cir.1983) (employer acted in bad faith in forcing union to go to court to enforce a valid arbitration award, and was forced to pay the union's attorneys' fees) (citing *Alyeska Pipeline Serv. Co. v. Wilderness Soc'y*, 421 U.S. 240, 258-59 (1975)).

[600] Alternative Dispute Resolution Act of 1998, § 2, Pub. L. 105-315, 112 Stat. 2998.

[601] Judicial Improvements and Access to Justice Act, Pub. L. 100-702, §§ 901-07, 102 Stat. 4642, 4659-64.

[602] 28 U.S.C. § 652 (a) (1988).

[603] Judicial Improvements and Access to Justice Act, § 906.

[604] *See* A bill to extend arbitration under the provisions of chapter 44 of title 28, United States Code, and for other purposes, Pub. L. 103-192, 107 Stat. 2292.

[605] Pub. L. 105-315, 112 Stat. 2998. Prior to the ADRA was the Civil Justice Reform Act of 1990, which required federal district courts to consider several case management strategies, including ADR, as a means of cost and delay reduction. Pursuant to this statute, many district courts implemented ADR procedures and hired ADR staff. DONNA STIENSTRA, FED. JUDICIAL CTR., ADR IN THE FEDERAL DISTRICT COURTS: AN INITIAL REPORT 1-2 (2011), *available at* http://www fjc.gov/public/pdf.nsf/lookup/adr2011.pdf/$file/adr2011.pdf.

[606] 28 U.S.C. § 651.

[607] The ABA, for example, explained that while it "has long supported voluntary arbitration in the federal courts, it strongly opposes mandatory arbitration programs, even if nonbinding, where involuntary participation is required before litigants are allowed a trial before a jury or federal judge." *Alternative Dispute Resolution and Settlement Encouragement Act; Federal Courts Improvement Act, and Need for Additional Federal District Court Judges: Hearing on H.R. 2603 and H.R. 2294 Before the H. Comm. on the Judiciary*, 105th Cong. 59 (1997) (statement of Mitchell F. Dolin).

[608] 28 U.S.C. § 654(b).
[609] *Id.* at § 651.
[610] *Id.* at § 652(a).
[611] *Id.* at § 652(b) ("Each district court may exempt from the requirements of this section specific cases or categories of cases in which use of alternative dispute resolution would not be appropriate.").
[612] *Id.* at § 654(a).
[613] DONNA STIENSTRA, FED. JUDICIAL CTR., ADR IN THE FEDERAL DISTRICT COURTS: AN INITIAL REPORT 5 (2011), *available at* http://www fjc.gov/public/pdf nsf/lookup/adr2011.pdf/$file/adr2011.pdf.
[614] *Id.* at 7.
[615] *Id. But see id.* at 6 (not every district court considers the settlement conference a form of ADR, and so not every court included its usage in its ADR provisions).
[616] STIENSTRA, at 9.
[617] *Id.* at 15.
[618] U.S. District Ct., N.D. CAL. ADR L.R. 3. Note that private ADR proceedings are not subject to enforcement, immunity, or other provisions of the local ADR rules. N.D. CAL. ADR L.R. 3-4(b).
[619] U.S. District Ct., N.D. Cal., *Statistics: ADR Referrals of All Civil Cases by Calendar Year Filed* (2011), http://www.cand.uscourts.gov/statistics.
[620] *Id.*
[621] CLA, *Certified Lawyer Referral Service*, http://www.calawyersforthearts.org/Lawyer_Referral (the administrative fee is $35 or $20 for CLA members).
[622] Alma Robinson, *Small Copyright Claimants Need Access to Justice* (Feb. 20, 2013 1:06 PM), http://www.calawyersforthearts.org/california_arts_blog?mode=PostView&bmi=1213811.
[623] CLA, *A.A.M.S. Fees and Services*, http://www.calawyersforthearts.org/AAMS_Fees (last visited Sept. 11, 2013).
[624] VLA Third Notice Comments at 1.
[625] *Id.*
[626] VLA, *Pro Bono Legal Services*, http://www.vlany.org/legalservices/probono.php.
[627] *Id.*
[628] *Id.*
[629] *Id.*
[630] N.D. Cal., *FLASH*, http://www.cand.uscourts.gov/helpcentersj ("FLASH does not provide help with: bankruptcy, habeas corpus, prisoner, appeals, state court, and/or criminal questions, or any question concerning a case not pending in the United States District Court for the Northern District of California—San Jose division.").
[631] *Id.*
[632] *Id.*
[633] FLASH Third Notice Comments at 2, n.6.
[634] *Id.* at 2 (note that this statistic is not limited to copyright cases).
[635] *Id.* at 1.
[636] JUDICIARY OF ENG. AND WALES INTELLECTUAL PROP. COURT USERS' COMM., WORKING GROUP'S FINAL REPORT ON PROPOSALS FOR REFORM OF THE PATENTS COUNTY COURT 6 (2009), *available at* http://new.judiciary.gov.uk/NR/rdonlyres/24E06162-8F8F-4117-92D2-3446CD75ECA1/0/report_wgf_reform_of_county_court.pdf.
[637] *Id.*
[638] RIGHT HONOURABLE LORD JUSTICE RUPERT JACKSON, REVIEW OF CIVIL LITIGATION COSTS: FINAL REPORT (2009), *available at* http://www.judiciary.gov.uk/NR/rdonlyres/8EB9F3F3-9C4A-4139-8A93-56F09672EB6A/0/jacksonfinalreport140110.pdf ("Jackson Report").
[639] IAN HARGREAVES, DIGITAL OPPORTUNITY: A REVIEW OF INTELLECTUAL PROPERTY AND GROWTH (2011), *available at* http://www.ipo.gov.uk/ipreview-finalreport.pdf ("Hargreaves Report").
[640] Jackson Report, at xx.
[641] Hargreaves Report, at 67.
[642] *Id.* at 83.
[643] Jackson Report, at xx; Hargreaves Report, at 83.
[644] Jackson Report, at xx; Hargreaves Report, at 85. Despite its name, the Patents County Court does not hear patent cases in its small claims track, though it does on its multitrack.
[645] HM GOV'T, THE GOVERNMENT RESPONSE TO THE HARGREAVES REVIEW OF INTELLECTUAL PROPERTY AND GROWTH 12 (2011) ("access to the courts at a proportionate cost should act as an incentive to settle or arbitrate as well as being a means of resolving less tractable but straightforward disputes"), *available at* http://www.ipo.gov.uk/ipresponse-full.pdf.
[646] *See* CPR 63.28.
[647] *Id.* 63.27(1)(b). The original limit was £5,000, which increased to £10,000 with a proposed general increase in 2013. THE INTELLECTUAL PROP. OFFICE, GOVERNMENT RESPONSE TO THE CALL FOR EVIDENCE ON INTRODUCING A SMALL CLAIMS TRACK INTO THE PATENTS COUNTY COURT 4 (2012), *available at* http://www.ipo.gov.uk/hargreaves-enforce-c4e-pcc-response.pdf ("IPO Response"). The limit could increase

to £15,000 after an evaluation of the increase to £10,000, equating the monetary limit to the limit for general civilclaims that may be eligible for other small claims procedures. *Id.* at 15.

[648] CPR 26.8(c).

[649] THE INTELLECTUAL PROP. OFFICE, INTRODUCING A SMALL CLAIMS TRACK INTO THE PATENTS COUNTY COURT 9 (2012), *available at* http://www.ipo.gov.uk/hargreaves-enforce-c4e-pcc.pdf.

[650] HM COURTS & TRIBUNALS SERV., GUIDE TO THE PATENTS COUNTY COURT SMALL CLAIMS TRACK 3 (2012),*available at* http://www.justice.gov.uk/downloads/courts/patents-court/patents-court-small-claims.pdf ("PCCGuide").

[651] *Id.* at 3.

[652] Though the Jackson Report advocated using model pleadings, this recommendation was not adopted. Jackson Report, at 254 (2009).

[653] PCC Guide, at 3.

[654] CPR 63.27(3)(b). One reason that the judge makes the ultimate decision on the appropriate track is that there was a concern that well-funded defendants would "bully" claimants out of small claims and into the multi-track. IPOResponse, at 7.

[655] PCC Guide, at 3.

[656] CPR 27.10 (there is no hearing if parties agree).

[657] CPR Practice Direction 27 ¶ 3.2; *see also* PCC Guide, at 4.

[658] CPR 27.2(1)(b).

[659] *See id.* 27.4(1)(b) ("After allocation the court will … give special directions …."); *id.* 27.2(3) ("The court of itsown initiative may order a party to provide further information if it considers it appropriate to do so.").

[660] *Id.* 27.8(2).

[661] *Id.* 27.8.

[662] PCC Guide, at 6.

[663] CPR 27.3 ("The court may grant any final remedy in relation to a small claim which it could grant if the proceedings were on the fast track or the multi-track.").

[664] *Id.* 63.27(4); PCC Guide, at 2.

[665] THE INTELLECTUAL PROP. OFFICE, INTRODUCING A SMALL CLAIMS TRACK INTO THE PATENTS COUNTY COURT 10 (2012), *available at* http://www.ipo.gov.uk/hargreaves-enforce-c4e-pcc.pdf.

[666] *See id.* at 10; *see also* IPO Response, at 19.

[667] *See* PCC Guide, at 4.

[668] CPR 27.14 (except under certain circumstances "the court may not order a party to pay a sum to another party in respect of that other party's costs, fees and expenses, including those relating to an appeal ….").

[669] *See id.*; PCC Guide, at 4.

[670] CPR 27.14(2)(b).

[671] *Id.* 27 ¶ 7.2.

[672] PCC Guide, at 7.

[673] PCC Guide, at 7; Email from Philip Horswill, Copyright and Enforcement Directorate, Intellectual Property Office (U.K.), to John Riley (Sept. 23, 2013) (email on file with U.S. Copyright Office).

[674] Court of Session Act, 1998, § 40 (Scot.), *available at* http://www.legislation.gov.uk/ukpga/1988/36/contents.

[675] Act of Sederunt (Rules of Court of Session Amendment No. 5) (Miscellaneous) 2012 (Scot.), *available at* http://origin-www.legislation.gov.uk/ssi/2012/275/pdfs/ssi_20120275_en.pdf.

[676] Rules of the Court of Session 1994, § 55.2E(2)(b)(ix) (Scot.), *available at* http://www.scotcourts.gov.uk/docs/default-source/equality/chap55-causes-relating-to-intellectual-property.pdf?sfvrsn=0.

[677] *Id.* § 55.2E(2)(b) & § 55.2D(5)-(7) (Scot.).

[678] *Id.* § 55.3(2)(e) & (g) (Scot.).

[679] *Id.* § 55.2E(2)(e) (Scot.).

[680] *Id.* § 55.5B (Scot.).

[681] Copyright Act, R.S.C. 1985, c. C-42 (Can.), § 34(4)(a), *available at* http://laws-lois.justice.gc.ca/PDF/C-42.pdf.

[682] *Id.* § 34(4).

[683] Federal Court Rules, SOR/98-106 (Can.) §§ 306-307, *available at* http://laws-lois.justice.gc.ca/PDF/SOR-98-106.pdf.

[684] *Id.* § 308.

[685] *Id.* § 316.

[686] Ley Federal del Derecho de Autor [LFDA] [Federal Law on Copyright], *as amended*, arts. 229-230, Diario Oficial de la Federacion [DO], 27 de Enero de 2012 (Mex.), *available at* http://www.wipo.int/wipolex/en/text.jsp?file_id=254993 ("Mexico Federal Copyright Law").

[687] Conciliation is a method of alternative dispute resolution similar to mediation, but where the conciliator "plays a relatively direct role in the actual resolution of a dispute and even advises the parties on certain solutions by making proposals for settlement." Alessandra Sgubini, Mara Prieditis, & Andrea Marighetto, *Arbitration, Mediation and Conciliation: differences and similarities from an International and Italian business perspective*, MEDIATE.COM (Aug. 2004) http://www mediate.com/articles/sgubinia2.cfm.

[688] Mexico Federal Copyright Law, art. 217.
[689] INDAUTOR, *Legal Department Frequently Asked Questions*, http://www.indautor.gob mx/ingles/preguntas/preguntas_juridica html.
[690] Mexico Federal Copyright Law, art. 218(I).
[691] Reglamento de la Ley Federal Del Derecho de Autor [Regulations under the Federal Copyright Law], *as amended*, art. 139(IV), Diario Oficial del la Federacion, 22 de Mayo de 1998, *available at* http://www.wipo.int/wipolex/en/text.jsp?file_id=255053 ("Mexico Copyright Regulations").
[692] INDAUTOR, *Legal Department Frequently Asked Questions*, http://www.indautor.gob mx/ingles/preguntas/preguntas_juridica html.
[693] Mexico Copyright Regulations, art. 140.
[694] Mexico Federal Copyright Law, art. 218(III).
[695] *Id.* 218(V).
[696] *Id.* art. 218(IV).
[697] *Id.* art. 218(VI).
[698] INDAUTOR, *Conciliation Statistics* (2013),http://www.indautor.gob mx/documentos_oficial/Graficasavenencias.pdf.
[699] *Id.*
[700] Mexico Federal Copyright Law, art. 220.
[701] *Id.* art. 222.
[702] *Id.* art. 224.
[703] Mexico Copyright Regulations, art. 147.
[704] *Id.* arts. 149, 153.
[705] Mexico Federal Copyright Law, art. 225.
[706] *Id.* art. 226.
[707] *Id.* art. 228.
[708] Copyright Act of 1957, Act No. 432, Jan. 28, 1957, art. 112, *amended by* Act No. 9625, Apr. 22, 2009, *available at* http://www.wipo.int/wipolex/en/text.jsp?file_id=190144; Korea Copyright Comm'n, *Service*, http://eng.copyright.or kr/ (follow "Service" hyperlink, then follow "Arbitration" hyperlink) ("Korea Copyright Act").
[709] *Id.* arts. 11-13.
[710] *Id.* arts. 16-22.
[711] *Id.* arts. 66-74, 78-81, 84-85.
[712] *Id.* arts. 75, 76, 76-2, 82, 83, 83-2
[713] *Id.* art. 93.
[714] Enforcement Decree of the Copyright Act, Presidential Decree No. 1482, Apr. 22, 1959, arts. 61(1) & (3) (S. Kor.), *amended by* Presidential Decree No. 23928, July 2, 2012, *available at* http://www.wipo.int/wipolex/en/text.jsp?file_id=281752.
[715] MINISTRY OF CULTURE, SPORTS AND TOURISM AND KOREA COPYRIGHT COMM'N, 2010 ANNUAL REPORT ONCOPYRIGHT IN KOREA 73 (2010).
[716] *Id.*
[717] Korea Copyright Act, arts. 115-116.
[718] *Id.* art. 117.
[719] Email from Soo Hyun Myung, Senior Deputy Director in Copyright Policy Division, Ministry of Culture, Sports and Tourism, to Catherine Rowland (June 18, 2013) (email on file with U.S. Copyright Office) (containing PowerPoint presentation by the Korea Copyright Comm'n, *Conciliation of Copyright Disputes*). In 2011, ninety-seven applications were submitted, and twenty-eight settlements reached. In 2010, sixty-two applications were submitted, and twenty-three resolved. In 2009, fifty-five applications were submitted in 2009 and twenty-nine resolved.
[720] Korea Copyright Act, art. 113-2(1).
[721] *Id.* art. 113-2(3)-(4).
[722] MINISTRY OF CULTURE, SPORTS AND TOURISM AND KOREA COPYRIGHT COMM'N, 2010 ANNUAL REPORT ON COPYRIGHT IN KOREA 72 (2010).
[723] Korea Copyright Comm'n, *Service*, http://eng.copyright.or.kr/ (follow "Service" hyperlink, then follow "Arbitration" hyperlink).
[724] *Id.*
[725] Perhaps the most ambitious suggestion for addressing the problem through the existing federal court system was submitted by Professor David Nimmer of UCLA School of Law on behalf of APA. Professor Nimmer's proposal would implement a voluntary procedure where disputes valued at under $80,000 would by heard by a magistrate judge. The rules of this proposal would require copyright owners and defendants to each make an offer of judgment at the outset of litigation. If the parties' offers diverged significantly, additional rounds of offers could take place to attempt to reach a settlement. If no settlement were reached, the award of attorneys' fees would depend upon a combination of which party prevailed and the relationship of the judgment amount

to the parties' offers. APA First Notice Comments at 4-7. Apart from its complexity, a problem with Professor Nimmer's proposal is that in some cases, small copyright owners who "bid" too high could end up paying attorneys' fees to a defendant who was found guilty of infringement yet assessed a damages award below the defendant's offer. In the Office's view, while well-intentioned, such a system could yield inequitable results.

[726] Kernochan Second Notice Comments at 1; *see also* NPPA, Comments Submitted in Response to Second Notice of Inquiry at 1 (Oct. 19, 2012) ("NPPA Second Notice Comments") ("In a perfect world the NPPA would prefer a new branch of Article III courts within the federal system . . . That said the NPPA recognizes the inherent political, financial and practical difficulties in creating such a new Article III court system."). Indeed, now might not be the ideal time to burden the federal district court system with additional responsibilities such as implementation of a small claims track for copyright cases. The judiciary is facing serious funding issues for the matters it already addresses, leading one court of appeals judge recently to warn that "[t]he federal courts are going to fall apart if [funding problems] continue[]." *Inadequate court resources hurt access to justice, say nation's top jurists*, ABA NEWS (Aug. 9, 2013), *available at* http://www.abanow.org/2013/08/inadequate-court-resources-hurt-access-to-justice-say-nations-top-jurists/#.UgWXnB0_bkY.twitter.

[727] *See supra* note 350 (listing states where most copyright cases are filed).

[728] *See supra* note 28 (providing statistics on copyright claims as a percentage of all federal civil claims). Indeed, other categories of claims arising under federal law – some of which result in more filings than copyright cases – might also benefit from a federal small claims court. *See, e.g.*, ADMINISTRATIVE OFFICE OF THE UNITED STATES COURTS, STATISTICAL TABLES FOR THE FEDERAL JUDICIARY: DEC. 2012, TABLE C-2, CIVIL CASES COMMENCED, BY BASIS OF JURISDICTION AND NATURE OF SUIT, DURING THE 12-MONTH PERIODS ENDING DECEMBER 31, 2011 AND 2012, *available at* http://www.uscourts.gov/uscourts/Statistics/StatisticalTablesForTheFederalJudiciary/2012/d ecember/C02Dec12.pdf (citing some of the more common federal court cases as involving prisoner petitions (54,402 or 20% of the total caseload), civil rights (37,391 or 13.9%), personal injury/product liability (33,851 or 12.6%), contract actions (28,252 or 10.5%), labor laws (18,629 or 6.9%), or social security laws (18,261 or 6.8%)).

[729] *See, e.g.*, APA First Notice Comments at 4 ("Consenting parties can have their positions quickly evaluated by a Magistrate Judge sitting in the appropriate United States District Court in which the case is pending."); NPPA Second Notice Comments at 4 ("Properly trained magistrates or staff attorneys could also be used effectively depending on their existing caseloads.").

[730] *See supra* Part III.C.4 (discussing magistrate judges generally) *and* Part IV.B.3 (discussing the Federal Magistrates Act).

[731] Another idea to improve access to federal courts that was raised but only briefly discussed would be to further empower organizations such as trade associations to litigate groups of smaller claims on behalf of their members. Because an association can aggregate hundreds or thousands of individual infringement claims, such cases are not "small" – either in procedural or economic terms – and therefore may be better suited to full-scale litigation in federal court. For example, the Independent Film & Television Alliance ("IFTA") urged that associations be allowed to act as "channeling associations" to pursue claims on behalf of a number of copyright owners. IFTA, Comments Submitted in Response to Second Notice of Inquiry at 5 (Oct. 19, 2012) ("IFTA Second Notice Comments"). The NPPA similarly supported the idea of allowing groups of copyright owners (either alone or through an association) to bring claims against multiple alleged infringers in one proceeding. NPPA Second Notice Comments at 13.

The propriety of associational standing in copyright cases owners currently is under review in the federal courts, and recent cases have yielded mixed results. As a general matter, the Supreme Court has held that "an association has standing to bring suit on behalf of its members when: (a) its members would otherwise have standing to sue in their own right; (b) the interests it seeks to protect are germane to the organization's purpose; and (c) neither the claim asserted nor the relief requested requires the participation of individual members in the lawsuit." *Hunt v. Wash. State Apple Adver. Com'n*, 432 U.S. 333, 343 (1977) (summarizing *Warth v. Seldin*, 422 U.S. 490, 511 (1975)). In the copyright context, associations have tended to limit their claims to injunctive relief, which does not require individualized proof of damages. *See, e.g.*, *Authors Guild v. Google, Inc.*, 282 F.R.D. 384 (S.D.N.Y. 2012) (organization suit seeking injunctive and declaratory relief for copyright infringement on behalf of individual members); *Author's Guild, Inc. v. Hathitrust*, 902 F. Supp. 2d 445 (S.D.N.Y. 2012) (same). But because ownership of a copyright is an element of an infringement claim under the Copyright Act, *see* 17 U.S.C. § 501(b), courts have diverged on the question of whether an association can seek to enforce its members' copyrights. *Compare Authors Guild v. Google*, 282 F.R.D. at 389, *vacated on other grounds and remanded*, 721 F.3d 132 (2d Cir. 2013) (in case involving mass digitization of copyrighted works, court upheld associational standing on ground that "the associations' claims of copyright infringement and requests for injunctive relief will not require the participation of each individual association member"), *with Authors Guild, Inc. v. Hathitrust*, 902 F. Supp. 2d at 452-54 (in another case involving mass digitization of copyrighted works, associational standing denied based on standing requirements of Copyright Act, which indicated to the court that "Congress did not intend for associations to enforce the rights of their members").

Separate and apart from an alternative small claims process, Congress may wish to consider amending the Copyright Act to clarify the nature and scope of copyright claims that associations may bring on behalf of their members. While such an amendment could be beneficial to many individual copyright owners, however, the Office does not view the possibility of associational standing as a satisfying answer to the problem of small copyright claims generally, if for no other reason than that many individual copyright owners do not belong to an association, and even if they do, the association may lack the resources or will to pursue litigation.

[732] 28 U.S.C. § 1338(a).

[733] *See* ASMP, Comments Submitted in Response to Second Notice of Inquiry at 5 (Oct. 16, 2012) ("ASMP Second Notice Comments"); Atkinson & Atkinson, Comments Submitted in Response to First Notice of Inquiry at 3; *see also* Tr. at 17:11-18 (Nov. 15, 2012) (Victor Perlman, ASMP) (noting that the "primary reasons" for ASMP's support of state court jurisdiction is that it would not require "significant congressional involvement and approval and funding.").

[734] ABA IP Section Second Notice Comments at 9 (noting lack of state court experience in copyright claims); AIPLA, Comments Submitted in Response to First Notice of Inquiry at 2 (Jan. 16, 2012) ("State courts ... lack expertise in adjudicating copyright matters, and state small claims courts have no experience whatsoever."); Authors Guild First Notice Comments at 4 ("Avoid delegating these proceedings to inexperienced state courts"); Google Inc., Comments Submitted in Response to First Notice of Inquiry at 2-3 (Jan. 17, 2012) ("Google First Notice Comments") (noting state court's inexperience with copyright claims); GAG First Notice Comments at 8 ("State court judges don't have extensive knowledge of copyright law or experience with copyright infringement cases."); PACA, Comments Submitted in Response to First Notice of Inquiry at 10 (Jan. 16, 2012) ("PACA First Notice Comments") (noting that the "amount of damages in a local small claims court is extremely limited," the lack of copyright expertise in state courts, and the concern that decisions would be inconsistent and arbitrary); SGA & NSAI First Notice Comments at 2 (agreeing that state courts do not have the necessary experience); APA, Comments Submitted in Response to Second Notice of Inquiry at 7 (Oct. 16, 2012) ("APA Second Notice Comments") ("APA does not believe a small infringement claims system should leave the federal court system and therefore does not believe a state court or a traditional small claims court should be incorporated."); Getty Images, Comments Submitted in Response to Second Notice of Inquiry at 6 (Oct. 19, 2012) ("Getty Images Second Notice Comments") ("Pursuing small claims through state court is not an adequate solution, in part due to jurisdictional issues."); NPPA Second Notice Comments at 15 ("[S]tate courts – especially small claims courts – don't have the resources to thoroughly research complex copyright issues. The end result could lead to conflicting decisions on important copyright issues. A copyright tribunal should have the required expertise and thus be able create appropriate and consistent caselaw."); Tr. at 67:15-68:16 (Nov. 15, 2012) (David Leichtman, VLA) (noting the low ceiling for monetary relief, unavailability of injunctive relief, and lack of expertise in state courts).

[735] ABA IP Section Second Notice Comments at 9 ("As federal courts have exclusive jurisdiction over copyright issues, the state courts have not had the opportunity to develop sufficient expertise to handle these cases."); Getty Images Second Notice Comments at 6 ("[S]tate courts do not have historical experience or expertise in copyright law").

[736] Illustrators' Partnership, Comments Submitted in Response to First Notice of Inquiry at 1 (Jan. 17, 2012) ("Illustrators' Partnership First Notice Comments") ("Copyright is a federal law and a small claims court would have to be administered on a local level. That means a) it's unlikely that local judges would have the expertise to properly administer the complexities of copyright law; and b) this would inevitably lead to hundreds or thousands of contradictory rulings, all constituting different interpretations of the same federal law."); IFTA, Comments Submitted in Response to First Notice of Inquiry at 4 (Jan. 17, 2012) ("IFTA First Notice Comments") ("copyright law is more complex than the types of cases on the docket of small claims courts"); New Media Rights First Notice Comments at 18 (noting that copyright law is "notoriously complex" and that "[w]hile the state small claims courts are well experienced in dealing with small disputes, they usually deal with contract and tort law which have clearer established doctrines and are easier to simplify into matters of equity.").

[737] It should be noted, however, that federal expertise in copyright law does not extend to every district. *See* LEX MACHINA, https://lexmachina.com/ (last visited May 30, 2013) (some federal districts hear very few copyright cases a year; for example, from 2000 to 2012, the Eastern District of Oklahoma averaged one copyright case a year, the District of Wyoming averaged 1.2 cases, and the District of Vermont averaged 2.8 cases).

[738] Tr. at 67:20-23 (Nov. 15, 2012) (David Leichtman, VLA).

[739] *See* Appendix D, at col. Attorney Representation.

[740] *See id.* at col. Jury Trials.

[741] *See id.* at col. Equitable Relief.

[742] *See, e.g.*, NWU First Notice Comments at 13 (noting that standard state court proceeding is "much more expensive").

[743] As noted above, the Supreme Court's jurisprudence concerning the constitutionality of non-Article III courts has shifted over time and undoubtedly will continue to evolve. *See supra* Part IV.B. A bankruptcy case currently pending before the Court, *Executive Benefits Insurance Agency v. Arkison*, 702 F.3d 553 (9th Cir. 2012), *cert*

granted, 81 U.S.L.W. 3702 (U.S. Jun. 24, 2013) (No. 12-1200), which concerns litigants' ability to consent to a non-Article III forum, could impact Congress's analysis of a voluntary alternative tribunal such as the one proposed here.

744 As discussed above, it is clear that litigants can waive both their personal right to a jury trial under the Seventh Amendment and to adjudication of a claim by an Article III court. *See supra* Part IV.A. At the same time, administrative tribunals must be appropriately limited in their jurisdiction and functions to avoid structural separation of powers issues under Article III, which are not personal in nature and cannot be waived. *See supra* Part IV.B.

745 Of course, as suggested above, Congress may wish to keep an eye on the *Executive Benefits Insurance Agency* case currently pending before the Supreme Court, as the Court's opinion may provide additional direction concerning the parameters of constitutionally valid consent to proceed before a non-Article III tribunal. *See supra* Part IV.B.4.

746 Tr. at 204:13-206:01 (Nov, 26, 2012) (Carolyn Wright, Law Offices of Carolyn E. Wright) (attorney who represents smaller photographer clients discussed use of Rule 4 and voiced a preference for a similar procedure in a small claims court).

747 Tr. at 143:24-144:02 (Nov. 15, 2012) (Randy Taylor, CDL) ("The vast majority of the infringers ignore the demand letters that are sent by the attorneys"); Tr. at 296:19-297:05 (Nov. 26, 2012) (Edward Hasbrouck, NWU) ("A common experience for us at the National Writers Union in working with our members who have grievances is that the infringer won't even talk to the victim, won't respond to attempts to negotiate or discuss the infringement. And they can do that now because they are confident that the infringer is impotent to sue because they aren't rich enough to sue. So they can with some confidence just literally ignore them."); Tr. at 300:13-17 (Nov. 26, 2012) (Michael Grecco, APA) ("I think the reality is no one takes you seriously until you file [a lawsuit]. … Every defendant I know in my own copyright cases are like 'Whatever.'").

748 Tr. at 360:25-361:07 (Nov. 16, 2012) (David Leichtman, VLA) ("[I]f the goal were to be to develop a body of default judgments for this tribunal . . . you would have to make it a mandatory process, but allow for an opt-out").

749 FED. R. CIV. P. 55(b).

750 FED. R. CIV. P. 55.

751 28 U.S.C. § 1446(b)(1) ("The notice of removal of a civil action or proceeding shall be filed within 30 days after the receipt by the defendant, through service or otherwise, of a copy of the initial pleading setting forth the claim for relief upon which such action or proceeding is based, or within 30 days after the service of summons upon the defendant if such initial pleading has then been filed in court and is not required to be served on the defendant, whichever period is shorter.").

752 ABA IP Section Second Notice Comments at 2 ("Parties could mutually elect or the Copyright Office may assign an adjudicator from a roster of experts in copyright law, one who is knowledgeable about the types of works in question."); AVA, Comments Submitted in Response to Second Notice of Inquiry at 4 (Oct. 19, 2012) ("The tribunal should be composed of individuals who are knowledgeable in this highly specialized area of the law and also have familiarity of the industry from which the claim results."); Getty Images Second Notice Comments at 3 ("the adjudicators could be administrative law judges or attorneys with specialized training and/or experience in copyright law"); IFTA Second Notice Comments at 3 (the judges should be a "panel of experts in copyright law"); NPPA Second Notice Comments at 4 ("The adjudicators should be attorneys well-versed in copyright law."); ASMP, Comments Submitted in Response to Third Notice of Inquiry at 3 (Apr. 10, 2012) ("ASMP Third Notice Comments") (any adjudicator is "ideally… knowledgeable about copyright"); VLA Third Notice Comments at 2 ("VLA envisions regional administrative panels of attorneys with copyright expertise… administered by the Copyright Office."); Tr. at 25:19-26:08 (Nov. 26, 2012) (Edward Hasbrouck, NWU).

753 Tr. at 51:10 (Nov. 15, 2012) (Jay Rosenthal, NMPA) (referring to music copyright issues)

754 Tr. at 97:08-11 (Nov. 26, 2012) (Michael Traynor, Cobalt LLP) (referring to fair use); *see also* 4 WEST'S FED. ADMIN. PRAC. § 4001 ("Current United States copyright law is quite complex, and the general practitioner has in essence two choices when confronted with all but the most basic and straight forward of copyright problems. He can seek help from competent copyright counsel at the outset, or he can plan to devote a substantial number of hours to reading through the 1976 Act, relevant portions of its legislative history, and cases interpreting the statutory provisions so that an understanding of the various sections of the Act and their interrelation is obtained. Any lesser effort exposes the practitioner to a minefield of hidden problems, and potentially exposes the client either to a loss of rights or to liability.").

755 Tr. at 24:15-21 (Nov. 26, 2012) (Timothy Cohan, Peermusic).

756 Tr. at 145:19-146:05 (Nov. 27, 2012) (Alicia Calzada, NPPA) ("If we have *pro se* plaintiffs, or maybe even *pro se* defendants, and there are these complicated questions about fair use and other issues, you really need a panel – one of the roles of attorneys is to educate the judges on the law. And if we don't have attorneys educating judges on the law, I think [the judges] need to be well versed [in copyright law].").

757 This approach is similar to the CRB, which requires the separate judges to have experience in copyright law, economics, or adjudications, arbitrations, or court trials. 17 U.S.C. § 802(a). Similarly, panelists in UDRP

proceedings usually have lengthy experience in intellectual property and related areas, rendering their somewhat brief review of sparse records more fruitful. For example, WIPO states that its panelists "come from different regions of the world and are well-reputed for their impartiality, sound judgment and experience as decision-makers, as well as their substantive experience in the areas of intellectual property law, electronic commerce and the Internet." WIPO Arbitration and Mediation Center, *WIPO Domain Name Panelists*, http://www.wipo.int/amc/en/domains/panel html.

[758] *See supra* at Part IV.D.

[759] Tr. at 126:10-20 (Nov. 26, 2012) (Alma Robinson, CLA); Tr. at 131:10-15 (Nov. 26, 2012) (George Clinton, musician) (raising possibility of Copyright Office-appointed attorney); Tr. at 41:02-43:04 (Nov. 27, 2012) (Art Neill, New Media Rights) (describing benefits of FLASH system).

[760] *See* N.D. Cal., *FLASH*, http://www.cand.uscourts.gov/helpcentersj; *see also* S.D.N.Y., *Role of the Pro Se Office*, http://www nysd.uscourts.gov/courtrules_prose.php?prose=office; DONNA STIENSTRA, ET AL., FED. JUDICIAL CTR, ASSISTANCE TO PRO SE LITIGANTS IN U.S. DISTRICT COURTS: A REPORT ON SURVEYS OF CLERKS OF COURT AND CHIEF JUDGES (2011), *available at* http://www.fjc.gov/public/pdf.nsf/lookup/proseusdc.pdf/ $file/proseusdc.pdf.

[761] *See* Federal Judicial Center, "*Who Does What, Chambers Staff: Judge's Law Clerk and Judicial Assistant,* http://wwwfjc.gov/federal/courts nsf/autoframe?OpenForm&nav=menu5b&page=/federal/courts nsf/page/ 351? open document ("Although the specific duties of judicial staff vary from judge to judge, the law clerks' duties usually include conducting legal research; preparing memoranda (including bench memos, which appellate judges use during oral argument); preparing draft orders and opinions; proofreading the judges' orders and opinions; and verifying citations.").

[762] *See, e.g.*, Authors Guild First Notice Comments at 4 ("The procedures, to the extent permissible within the requirements of due process, should be conducted by mail and telephone conference. Small copyright infringement claims can generally be adjudicated largely on documentary evidence – a submission of the plaintiffs [sic] registered work and the alleged infringing work. Such procedures will allow parties to press and defend claims without traveling to the court."); ABA IP Section Second Notice Comments at 3 (suggesting a process using electronically submitted documents, similar to the UDRP).

[763] *See* AVA Second Notice Comments at 6-7 (suggesting use of "e-mail, teleconference, fax, online videoconference platforms, or other virtual discussion forum"); Tr. at 204:03-08 (Nov. 15, 2012) (David Leichtman, VLA) (hearings should be available on a remote basis).

[764] Authors Guild First Notice Comments at 4 (linking a small copyright claims court to the Copyright Office "would help assure the competence of the court"); GAG First Notice Comments at 8 ("We would like to see this [proposed] system kept close to the Copyright Office."); SGA & NSAI First Notice comments at 2 ("[A] small claims court affiliated with the Copyright Office would be the best alternative."); ZipCourt, Comments Submitted in Response to First Notice of Inquiry at 6 (Jan. 17, 2012) ("ZipCourt First Notice Comments") ("[A] new online copyright adjudication system] would welcome an association with the Office to assure competencies in terms of quality control, user experience, and low cost.").

[765] PACA First Notice Comments at 10 (considering a new forum of decisionmakers or expanding the role of the CRB); ASMP Second Notice Comments at 6 (considering the possibility of the CRB or an entity similar to the CRB); IFTA Second Notice Comments at 4 (suggesting using the CRB as a model).

[766] APA First Notice Comments at 16 (where a complaint or counterclaim alleges something other than copyright infringement, the case "fails to qualify as an eligible small infringement claim"); IFTA Second Notice Comments at 6 ("The proposed administrative agency should be available to all copyrighted works, but limited to infringement claims …."); Association of Am. Publishers ("AAP"), Comments Submitted in Response to Third Notice of Inquiry at 2-3 (Apr. 12, 2013) ("AAP Third Notice Comments") (though suggesting contract and licensing analysis should be retained as a defense to infringement); PACA, Comments Submitted in Response to Third Notice of Inquiry at 3 (Apr. 12, 2013) ("PACA Third Notice Comments") (though suggesting ownership claims could fall within the scope of a small claims court for the purposes of determining whether a work was a work for hire).

[767] AVA Second Notice Comments at 4 (favor including violations of a license or similar contractual matters); GAG Second Notice Comments at 6 (favor including claims covering trademark infringement, contractual issues, ownership, and material misrepresentations in violation of the DMCA); NPPA Second Notice Comments at 4 (favor including contractual and DMCA claims).

[768] Google First Notice Comments at 7; James Cannings, Comments Submitted in Response to Second Notice of Inquiry at 2 ("Cannings Second Notice Comments"); GAG Second Notice Comments at 6; IFTA Second Notice Comments at 5; NPPA Second Notice Comments at 4; VLA Third Notice Comments at 5, n.2.

[769] Tr. at 92:22-94:04 (Nov. 26, 2012) (Carolyn Wright, Law Offices of Carolyn E. Wright).

[770] Commenting parties agreed that DMCA issues should not be overlooked in considering the problem of small copyright claims. *See, e.g.*, Google First Notice Comments at 7 ("An infringement action is not the only species of action under the Copyright Act that is deterred in practice by high litigation costs. If the Office is concerned that the cost of litigation is preventing people from vindicating their rights under the Act, then the small claims court should also hear actions under Section 512(f)."); GAG First Notice Comments at 4 ("In

some instances the ISP or host does not respond to or comply with a DMCA take-down notice, or allows the image to be reposted again later."); Eman Hegazy, Comments Submitted in Response to Second Notice of Inquiry at 1 (relating a story where in response to a DMCA takedown notice, a competitor issued allegedly fraudulent takedown notices against the author).

[771] The evidence that was received noted that secondary liability can bring an additional level of complexity to a small copyright claim. *See* Google First Notice Comments at 5 (suggesting that the judicial standards for secondary liability are too vague); PACA Third Notice Comments at 4 (suggesting that these claims are complicated, and that they could be added depending on how well a new system of litigating direct infringement works).

[772] Many stakeholders agreed with this concept, especially in a voluntary system that would require a defendant's consent. *See, e.g.*, ASMP Second Notice Comments at 7 ("All traditional defenses, such as fair use, should be permitted. Similarly, a defense based on a DMCA safe harbor argument would have to be allowed in order to avoid eviscerating the DMCA."); Cannings Second Notice Comments at 3 ("All defenses available to large claims must be allowed to small claims. Due Process must be the rule. In essence the Constitutional right of small claims must in no way be compromised."); Rochelle Dreyfuss, Comments Submitted in Response to Second Notice of Inquiry at 3 ("I believe any defense that could be asserted in district court should be available in this court. There is a strong possibility that the existence of this court will give right holders new opportunities to harass individuals. Disallowing important defenses would make this problem even more severe."); Getty Images Second Notice Comments at 3 ("The defendant should have an opportunity to present its defenses, including fair use, independent creation, non-infringement or any other statutory exception (including DMCA safe harbor)."); NPPA Second Notice Comments at 6 ("NPPA proposes that defendants compelled to participate in small claims court would be entitled to assert all defenses and counterclaims including fair use, independent creation or those claims arising under the DMCA."); PACA Second Notice Comments at 5 ("The respondent should have the opportunity to present its defenses, such as fair use, independent creation, non-infringement or any other statutory exception.").

[773] Google First Notice Comments at 4; NMPA, ASCAP, & SESAC, Comments Submitted in Response to First Notice of Inquiry at 2 ("NMPA, ASCAP, & SESAC First Notice Comments") ("We have great concern about litigating fair use defenses in a small claims court setting."); SGA & NSAI First Notice Comments at 3 (cases with "credible and substantial" fair use arguments should be removed to federal court); AAP, Comment Submitted in Response to Second Notice of Inquiry at 5 ("AAP Second Notice Comments") ("AAP is opposed to allowing … potentially complex defenses such as fair use to be raised in small claims proceedings.").

[774] Tr. at 168:14-17 (Nov. 15, 2012) (Eugene Mopsik, ASMP); *see also* Tr. at 164:11-17 (Nov. 15, 2012) (Nancy Wolff, PACA) ("So I don't think I have ever had a case where someone hasn't at least put in a defense of fair use, whether it could be legitimate or not. So I think that that should not be sort of a threshold to avoid an alternative resolution procedure that could be in place.").

[775] Tr. at 161:18-21 (Nov. 15, 2012) (David Leichtman, VLA). Other stakeholders made similar statements. *See, e.g.*, Tr. at 168:04-10 (Nov. 15, 2012) (Lisa Shaftel, GAG) ("[W]e realize that we don't think the defenses should be limited because otherwise the defendants would be able to opt out of the alternative copyright court in a substantial number of cases, and that would just weaken the effectiveness of the alternative court.").

[776] Tr. at 162:09-12 (Nov. 15, 2012) (David Leichtman, VLA).

[777] Although there was no unanimity, a number of participants were of the view that respondents should be able to bring counterclaims. *See* ABA IP Section Second Notice Comments at 8 ("Counterclaims should be permitted, but should not be compulsory, especially if they exceed the jurisdictional limit."); NPPA Second Notice Comments at 6 ("NPPA proposes that defendants compelled to participate in small claims court would be entitled to assert all defenses and counterclaims including fair use, independent creation or those claims arising under the DMCA.").

[778] *See, e.g.*, 37 C.F.R. §§ 2.106(b)(2)(i) & 2.114(b)(2)(i) (defense attacking the validity of certain registrations pleaded in the opposition (§ 2.106(b)(2)(i)) or petition for cancellation (§ 2.114(b)(2)(i)) is considered a compulsory counterclaim).

[779] *See* Tr. at 143:11-151:08 (Nov. 26, 2012) (various participants) (discussing that while voluntary counterclaims pose less of a problem as they can be preserved for a trial in federal court, mandatory counterclaims that are over the monetary limit of the small claims court pose a tension as the small claims forum may not be suited to best handle these larger claims).

[780] 17 U.S.C. § 411(a). This requirement applies only to United States works. Timely registration is, however, required for *all* works if the copyright owner wants to seek statutory damages, attorneys' fees, and/or costs. 17 U.S.C. § 412.

[781] *See, e.g.*, NPPA First Notice Comments at 8 ("Legal proceedings should be available to copyright holders regardless of when they registered their work. Registration as a prerequisite to bringing a claim is acceptable, but there should be no limits to a claim based on when that registration occurred.").

[782] ASMP First Notice Comments at 5 ("[O]ne of the impediments to professional photographers' access to the current copyright enforcement system is the requirement of copyright registration before litigation can be instituted (and earlier, for eligibility for an award of attorney fees and/or statutory damages)."); *see also* GAG

First Notice Comments at 4 ("Most visual works are not registered, and most of the business sector is aware of this."); Tr. at 41:02-04 (Nov. 15, 2012) (Nancy Wolff, PACA) ("When you have large amounts of images, it is difficult to register, particularly when you have the published versus unpublished."). *Cf.* Tr. at 186:21-187:03 (Nov. 15, 2012) (Mickey Osterreicher, NPPA) ("[P]hotographers are probably the worst at registering their works. And I would extend that to say that news photographers are probably the worst of all of the photographers just because the nature of their business in terms of they barely have time to bill in terms of operating the small business.").

[783] APA First Notice Comments at 25 ("[T]he ideal solution to the issue of small claims would dispense with the registration requirement [as a prerequisite to bring an infringement lawsuit]."); NWU First Notice Comments at 12 ("[T]he requirement for registration of copyright is entirely unnecessary and should be abolished. [The registration requirement] creates a perverse disincentive for first publication in the U.S. ...."); Tr. at 155:08-157:22 (Nov. 26, 2012) (Edward Hasbrouck, NWU) (summarizing various problems with the registration requirement); Tr. at 158:07-09 (Nov. 26, 2012) (Lorin Brennan, Linde Law Firm) ("[The registration requirement is] primarily a way to ... generate fees and waste time.").

[784] GAG First Notice Comments at 7 ("To ensure timely access to the ACC, we recommend that U.S. plaintiffs/rights holders be eligible to file their claims as soon as they have submitted application for copyright registration, as is the practice in many jurisdictions in federal court, rather than requiring them to have an issued copyright registration before filing. (Foreign authors would be exempt under Berne). There would be no prior registration or timely registration bars to obtaining ACC statutory damages."); Tr. at 184:04-09 (Nov. 15, 2012) (Victor Perlman, ASMP) ("So how you cut that Gordian Knot, is to do what some of the federal circuits currently do, which is to accept as the equivalent of a registration, proof of the filing of a petition for registration. And that seems, to me, to be a reasonable compromise.").

[785] *See Apple Barrel Prods., Inc. v. R.D. Beard*, 730 F.2d 384, 386–87 (5th Cir.1984) ("In order to bring suit for copyright infringement, it is not necessary to prove possession of a registration certificate. One need only prove payment of the required fee, deposit of the work in question, and receipt by the Copyright Office of a registration application."); *see also Chi. Bd. of Educ. v. Substance, Inc.*, 354 F.3d 624, 631 (7th Cir. 2003) (Posner, J.) (describing an argument that only an application had been filed, and there was thus no registration, as being "frivolous"). The Office is *not* suggesting that the mere filing of an application be sufficient for existing federal court litigation, which is much more formal than the small claims system envisioned in this Report.

[786] Cannings Second Notice Comments at 2.

[787] APA First Notice Comments at 4.

[788] ABA IP Section Second Notice Comments at 8; ASMP Second Notice Comments at 7; Getty Images Second Notice Comments at 3 ("$30,000 at the most"); Kernochan Second Notice Comments at 4; GAG Second Notice Comments at 6-7; MPAA Third Notice Comments at 3; NPPA Second Notice Comments at 5.

[789] Tr. at 36:05-09 (Nov. 15, 2012) (Charles Sanders, SGA).

[790] ABA IP Section Second Notice Comments at 7. The same evidence indicated, however, that some cases being tried resolved for between $50,000 and $100,000. *Id.* at 7-8.

[791] 17 U.S.C. § 504(a).

[792] *Id.* § 504(c).

[793] *See* Public Knowledge, Electronic Frontier Foundation, & Future of Music Coalition, Comments Submitted in Response to U.S. Copyright Office's Oct. 27, 2011 Notice of Inquiry at 7 ("Exposing defendants to [possibility of punitive and excessive statutory damages awards] in an abbreviated proceeding is likely to jeopardize their due process rights."); AAP Second Notice Comments at 7 (removing statutory damages offers a "powerful incentive for potential defendants to work within the system instead of opting for transfer to federal court.").

[794] *See Sony BMG Music Entm't v. Tenenbaum*, 719 F.3d 67, 71 (1st Cir. 2013) ("[Defendant] Tenenbaum argues that the award of $675,000 [for copyright infringement of thirty songs] violates due process because it is not tied to the actual injury that he caused, which he estimates to be no more than $450, or the cost of 30 albums at $15 each. But this argument asks us to disregard the deterrent effect of statutory damages, the inherent difficulty in proving damages in a copyright suit, and [plaintiff] Sony's evidence of the harm that it suffered from conduct such as Tenenbaum's."); *Capitol Records v. Thomas-Rasset*, 692 F.3d 899, 908 (8th Cir. 2012) ("Congress no doubt was aware of the serious problem posed by online copyright infringement, and the 'numberless opportunities for committing the offense,' when it last revisited the Copyright Act in 1999. To provide a deterrent against such infringement, Congress amended § 504(c) to increase [statutory damages]."). *But see* Pamela Samuelson & Tara Wheatland, *Statutory Damages in Copyright Law: A Remedy in Need of Reform*, 51 WM. MARY L. REV. 439, 495-96 (2009) ("Excessive copyright statutory damage awards are...likely to have other negative spillover effects, such as chilling lawful...uses of copyrighted works, especially those that would promote...the development of innovative new technologies and services.").

[795] Tr. at 151:23-152:22 (Nov. 15, 2012) (David Leichtman, VLA); Tr. at 262:08-15 (Nov. 16, 2012) (Rachel Fertig, AAP).

[796] Tr. at 144:03-09 (Nov. 15, 2012) (Randy Taylor, CDL) ("[T]he statutory damage [award] is the primary tool by which the infringer is likely settled. So if statutory damages are limited or removed from any type of alternative process, the effectiveness is going to be dramatically reduced.").

[797] Tr. at 254:09-22 (Nov. 16, 2012) (Nancy Wolff, PACA); Tr. at 256:14-257:04 (Nov. 16, 2012) (Victor Perlman, ASMP).

[798] *See* Tr. at 229:22-230:3 (Nov. 26, 2012) (Edward Hasbrouck, NWU) (noting that statutory damages are relatively simple, and without statutory damages, more discovery is needed); Tr. at 144:22-23 (Nov. 15, 2012) (Randy Taylor, CDL) (asserting that the only reason infringers respond to demand letters is the threat of statutory damages).

[799] Claimants with timely registrations who wished to seek higher amounts of statutory damages would, of course, continue to have the option of proceeding in federal court.

[800] VLA Third Notice Comments at 17 ("VLA sees no reason to eliminate an innocent infringer defense because it would fall well below the cap proposed and would remove an incentive for defendants who might assert such defense.").

[801] Tr. at 189:22-190:20 (Nov. 26, 2012) (Lorin Brennan, Linde Law Firm) (noting that including a finding of willfulness requires submitting evidence of willfulness and that involves discovery and disclosure by the defendant, all of which can be too cumbersome for a small claims tribunal).

[802] PACA Third Notice Comments at 5.

[803] 17 U.S.C. § 502.

[804] *Id.* § 503.

[805] Tr. at 31:12-18 (Nov. 15, 2012) (David Leichtman, VLA); *see also* Tr. at 284:19-24 (Nov. 16, 2012) (David Leichtman, VLA) ("But I think from the standpoint of indigent artists, the injunctive relief is absolutely critical. And what we see more often than not is folks that come in to our offices who really just want their stuff back, or taken down, or the infringement to stop."); Tr. at 59:21-60:01 (Nov. 27, 2012) (Molly Knappen, designer and developer) ("If you take injunctions out of the equation for the true small claims, you take the teeth out of it."); Tr. at 49:05-06 (Nov. 27, 2012) (Edward Hasbrouck, NWU) ("Injunctive relief is vital for our members ....").

[806] Tr. at 49:05-16 (Nov. 27, 2012) (Edward Hasbrouck, NWU).

[807] *eBay Inc. v. MercExchange, L.L.C.*, 547 U.S. 388, 391-92 (2006) (though this case involved patents, the Court noted the same standard applies to copyright cases).

[808] *See, e.g.*, *Salinger v. Colting*, 607 F.3d 68 (2d Cir. 2010) (holding that *eBay* injunction test "applies with equal force to preliminary injunctions issued on the basis of alleged copyright infringement").

[809] Google First Notice Comments at 6 ("In District Court, an injunction can only be obtained after a rigorous evidentiary showing, but a small claims court will not have the ability to collect or hear such extensive evidence."); Tr. at 58:13-19 (Nov. 27, 2012) (Lorin Brennan, Linde Law Firm) ("[T]o have small claims courts issuing preliminary injunctions ... you are probably going to want to have only an injunction after you have had the mini trial where you could have all of the evidence presented that justifies the injunction. And that is a substantial showing here.").

[810] *See, e.g.*, PACA First Notice Comments at 7 ("An injunction to prevent the continued infringement or to enforce the removal of content online may be appropriate if a work is not so incorporated within another creative work that it would cause disproportionate economic harm to a work containing the infringing was enjoined. For example if the infringing work is merely displayed on a website, in addition to damages, it would be appropriate to enjoin continued use of the infringing work by the defendant, to avoid multiple claims for the same use by a plaintiff against the same party.").

[811] Tr. at 295:11-16 (Nov. 16, 2012) (Nancy Wolff, PACA) ("[I]f images are displayed on a web site, there really wouldn't be any harm to make sure it wasn't continued. But, for example, if there was one image that was in a documentary film, it may cause a lot of harm to have someone redo an entire documentary film."); Tr. at 56:15 57:01 (Nov. 27, 2012) (Lorin Brennan, Linde Law Firm) (raising the example of the monetary damages of enjoining the release of a motion picture exceeding the small claims forum limits).

[812] *See* Tr. at 51:15-18 (Nov. 27, 2012) (Kim Tommaselli, IFTA) (". . . to get an injunction to halt the production or distribution of a film would cause great financial stress on that company through such a small claims procedure").

[813] FED. R. CIV. P. 65 (granting federal courts the authority to enforce injunctions); *see Grupo Mexicano de Desarrollo S.A. v. Alliance Bond Fund, Inc.*, 527 U.S. 308, 318 (1999) ("The Judiciary Act of 1789 conferred on the federal courts jurisdiction over 'all suits ... in equity.'").

[814] VLA Third Notice Comments at 16 ("[*D*]*e novo* review [of an injunction by a district court] would defeat the purpose of the Small Claims Tribunal in the first place."); Tr. at 338:18-339:17 (Nov. 16, 2012) (Rachel Fertig, AAP) (explaining that if injunctions were allowed in this system with an appeal to district court, this would increase the probability of appeals and would create a problem that we are trying to avoid in the first place).

[815] 17 U.S.C. § 505.

[816] *See supra* at Part III.

[817] *See, e.g.*, *Garcia-Goyco v. Law Envtl. Consultants, Inc.*, 428 F.3d 14 (1st Cir. 2005) (upholding award of attorneys' fees to prevailing defendant); Tr. at 285:09-289:13 (Nov. 16, 2012) (David Leichtman, VLA).

[818] *See, e.g.*, *Thoroughbred Software Int'l, Inc. v. Dice Corp.*, 529 f. supp. 2d 800, 803 (E.D. Mich. 2007) (refusing to award attorneys' fees to plaintiffs because defendant's "position at trial was not frivolous and was objectively reasonable," they did not "act with an improper motivation," and did not profit from their activities, among other things).

[819] Tr. at 318:19-321:12 (Nov. 16, 2012) (Bruce Lehman, Former Asst. Sec'y of Commerce and Comm'r of Patents & Trademarks) (discussing importance of incentivizing lawyers to represent clients in a small copyright claims proceeding).

[820] *See* Tr. at 310:01-12 (Nov. 16, 2012) (Victor Perlman, ASMP) ("[M]y concern is that you may have a corporate defendant who's running up a significant legal bill. And I guess the way to deal with that situation is to use a sort of system that [has] attorneys' fees, but to cap the fees at some level so that, for instance, a photographer or an artist isn't faced with the prospect of a five figure award or more, legal bills being assessed against him if he loses."); Tr. at 311:09-12 (Nov. 16, 2012) (Mickey Osterreicher, NPPA) (suggesting a cap on attorneys' fees "[s]o you don't have a corporate defendant coming in and having a fee request that dwarfs what's looked for in terms of any recovery").

[821] *See* Tr. at 151:03-152:22 (Nov. 15, 2012) (David Leichtman, VLA) (noting that system would have to "mak[e] sense financially from the standpoint of the defense side" and proposing damages cap with no attorneys' fees); Tr. at 62:04-07 (Nov. 15, 2012); (Lisa Willmer, Getty Images) (defendants could be incentivized to submit to voluntary process by limiting attorneys' fees); *see also* Tr. at 150:09-13 (Nov. 15, 2012) (Nancy Wolff, PACA) ("[O]nce the attorneys' fees have to get factored in the amount, … there's always going to be a lot of work, and then the settlement amount and demands become much higher.").

[822] Tr. at 288:21-289:13 (Nov. 16, 2012) (David Leichtman, VLA) ("And we have lots of clients in these kinds of situations where you have a close case, where there may be a fair use defense. And, you know, as a lawyer advising the client, you have no idea how that's going to come out, and yet you have to say to the client, 'I can bring your case in federal court for you, we have a 55 percent, 75 percent chance of winning the case, but what I have to tell you is, you are at risk. You know, you are not even asking for money, you are just looking for an injunction to get the infringement to stop, but you are at risk of – you don't have to pay my fees because I am the pro bono lawyer, but you are at risk of having to pay the other side's attorneys' fees.'").

[823] Tr. at 309:04-11 (Nov. 16, 2012) (Charles Sanders, SGA).

[824] Comments submitted by APA suggested a rather novel fee-shifting system. To incentivize settlement, parties would be required to exchange offers of judgment before trial. If the plaintiff won at trial and were awarded more than his or her demand, the plaintiff would receive attorneys' fees. But if the plaintiff, even though prevailing, were awarded less than what the defendant had offered, the plaintiff would be required to pay attorneys' fees to the defendant. Conversely, a defendant who offered less than what the plaintiff received would be assessed fees. APA First Notice Comments at 6-7 (comments submitted by David Nimmer on behalf of the APA). As suggested above, such a system could yield a rather harsh result for a plaintiff who is injured by an infringer and forced to pursue an action but who is overly optimistic about the ultimate award of damages. *See supra* note 725.

[825] ASMP First Notice Comments at 9 ("[V]irtually everyone in the copyright world has long recognized that photographers are uniquely disenfranchised from access to the copyright protections to which they are legally entitled. Anything that the Copyright Office and Congress can do to help correct that situation would be of great benefit to working photographers and greatly appreciated by them."); GAG Second Notice Comments at 28 (in a survey, it was estimated that over 80% of GAG members would use a small claims copyright tribunal); IFTA First Notice Comments at 3; NWU First Notice Comments at 2 (calling the subject of this report a "vital copyright reform initiative"); SGA, Comments Submitted in Response to Second Notice of Inquiry at 1 (Oct. 19, 2012) ("[I]t would be extremely important for individual songwriters to have an alternative to the current legal system through which they could enforce their rights effectively and inexpensively when a small claim is involved.").

[826] Tr. 111:04-05 (Nov. 15, 2012) (David Leichtman, VLA).

[827] *See* ASCAP, A2IM, BMI, NMPA, RIAA, and SESAC, Comments Submitted in Response to Second Notice of Inquiry. The RIAA's position is notable because it pursued some 35,000 infringement cases against individual defendants for unauthorized file-sharing during the mid-2000s in which it typically sought relatively modest damages (at least at the pretrial stage). By the end of 2008, however, the RIAA had discontinued this litigation strategy. *See Recording Industry Begins Suing P2P File Sharers Who Illegally Offer Copyrighted Music Online, Recording Industry Ass'n of America*, (Sept. 8, 2003), http://riaa.com/newsitem.php?id=85183A9C-28F4-19CE-BDE6-F48E206CE8A1; Sarah McBride & Ethan Smith, *Music Industry to Abandon Mass Suits*, WALL ST. J. (Dec. 19, 2008), *available at* http://online.wsj.com/article/SB122966038836021137.html.

[828] For example, at the hearings, participants discussed instances of frivolous claims of ownership of iconic songs like the Beatles' "Hey Jude." *See* Tr. at 88:03-12 (Nov. 15, 2012) (Christos Badavas, HFA) ("'Hey, Jude' was written by Paul McCartney on his way to visit Julian Lennon shortly after the divorce of his father and his mother. And based on the number of letters and claims I received in my years of working at EMI, which was a

Beatles distributor and now Harry Fox, related to, hey, who owns 'Hey, Jude,' there must have been several hundred people riding in that car with Paul McCartney.").

[829] Tr. at 82:10-83:23 (Nov. 15, 2012) (Jay Rosenthal, NMPA) (discussing complexities of ownership claims regarding publishers).

[830] SGA & NSAI First Notice Comments at 1.

[831] Tr. at 91:18-20 (Nov. 15, 2012) (Charles Sanders, SGA); *see also* Tr. at 60:08-61:01 (George Clinton, musician) (agreeing that music owners should be able to participate in a small copyright claims procedure).

[832] *See* 17 U.S.C. §§ 203, 304 (setting forth provisions allowing copyright owners to terminate grants).

[833] Tr. at 73:11-20 (Nov. 26, 2012) (Alma Robinson, CLA) ("Again, on behalf of California Lawyers for the Arts, I just want to share the observation that many songwriters and musicians are now self-publishing and distributing their own work and subject to the hazards of the internet. And I think that it would really be important to allow those folks access ... to whatever potential system we're saying we're thinking about.").

[834] VLA Third Notice Comments at 4.

[835] Tr. at 50:22-51:02 (Nov. 26, 2012) (Timothy Cohan, Peermusic).

[836] Small Claims Act, CAL. CIV. PROC. CODE § 116.530.

[837] Tr. 302:11-303:09 (Nov. 16, 2012) (Lisa Shaftel, GAG).

[838] Tr. at 305:24-306:03 (Nov. 16, 2012) (Bruce Lehman, Former Asst. Sec'y of Commerce and Comm'r of Patents & Trademarks); Tr. at 310:19-24 (Nov. 16, 2012) (Mickey Osterreicher, NPPA) (noting importance of right to counsel). *Cf.* VLA Third Notice Comments at 16-17 ("VLA sees no reason to bar attorneys from the small claims process. VLA and other similar organizations throughout the country routinely provide access to either pro bono legal services or referrals to low cost legal representation, which VLA feels will only be encouraged with the addition of a streamlined, expedited small claims process.").

[839] IFTA First Notice Comments at 4 ("While small claims courts typically do not allow parties to be represented by counsel, copyright law is more complex than the types of cases on the docket of small claims courts so the parties should be entitled to be represented by counsel."); New Media Rights First Notice Comments at 18 ("If copyright law is full of issues that even fully trained attorneys struggle with, how will the average small-time plaintiff or defendant successfully represent themselves?").

[840] Tr. at 233:19-25 (Nov. 15, 2012) (Nancy Wolff, PACA) (noting danger of frivolous claims by unrepresented parties).

[841] *See* 9A WILLIAM MEADE FLETCHER ET AL., FLETCHER CYCLOPEDIA OF THE LAW OF PRIVATE CORPORATIONS § 4463, (perm. ed., rev. vol. 2013) ("Generally, a corporation cannot appear in person, and hence it must appear through an attorney admitted to practice in the jurisdiction in which the action is pending.").

[842] Tr. at 214:12-19 (Nov. 15, 2012) (Jay Rosenthal, NMPA) (stressing importance of making "instructions up front as clean and clear as possible"); Tr. at 133:10-16 (Nov. 26, 2012) (Alma Robinson, CLA) (suggesting "self-help guides in some of the more esoteric things we have talked about today, additional media, Copyright Act, or peer use, and so forth").

[843] *See, e.g.*, IFTA First Notice Comments at 5 ("Basic information as to the responsibilities and jurisdiction of the Specialized Court as well as sample forms, including a complaint and a notice of complaint to be served on defendant, should be publicly available for ease of claim filing."); Barry Rosen, Comments in Response to First Notice of Inquiry at 2 ("The court could function by using Magistrates specially designated to deal specifically with copyright issues and filings could be done via a set of easy to use streamlined forms that could be done by any layman."); ABA IP Section Second Notice Comments at 3 ("Sample claim forms and responses would be useful in creating a more streamlined process."); Tr. at 133:19-134:09 (Nov. 26, 2012) (Alicia Calzada, NPPA).

[844] *See* Cal. Dep't of Consumer Affairs, The Small Claims Court A Guide to Its Practical Use, *available at* http://www.dca.ca.gov/publications/small_claims/; *see also* Plaintiff's Claim and Order to Go to Small Claims Court, *available at* http://www.courts.ca.gov/documents/sc100.pdf.

[845] *See* WIPO Arbitration and Mediation Center, *eUDRP Model Complaint and Filing Guidelines*, *available at* http://www.wipo.int/amc/en/domains/complainant/; WIPO Arbitration and Mediation Center, *Model Response and Filing Guidelines*, *available at* http://www.wipo.int/amc/en/domains/respondent/.

[846] *See* FED. R. CIV. P. 4.

[847] Google First Notice Comments at 4 (agreeing that copyright owner should provide a *prima facie* case before a defendant must appear); FLASH Third Notice Comments (agreeing "that defendants should not have to engage in litigation or even submit an answer until the plaintiff has proven their prima facie case."); VLA Third Notice Comments at 5-6; Tr. at 197:22-198:12 (Nov. 15, 2012) (Lisa Willmer, Getty Images); Tr. at 198:13-199:04 (Nov. 15, 2012) (Rachel Fertig, AAP).

[848] Tr. at 231:19-232:16 (Nov. 15, 2012) (Rachel Fertig, AAP).

[849] Tr. at 194:19-23 (Nov. 15, 2012) (Rachel Fertig, AAP); *see also* Microsoft First Notice Comments at 3 ("Some mechanisms that may help ensure the right incentives are in place include ... meaningful filing fees that help fund the system and discourage nuisance claims but reasonable enough for copyright owners with legitimate disputes."); AAP Third Notice Comments, at 2 (calling filing fees a "safeguard"); NMPA, HFA, CMPA, ASCAP, BMI, & SESAC, Comments Submitted in Response to Third Notice of Inquiry at 9 (not including a

filing fee "would encourage parties to bring questionable claims in a cheaper small claims court process ...."); Tr. at 186:14-16 (Nov. 25, 2012) (Alma Robinson, CLA) ("[P]eople have to have some skin in the game. It eliminates some frivolous claims if there is a filing fee.").

[850] NPPA Second Notice Comments at 5 ("It should be the plaintiff's sole prerogative whether to pursue multiple claims against the same defendant in one proceeding."), 13 ("[W]e support permitting multiple copyright owners or entities acting on behalf of groups of copyright holders to pursue multiple claims against one or more defendants."); Tr. at 178:03-07 (Nov. 15, 2012) (Lisa Shaftel, GAG) ("We do think that multiple copyright owners should be allowed to act together to pursue multiple infringement claims if their work was infringed by the same user for the same use.").

[851] FED. R. CIV. P. 13(a) ("A pleading must state as a counterclaim any claim that–at the time of its service–the pleader has against an opposing party if the claim: (A) arises out of the transaction or occurrence that is the subject matter of the opposing party's claim; and (B) does not require adding another party over whom the court cannot acquire jurisdiction."); *id.* 19 (Required Joinder of Parties).

[852] *See generally*, *id.* 12(b)(7) & 19; *Escamilla v. M2 Tech., Inc.*, 2013 U.S. App. LEXIS 14385 (5th Cir. 2013).

[853] These counterclaims are similar to those required by Rule 13(a) of the Federal Rules of Civil Procedure, although they would not be mandatory and, as discussed below, omitting them would not have any preclusive effect on future litigation.

[854] *See, e.g.*, *Arista Records LLC v. Does 1-27*, 584 F.Supp. 2d 240, 247 (D. Me. 2008) (denying a motion to quash a subpoena seeking to discover the identity of unknown online infringers as the "DMCA specifically sanctions the disclosure of anonymous internet users' identities").

[855] *See* 17 U.S.C. § 803(b)(6)(C)(ix); *see also* Copyright Royalty Judges' Authority to Subpoena a Nonparticipant to Appear and Give Testimony or to Produce and Permit Inspection of Documents or Tangible Things, 75 Fed. Reg. 13,306 (Mar. 19, 2010) (noting in a Final Order that the issue of whether the CRJs can issue a non-party subpoena has not been determined in prior decisions, determinations, or rulings).

[856] *See, e.g.*, TENN. CODE ANN. § 24-9-102(a) ("Discovery ... excluding physical and mental examinations ... may be taken in all civil cases pending in the courts of general sessions in the discretion of the court after motion showing both good cause and exceptional circumstances and pursuant to an order describing the extent and conditions of such discovery."); *see also* Appendix D.

[857] *See, e.g.*, AAP Second Notice Comments at 7 (including "(1) limit discovery to 90 days; (2) allow only written discovery; (3) limit interrogatories, requests for admission and document requests; and (4) allow good faith discovery motions, but require resolution through phone conference"); Getty Images Second Notice Comments at 4 ("Limited discovery should be permitted in the form of written depositions and interrogatories to allow the plaintiff to establish its infringement claim and to allow the defendant to establish its defense(s)."); IFTA Second Notice Comments at 5; Kernochan Second Notice Comments at 2 ("Discovery should be permitted to allow for those cases in which critical information resides with the opposing party, but it should be very limited in time and scope.").

[858] Tr. at 228:06-11 (Nov. 26, 2012) (Alicia Calzada, NPPA).

[859] Tr. at 229:15-19 (Nov. 26, 2012) (Edward Hasbrouck, NWU).

[860] *See, e.g.*, NPPA Second Notice Comments at 10 ("Discovery should be limited and could include interrogatories, requests for admissions, and limited requests for production of documents relevant to the issue of liability and damages. Testimony should be in affidavit form unless a hearing is granted, in which case oral sworn testimony could be allowed.").

[861] *See* Tr. at 211:22-24 (Nov. 15, 2012) (David Leichtman, VLA) ("We don't think except in maybe very rare circumstances that depositions would be appropriate."); Tr. at 235:07-09 (Nov. 26, 2012) (Carolyn Wright, Law Offices of Carolyn E. Wright) ("I think that no depositions likely would be allowed without leave of court.").

[862] *See, e.g.*, Tr. at 235:01-09 (Nov. 26, 2012) (Carolyn Wright, Law Offices of Carolyn E. Wright) (suggesting no depositions without leave of court); Tr. at 232:20-22 (Nov. 26, 2012) (Lorin Brennan, Linde Law Firm) (suggesting discovery should be limited and noting that "[o]ftentimes depositions just become a way to torture one of the parties in wasting time taking endless depositions that go nowhere").

[863] FED. R. CIV. P. 33 (interrogatories), 34 (requests for production of documents), & 36 (requests for admissions).

[864] Tr. at 233:14-234:03 (Nov. 26, 2012) (Lorin Brennan, Linde Law Firm).

[865] *See, e.g.*, Authors Guild First Notice Comments at 4 ("Small copyright infringement claims can generally be adjudicated largely on documentary evidence – a submission of the plaintiffs [sic] registered work and the alleged infringing work."); Getty Images Second Notice Comments at 3 ("In many cases, the parties could submit their positions and evidence in writing, without need for personal appearance."); Tr. at 217:19-20 (Nov. 15, 2012) (Lisa Willmer, Getty Images) (start with presumption that proceedings are based on submitted papers).

[866] Illustrators' Partnership First Notice Comments at 2 (opposing limitation of expert witnesses); Getty Images Second Notice Comments at 4 ("Expert witnesses should not be permitted due to the expense and complexity of assessing their expert role. If an expert is required, the matter is not suitable for the small claims process."); Cannings Second Notice Comments at 4 (supporting inclusion of expert witnesses); Tr. at 89:20-22 (Nov. 15,

2012) (Christos Badavas, HFA) (relating reliance on expert witnesses); Tr. at 168:19-25 (Nov. 15, 2012) (Eugene Mopsik, ASMP) (concerned that expert witnesses will drive up the cost); Tr. at 174:22-175:06 (Nov. 15, 2012) (David Leichtman, VLA) (advocating for limited use of experts for fair use determinations); Tr. at 207:08-11 (Nov. 15, 2012) (Lisa Shaftel, GAG) (advocating for limited use of expert witnesses, at least to determine customary license fees).

[867] CPR 27.5 (In the small claims track, "[n]o expert may give evidence, whether written or oral, at a hearing without the permission of the court.").

[868] Google First Notice Comments at 4.

[869] Tr. at 277:20-278:05 (Nov. 26, 2012) (Alma Robinson, CLA) ("[W]e do get a number of frivolous inquiries in our office, people who wrote all of Michael Jackson's music or et cetera, wrote the latest blockbuster movies, the scripts. And so I think having some sort of screening, we discussed legal advisers at the front door that would help people self-evaluate and decide that they didn't really have the evidence to pursue this would be helpful.").

[870] Such an approach, for example, was proposed by NPPA. Tr. 266:12-267:01 (Nov. 26, 2012) (Alicia Calzada, NPPA) (suggesting capped fee awards for "truly, truly frivolous claims").

[871] PACA Third Notice Comments at 6.

[872] ZipCourt First Notice Comments at 3, 6 (suggesting that a small copyright claims tribunal would benefit from being an arbitration, because it would be covered by the FAA); VLA Third Notice Comments at 16 (suggesting use of the FAA to both affirm awards and as a standard for overturning awards).

[873] 9 U.S.C. § 9.

[874] *Id.* If the enforcement of the arbitration was agreed to by the parties and was timely, "the court must grant such an order unless the award is vacated, modified, or corrected as prescribed in sections 10 and 11 of this title."); *see also Denver & Rio Grande W. R.. Co. v. Union Pac. R. Co*., 868 F. Supp. 1244, 1252 (D. Kan. 1994) ("If an arbitration award cannot be vacated pursuant to 9 U.S.C. § 10, or modified pursuant to 9 U.S.C. § 11, it must be confirmed pursuant to 9 U.S.C. § 9.").

[875] Tr. at 53:21-23 (Nov. 15, 2012) (Joseph DiMona, BMI) ("[Collecting a judgment] costs money, and it is not always the easiest thing to do either ...."); Tr. at 348:20-350:09 (Nov. 16, 2012) (David Leichtman, VLA) (discussing the problems that plaintiffs in small claims proceedings have collecting judgments); Tr. at 358:08-21 (Nov. 16, 2012) (Lisa Willmer, Getty Images) (suggesting that the enforcement issue is not unique to small claims proceedings, and enforcement challenges may be lessened that if the small claims copyright tribunal were voluntary).

[876] FED. R. CIV. P. 64 (allowing garnishment as a remedy).

[877] *See* Tr. at 347:05-12 (Nov. 16, 2012) (Nancy Wolff, PACA) ("I think the idea of giving a *pro se* party the federal rules to look at and to wind their way through the appeals, and even the fonts they have to do, the amount of footnotes and the page limits, the requirements to cite would just – I can't even begin to imagine how hard that would be for – particularly for a creative person.").

[878] Tr. at 242:04-07 (Nov. 26, 2012) (Michael Grecco, APA).

[879] Tr. at 325:25-326:06 (Nov. 16, 2012) (Charles Sanders, SGA).

[880] 17 U.S.C. § 803(c)(4) ("The Copyright Royalty Judges may issue an amendment to a written determination to correct any technical or clerical errors in the determination or to modify the terms, but not the rates, of royalty payments in response to unforeseen circumstances that would frustrate the proper implementation of such determination."); FED. R. CIV. P. 59 (allowing motions to alter or amend judgments).

[881] Some stakeholders supported creating appeals procedures within the Copyright Office itself. IFTA Second Notice Comments at 4 (supporting the right to a limited appeal to the Register similar to the rules governing the CRB); Tr. at 328:17-329:02 (Nov. 16, 2012) (Lisa Shaftel, GAG) (proposing an *en banc* style of appeal within the small claims copyright court); Tr. at 339:18-340:03 (Nov. 16, 2012) (Rachel Fertig, AAP) (suggesting an internal appeals system for motions to reconsider).

[882] 9 U.S.C. § 10(a) (grounds for vacation); *see also*, Tr. at 331:03-05 (Nov. 16, 2012) (David Leichtman, VLA) (suggesting that any challenges to awards granted by the small copyright claims tribunal could be judged by the same the standards found under the FAA).

[883] ASCAP & SESAC, Comments Submitted in Response to First Notice of Inquiry at 6 ("[T]he Office should ensure that decisions and opinions of any such adjudication body be limited to that case and not serve as precedent for any other action, including specifically for any action brought in a federal or state court."); Microsoft First Notice Comments at 3 ("[A]ny findings or opinions that result from a system should be limited to the works at issue, and non-precedential except as between the parties, particularly on fact-specific issues involved in the dispute, such as application of fair use or other exemption."); PACA First Notice Comments at 11 ("[D]ecisions would... have no precedential value in future cases."); Traynor *et al.* First Notice Comments at 8 ("[Decisions] should *not* have precedential or *stare decisis* effects in other or future cases."); AAP Second Notice Comments at 9 ("[W]e oppose giving the decisions any precedential value."); GAG Second Notice Comments at 11 ("A decision of the small claims tribunal should not be published and/or carry any precedential weight."); Getty Images Second Notice Comments at 5 ("[Decisions of the tribunal] should not be precedential, other than as between the same parties with respect to the same alleged infringement."); MPAA

Third Notice Comments at 5 ("In a system where quick, cheap resolution of claims is the primary goal, judges' main goal should be to do justice – perhaps even rough justice – for the parties before them" and "[s]mall claims decisions should also have no precedential effect."). *But see* Cannings Second Notice Comments at 5 ("The decision should be published, and carry precedential weight.").

884 Google First Notice Comments at 4.

885 PACA Third Notice Comments at 4.

886 *See, e.g.*, 5 U.S.C. 554(a) (the Administrative Procedure Act, for example, applies "in every case of adjudication required by statute to be determined on the record after opportunity for an agency hearing"); *see also* Tr. at 352:21-25 (Nov. 16, 2012) (Randy Taylor, CDL) ("Another possibility has been discussed about whether or not these outcomes should be disclosed publicly or not. That might be an interesting deterrent, that if you refuse to pay in a certain period of time, that outcome would become public."); Tr. at 263:7-20 (Nov. 26, 2012) (Alicia Calzada, NPPA) (in support of a public record); Tr. at 264:8-12 (Nov. 26, 2012) (Edward Hasbrouck, NWU) ("Especially given whatever kinds of limitations on damages, the naming and shaming are an important function of this tribunal. And that can't be carried out if its decisions aren't a public record."). *But see* GAG Second Notice Comments at 11 ("A decision of the small claims tribunal should not be published and/or carry any precedential weight.").

887 Tr. at 300:13-17 (Nov. 26, 2012) (Michael Grecco, APA); *see also* Tr. at 305:19-306:02 (Nov. 26, 2012) (Kim Tommaselli, IFTA) ("[W]e wouldn't find mediation particularly helpful because it is important for [our members] to get something enforceable, an award, quickly in order to preserve their rights and stop any damage that has already occurred."); Tr. at 297:16-298:03 (Nov. 26, 2012) (Edward Hasbrouck, NWU) ("The[se cases] would settle if and only if infringers have come to learn that they're actually going to lose and it is actually going to be costly to them if they pursue these matters to a small claims adjudication.").

888 *See, e.g.*, Tr. at 307:16-21 (Nov. 26, 2012) (Lorin Brennan, Linde Law Firm) ("I don't think that any sort of mandatory prefiling procedures for mediation, et cetera, would have it benefit. It only increases costs and increases the glue and the procedural hurdles you have to jump through to go through a case."); Tr. at 296:03-17 (Nov. 26, 2012) (Alicia Calzada, NPPA) ("We do support making mediation a part of the process. But, again, we just want to make sure that it doesn't become a burdensome part of the process.").

889 Tr. at 284:01-288:02 (Nov. 26, 2012) (various participants).

890 Tr. at 295:19-22 (Nov. 26, 2012) (Alma Robinson, CLA) ("[Mediation] can be effective. Again, if people are there in good faith, if they really want to resolve it, if they want to explore other options, then it can be effective.").

891 *See* 28 U.S.C. § 651(b).

892 Tr. at 137:21-22 (Nov. 27, 2012) (Art Neil, New Media Rights); *see also* Tr. at 225:13-16 (Nov. 26, 2012) (Alma Robinson, CLA) ("I would think that we have heard the idea of a pilot project to test some of these concepts. And if it's available to everybody around the country, I think it would [be] more useful."); Tr. at 413:02-04 (Nov. 16, 2012) (Nancy Wolff, PACA) ("So I think even if it was just a pilot program, I think get it started very quickly, that would be helpful.").

893 *Remedies for Small Copyright Claims, Before the Subcomm. on Courts, the Internet, and Intellectual Property of the H. Comm. on the Judiciary,* 109th Cong. (2006), available at http://frwebgate. access.gpo.gov/cgi-bin/getdoc.cgi?dbname=109_house_hearings&docid=f:26767.pdf.

894 *Remedies for Small Copyright Claims, Before the Subcomm. on Courts, the Internet, and Intellectual Property of the H. Comm. on the Judiciary,* 109th Cong. (2006) (statement of the United States Copyright Office), available at http://www.copyright.gov/docs/regstat032906.html.

895 United States Copyright Office, *Report on Orphan Works* 1 (2006), available at http://www.copyright.gov/ orphan/orphan-report-full pdf.

896 Proposed bills include the Shawn Bentley Orphan Works Act of 2008, S. 2913, 110th Cong. 2008), which was passed by the Senate; the Orphan Works Act of 2008, H.R. 5889, 110th Cong. (2008); and the Orphan Works Act of 2006, H.R. 5439, 109th Cong. (2006).

897 Federal Judicial Caseload Statistics, March 31, 2010, Office of Judges Programs, Statistics Division, Administrative Office of the United States Courts, Table C–5, *available at* http://www.uscourts.gov/ Viewer.aspx?doc=/uscourts/Statistics/FederalJudicialCaseloadStatistics/2010/tables/C05Mar10.pdf. The time frame differs significantly between districts—from 11.1 months in the U.S. District Court for the Eastern District of Virginia to 41.2 months in the U.S. District Court for the District of Columbia.

In: Small Copyright Claims: Challenges and Proposals
Editor: Sabrina Loftus
ISBN: 978-1-63117-313-4

Chapter 2

REMEDIES FOR SMALL COPYRIGHT CLAIMS: COMMENTS SUBMITTED BY THE GRAPHIC ARTISTS GUILD*

Lisa Shaftel

INTRODUCTION

From the moment you get up in the morning, you are surrounded by graphic art. A graphic artist's job and talent is to translate society's ideas and messages from the market to you in visual form. Your sheets are designed by a textile artist, as are the fabrics you wear. The enticing labels on the food you buy at the grocery store, or the bags and containers that you get from a fast-food restaurant, are designed by graphic artists. Your morning newspaper (in print or online) or TV news program was formatted by a graphic designer or broadcast designer. The book, magazines, or newspaper you read as you commute to work are designed by graphic designers, and illustrated by artists and photographers. The logos, letterheads and brochures you see at work present visual images that enhance the written messages you receive and were also created by graphic artists. Indeed, the type fonts used in these documents were developed by graphic artists. Our society depends upon the work of graphic artists to make our products and messages interesting and attractive. Virtually all areas of commerce and communications use graphic artists.

Because graphic art is so integral to the American economy, the graphic art industry is uniquely vulnerable to copyright infringement. Protecting the creative works of graphic artists should be a vital, necessary, integral part of U.S. law. Graphic artists' livelihoods depend on their ability to claim authorship of the work they produce, and to control and set fees for use of their works in the marketplace. The ability to sell or license limited usage, or limited rights, to a creative work for a fee is not only an issue of basic fairness; it is the economic essence of copyright law that sustains the productivity of American creative professionals.

---

* This is an edited, reformatted and augmented version of comments submitted January 16, 2012 in response to U.S. Copyright Office's October 27, 2011 Notice of Inquiry.

The Graphic Artists Guild supports the creation of an alternate dispute resolution, small-value, copyright infringement court within the federal district court system so that rights holders can take meaningful action against infringers. The Copyright Office began looking into this concept in 2006. The Guild endorsed it then as one of the possible solutions to the orphan works situation, and we continue to support the establishment of a practical alternative to the current federal district court system, which in practice is only viable for large-value infringement cases, irrespective of any legislative action addressing orphan works.

In 2007, Stephen Tepp was working at the Copyright Office on this issue, and proposed the possibility of gathering information from authors and creators through professional organizations such as the Graphic Artists Guild. Our National Advocacy Committee prepared a survey applicable to all authors and creators of copyrightable works to collect information regarding how rights holders had experienced infringement of their works, and if, or how, they took action against the infringer including whether they used the federal court system; if not, why they didn't, and if they would consider using an alternate court system for small-value copyright infringement. The survey would ask how authors would like such an alternate court system to work, and what the ceiling for monetary damages should be.

We would be honored to conduct this survey online to contribute to the Copyright Office's current study and information. We believe that authors and creators may respond more positively and constructively to a survey conducted by a creators' organization than inquiries by a governmental agency.

Visual art organizations including the Graphic Artists Guild [GAG], American Society of Media Photographers [ASMP], Picture Archive Council of America [PACA], Professional Photographers of America [PPA], North American Nature Photography Association [NANPA] and the American Photographic Artists [APA] have formed a joint committee to work on this issue and other legislative issues of concern to visual creators. We look forward to working with the Copyright Office in finding a workable solution to this important issue. Although we are filing individual Comment Letters, we share the common goal of establishing a new system to facilitate fair, expeditious, affordable and easily accessible legal enforcement of the economic rights of copyright owners.

CHALLENGES OF THE CURRENT LEGAL SYSTEM

Copyright infringement is rampant, especially by copying of digital works and the scanning visual works into digital format. Infringing uses rob rights holders – both businesses and individuals - of licensing income. As a practical matter, except for large corporate copyright owners, our current copyright laws are virtually unenforceable when it comes to the infringement of visual works. Too often when an infringement is discovered, there is little or nothing a rights holder can do to stop the infringing use or recoup financial damages. Litigation in federal district courts is too costly, and completely financially impractical for damages under $30,000.

We hear from our organization's members and other visual creators that most infringing uses of their images result in actual damages of less than $15,000. That's not much to big business, but to self- employed independent contractors and small studios this is a significant loss of income. Attorneys will not take on these infringement cases even if the work is registered, particularly if it's clear that the infringer would never be able to pay actual damages, statutory damages *AND* the rights holder's legal fees. We also hear from visual creators that often their work was not registered prior to the infringement, making legal action completely economically impractical because the cost of litigation would be far greater than recoverable damages. This relatively "small-value" infringement happens to nearly every professional illustrator and graphic artist during his or her career, causing economic harm to small businesses and families.

Most Americans don't understand copyright, and that includes clients who license graphic art - both individual clients and employees of large businesses. It is not unusual for a client to make additional unauthorized use of an illustration or graphic design beyond the original license for the project. Clients mistakenly presume that either they've purchased the copyright when they haven't, or that whatever fee they've paid grants them unlimited use. Sometimes the illustrator or graphic artist is able to bill the client for the additional usage and successfully collect, but often the client refuses to pay.

A significant infringement problem for visual creators is unauthorized copying and use of our images online; both the unauthorized sale of images and unauthorized display without sales of the images. Infringers rarely respond to or comply with a cease & desist letter sent by the creator. In some instances the ISP or host does not respond to or comply with a DMCA take-down notice, or allows the image to be reposted again later. The visual creator may have typically charged a usage fee for such online use, and ought to be able to pursue an infringer for a licensing fee for use already made, regardless of whether the infringer complied with a demand to remove the image. Injunctive relief, particularly for online use, is equally important to visual creators. Unauthorized uses of images are found on every variety and purpose of website.

Most visual works are not registered, and most of the business sector is aware of this. Many businesses take a calculated risk when they deliberately make infringing use of an image, presuming that the image has not been registered, and that in the event the visual creator discovers the infringement, he/she will not be able to take legal action. Currently, if a work was not registered before the infringement occurs (or within the 3-month grace period), the copyright owner may recover only actual damages, and that typically would not even pay the visual creator's legal fees. [See 17 U.S.C. § 412]

ALTERNATIVES FOR SMALL COPYRIGHT CLAIMS- THE GUILD'S RECOMMENDATIONS

To begin, we would like to express that we have found use of the name "small claims court" in association with an alternate, small-value, copyright claims system to be problematic when discussing this issue with artists. It is already associated with an established court system and will be confusing to some people. We suggest the name "Alternate Copyright Dispute Court," or even simply, "Copyright Court."

The Graphic Artists Guild opines that the goal of an alternate, small-value, copyright infringement court system ("alternate copyright court" or "ACC") is to encourage proper business practices and the licensing of copyrighted works, as well as discourage unauthorized use. The procedure and system ought to be easy to use by both parties, with expeditious results and lower costs for the process, and with evidentiary requirements to deter false claims. More rights holders will be able to get monetary compensation from unauthorized users. Users will be aware that it is more cost-effective to contact the rights holder and pay a licensing fee rather than infringe, because rights holders will have easier access to legal recourse.

Determination of "Small" Copyright Claims

We believe that infringements of visual works would be well suited to an alternate copyright court system. In an ACC, it should be easy enough for creators to produce digital files, scans, photocopies or hard copy prints of their work and any necessary documentation to present either in person or by mail as evidence. Federal judges or magistrates with copyright law expertise should be able to review this evidence of visual works much the same as they do in the current system. The Graphic Artists Guild cannot speak for the concerns of other creators such as software engineers as to whether other classes of copyrighted works could be properly and expertly reviewed, and perhaps certain classes of works would be excluded from an ACC system. We would defer to the opinions of professional organizations representing authors and creators in other classes of works as to what would be best for those works. A limitation of the available damages to be awarded, such as $30,000, will serve as a guide for rights holders to determine for themselves whether the ACC is appropriate and satisfactory for their particular infringement situation. Where a larger profit was made on the infringement, or more incidences of infringing use would result in higher damages, or complicated evidentiary issues exist, the rights holder may choose to file suit in the regular federal district court system.

Voluntary or Mandatory

Would participation in an alternate copyright court system be mandatory or voluntary for both parties? We would like to see the rights holder/plaintiff have the option to choose ACC or federal district court; however the infringer/defendant must comply with the rights holder's choice of court system. The incentive for the rights holder to use ACC is obvious; it would be less costly, faster, and hopefully afford action against an infringer for damages too low for full-scale legal action in federal district court. In the event that the process is not mandatory for the defendant once elected by the plaintiff, the ACC should offer incentives to deter defendants from rejecting the ACC or removing the case to federal district court. We suggest that if the rights holder/plaintiff chooses ACC and the infringer/defendant objects, the infringer/defendant would be required to pay a monetary penalty AND the rights holder's/plaintiff's costs and legal fees in federal district court. This would motivate infringers to comply rather than stonewall the rights holder with the hopes that the rights holder would not pursue the infringer in federal district court. If an infringer/defendant does not appear or participate after both parties have agreed to ACC, the defendant should lose the case by a streamlined process for default judgment. We hope that the significantly lower cost of ACC would be incentive enough for participation. Perhaps in the future, if the ACC system proves to be popular and successful, it could also be an available recourse to authors/creators of works not registered prior to infringement (timely registration). We hope that this would be a faster, easier way for rights holders to get recourse for an uncomplicated clear infringement, rather than potentially adding another step in the process. We do not think there should be an incentive to arbitration, because arbitrators are not familiar with copyright law or the business of visual art. We think there should be an incentive to choose ACC for both parties involved.

Available Remedies

Remedies should always include monetary relief. The ACC should have authority to grant statutory damages in excess of plaintiffs' actual damages or lost profits, or defendants' profits, to compensate plaintiffs for the costs of pursuing the claim (including attorneys' fees if attorneys are allowed to practice in the ACC), to deter infringements and to incentivize infringers to negotiate in good faith for licensing rights to artwork rather than forcing creators to take them to court.

Conditional injunctive relief should be available on a case by case basis. Continued use of infringing derivative works may be permitted if damages are paid promptly to be determined by the Court on a case by case basis. We understand that just like some uses of orphan works, there are situations of usage in collective and derivative works where it would be impossible or financially devastating for the user/infringer to remove the infringed work, but these should always be balanced against detrimental effects on the rights holder's market for the work, and damages for any allowed continued use should be determined accordingly. There should also be remedies for the destruction of goods, particularly if the infringing use conflicts with pre-existing legitimate licensing agreements between the creator and clients, or is detrimental to the creator's professional image.

Visual creators earn significant income from the licensing of our images. Often the initial use is licensed to our clients on a nonexclusive basis, and there is a robust market for secondary licensing after the initial license expires. Obtaining exclusive use of an image is of great value to our clients, who pay considerably more for exclusive rights. When infringers use images without authorization, their use frequently conflicts with the terms of the legitimate licensee's rights, cause economic harm to our clients, devalue the work or product, and/or market confusion or saturation. It is crucial that the ACC give significant consideration to any existing licensing agreement from a rights holder granting exclusivity of use to particular parties when considering injunctive relief. Simply paying a usage fee may not be satisfactory, even if an injunction would be financially harmful or difficult for the infringer. Under U.S. copyright law, an author/creator/rights holder should always have the right to determine licensing/usage terms and fees, not an infringer. The legitimate licensee's rights and economic interests should be considered, too.

At this time, the Guild recommends that the limit of monetary damages be $30,000, separate from any legal fees and court costs. However, we would like to survey authors and creators on this point. $30,000 references the ceiling of statutory damages currently awarded for single non-willful infringements, and in practice seems to be a threshold of complexity of the infringement and willingness of attorneys to represent a rights holder in federal district court. The amount of monetary damages should be adjusted periodically in accordance with the cost of living index.

Payment of damages ought to occur in a timely manner, such as 30 days. Late payment penalties would encourage the infringer/defendant to pay expeditiously. To ensure timely access to the ACC, we recommend that U.S. plaintiffs/rights holders be eligible to file their claims as soon as they have submitted application for copyright registration, as is the practice in many jurisdictions in federal court, rather than requiring them to have an issued copyright registration before filing. (Foreign authors would be exempt under Berne). There would be no prior registration or timely registration bars to obtaining ACC statutory damages. Discovery of evidence would need to be simplified, conducted remotely by mail or teleconferencing, and more accessible to both parties without legal representation. There should be limited pre-trial discovery, such as documents that could be provided as hard copies and digital files. Similar practices for opposition and cancellation actions in the Trademark Trial and Appeal Board ("TTAB") may provide helpful examples. As in federal district court, rights holders would need to present documentation that they are the copyright owner of the work(s) at issue, such as the registration certificate or their working files evidencing their creation of the work. The user or person legally responsible for the use of the work at issue (defendant) would be required to disclose and document all of his/her uses of the work. Rights holders would need to present a history of his/her fees and licenses, or standard industry fees for analogous uses, to support the amount of damages requested. The user/defendant would have to provide documentation of any profits made. The defendant would also have the opportunity to present a defense on all grounds available under copyright law, including fair use, independent creation, or other permitted use as described by law or contract. There should be penalties for providing false information.

Location of Federal Court/Tribunal, Defendants' Appearance and Jurisdiction Issues

We recommend that infringement claims of visual works could be handled by submitting documents to a central ACC location without personal jurisdictional requirements. As in the TTAB, hearings conducted by phone or video conferencing, mail, and email would work for visual works. Hearings could allow both the appearance in person of parties that can attend and participation by phone or video conferencing. People who live far from cities where courts would logically be located might be too inconvenienced by time and cost of travel to appear in person. This is already a significant problem with the current federal district court system. Again, we would like to gather information from authors and creators through a survey as to how they'd like this to work.

We believe parties should not be represented by legal counsel and should participate *pro se*. That would keep the ACC process simple, keep costs down for both parties, and create a level playing field for all involved. Ideally, the ACC system should be simple and straightforward enough for people to handle themselves.

State Court or Federal Court

We don't think state courts should be involved. State court judges don't have extensive knowledge of copyright law or experience with copyright infringement cases. Federal court judges or magistrates with copyright law expertise, or new ACC judges appointed from the copyright bar would be best able to determine issues unique to copyright jurisprudence, including important defenses such as fair use.

Affiliation with the Copyright Office or Copyright Royalty Board

We would like to see this ACC system kept close to the Copyright Office. We recommend that the existing Copyright Review Board review claims with assistance from the Copyright Office. We also recommend that industry professionals with expertise in certain classes of works or businesses act as consultants on particular claims based on guidelines with the Copyright Royalty Board.

Review and Evaluation

As with any new system or procedure, this ADR ought to be reviewed and evaluated after a few years in practice –possibly 4 years?- with recommendations for changes.

About the Graphic Artists Guild

In the course of its 44-year history, the Graphic Artists Guild has established itself as the leading advocate for the rights of graphic artists on a wide range of economic and legislative issues, from copyright to tax law. Through its publication of the *Handbook: Pricing & Ethical Guidelines* (now in its 13th edition), the Guild has raised ethical standards in the industry, and provides an invaluable resource on pricing information that is relied on by both artists and clients. The Guild's newsletter, the *Guild News*, provides lively, provocative, and useful coverage of developments in the visual communications industry for its readers.

The Guild also provides a wealth of services and benefits for its members, including educational programs, discounts on a multitude of products and services, a legal referral network, and grievance handling. The Guild's website offers up-to-date information on Guild activities, updates on advocacy issues, members' portfolios, individual chapters, and links to related organizations.

The Guild also has a blog, *All Things Copyright* (www.allthingscopyright.com) that posts relevant and pertinent information regarding copyright related issues and how they impact the visual arts.

Thank you for your consideration.
Respectfully,
Lisa Shaftel
National Advocacy Committee Chair
Graphic Artists Guild
advocacy@gag.org

In: Small Copyright Claims: Challenges and Proposals
Editor: Sabrina Loftus
ISBN: 978-1-63117-313-4

Chapter 3

REMEDIES FOR SMALL COPYRIGHT CLAIMS: ADDITIONAL COMMENTS SUBMITTED BY THE ASSOCIATION OF AMERICAN PUBLISHERS*

Allan Adler

Register of Copyrights
United States Copyright Office
101 Independence Ave. S.E.
Washington, DC 20559

RE: Notice of Inquiry—Remedies for Small Copyright Claims: Additional Comments

To the Register of Copyrights:

Pursuant to the Notice of Inquiry ("NOI") published in the Federal Register on August 23, 2012 (77 Fed.Reg. 51,068), I submit these comments on behalf of the Association of American Publishers ("AAP") regarding the Copyright Office's efforts to assess the feasibility of creating an alternative copyright enforcement method for claims of small economic value ("small copyright claims").

AAP's core mission is to support publishers—copyright owners—by promoting respect for copyright. As the principal national trade association of the U.S. book publishing industry, AAP represents more than 250 member companies and organizations that include most of the major commercial book publishers in the U.S., as well as many small and non-profit publishers, university presses and scholarly societies. Thus, our members have a diversity of perspectives about the best way to structure the adjudication of small copyright claims, which should serve to strengthen copyright protection as a whole.

As noted in our first filing on this issue, larger publishers, in general, are apprehensive about a potential surge in frivolous claims surrounding legitimate uses of third-party works as

* This is an edited, reformatted and augmented version of comments submitted October 19, 2012 in response to U.S. Copyright Office's August 23, 2012 Notice of Inquiry.

free-standing publications, inserts within publications, or contributions to collective works. Yet, our smaller publishers can face *de-facto* non-enforcement of their copyrights under the current system.

Appreciating these differences, AAP welcomes the opportunity to provide the Copyright Office with feedback concerning a number of issues integral to forming an alternative forum for adjudicating small copyright claims. In Section I, we have listed our suggestions in parallel format with the NOI. In Section II, in order to illustrate the balance between easing small claims enforcement and preventing a surge of frivolous suits, AAP provides a sample case detailing how our suggestions would be applied.

Before moving to our suggestions, AAP wants to be clear that we are not yet endorsing the creation of an alternative copyright adjudication process. However, should the Copyright Office decide, after carefully reviewing public comments, that it can and should create a small claims process, AAP suggests adopting the following approach based on views received[1]from our members:

SECTION I

Overarching Approach

Copyright claims are the exclusive province of federal courts.[2] Devising an alternative method for adjudicating a subset of copyright claims having small economic value deserves the utmost care to achieve a result that strengthens copyright enforcement, rather than compromising it. Therefore, when assessing each of the following components that may form the bases of a small claims process, AAP urges the Copyright Office to consciously evaluate the ways in which streamlining procedures to make filing small claims cost-effective can be balanced by measures that prevent opening the floodgates to frivolous claims.

Nature of Tribunal/ Process

AAP is in agreement with the majority of respondents to the Copyright Office's 2011 NOI[3] that oppose vesting state courts with authority to adjudicate small copyright claims.[4] Earlier comments highlighted the issues engendered by state court lack of expertise, experience with copyright law, and consistency; thus AAP will not re-hash these concerns. With state court adjudication removed from consideration, AAP supports consideration of processing small copyright claims through an informal administrative body, potentially modeled on the Trademark Trial and Appeals Board (TTAB).

More specifically, the Accelerated Case Resolution process of resolving disputes under the TTAB offers a useful example of the type of expedited proceeding that may be suitable for adjudicating small copyright claims.[5] More detailed reference to ACR processes will be made throughout this comment under the appropriate topic subheadings. As a general proposition, however, AAP believes that "the accelerated timelines, and limitations on discovery, motion practice and the methods of presentation of evidence" under ACR embody a reasonable approach to adjudicating small copyright claims.[6]

Voluntary versus Mandatory Participation

There is broad consensus among publishers and other respondents that any small copyright claims process, provided as an alternative to federal district court adjudication, must be strictly voluntary. However, because of the diversity within the publishing industry, AAP appreciates that good faith claimants may desire mandatory jurisdiction over potential defendants in order to prevent removal to federal court, which would result in continued *de facto* non-enforcement of small copyright claims.

Keeping the needs of all copyright owners in mind, AAP would urge the Copyright Office to make participation voluntary for both parties, while creating incentives and, potentially, penalties to encourage parties to keep their claims in the small claims forum. This balanced approach could involve incentives such as a low damages cap and only allowing monetary damages, which would encourage defendants to remain in the small claims forum.

Settlement

AAP supports creation of a small claims process that does not disturb incentives for settling claims out of court. The extent to which such incentives should be incorporated into the adjudicatory process itself is a topic that merits further discussion. Preliminarily, however, one such incentive could be penalizing a party that rejects a reasonable settlement offer, if the rejecting party does not substantially prevail in the case.

Location of Tribunal(s)

AAP recognizes that the high cost of pursuing a claim in federal court is one of the primary factors leading to *de facto* non-enforcement of small copyright claims. In fact, AIPLA's 2011 Economic Survey calculated the median cost of a small copyright case to be \$350,000.[7] More importantly, AIPLA's survey highlights just how many costs go into federal litigation: "cost of…counsel, associates, paralegals, travel and living expenses, fees and costs for court reporters, photocopies, courier services, exhibit preparation, analytical testing, expert witnesses…surveys, jury advisors," etc.[8]

Cutting down on these expenses is both necessary and appropriate in creating a small claims process that would be cost-effective for pursuing small copyright claims. AAP supports appropriate measures to reduce the cost of enforcing copyrights, provided that counter-measures to limit frivolous suits are paired with such measures. As such, our members that support adjudicating small copyright claims through an administrative proceeding are in favor of establishing a centralized forum location, which uses video- and/or teleconferencing to resolve motions, conduct hearings, and fulfill appearance requirements, if any.

A centralized forum location with remote conferencing would not only eliminate travel costs and living expenses for attorneys, witnesses, parties, etc., but would also promote a host of other benefits that would increase the effectiveness of the small claims tribunal. Such benefits, at a minimum, include: (1) development of the tribunal's expertise; (2) consistency of decisions; (3) elimination of forum shopping; and (4) centralization of information for potential claimants and defendants.

Permissible Claims

In order to meet the Copyright Office's stated goal "to improve the adjudication of" small copyright claims, simplicity will be crucial to creating efficiency. Therefore, AAP suggests that only "pure" copyright infringement claims should be permitted in this process. Although many licensing claims and fair use defenses seem straightforward, such claims and defenses have the potential to become extremely complex.[9] Moreover, AAP strongly opposes inclusion of contract claims within the jurisdiction of the small claims forum, given that such claims typically raise state law issues and thus detract from the forum's focus on developing expertise regarding copyright claims. Allowing these potentially complex claims and defenses to be raised in what is intended to be an efficient and cost-effective forum will only hinder *bona fide* claimants from enforcing their copyrights.

That said, AAP agrees with many of the respondents from the prior round of comments that it will be difficult to define a narrow category of claims that are "simple" enough to be quickly adjudicated in the small claims forum. As a starting point, however, the Copyright Office should consider the following aspects of a claim as threshold requirements: (1) the amount in controversy should be less than or equal to the cap on damages; (2) adjudication of the claim should be compatible with accelerated proceedings; (3) adjudication of the claim does not require extensive discovery;[10] and (4) the claim is separable from tangential contract and licensing issues. To be sure, this is not a complete list, but AAP supports efforts to improve the functioning of copyright enforcement for all rights holders and is therefore willing to work with the Copyright Office and other stakeholders to devise realistic parameters for the jurisdiction of a small claims forum.

Lastly, AAP appreciates the concern introduced in first-round comments that potential defendants may raise complex defenses or counterclaims, beyond the jurisdiction of the small claims forum, in order to "game the system" and remove the case to federal court. Thus, AAP acknowledges that penalties for frivolous defenses and counterclaims should accompany other measures that narrow the jurisdiction of the small claims forum.

Permissible Claim Amount

AAP agrees with the Copyright Office that there must be a cap on damages available through the small claims forum. Beyond this basic requirement, our members understand that creating an alternative system for adjudicating small copyright claims must balance its appeal to claimants against the possibility of increasing frivolous suits. With these counterweights in mind, AAP offers the following suggestions as topics for discussion at upcoming roundtables: (1) a damages cap per work; (2) a $50,000 aggregate damages cap; (3) a damages cap per work and in aggregate.

Permissible Defenses and Counterclaims

As discussed above, AAP believes the best way to create a cost-effective, efficient and fair process for addressing small copyright claims is to keep the cases simple. Therefore, AAP is opposed to allowing counterclaims, non-Copyright Act defenses, or potentially complex defenses such as fair use to be raised in small claims proceedings. AAP acknowledges that, standing alone, prohibiting such defenses and counterclaims provides a quick "opt-out" mechanism to potential defendants. However, a holistic viewing of the various factors underpinning a small claims forum – such as the damages cap, the unavailability of injunctive relief, and penalties for frivolous defenses – points to a number of potential risks and rewards that can establish a workable process while eliminating opportunities for gamesmanship.

Registration

Starting from the proposition that statutory damages and attorneys' fees will not be available in the small claims forum, AAP could support allowing claims where registration was not effective at the time of infringement. Specifically, AAP supports the current standard under federal law where a copyright owner can seek actual damages in federal court so long as he files for registration after discovering the infringement and before commencing any legal action.

To be clear, however, AAP does not support waiving registration as a pre-requisite to statutory damages or attorneys' fees. Registration is required in federal court and to eliminate this requirement within an accelerated small claims forum would likely lead to an unmanageable surge in cases and formalistic, instead of realistic, determinations of liability against defendants deprived of the basic notice that copyright registration provides.

Filing Fee

In developing a small claims process, the Copyright Office could find that a reasonable filing fee would be a useful tool to help strike a balance between the system's appeal to claimants and the risk of spawning frivolous suits. For example, the TTAB maintains a $300 filing fee per class per claim,[11] which would equate to $300 for each allegation of infringement of separate copyrights (e.g., if a photographer makes a claim for infringement of 6 photos, the filing fee to address each of those works in a single case would be 6 x $300 = $1800).

Initiation of Proceedings

AAP agrees with many respondents that a copyright owner should be required to establish a *prima facie* case of infringement before the defendant is required to respond.[12] In keeping with the goal of creating a simplified avenue for effective copyright enforcement,

AAP suggests that a claimant would attempt to meet his *prima facie* burden by submitting to the court the evidence upon which he intends to rely.

For example, a plaintiff claiming copyright infringement based on unauthorized copying of a work would need to submit the following to meet his *prima facie* burden: (1) ownership of a valid copyright; and (2) evidence of actionable copying.[13] As usual, a certificate of copyright registration would establish a rebuttable presumption of ownership of a valid copyright. Assuming that statutory damages and attorneys' fees would not be available in this forum, a claimant lacking proof of an effective registration could offer proof of filing for registration, along with a showing of the originality and copyrightability of the work. To establish actionable copying, the claimant would need to show: (1) factual copying, and (2) the "substantial similarity" of the works. *Prima facie* evidence of these factors could include: (1) proof that the defendant used the copyrighted material in another work; or (2) proof of access[14] to the infringed work and its probative similarity to the claimant's work; or (3) that the works are strikingly similar.[15]

Cases that are truly amenable to an accelerated proceeding with limited discovery should be able to establish a *prima facie* case using only a few documents to convey the viability of the infringement claim. Thus, in this abbreviated context, if the evidence is insufficient to establish a *prima facie* case of infringement, AAP would support dismissing the claim without prejudice. This initial screening process should facilitate the aim of funneling only simple cases into the small claims forum, while reserving more complex cases for a more appropriate form of adjudication in federal court.

Representation

As noted in our previous filing, AAP's membership includes many small and independent publishers that face challenges in pursuing small copyright claims. AAP understands that the cost of hiring an attorney is often a key factor that dissuades copyright owners from taking legal action to protect their copyrights.[16] Therefore, AAP supports creation of a small claims process that encourages *pro se* representation, but still allows attorney representation, provided that presiding judges have authority to issue sanctions against attorney and non-attorney representatives alike for bringing frivolous claims.

Conduct of Proceeding

Without question, the bottom line from the first round of comments was that two factors underlie the current failure to pursue enforcement of many small copyright claims in the federal courts—time and money.[17] As noted above, the median cost to litigate a relatively small copyright claim is $350,000.[18] Thus, any small claims forum must adopt procedures that streamline adjudication in a manner that reduces the time and money required to pursue a claim to resolution. For this reason, AAP is willing to support a system that relies on all-paper filings (through e-mail); uses video and tele-conferencing to eliminate travel costs; requires expedited filing, discovery, and adjudication schedules; and, limits motion and discovery procedures.

AAP anticipates that these streamlined procedures could be the keystones for an efficient and effective small copyright claims system. However, the benefits of this system will not come to fruition if it is bogged down by frivolous claims. Therefore, a fair and workable approach for both claimants and defendants requires that these streamlined procedures be adopted only in conjunction with measures that stave off meritless suits. To this end, AAP proposes that the Copyright Office require: (1) filing fees; (2) good faith declarations [or oaths on penalty of perjury]; (3) verification measures for paper filings;[19] and (4) sanctions for delaying proceedings or abusing the discovery process.

In the abstract, a balance between streamlining measures and those to prevent frivolous suits can be hard to see. Thus, following the topic-by-topic explanation of AAP's views, we have provided an example of a model small copyright claims proceeding, incorporating the key issues discussed in our comment.

Discovery

AAP supports limiting discovery as much as possible, while still allowing parties to gather evidence essential to proving simple infringement claims within the forum's jurisdiction. While the time may not yet be ripe to explore all the minutiae of how to limit discovery, AAP offers the following suggestions, which are put in context in the model case described below: (1) limit discovery to 90 days; (2) allow only written discovery; (3) limit interrogatories, requests for admission and document requests;[20] and (4) allow good faith discovery motions,[21] but require resolution through phone conference.

Damages

Damages will be a crucial factor in shaping the overall viability of an alternative process for adjudicating small copyright claims. The types and amount of damages available under a small copyright claims system could provide a powerful incentive for potential defendants to work within the system instead of opting for transfer to federal court. Thus, AAP suggests removing statutory damages from the realm of possible awards available through the small claims forum.

However, as copyright owners, publishers are aware that *actual* damages can be difficult to prove in infringement cases. Moreover, as many of the comments pointed out, artists, independent publishers, and authors alike are most often seeking remuneration for unauthorized use of a work that they would have been willing to license. Therefore, AAP proposes that "reasonable compensation"[22] should serve as the primary small claims forum award for a prevailing claim. As explained by the Copyright Office, reasonable compensation "represent[s] the amount the user would have paid to the owner had they engaged in negotiations before the infringing use commenced."[23]

Although higher damages awards, such as statutory damages, are available in federal court, it is AAP's position that such potentially high damages should not be allowed in an expedited proceeding that establishes a relatively thin evidentiary record. Furthermore, although photographers, illustrators and graphic artists have noted concerns with limiting damages to reasonable compensation when this same issue was discussed as a remedy in the context of orphan works legislation, the rationale was that such compensation would be so low in comparison to the high costs of hiring an attorney to litigate the claim that it would be inefficient to enforce their copyrights.[24] The Copyright Office's proposed small claims system, however, should solve this inefficiency, and thus validate reasonable compensation as a fair outcome.

Limiting damages to reasonable compensation will promote the protection of all copyrights, facilitate honest bargaining between the parties, and ensure that the expedited process does not impose unnecessarily high levels of liability based on minimal evidence.

Equitable Relief

AAP opposes authorizing the small claims forum to award any type of injunctive relief because "the decision whether to grant or deny injunctive relief rests within the equitable discretion of the district courts."[25] The rightful aim of the small claims proceedings will be to determine instances of copyright infringement. However, the Supreme Court "has consistently rejected invitations to replace traditional equitable considerations with a rule that an injunction automatically follows a determination that a copyright has been infringed."[26]

Awarding injunctive relief on the basis of the necessarily thin evidentiary record in small claim cases would work a substantial injustice against the enjoined, even if not automatically imposed following a finding of infringement, because the traditional rigors of the four-factor balancing test could not be meaningfully applied.

Moreover, as a practical matter, an injunction can be worth much more than a monetary damages award considering the losses a movie, song, or book producer could suffer if a claimant was allowed to hamstring the release of a work by securing an injunction through a simplified administrative proceeding. Thus, in order to preserve the equity considerations articulated by the Supreme Court, as well as the vitality of the damages cap, injunctive relief cannot be part of the small claims system.

Effect of Adjudication

Decisions of the small claims tribunal should be final, enforceable, and appealable. And while AAP supports giving the decisions *res judicata* and collateral estoppel effect, we oppose giving the decisions any precedential value. *Res judicata* and collateral estoppel ensure that there is finality to the decisions reached concerning disputes between the parties to the litigation. Precedent, on the other hand, applies to unrelated parties and should not be afforded to decisions from the small claims forum.

All of the administrative law judges (ALJs) that would decide small claims cases in the forum would have equal weight to their decisions. Therefore, just as trial court decisions are not binding precedent on other trial court judges, decisions of fellow ALJs should not constitute precedent either. That said, federal appeals court rulings should still be binding precedent governing small claims disputes because appeals court rulings are a higher authority by law and are intended to clarify the meaning of federal laws, including copyright.

Review/Appeals

AAP supports including a right to appeal decisions of the small claims forum. Options for appeal could include: (1) an abuse of discretion review by a larger panel of ALJs from the forum; and/or (2) review by a federal court.[27] Additionally, while not endorsing the suggestion, AAP appreciates that requiring the appellant to post a bond may be a reasonable mechanism for dis- incentivizing gamesmanship surrounding the adjudication of small copyright claims.

Frivolous Claims

Throughout this comment, AAP suggests various mechanisms that could help stymie the potential for opening the floodgates to frivolous claims. These suggestions include: (1) filing fees; (2) verification procedures for electronically submitted paper filings; (3) good faith requirements for proposing claims and defenses; and (4) requiring the claimant to establish a *prima facie* case of infringement.

Moreover, devising sanctions to award against parties that raise frivolous claims, defenses, and counterclaims (if allowed) would be integral to creating a workable small claims system. A party could be required to pay a percentage of the alleged claim's value to the defendant, if the judge determines that the party raised a frivolous claim. And, on balance, a similar sanction could be assessed against a defendant for raising a frivolous defense.

Aside from specific sanctions, however, AAP would remind the Copyright Office, and all stakeholders, that each component of the small claims system presents an opportunity to strike a balance between facilitating simplified copyright enforcement and unleashing a flood of frivolous suits.

Evaluation of Small Claims System

As the detailed questions within the second NOI demonstrate, creating an alternative method to adjudicate small copyright claims in an efficient, effective, and just manner will be a complex task, to say the least. Therefore, AAP strongly supports launching the system as a pilot program. Starting on a small scale, reviewing procedures, and amending qualifications and processes before expanding to a full-scale system will allow stakeholders to revise and improve the system so that small copyright claims are no longer subject to *de facto* non-enforcement.

AAP assumes that creating the small claims tribunal would require the Copyright Office to recommend proposed legislation to Congress, to be followed by public hearings on the legislative embodiment of the proposal. AAP supports this approach and would suggest providing a 3 year time-frame for the pilot version of the small claims tribunal, followed by the Copyright Office's review and request for public comment on its functioning and further refinement or, potentially, discontinuation.

SECTION II

As noted above, AAP views the expedited trial format of the TTAB's Accelerated Case Resolution process as a potentially reasonable model for creating a small claims forum. The following timeline provides a step-by-step illustration of the application of this model to a hypothetical copyright infringement case where a photographer alleges that a publisher made unauthorized copies of four photographs by including them in a book that is scheduled for release in three months. Additionally, AAP gives our rationale for suggestions that will provide balance to the streamlining measures, such as centralization, all-paper filings, teleconferencing and limited discovery, which could encourage genuine as well as frivolous claims.

Adjudication Phase	Party Action	AAP Rationale
Initiating Case: Filing Fee	Claimant pays $300 per work he alleges the defendant infringed: $300 x 4 photos = $1200	Requiring a modest filing fee is an important threshold that will dis-incentivize filing frivolous claims.
Pleading:	Complaint: Plaintiff establishes *prima facie* case of copyright infringement. If No = Case Dismissed Without Prejudice If Yes = Defendant Responds Answer: Defendant files an Answer only after notification from the forum that the Plaintiff has met its *prima facie* burden.	The *prima facie* burden on the plaintiff is another step that filters out meritless suits. Upon filing the Complaint and all other trial documents, forum rules must establish that electronic signatures represent certification of good faith filing. Discovery of violation of the requirements of good faith filing should result in varying levels of sanctions.
Discovery Conference	Parties meet to discuss possibility of settlement and agree to the limited discovery and motion procedures of the small claims forum.	As stated above, AAP supports creation of a forum that promotes settlement. The extent to which unfruitful settlement discussion should result in penalties based on the result of the trial is a matter in need of more discussion. Important to note, if injunctive relief was available in the small claims forum, the photographer in this example could leverage the publishers' relatively large losses that would result from an injunction to force the publisher to settle a meritless suit. If a small claims forum is to have a meaningful damages cap, which it must, injunctive relief cannot be a possible remedy.

Adjudication Phase	Party Action	AAP Rationale
		Given that AAP supports creating a completely voluntary forum, we expect parties that agree to adjudicate claims within the forum to uphold the agreement to limited discovery as it leads to lower costs and speedier resolution of the claim for both parties.
Discovery Period: 90 Days	Only written discovery; Limited interrogatories, requests for admission and document requests; and (3) Good faith discovery motions.	An accelerated timeline coupled with limited discovery requests will significantly reduce the cost of pursuing a copyright infringement claim. However, as explained by the TTAB, these cost and time savings are not realized if parties do not uphold a "Duty to Cooperate," which requires parties to focus only on relevant requests and ways to narrow the issues, instead of gamesmanship.
Submission of Evidence: 75 Days	Plaintiff and Defendant have opportunity to electronically submit evidence.	Parties, again, must certify through an electronic signature that documents are submitted in good faith. In a forum that does not require personal appearances, verification and authentication procedures, with meaningful penalties for violation, are essential for creating a just system.
Trial Briefing: 75 Days	Plaintiff has 30 days after the close of discovery to file its trial brief. Defendant has 30 days to file its response. Plaintiff has 15 days to file a reply brief.	In addition to verification procedures, the ALJs should be empowered to sanction any representative that proposes frivolous arguments in the pleadings as well as the briefs.
Decision: 50 Days	Decisions should be final between the parties (*res judicata* and collateral estoppel); enforceable; and appealable. Decisions should not serve as precedent within the forum, and especially not in federal courts.	Affording forum decisions *res judicata* and collateral estoppel status ensures that dissatisfied (or victorious) claimants will not bring the same infringement action against the defendant in district court.
Appeal: 30 Days	Parties may file a Motion for Rehearing, and if granted, the case goes to a panel of ALJs to review the record under an abuse of discretion standard.	

CONCLUSION

AAP is committed to representing the best interests of all of our members. This includes a category of members that share the frustration that pursuing small copyright claims through the federal court system does not provide a practical enforcement mechanism. Specifically, AAP represents numerous small and non-profit publishers, university presses, and scholarly societies. Conversely, AAP also represents publishers that have been successful in enforcing their copyrights using currently available methods, ranging from private settlements to full-scale litigation.

In general, the above mentioned views represent a baseline within the publishing industry. However, as discussions continue, AAP members representing diverse viewpoints within the book and journal publishing industry may raise their specific concerns in response to more defined proposals.

We appreciate the Copyright Office's attention to detail in reviewing suggestions for an alternative system to adjudicate small copyright claims. Hence, AAP reiterates that the importance of crafting a just and efficient system requires consciously evaluating the ways in which streamlining procedures to make filing small claims cost-effective can be balanced by measures that stave off meritless claims.

AAP looks forward to working with the Copyright Office to formulate a solution that strengthens copyright protections and provides this fair and adequate enforcement mechanism for all, without potentially opening the floodgates to frivolous suits, or continuing the pattern of *de facto* non-enforcement for holders of small copyright claims.

Sincerely,

Allan Adler

General Counsel
Vice President for Government Affairs
Association of American Publishers
455 Massachusetts Ave., NW, 7th Floor
Washington, D.C. 20001
(phone) 202/220-4544 (fax) 202/347-3690
(email) adler@publishers.org

End Notes

[1] AAP notes that we do not represent all publishers in the U.S. Moreover, our comment is a reflection of the feedback we received and does not take into account views of our membership that were not communicated to AAP.

[2] 28 U.S.C. § 1338 (2012).

[3] Notice of Inquiry, 76 Fed. Reg. 66,758 (Oct. 27, 2011).

[4] *See generally* Google, AIPLA, and Authors Guild comments re: Notice of Inquiry, 76 Fed. Reg. 66,758 (Oct. 27, 2011).

[5] *See generally TTAB Accelerated Case Resolution FAQ*, available at http://www.uspto.gov/trademarks/process/appeal/accelerated_case__resolution_acr_faq.doc (last visited, Oct. 17, 2012).

[6] *TTAB ACR Options*, uspto.gov, available at http://www.uspto.gov/trademarks/process/appeal/TTAB_ACR _Options.jsp (last visited, Oct. 18, 2012).

[7] *See* AIPLA, *Comments Concerning Development of the Joint Strategic Plan on IP Enforcement*, 3 (August 10, 2012), available at http://www.aipla.org/advocacy/executive/Documents/AIPLA%20Comments%20to%20 IPEC%20on%20Joint%20St rategic%20Plan%20on%20IP%20Enforcement%20-%208.10.12.pdf (last visited, Oct. 17, 2012). "Small" is relative to the value of copyright cases for which AIPLA sought litigation cost data, the range being divided into (1) less than $1 million (2) $1-25 million and (3) greater than $25 million at risk in the litigation. It is unclear how small the claims in the "less than $1 million" category were, but this category would necessarily include all of the small claims cases at issue in this filing.

[8] *Id.* at 2.

[9] For example, whether digital rights were conveyed in a pre-digital licensing agreement that covered all rights.

[10] By non-extensive discovery, AAP means the limited discovery methods commonly associated with ACR proceedings at the TTAB, which are explained in this comment under "Discovery."

[11] *See* 37 C.F.R. §2.6(a)(16)-(18) (detailing the filing fees for mark opposition, cancellation, etc. handled by TTAB).

[12] *See generally* Google, Public Knowledge/Electronic Frontier Foundation/Future of Music Coalition, and Authors Guild comments re: Notice of Inquiry, 76 Fed. Reg. 66,758 (Oct. 27, 2011).

[13] *See* 18 AM. JUR. 2d Copyright and Literary Property §225 (2012).

[14] *See* AM. JUR. 2d Copyright and Literary Property §228 (2012) (noting that access could be shown by a "reasonable opportunity to see or hear the plaintiff's work."

[15] *See* 18 AM. JUR. 2d Copyright and Literary Property §225 (2012).

[16] *See generally* Graphic Artists Guild, Picture Archive Council of America, American Photographic Artists comments re: Notice of Inquiry, 76 Fed. Reg. 66,758 (Oct. 27, 2011).

[17] *See generally* Alliance of Visual Artists and American Photographic Artists comments re: Notice of Inquiry, 76 Fed. Reg. 66,758 (Oct. 27, 2011).

[18] *See supra* FN 7.

[19] *See* 37 C.F.R. § 10.18(a)-(d) (explaining the verification measures for electronically filed documents in TTAB proceedings).

[20] *See AIPLA ACR Options*, uspto.gov, available at http://www.uspto.gov/trademarks/process/appeal/AIPLA_ACR_ Options.jsp (last visited, Oct. 17, 2012) (promoting ACR procedures that limit parties to 20 interrogatories, 10 request for admission, and 10 document requests based off previous ACR discovery agreements).

[21] *See* USPTO, TRADEMARK TRIAL AND APPEAL BOARD MANUAL OF PROCEDURE § 408.01 (3d ed., 2012) available at http://www.uspto.gov/trademarks/process/appeal/tbmp_3rd_ed_rev_1_chapter_400.pdf (last visited, Oct. 19, 2012) (detailing the "Duty to Cooperate" in regards to discovery, which requires parties to only seek discovery and file motions that are truly relevant to resolving the case).

[22] *See* COPYRIGHT OFFICE, REPORT ON ORPHAN WORKS 115-117 (2006).

[23] *Id.* at 116.

[24] *Id.* at 117.

[25] *eBay, Inc.* v. *MercExchange, L.L.C.*, 547 U.S. 388, 392 (2006).

[26] *Id.* at 390.

[27] AAP respects the constitutional requirement of making a jury trial available and appreciates the comments from the Kernochan Center at Columbia University to the first NOI, which suggest the possibility of an appeal to federal court as a method of safeguarding this right, while also noting that waiver of the right by voluntary use of the small claims system may obviate the need to provide an appeal to a federal court.

In: Small Copyright Claims: Challenges and Proposals ISBN: 978-1-63117-313-4
Editor: Sabrina Loftus

Chapter 4

REMEDIES FOR SMALL COPYRIGHT CLAIMS: RESPONSE TO THIRD REQUEST FOR COMMENTS SUBMITTED BY AMERICAN PHOTOGRAPHIC ARTISTS*

James Lorin Silverberg

COPYRIGHT OFFICE STATEMENT

The Copyright Office is studying whether and, if so, how the current legal system hinders or prevents copyright owners from pursuing copyright claims that have a relatively small economic value and will discuss, with appropriate recommendations, potential changes in administrative, regulatory, and statutory authority. At this time, the Office seeks additional comments on possible alternatives to the current system to improve the adjudication of such claims.

APA COMMENT

The Office's inquiry stems from the fact that the existing legislative scheme does not provide adequate remedies for copyright infringement. This is true for cases of higher value. But it is especially true for cases of nominal value considering the impracticality of legal proceedings, in cases of nominal value, where the legal costs may be high. As a result of these costs, only a small number of infringement cases, large or small, are pursued. And as a further result, copyright infringement is widespread and flagrant.

In explicating some of the obstacles imposed by the current legal system to infringement claims, one comes to easily understand why copyright law has become ineffective, why infringement is rampant, and why many valid copyright claims are ignored.

* This is an edited, reformatted and augmented version of comments submitted April 12, 2013 in response to U.S. Copyright Office's February 26, 2013 Notice of Inquiry.

I. The Inadequacy of Damages under the Current Legislative Scheme

The first and most obvious problem lies in the existing statutory scheme for awarding damages.

A. Statutory Damages

As a preliminary matter, only works registered prior to an infringement qualify for statutory damages pursuant to 17 U.S.C. Section 505, subject to certain exceptions (See, e.g., 17 U.S.C. Section 412). This archaic registration requirement has never proven to effectively encourage registration of rights, particularly in cases where non-corporate, individual rights owners are involved. And in any case, registration could be better incentivized by simplifying the registration requirement, by permitting multiple and group registrations so that more works could be registered with less effort and with lower cost, by permitting published and unpublished works to be registered together to simplify the registration procedure, and by reducing registration filing fees to make registration more affordable. Were these procedures to be adopted, rights owners would be better able to qualify for attorney's fees, and would be better able to pursue their claims, large or small. Another answer would be to eliminate the requirement of registration for statutory damage awards entirely. Yet another solution would be to make work eligible for statutory damages once the work is registered, even though an infringement has already commenced, thereby accomplishing any purpose that registration may serve, while still providing the rights owner with the attorney's fees that make proceedings viable. Alternatively, and to specifically address small clams, attorney's fees could be made available without registration for claims under a certain ceiling, e.g. $80,000 (excluding fees). In this manner, the rights owner would be able to, and would be encouraged to, proceed with counsel to prosecute infringement claims, provided that they limit the relief being requested.

Another and also obvious problem with the statutory scheme for pursuing copyright claims lies in the fact that the statutory awards are currently capped at $150,000 for willful infringement, and $30,000 where the infringement is not willful. See 17. U.S.C. Section 504 (c). That said, in awarding statutory damages, courts generally award amounts which conservatively enhance actual damages. In certain cases, the infringer may seek to reduce the award to as little as $250 for an innocent infringement. (See 17 U.S.C. Section 504(c)(2). Consequently, the law gives prospective infringers an incentive to infringe because the prospective infringers pay only a nominal increase over the actual damages or licensing costs where statutory fees are awarded. If the law truly wishes to protect rights owners against infringement, the law should not be providing any escape hatch for infringers. Only by compelling infringers to take licenses will the law make licensing as an option more attractive than infringing. The real solution to this problem is clear: to both increase the statutory caps under 17 U.S.C. Section 504; but also to substantially increase the statutory minimums, and to eliminate entirely the statutory reduction for "innocent infringement." In this regard, Chapter 5 remedies should be raised above the current Chapter 12 minimum remedies for infringement ($2,500 per infringement); currently they fall well below that level. (Cf. 17 U.S. C. Section 1203(c)(3).

B. Profits as Actual Damages

An additional and critical problem with the current system for computing damage awards lies in the means by which actual damages are calculated. In profit recovery cases (for which a pre-infringement registration is not required), and which is one of the few remedies currently allowed the rights owner in the majority of cases in which they have not registered their work, the plaintiff is required to prove gross revenue for the infringement, and the infringer is required to prove the expenses attributable to infringement. 17 U.S.C. Section 504(b). This frequently results in a more complex legal proceeding designed to prove what is, and what is not, net profit. This typically involves the expense of discovery, interrogatories, document production requests, and complex procedures to protect the parties' confidential business information. This typically involves the retention of expensive experts, on both sides, as well as the time and expense of depositions to obtain explanations of complex financial information, and to conduct an analysis of infringer costs, frequently detailing the exact manner and rational for why any given expense should be or should not be deductible. For the rights owner, and in many cases, it is therefore only at considerable expense that they can pursue the infringers' profits, a scenario under which they may find that they have spent more to recover than what the recovery itself amounts to in the end. And ironically, when followed to fruition, this procedure only disgorges from the infringer the profits they obtained. In other words, if the infringe does not get caught, they profit from their activity, and if they are caught and sued, they lose nothing. Infringement, at worst, is a zero sum game. In any case, it is the mere cost of adducing evidence, and computing the revenues, that makes the proceedings costly, and impractical for the rights owner.

There are several possible answers. The first would be a mandatory requirement that the defendant in any infringement case make a full disclosure of their net profits taking into account actual sales and direct expenses. Another possibility is to compensate the rights owner, if not with the profits (if any) ultimately computed through the proceedings, then with the fees incurred in order to undertake the computation. Yet another is to make the alternative "statutory" damage awards available, and to assure that there is a minimum damage award that is truly compensatory. Another possibility is to treble the profits, once they are established.

C. Reasonable Royalties

Another significant problem with the current scheme of determining the rights owner's damage award is in the means by which reasonable royalties are computed. Under current law, the rights owner can recovery under the rubric of "actual loss" a reasonably royalty in certain cases where the owner can establish that a license may have applied. (17 U.S.C. Section 504(b). As is the case with profits, it is currently to the infringer's benefit to infringe. If they get caught, they lose nothing, and in the case of a royalty recovery, the infringer pays nothing more than the royalty they would have paid in an arms length transaction. And this assumes that the rights owner convinces the court that a royalty award is warranted. The answer to this problem would be to treble the reasonable royalty so that it costs the infringer more to infringe than it would to license the work, and thereby encourage the licensing to take place. The larger award possibility would thereby deter infringement and would increase the benefit of proceeding, thereby allowing room for rights owner to compensate counsel and to pay costs.

D. Attorney's Fees

The fact that the rights owner's attorney's fees will exceed their recovery is probably the single foremost impediment to their proceeding with an infringement claim. Attorney's fees must therefore be made available to a prevailing plaintiff in all cases; not only where the work was registered prior to infringement. Unless this obstacle is removed, there is little hope that copyright owners will really be able to pursue their claims because in the vast majority of cases, it will cost more to do so than they will be likely to recover, particularly under the currently inadequate and limited damage awards that are possible.

E. Apportionment

Yet another stumbling block is interposed by the rules for "apportionment." Under the law of apportionment, 17 U.S.C. Section 504(b), the damage recovery in copyright cases may be apportioned for any profits not "attributable" to the infringing work. The apportionment rules have, on the one hand, turned intentional infringement in the marketplace into a science. The use of multiple images or copyrightable contributions, even additional infringing work, guarantees the infringer that they will pay only a faction of the damages awardable to any one infringed rights owner once an apportionment is performed. As a result, multiple infringements are frequently found in one infringing article based on the infringer's knowledge that, if caught, the infringer will pay only a portion of the damages or profits from their work to any one rights owner, as long as they take pains to infringe many other works at the same time. Unless all of the rights owners are found, this makes fractional the recovery for any one infringement. One solution to this problem is to limit apportionment to non-infringing works, which may be included in the infringing article. Another is to cap apportionments to no more than 50% of the net profits, in any case, so as to guaranty that the copyright infringement will find a meaningful remedy.

F. Attorney's Fees for the Prevailing Defendant

Were the foregoing impediments to proceeding with a claim not more than sufficient to deter the rights owner from proceeding, the law adds yet a further obstacle: the threat that were the rights owner to lose their case, they confront the possibility of an attorney's fee award against themselves, in favor of the defendant. While there currently exists a registration precondition for the rights owner to obtain their attorney's fees if they prevail, a prevailing defendant has no formal pre-requisite to obtaining an award of attorney's fees should they win against the rights owner. This creates a manifest imbalance between the rights owner and infringer in legal proceedings, weighing heavily in the infringer's favor. Were the rights owner to lose, even as a result of a technical problem such as a registration error, or an unforeseen statute of limitations issue, the results could be financially devastating if a fee award against the rights owner were granted. As a result, the rights owner faces a significant disincentive to proceed, while the law empowers the infringer with retaliatory tools should the rights owner decide to move forward. If there is any rational in the law for this imbalance, the net effect of it is to advance the interests of infringers over anyone wishing to protect their rights.

G. Fed.R.Civ.P. Rule 68

Rule 68 of the Federal Rules of Civil Procedure currently awards costs to a defendant in any case in which the plaintiff does not obtain by judgment or settlement an amount exceeding the defendants Rule 68 award. While the current status of Rule 68 remains somewhat in flux, and there are complications in its application, there are at least some judicial pronouncements that award attorney's fees to defendants as part of costs in copyright cases under Rule 68. Under these cases, even if the plaintiff rights owner prevails, they still must pay the defendant's costs, possibly including attorney's fees under at least some cases, unless they also win an amount that is more than what the defendant offered. Such a possibility must be eliminated if copyright enforcement is to be a practical reality.

II. Structural Impediments in the Legal System

For those copyright owners who are prepared to brave the currently available legal remedies, there is some good news. Under the current system the parties to litigation are afforded the opportunity to design a case plan that is sometimes efficient and that will often meet the needs of their case. This derives from Rule 26, and Rule 16, of the Federal Rules of Civil Procedure, which require the parties to meet and confer early in the case, to formulate a plan for joinder of parties, amendment of pleadings, discovery including document production, interrogatories, and depositions, time for filing dispositive motions, time for designation of experts, submission of pretrial statements, and other case management issues, and pursuant to which the Court issues a scheduling order. In addition, Rule 26 requires at least the disclosure, early in the case, of witnesses and the identity of documents, which may be used to support a party's claims or defenses. Unfortunately, the prospect of a scheduling order, and case management plan, conducive to a resolution of a case, does not necessarily encourage the litigant with a smaller claim to proceed in seeking a judicial remedy due to the various other obstacles identified above. However, Rule 26 does add some certainty and the possibility of streamlining proceedings, to make case processing more orderly, and less expensive in some instances.

III. APA's Proposal

As outlined in APA's previous submissions, APA endorses the use of magistrates, for cases designated by the plaintiff as having an $80,000 maximum, under a voluntary system for claims resolution. Having pointed out, above, the need to eliminate the registration requirements as a condition for obtaining attorney's fees, this procedure would be available to current registrants, until such time as the registration requirement for fees is eliminated. The qualifying case would require a waiver of equitable relief (of prospective benefit the copyright defendant), and waiver of a jury trial, and would involve an expedited timeline. The plan would provide attorney's fees to losing defendants who make a judgment offer, unless the plaintiff recovered more than the defendant's offer. The Plaintiff would be required to make an offer and would recover attorney's fees if they recovered what they offered or more.

If the recovery was between the plaintiff's and defendant's offer the court would have discretion to award attorney's fees to the plaintiff.

In recommending its small claim procedure, APA does not mean to suggest that it is a substitute for enhancing the recoverable damages in a copyright case, for a statutory revision allowing prevailing copyright owners their attorney's fees, or for a simplification and liberalization of existing registration procedures, or improvement in procedures for damage computations. All of these are crucial to an effective copyright law. Pending that, APA is merely suggesting what APA envisions as enhancements to the current process to expedite small claims.

In order to achieve an expedited ruling, APA specifically suggests that the parties be required to disclose the financial information necessary to resolve the case early in the proceeding. More specifically APA recommends that in addition to the currently required Rule 26 disclosures, the parties in the proceeding make additional disclosures that otherwise might require extensive and time consuming discovery, and which would shed light on the financial dimensions of a case. These "sunshine" disclosures would be made with other Rule 26 disclosures.

a) This would include a statement of the basis for each party's claims regarding copyright ownership, or lack thereof, without a formal discovery demand from the opposing party.
b) This would also include the plaintiff's and defendant's disclosure of any royalty fee information either may use in support of claim for a royalty, without a formal discovery demand from the opposing party.
c) This would also include the defendant's disclosure in any case for which profits were sought of an accounting for all monies received from the infringement, and a detailed, itemized account of all of the expenses claimed and how they were computed, when they were incurred, and which expenses were direct or indirect expenses associated with the infringement.
d) This would also include the defendant's disclosure in any case for which profits were sought of an accounting for any apportionment claimed, and a description of the basis for the apportionment, without any formal discovery demand.
e) This would also include the names and addresses of any John Does.

After the provision of this supplemental information each party would be permitted to verify the opposing party's information through proceedings approved by the magistrate, whether that be through interrogatories, document production requests, depositions and or other discovery.

After such verification, each party would be required to make their judgment offer.

The expedited provision of the supplemental Rule 26 information would greatly enhance each party's' ability to understand the issues affecting case valuation, and would greatly expedite a resolution of the claim. Additionally, defendants would have an incentive to make financial disclosures early in the case, because doing so would theoretically apprise the plaintiff of any limitations on the plaintiff's damage claims, and put the plaintiff in a position to determine the reasonableness of the defendant's judgment offer. Further, it would allow defendant recovery of attorney's fees, if their offer, based on this information, were not exceeded. There is, therefore, a significant incentive for the infringing defendant to empower the rights owner with the information required, even if it reduces the rights owner's expense, because doing so would entitle the defendant to fees from any opportunistic rights owner who sought to recover more than their case was worth. While additional damage remedies are needed, along with reforms for computing copyright damages, the implementation of such an interim procedure would at least help reduce the current costs of proceeding and -- subject to the existing limitations which the rights owners now confront -- help to at least reduce the obstacles and costs associated with case proceedings and case valuation, particularly in the small claims context.

It is noted that many federal courts have introduced Alternative Dispute Resolution (ADR) as a mandatory, or at least a voluntary, proceeding, where a case can undergo an early Neutral evaluation, or can go through Mediation, or Arbitration. These programs have been highly successful for the federal courts. While APA's proposal is intended as an alternative to these programs, APA does not seek to supplant any of these programs where they are already being practiced as these programs already present positive possible solutions for small claims holders in federal cases. The ADR programs already used by the courts should be mandatory in all federal copyright cases.

Responding, seriatim, to the Copyright Offices specific requests for comments, APA's recommended procedure would not utilize a new adjudicative body, would employ the existing system, and would not supplant arbitration or mediation. It would be 1) Voluntary, 2) apply to all works, 3) would not consider other claims, 4) require waiver of injunctive relief, 5) would not change the requirement for secondary liability, 6) would employ attorneys for obtaining a solution) 7) would follow existing law, 8) would be binding, 9) would not depend on a finding of innocence or willfulness, 9) use existing means of service, 10) Would eliminate application of Rule 68, 11) allow default, 12) use existing means of enforcement, 13) require john doe identification (as part of the Rule 26 disclosures), 14) utilize the existing tracking systems 15) avoid constitutional issues, 16) does not implicate international issues, and 17) should be tested to obtain empirical data.

The APA has a core value of advocacy for its members, as well as for the benefit of all photographers. The organization greatly appreciates the Copyright Office's request to submit comments on the issue of small infringement claims. Towards that end, the APA has participated with other visual art organizations in discussions on the subject of Remedies for Copyright Small Claims. Those organizations include Graphic Artists Guild (GAG), Professional Photographers of America (PPA), Picture Archive Council of America (PACA), American Society of Media Photographers (ASMP), North American Nature Photography Association (NANPA) and National Press Photographers Association (NPPA).

Some of those other organizations are anticipated to file their own comments with the Copyright Office, at times expressing divergent recommendations from those highlighted herein. Nonetheless, APA shares with each of those entities the goal of protecting the copyright of all members, along with all copyright holders in general. The APA and the other trade organizations listed above are all jointly committed to achieving a fair system that provides more opportunity for copyright holders whose rights are infringed to be able to vindicate their rights in a court of law.

INDEX

A

B

C

D

N

O

P

Q

R

S